Past and Present Publications

Crowds and History

Past and Present Publications

General Editor: PAUL SLACK, *Exeter College, Oxford*

Past and Present Publications comprise books similar in character to the articles in the journal *Past and Present*. Whether the volumes in the series are collections of essays – some previously published, others new studies – or monographs, they encompass a wide variety of scholarly and original works primarily concerned with social, economic and cultural changes, and their causes and consequences. They will appeal to both specialists and non-specialists and will endeavour to communicate the results of historical and allied research in readable and lively form.

For a list of titles in Past and Present Publications, see end of book.

Crowds and History

Mass Phenomena in English Towns, 1790–1835

MARK HARRISON

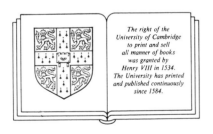

The right of the
University of Cambridge
to print and sell
all manner of books
was granted by
Henry VIII in 1534.
The University has printed
and published continuously
since 1584.

CAMBRIDGE UNIVERSITY PRESS

Cambridge

New York   New Rochelle   Melbourne   Sydney

Published by the Press Syndicate of the University of Cambridge
The Pitt Building, Trumpington Street, Cambridge CB2 1RP
32 East 57th Street, New York, NY 10022, USA
10 Stamford Road, Oakleigh, Melbourne 3166, Australia

First published 1988

Printed in Great Britain
at the University Press, Cambridge

British Library cataloguing in publication data

Harrison, Mark.
Crowds and history: mass phenomena in
English towns, 1790–1835 / – / (Past and
present publications).
1. England. Towns. Crowds. Behaviour, 1790–
1835. Sociopolitical aspects
I. Title   II. Series
302.3′3

Library of Congress cataloguing in publication data

Harrison, Mark.
Crowds and history: mass phenomena in English towns, 1790–1835 /
Mark Harrison.
        p.   cm. (Past and present publications)
Originally presented as the author's thesis (Ph.D. – Cambridge
University) under title: The crowd in Bristol, 1790–1835.
Bibliography.
Includes index.
ISBN 0 521 30210 2
1. Great Britain – History – 1789–1820. 2. Great Britain –
History – 1800–1837. 3. Crowds – History. 4. Cities and towns –
England – History. 5. England – Social conditions – 19th century.
6. England – Social conditions – 18th century. I. Title
DA520.H38   1988
942.07 – dc 19   88-1728   CIP

ISBN 0 521 30210 2

For
Coral and Geoff
and for
Rona and Bill

Contents

Illustrations

Figures, maps and tables

Preface

Other people exist in crowds. Our association of differentness and foreignness – of the alien and the threatening – with the existence of frenzied and faceless far-away hordes is an aspect of human psychology with crucial implications for the formulation of social policy and foreign relations the world over. The supposed intimidation represented by mythical packs of strangers is what makes possible international and intercultural mass violence; it facilitates the process of dehumanisation essential to the lifting of moral constraints against violence and persecution. Less dramatically, our willingness as citizens in western democracies to accept domestic policies which advantage ourselves or our beliefs at the expense of large numbers of others is all about our ability to view other people not as individuals but as part of an invisible crowd.

Human beings are gregarious, and yet, peculiarly, our association in large numbers has come to hold numerous negative connotations. Equally strangely, historians, who deal all the time with masses of other people existing in the foreign territory of the past, have been incurious about the way in which our attitudes towards mass have developed. Some have looked closely at the rioting masses, but through such exclusive attention they have only confirmed the general belief we all seem to carry that people gathered in large numbers and close proximity are dangerous.

This book is an attempt, part tentative and selective, part assertive and comprehensive, to question our presumptions about crowds, and to establish some historical ground-rules for the contemplation of, and evolution of, attitudes towards the masses in public. In so doing, it bites the conceptual hand that fed it. The original motivation for this book lies in my reading, as an undergraduate student, of the work of E.P. Thompson, George Rudé and Eric Hobsbawm. Like many other young history students, I was captivated by their discussions of rioting and protesting crowds, and by their effective and entertaining refutation of generations of ill-informed historical presentations of the 'mindless mob'. Now, several years later, I find myself making some criticisms of this famous trio of 'crowd historians'; I hope my sharper words will be seen as stemming from a desire to carry their excellent and invigorating research a little further. Would that I could do it with their style.

In the course of years of work I have accumulated many debts, of different kinds, to many people.

I am grateful for the assistance and advice I have received from the staffs of a number of libraries and records offices, particularly: Bristol Reference Library; Bristol Record Office; Liverpool Records Office; Norwich Public Library; Colindale Newspaper Library; the Public Records Office at Kew; and Cambridge University Library.

This work began in the form of a Cambridge University PhD thesis, titled 'The crowd in Bristol, 1790–1835', and funded by a Social Science Research Council Quota Award. I am grateful to the Provost and Fellows of King's College, Cambridge, who enabled me to develop the work by appointing me to a junior research fellowship.

In the early stages of research I received encouragement and advice from Michael Ignatieff and Alan Macfarlane, and later from Roy Porter. Roy Foster has kept me in touch over the last couple of years; and William Davies, at Cambridge University Press, has been extremely patient over the same period of time. My colleagues at the BBC have similarly suffered in the final stages of preparation of this book, and I am grateful to Amanda Theunissen, who helped me find the time, and Anna Thomas, who prepared the final draft of two of the chapters. Most of the rest of the final version was prepared with great speed and efficiency by Sue Prestridge. At the very beginning Jonathan Barry was generous in sharing his knowledge of records relating to eighteenth-century Bristol, and at the very end Sheena Stoddard kindly gave me access to Bristol Museum and Art Gallery photographs of early nineteenth-century processions. The remainder of the photographs were taken, with great skill, by Gordon Kelsey. My family have been ceaseless in their support, throughout.

There are three people to whom I am particularly grateful. The first is Linda Colley, who taught me as an undergraduate and supervised the first year of my PhD thesis. It was largely due to her excellent teaching that I took up research. The second is David Cannadine, who supervised the remainder of my graduate work, and who has continued to be a great source of advice and encouragement. The completion of this book owes a huge amount to his knowledge, energy and infectious enthusiasm.

The third is Nicola Davies, to whom I give my thanks with all my love.

Acknowledgements

Chapter 5 is a revised and extended version of my article, 'The ordering of the urban environment: time, work and the occurrence of crowds, 1790–1835', which appeared in *Past and Present*, no. 110 (Feb. 1986), pp. 134–68 (world copyright: The Past and Present Society, 175 Banbury Road, Oxford). I am grateful for their permission to include material from that article, including graphs and tables.

Chapter 6 is a revised version of my article, 'Symbolism, "ritualism" and the location of crowds in early nineteenth-century English towns', which appeared in Denis Cosgrove and Stephen Daniels (eds.), *The iconography of landscape: essays on the symbolic representation, design and use of past and environments* (Cambridge, 1988). The first part of chapter 11 draws on material in my article, ' "To raise and dare resentment": the Bristol Bridge Riot of 1793 re-examined', which appeared in *Historical Journal*, XXVI, 3 (1983), pp. 557–85. I am grateful to Cambridge University Press for permission to include material from these articles, including maps for chapter 6.

I am also very grateful to Bristol Reference Library for permission to reproduce illustrations 1, 2, 3, 5, 12, 14, 15; to the City of Bristol Record Office for permission to reproduce illustrations 4, 9, 10, 11, 13; and to the City of Bristol Museum and Art Gallery for permission to reproduce illustrations 6, 7, 8, and the front cover illustration.

Abbreviations

Libraries and records offices

BRL	Bristol Reference Library
BRO	Bristol Record Office
BUL	Bristol University Library
LRO	Liverpool Records Office
NPL/LS	Norwich Public Library, Local Studies Department
NRO	Norfolk Record Office
PRO	Public Records Office, Kew

Bristol Corporation records, deposited in Bristol Record Office

LMP/BRO	Common Council letters and miscellaneous papers
CCP/BRO	Common Council proceedings
PO/BRO	Public orders
SP/BRO	Sessions papers
PMA/BRO	Proceedings of mayor and aldermen
LB/BRO	Common Council letter books

Collections

Jefferies MSS	'Collection of MSS of C.T. Jefferies', vols. I–XVI, Bristol Reference Library
Seyer MSS	'Seyer MSS relating to the history of Bristol: chronicle of events, 1760–1813', Bristol Reference Library
PP/BUL	Pinney Papers, Bristol University Library

Government records, deposited in Public Records Office, Kew

HO	Home Office
WO	War Office

Newspapers

All newspapers are referred to by the short version of their title (see bibliography, below). In addition, the following abbreviations are used:

BMBJ	*Bonner and Middleton's Bristol Journal*
FFBJ	*Felix Farley's Bristol Journal*
SFBJ	*Sarah Farley's Bristol Journal*

Part 1   *Theory and method*

1. *The crowd and History: problems of historiography*

We may exclude from our present considerations crowds that are casually drawn together, like sight-seers; crowds assembled on purely ceremonial occasions or crowds taking part in religious or academic processions.
(George Rudé, *The crowd in history 1730–1848: a study of popular disturbances in France and England* (1964; revised edn London 1981), p. 4)

What is . . . striking . . . is the continuing prevalence of Rudé's protest framework at the expense of other forms of crowd organisation and behaviour.
(Robert J. Holton, 'The crowd in history: some problems of theory and method', *Social History*, III, 2 (1978), p. 225)

An air of mystery surrounds the crowd. That mystery has been lovingly perpetuated by generations of social commentators, sociologists, social psychologists and historians. For some, such as Gustave LeBon, the crowd is always to be feared: 'by the very fact that he forms part of an organised crowd, a man descends several rungs in the ladder of civilisation. Isolated, he may be a cultured individual; in a crowd he is a barbarian – that is, a creature acting by instinct.'[1] For others, such as Elias Canetti, it is revered: 'It is for the sake of . . . equality that people become a crowd and they tend to overlook anything which might detract from it. All demands for justice and all theories of equality ultimately derive their energy from the actual experience of equality familiar to anyone who has been part of a crowd.'[2]

Both these writers, like most who discuss mass phenomena, are fascinated by the single most striking characteristic of crowds: that

[1] Gustave LeBon, *The crowd: a study of the popular mind* (London, 1896), p. 13.
[2] Elias Canetti, *Crowds and power*, trans. Carol Stewart (Harmondsworth, 1973), p. 32.

3

when tens, hundreds, thousands of individuals join together, their individualities appear to be lost, subsumed, transformed into one, discrete, homogeneous body. The sea of faces becomes, paradoxically, a single-headed collectivity. This, to some, almost magical transmutation of the many into the single facilitates the discussion of the crowd as if, indeed, it was an individual itself: the crowd does this, the crowd does that; it becomes hostile, it becomes angry; it is placated, it is calmed; it becomes friendly.

The susceptibility of a crowd to characterisation as a single, describable, individual is one of the means by which those who commentate upon crowds attempt to make sense of them. Large crowds have been a regular feature of urban life in England for at least the last two centuries. In the early nineteenth century some crowds were immense. In 1831 meetings of the Birmingham Political Union were said to have drawn 150,000;[3] some estimates put the attendance at the London Corresponding Society meetings in Copenhagen Fields, Islington, in October 1795, at the same figure.[4] The celebration of George III's golden jubilee in Liverpool was watched by 50,000 people;[5] 80,000 of the town's inhabitants watched a balloon ascent in 1819.[6] In Manchester around a third of the population turned out for the visit of Henry Hunt in 1831,[7] while a public execution in Bristol in 1835 was apparently attended by half the city.[8] There were numerous occasions for the formation of crowds: sporting events, civic ceremonials, public executions, parliamentary and local elections, political meetings, riots, the celebrations of national anniversaries and military victories, and so on.

The gathering together of so many people provided problems of organisation: consequently, the history of crowds in English towns is in some respects a history of crowd control and the ordering of the urban environment. But such gatherings were also dramatic events which offered the opportunity for claims to be made regarding the effect and implications of bringing together so many people. Those claims might be in terms, on the one hand, of confrontation, or, on the other, of social unity. A radical political meeting, for example, could be depicted as representative of the will of the people in

[3] Asa Briggs, *The age of improvement, 1783–1867* (London, 1959), p. 252.
[4] John Stevenson, *Popular disturbances in England, 1700–1870* (London, 1979), pp.172–3.   [5] *Liverpool Courier*, 1 Oct. 1809.
[6] 'Ascent of Messrs Livingstone and Sadler in a balloon', *The Imperial Magazine*, vol. I (Liverpool, 1819), pp. 780–2.
[7] *Manchester Times*, 9 April 1831.   [8] *Bristol Gazette*, 11 April 1835.

opposition to an entrenched executive. A coronation celebration, for its part, might be seen as representative of a unified, loyal and patriotic populace. These are big claims, made possible by the ways in which crowds are characterised: reduced to a single, coherent, entity, they are presented, either by their spokespeople or by outside commentators, as representative of a single, coherent, *belief.*

Crowds are, and for a long time have been, used to proclaim the existence of certain views and values. When thousands of people present themselves on the street, their individual value systems are reduced, condensed, filtered and reinterpreted by those who comment upon them. That process (effectively, the extra-politicisation of gatherings) may be carried out by the description of masses in individualistic terms. This, however, is only a part of a broad and complicated language for the description and characterisation of crowds. Specific terms have come to be allocated to different sorts of gatherings. We speak of mobs, of gangs, of assemblies, of processions, of audiences, of rioters, of spectators. There are distinct contexts in which each term is employed: whoever heard of a seated mob? Those people watching a football match are termed a crowd, but those gathered at the Albert Hall are referred to as an audience. Skinheads are said to roam in gangs, company directors assemble in groups. A large number of pickets behaving in a threatening manner may be termed a mob, but a large number of policemen charging with batons will almost never be so described. Crowds occur almost entirely outdoors: a room may be described as crowded, but those inside will only in certain, specific, circumstances be termed a crowd.

The language of crowd description is constantly changing; it changes because the significance of crowds, and of certain kinds of crowds, changes. Indeed, the language employed by historians in their discussion of crowds is the product not only of ideological and methodological approach, but of the long-term influence of characterisations imposed by successive generations of social commentators. This chapter will examine the present state of discussion concerning crowds, and attempt to evaluate the usefulness of the existing historiography for a general analysis of the position and perception of crowds in the early nineteenth century. It will be argued that, despite a formidable challenge to late nineteenth-century views of the crowd as an uncritical, instinctual and anti-social phenomenon, the presumption that crowds are inherently violent and disruptive has continued to prevail. The wider historiographical context for the discussion of crowds in this period has been in terms primarily of a supposed 'transition to order' around the middle of the nineteenth century (a transition made possible in part by the 'taming' of crowds); and the notion of such a transition, it will be suggested, is both the product and the producer of a narrow and deterministic conception of crowds.

The search for a conception which is at once broader and more sophisticated finds little reward, the argument will continue, in the sociological and social psychological literature relating to mass phenomena, since here also there exists the premise that crowds are (often violently) disruptive. The body of work which does seem, more or less consciously, to invite a broader examination of mass events is that relating to ceremonial, and, ironically, to ritualised violence. The concentration in this work is upon aggression in a ritualised or a concealed form, and this inevitably continues to connect crowds with disruption. But it does so only in the broadest sense – one which relates to theoretical approaches to the concept of social order, and which will be dealt with later in the book. Of greater significance at this stage is the willingness in this literature to examine crowd events which do not appear to belong to the framework of riot and protest. Rather, these historians (and sociologists) discuss crowds which might appear at first glance to be 'non-political', 'conservative' or 'consensual': they discuss sports crowds, crowds attending public spectacles, religious crowds and crowds celebrating local or national events. Furthermore, their concern is rather less with crowd occurrences as part of a picture of transition and change, and rather more with immediate historical contexts, and the perceptions and interpretations of contemporary participants and observers. Consequently, this chapter will conclude, it is the methodologies employed by these scholars as much as those of the so-called 'crowd historians' that are of use in the historical examination of crowds.

I

Throughout the nineteenth century there was, in both England and France, a concern among social observers regarding the alienation and social disorganisation which seemed to derive from industrialisation and urbanisation. In England, such concern manifested itself around questions of public order, disturbance, housing and the classification of poverty and criminality. In the course of the century there evolved a detailed vocabulary, used widely, and further stimulated by the classifications employed in the investigative work of Mayhew, Booth, Rowntree and others, which attempted to separate the dangerous from the unfortunate, the deserving from the undeserving, the petty from the malicious.[9] In France, similar concerns (further fuelled by events surrounding the Paris Commune, the growth of working class militancy, and, later, the inauguration of the May Day parade) produced discussions of crowd psychology and collective behaviour by Taine (1887–8) and the novelist Emile Zola (notably *Germinal*, in 1885). These discussions, together with the examination of supposed 'invisible communication', by Alfred Espinas (1878), and the influence of Italian criminal anthropologists Cesare Lombroso and Enrico Ferri spawned further work in France, by Alexandre Lacassagne, Gabriel Tarde and Henry Fournial.[10]

It took a non-specialist, Gustave LeBon, to bring the conclusions of these crowd psychologists and self-styled social scientists into popular currency. LeBon spoke for them all in characterising the crowd as awesome, terrifying, savage, instinctual, bestial, capricious – and violent. He argued that the crowd represented an evolutionary regression in human civilisation, a last stage of human development, and the accession of mass irrationality.[11] LeBon's definition of the crowd was broad. He employed two classifications. The first was the heterogeneous crowd, which in turn consisted of 'anonymous crowds' (street crowds for example), and 'crowds not anonymous' (juries, parliamentary assemblies, and so on). The second classification was the homogeneous crowd, consisting of political and religious sects, military and working castes, and social classes.[12] The

[9] Gareth Stedman Jones, *Outcast London: a study in the relationship between the classes in Victorian society* (Oxford, 1971); J.A. Banks, 'The contagion of numbers', in H.J. Dyos and Michael Wolff (eds.), *The Victorian city: images and realities*, 2 vols. (London, 1973), vol. 1, pp. 105–22; Asa Briggs, 'The human aggregate', repr. in *The collected essays of Asa Briggs* (Brighton, 1985), vol. 1, pp. 55–83; Anthony S. Wohl, *The eternal slum: housing and social policy in Victorian London* (London, 1977), esp. chs. 1, 2; Raymond Williams, *Culture and society 1780–1850* (Harmondsworth, 1963), conclusion.

[10] Susanna Barrows, *Distorting mirrors: visions of the crowd in late nineteenth-century France* (New Haven, 1981), chs. 1–5; Robert A. Nye, *The origins of crowd psychology: Gustave LeBon and the crisis of mass democracy in the third republic* (London, 1975); Eric Hobsbawm, 'Mass-producing traditions: Europe, 1870–1914', in Eric Hobsbawm and Terence Ranger (eds.), *The invention of tradition* (Cambridge, 1983), esp. pp. 164–9, 283–7.

[11] LeBon, *The crowd*; Barrows, *Distorting mirrors*, ch. 7; Nye, *Origins of crowd psychology*, ch. 4.   [12] LeBon, *The crowd*, book III, ch. 1.

crowd, for LeBon, was not simply 'the mob'; it was rather the fickle, infectious, aggressive and ignorant characteristics of *all* crowds that gave each a mob-like attitude. Once LeBon had extended his argument so far as to classify a jury as a crowd, and to portray it as displaying a susceptibility to suggestion, a slight capacity for reasoning, and a tendency to be guided by unconscious sentiment, the threatening and irrational element of crowds had become the dominant, and all-pervading, characteristic.[13]

Among sociologists, and particularly in America, it was the 'deviant' aspect of collective behaviour which received attention in the wake of LeBon.[14] Robert E. Park, for example, writing in 1904, was concerned with what he perceived as the separation of crowds from the institutional order, and thereby from the social stability offered by common customs and traditions: 'Precisely because the crowd proves to be a social power whose effect is always more or less disruptive and revolutionary, it seldom arises where there is social stability and where customs have deep roots. In contrast, where social bonds are removed and old institutions weakened, great crowd movements develop more easily and forcefully.'[15] Among English historians the influence of LeBon and others was of a quite particular kind. Susanna Barrows, in her book *Distorting mirrors: visions of the crowd in late nineteenth-century France*, observes that although a crowd in France at that time could, of course, include patriotic parades, funerals, religious processions or concert audiences, nevertheless most of the crowd psychologists conceived of *la foule* as a violent and raucous assembly of the lower classes.[16] It is this exclusive conception which has endured among historians of England.

Examples abound, but the notion of the crowd as 'rabble' is typified by Conrad Gill, who, on examining the Birmingham riots of 1791, advised that 'we should take into account . . . the multitude of untaught minds which found in looting and civil disorder an excitement similar to that of bull-baiting or tavern brawls'.[17]

---

[13] *Ibid.*, pp. 178–84.

[14] Jerry D. Rose, *Outbreaks: the sociology of collective behaviour* (New York, 1982), ch. 2; A.P. Donajgrodzki (ed.), *Social control in nineteenth-century Britain* (London, 1977), pp. 9–26; Jesse R. Pitts, 'Social control: the concept', in David L. Stills (ed.), *International encyclopedia of the social sciences*, vol. 14 (1968), pp. 381–96.

[15] Robert E. Park, *The crowd and the public, and other essays*, trans. Charlotte Elsner (Chicago, 1972), p. 47.   [16] Barrows, *Distorting mirrors*, p. 24.

[17] Conrad Gill, *History of Birmingham*, vol. 1: *Manor and borough to 1865* (London, 1952), p. 129.

Christopher Hibbert emphasised that the Gordon riots of 1780 were 'encouraged by trouble-makers, prostitutes and runaway apprentices and led by criminals'.[18] W.L. Burn, author of the influential book *The age of equipoise*, informed us that 'the Englishman' of the 'lower ranks', in the mid-Victorian years, 'remained potentially and often showed himself in practice a very ugly customer', indulging in 'a vast amount of casual rowdyism', and with an 'instinct for violence' that 'could be satisfied, in part, by reading the considerable mass of semi-pornographic "horror" tales and, of course, by witnessing public executions'.[19] David D. Cooper, writing ten years later, still regarded crowds at executions in the eighteenth and nineteenth centuries in the same light.[20] A.G. Rose, meanwhile, in his account of the Lancashire Plug riots of 1842, typifies an approach taken by many historians when he describes the authorities attempting to 'master' 'the mob' much as if they were coping with a natural disaster or a maddened beast.[21]

In 1945 Robert F. Wearmouth, writing under the title of *Methodism and the common people of the eighteenth century*, began what was later to be seen as a concerted challenge to such views. Wearmouth argued, with a formidable volume of evidence to support him, that working people in the eighteenth century made selective and rational appeals for the rectification of some grievances related to economic distress through collective action. He also claimed that far from being violent themselves, these people were frequently the subject of brutal insensitivity from those in power.[22] In essence, Wearmouth was lamenting the shortcomings of a paternalistic system which should and could, in his opinion, have shown greater benevolence.[23] His arguments were taken up, focused and developed by a (now well-known) group of historians some years later. They, however, were approaching the subject from a rather different perspective.

Writing in the late 1950s and early 1960s, E.J. Hobsbawm, R.B. Rose, George Rudé and E.P. Thompson demonstrated that protest-

---

[18] Christopher Hibbert, *King mob: the story of Lord George Gordon and the riots of 1780* (London, 1958), p. 61 and *passim*.

[19] W.L. Burn, *The age of equipoise: a study of the mid-Victorian generation* (London, 1964), pp. 82–3.

[20] David D. Cooper, *The lesson of the scaffold* (London, 1974), esp. ch. 1.

[21] A.G. Rose, 'The Plug riots of 1842 in Lancashire and Cheshire', *Transactions of the Lancashire and Cheshire Antiquarian Society*, LXVII (1957), pp. 75–112, and esp. p. 96.

[22] Robert F. Wearmouth, *Methodism and the common people of the eighteenth century* (London, 1945), chs. 1–3.   [23] *Ibid.*, ch. 3.

ing crowds between 1700 and 1835 were composed of working people who possessed clear notions of the prerequisites for social order, and who undertook collective action in order to rectify, rather than to challenge, that order. Crowds' targets were specific; their pre-organisation minimal; their action (based upon well-established norms for mass response) disciplined and restrained; their violence towards property considerable, but their violence towards people almost non-existent. Indeed, such ideological and physical cohesion (these historians argued), although it sometimes met with violent response, was generally well understood by those in authority: it functioned as a bargaining tool in its own right. The threat of action was as integral to protest, and as forceful, as the action itself. By this means working people defended what they perceived to be their 'rights' in the face of the challenge to established practices posed either by the emergent industrial capitalist economy, or from the perceived intrusion of foreigners and their religion.[24]

There are a number of important elements in the work of these historians, some of which will be discussed later in the context of arguments concerning supposed transitions in the form and frequency of popular disturbance. But first it is necessary to examine two publications which solidified the arguments of the so-called 'crowd historians'. The first was a synthesis, by George Rudé, in 1964, of the riot studies of the previous years, under the title *The crowd in history*. The second was a highly influential article, published in *Past and Present* in 1971 by E.P. Thompson, and titled 'The moral economy of the English crowd in the eighteenth century'.

In *The crowd in history* Rudé launched an onslaught against both the crass liberal depiction of the crowd as 'the people', and the perniciously conservative characterisation of the crowd as 'rabble'. Both interpretations, argued Rudé, presented the crowd as a 'disembodied abstraction'. Rudé sought to give faces to members of

---

[24] E.J. Hobsbawm, *Primitive rebels: studies in archaic forms of social movement in the nineteenth and twentieth centuries* (Manchester, 1959), ch. 7; R.B. Rose, 'The Priestley riots of 1791', *Past and Present*, no. 18 (Nov. 1960), pp. 68–88; R.B. Rose, 'Eighteenth-century price riots and public policy in England', *International Review of Social History*, VI, 2 (1961), pp. 277–92; George Rudé, 'The Gordon riots: a study of the rioters and their victims', *Transactions of the Royal Historical Society*, 5th series, VI (1956), pp. 93–114; George Rudé, 'The London "mob" of the eighteenth century', *Historical Journal*, II, 1 (1959), pp. 1–18; George Rudé, *The crowd in the French revolution* (Oxford, 1959); George Rudé, *Wilkes and liberty* (Oxford, 1962); E.P. Thompson, *The making of the English working class* (Harmondsworth, 1963), ch. 3.

the crowd: to escape stereotypical characterisations by analysing the composition and motivation of crowds.[25] At the very outset Rudé stated his definition of the crowd; and, extraordinarily for an historian who became renowned for his argument that it was through the minutiae of popular disturbance that we would come to understand their function, motivation and composition, that definition proved to be exclusive in the extreme:

in general [Rudé announced] we may exclude from our present considerations crowds that are casually drawn together, like sight-seers; crowds assembled on purely ceremonial occasions; or crowds taking part in religious or academic processions; or 'audience' crowds (as they have been termed) who gather in theatres or lecture halls, at base-ball matches or bullfights, or who used to witness hangings at Tyburn Fair or in the Place de Grève in Paris. Equally, we should generally exclude those more active, or 'expressive' crowds that come together for Mardi Gras, participate in dancing orgies or student 'rags', or who attend revivalist meetings to hear Billy Graham or Father Divine, as they listened two hundred years ago to George Whitefield and the Wesleys . . . In fact, our main attention will be given to political demonstrations and to what sociologists have termed the 'aggressive mob' or the 'hostile outburst' – to such activities as strikes, riots, rebellions, insurrections, and revolutions.[26]

The only explanations for this statement of methodological exclusivity were in terms of Rudé's personal conception of what was historically 'interesting' and 'significant', and the necessity of limiting the amount of material that could be discussed in the course of the book. Certainly Rudé gave himself the space to demolish many preconceptions about riotous and protesting crowds, but to assume the title 'the crowd in history' was little short of pretentious. Nevertheless, Rudé's rather casual justification for the scope of his study became (perhaps because of the many valuable conclusions which the book did contain) entrenched in historians' conception of the crowd. From 1964, 'the crowd', to historians, was, quite simply, the 'protesting crowd', and, more usually, 'the rioting crowd'. The tenacity of this conflation cannot be overstated. What is particularly ironic, however, is that although Rudé sought, quite explicitly, to

---

[25] George Rudé, *The crowd in history 1730–1848: a study of popular disturbances in France and England* (New York, 1964; revised edn London, 1981), pp. 7–11.

[26] *Ibid.*, p. 4. The definition seems peculiarly retrograde in the light of Rudé's earlier remarks regarding the transformation, during the French revolution, of casual and processional crowds into riots: *Crowd in the French revolution*, pp. 219–20.

explode the myths created by LeBon, he in fact strongly reinforced the tendency in LeBon's work towards an assumption that crowds are violent phenomena. But, whereas LeBon, rather than seeing all crowds as mobs, preferred to argue that all crowds had mob-like qualities, Rudé, in his linguistic conflation of crowd and riot, created the impression that crowds were, in essence, mobs. He gave a face to the crowd, but it was the face only of anger; he established the 'respectability' of the mob, but it was a mob just the same.

In his 1971 article on 'The moral economy of the English crowd', E.P. Thompson, inadvertantly, narrowed the definition of mass phenomena in eighteenth- and early nineteenth-century England still further. Thompson was developing remarks he had made in *The making of the English working class*.[27] He argued that eighteenth-century food crowds possessed a specific, and coherent, conception of social and economic justice, and he termed that notion the 'moral economy'. Crowds of working people, Thompson explained, took actions to fix the price of bread, to regulate food supplies and to encourage the authorities to intervene during economic crisis, which were all part of a long-established concept of 'Englishmen's rights'. Those rights, says Thompson, served to legitimise collective action. Food crowds were well disciplined and serious minded, operated within a well-understood tradition of collective action and regarded their action as a process both of rectification and cultural assertion. Their acts were not 'radical' in the sense that they offered no alternative formulations for how society should be organised, but neither were they mindless, unaware or entirely deferential. The coherence of riot action of this sort served to constrain those who sought to usher in the market economy; and it served to override the fear and deference that could otherwise govern social relations.[28]

The moral economy article has, quite rightly, become one of the best-known publications in English social history. It is quoted, respectfully, by almost every historian working on disturbance, irrespective of period or location. It is Thompson at his eloquent best; and it identifies him as one of the few historians who can successfully combine original research with an assertiveness amounting almost to

[27] Thompson, *The making*, pp. 65–6, 72–3.
[28] E.P. Thompson, 'The moral economy of the English crowd in the eighteenth century', *Past and Present*, no. 50 (Feb. 1971), esp. pp. 78–9, 98, 107–8, 120.

polemic. That forcefulness, however, seems to have overwhelmed the critical faculties of many other historians: repeated summaries of the article have produced a garbled and vulgarised version of the argument. It is a sort of historians' Chinese whisper that has reduced Thompson's claims almost to absurdity: the article has become about 'the crowd' in the eighteenth century, about the motivation of 'pre-industrial crowds' in general, and about 'traditional' protest. Certainly Thompson is in some respects to blame: although, if the article is read closely, it contains subtleties that others have overlooked, there is little in the text itself that actually runs counter to be vulgarised version.

Thompson's article has a number of shortcomings, which will be examined more fully in chapter 6. It is sufficient to note here, first that he applied the term 'the English crowd' to what was, in fact, a very specific category of mass formation, and in so doing solidified Rudé's conflation of crowd and riot; and second, that the eagerness of his argument perhaps gives a false impression of the frequency of disturbance in eighteenth-century England. As Dale Edward Williams has recently pointed out, food riots were in fact very rare: most market towns had experience of no more than one such riot in the course of a century.[29] This is of great relevance when discussing trends in violence since 1700: was riot really as common pre-1830 as it is presented as having been? Or, to put it another way, does it 'matter' if riot was statistically more frequent pre-1830 if it was nevertheless rarely experienced by most individuals?

Thompson is guilty of sins of omission – an offence of which almost every writer could be accused. It is unreasonable to condemn him for the overextrapolation of his material by others. But what Thompson did do, intentionally or otherwise, was, following Rudé, to encapsulate the vast subject of 'the English crowd' within the quite specific study of eighteenth-century popular protest. There have, in recent years, been numerous studies of 'the crowd', a number of which lend further weight to the cohesive characteristics of eighteenth- and early nineteenth-century popular protest identified by Rudé *et al.* And, needless to say, all of them are, in fact, studies of

[29] Dale Edward Williams, 'Morals, markets and the English crowd in 1766', *Past and Present*, no. 104 (Aug. 1984), pp. 69–70. The infrequency of riot is also noted by J.M. Beattie, 'The pattern of crime in England, 1660–1800', *Past and Present*, no. 62 (Feb. 1974), pp. 66–7.

riot. Together they have helped the formation of what is now a formidable, highly influential and slightly stagnant orthodoxy.[30]

II

So far the discussion of Rudé, Hobsbawm and Thompson has been in terms of their challenge to previously accepted images of the crowd as 'rabble'. There is, however, a broader context for their work: the notion of a transition from pre-industrial to industrial protest, and, within this, from pre-industrial to industrial crowd activity. Although Thompson's work is concerned with the 'pre-industrial crowd' and with the years 1790–1835 as a transition period in English history, he is far less concerned than Hobsbawm and Rudé with the distinction between pre-industrial and industrial protest. For Rudé

[30] For instance: Alan Booth, 'Food riots in the north-west of England, 1790–1801', *Past and Present*, no. 77 (Nov. 1977), pp. 84–107; Joyce Ellis, 'Urban conflict and popular violence: the Guildhall riots of 1740 in Newcastle upon Tyne', *International Review of Social History*, XXV, 3 (1980), pp. 332–49; Geoffrey Holmes, 'The Sacheverell riots: the crowd and the church in early eighteenth-century London', *Past and Present*, no. 72 (Aug. 1976), pp. 55–85; Philip D. Jones, 'The Bristol bridge riot and its antecedents: eighteenth century perceptions of the crowd', *Journal of British Studies*, XIX, 2 (1980), pp. 74–92; Robert W. Malcolmson, '"A set of ungovernable people": the Kingswood colliers in the eighteenth century', in John Brewer and John Styles (eds.), *An ungovernable people: the English and their law in the seventeenth and eighteenth centuries* (London, 1980), pp. 85–127; Norman McCord and David E. Brewster, 'Some labour troubles of the 1790s in north east England', *International Review of Social History*, XIII, 3 (1968), pp. 366–83; John Walsh, 'Methodism and the mob in the eighteenth century', in G.J. Cuming and Derek Baker (eds.), *Studies in church history*, vol. 8 (Cambridge, 1972), pp. 213–27; Roger Wells, 'The revolt of the south west, 1800–1801: a study in English popular protest', *Social History*, II, 3 (1977), pp. 713–44; John Wigley, 'Nottingham and the Reform Bill riots of 1831: new perspectives, Part II', *Transactions of the Thoroton Society of Nottinghamshire*, LXXVII (1973), pp. 95–103; Dale Edward Williams, 'Midland hunger riots in 1766', *Midland History*, III, 4 (1976), pp. 256–97; Gwyn A. Williams, *The Merthyr rising* (London, 1978); David L. Wykes, 'The Leicester riots of 1773 and 1787: a study of the victims of popular protest', *Transactions of the Leicestershire Archaeological and Historical Society*, LIV (1978–9), pp. 39–50. Other studies owing much to the 'crowd historians', include: E. Abrahamian, 'The crowd in Iranian politics, 1905–53', *Past and Present*, no. 41 (Dec. 1968), pp. 184–210; Michael Feldberg, 'The crowd in Philadelphia history: a comparative perspective', *Labour History*, XV, 3 (1974), pp. 323–36; Pauline Maier, 'Popular uprisings and civil authority in eighteenth-century America', *William and Mary Quarterly*, XXVII, 1 (1970), pp. 3–35; David Pinkney, 'The crowd in the French revolution of 1830', *American Historical Review*, LXX (1964), pp. 1–17; William M. Reddy, 'The textile trade and the language of the crowd at Rouen, 1752–1871', *Past and Present*, no. 74 (Feb. 1977), pp. 62–89; Gordon S. Wood, 'A note on mobs in the American revolution', *William and Mary Quarterly*, XXIII, 4 (1966), pp. 635–42.

and Hobsbawm there was, around 1831, and certainly by 1848, a transition in the form and content of collective protest. The notion of such a transition, taking place around the second quarter of the nineteenth century, has now become entrenched in virtually all historical writing relating to protest, crowds and public order in nineteenth-century England.

The transition argument is relatively straightforward: in the eighteenth and early nineteenth centuries, it is argued, protest was frequently riotous, involved a significant degree of violence against property, and was defensive. It sought to protect and uphold what were regarded as common rights; but it was not informed by a programme for change, or a set of demands relating to the betterment, rather than merely the maintenance, of the worker's economic position. Industrial movements in manufacturing districts, such as the National Association for the Protection of the Working Classes, founded in June 1830, did possess the forward looking aims of protecting labour and improving wages, but they were counterbalanced by lingering 'luddite' methods of bargaining, by the failure of the middle class to provide leadership and by the backward looking concerns of agricultural labourers.[31] Despite Rudé's and Hobsbawm's attempts to explain and give respectability to riotous protest in the late eighteenth and early nineteenth century, they are fairly explicit in their sympathies: pre-industrial protest, when still to be found as late as 1830–1, was sorry evidence of class unconsciousness, while industrial protest represented the attainment of consciousness and thereby the realisation of the correct method of protest within industrial society. Consequently, the major riots related to reform in Derby, Nottingham and Bristol, in 1831, for instance, were merely backward – the riots in Bristol being, according to Rudé, 'the last great urban riot in English history' (he was writing before 1981).[32] Similarly, the agricultural disturbances in 1831 were said to have relied upon the 'traditional' 'direct action' methods of 'pre-industrial' England.[33]

An approach such as this has received the support of John

---

[31] George Rudé, 'English rural and urban disturbances on the eve of the first reform bill, 1830–1', *Past and Present*, no. 37 (July 1967), pp. 91–3, 100–1. See also: Rudé, *Crowd in the French revolution*, pp. 235–9; Rudé, 'The "pre-industrial" crowd', repr. in Rudé, *Paris and London in the eighteenth century* (London, 1974), pp. 17–34; Hobsbawm, *Primitive rebels*, ch. 7.

[32] Rudé, 'English rural and urban disturbances', p. 98.

[33] *Ibid.*, p. 90. See E.J. Hobsbawm and G. Rudé, *Captain Swing* (London, 1969).

Stevenson, in his important 'textbook' *Popular disturbances in England, 1700–1870*. Stevenson, however, is a rather sophisticated proponent of the view, being well aware of the contingent elements of disturbance. Indeed the subtlety of the book is such that the simple section headings relating to 'the transition to order' come as something of a surprise. The approach is also be to found in Gwyn Williams' *Merthyr rising*.[34] But perhaps the best-known advocate of the transition, or modernisation, thesis is Charles Tilly, who brings a sociological perspective to the history of mass protest. His well-known article 'Collective violence in European perspective', published in 1969, began by disputing the assumption (to be found in the writing of the 'crowd psychologists') that collective violence was linked to, and indeed created by, the impact of industrialisation.[35] Tilly preferred to argue that in industrial society struggles take place for established places within the power structure, and that it is those groups that fail to acquire or that lose power within the established structure that resort to violence. Those groups that are successful, on the other hand, take advantage of their proximity to the seats of power, and campaign through institutional channels. From this starting point Tilly went on to argue that those groups that were losing their position under industrialisation, and that sought to preserve their old status, were backward looking in their protest, and communal in their means of organisation. Meanwhile, those groups that sought rights due to them, but not yet enjoyed, formed into specialist associations, with well-defined objectives. The reactionary, and communal, form of protest challenges the claims of the national state and the national economy; the modern, associational, forms assume the state is durable. In England, Tilly contends, reactionary forms declined from around the 1830s; and, consequently, so did collective violence. He concludes, therefore, that, contrary to some views, there may be a negative correlation between industrialisation and violence.

Tilly has, more recently, elaborated his argument, attempting to chart the rise of the 'social movement' through shifts in the forms and language of mass protest.[36] This recent work confirms one of the

[34] Williams, *Merthyr rising*, esp. ch. 10.
[35] Charles Tilly, 'Collective violence in European perspective', in Hugh Davis Graham and Ted Robert Gurr (eds.), *The history of violence in America: historical and comparative perspectives* (New York, 1969), pp. 4–45.
[36] Charles Tilly, 'Britain creates the social movement', in James E. Cronin and Jonathan Schneer (eds.), *Social conflict and the political order in modern Britain* (London, 1982), pp. 21–51.

major problems with Tilly's work, namely, his research methods. Despite his recent claim that analysis of collective action must be historically specific, [37] he continues to employ a method for search for data related to collective behaviour which is designed to satisfy the retrieval needs of the computer, rather than a rich appreciation of context.[38] Undoubtedly, Hobsbawm and Stevenson would both have grave reservation about these methods, since both have expressed an awareness that by searching only for incidents of violence, the historian fails to identify all those occasions on which there was last minute reconciliation: the resulting picture is one only of outbursts, and not of contention.[39]

Returning more specifically to the transition theory as deployed by Tilly, Rudé, *et al.*, criticisms can be made from two perspectives. The first concerns the ideology of 'social movements' pre-1850. Gareth Stedman Jones has presented a persuasive challenge to the view that Chartism represented the first class conscious popular movement.[40] Through an analysis of the language of Chartism, Stedman Jones demonstrates that radical thought up to at least 1848 continued to concentrate on the notion that political power was the basis for economic power:

Radical and Chartist politics make no sense if they are interpreted as a response to the emergence of an industrial capitalism conceived as an objective, inevitable, and irreversible economic process. The radical picture was of a far more arbitrary and artificial development whose source was to be found not in the real workings of the economy, but in the acceleration and accentuation of a process of financial plunder made possible by the political developments of the preceding fifty years.[41]

In short, insofar as 'new' methods of protest were developed in the second quarter of the nineteenth century, they were the methods of a movement informed not by a 'new' proto-Marxist consciousness, but by the radical critique of the eighteenth century.

The second area of criticism relates to the methodological approach invited by the implicit determinism of the transition theory:

---

[37] Charles Tilly, intro. to Louise A. Tilly and Charles Tilly (eds.), *Class conflict and collective action* (London, 1981), p. 16.

[38] Tilly, 'Britain creates the social movement', esp. pp. 32–48.

[39] E.J. Hobsbawm, 'Political violence and political murder: comments on Franklin Ford's essay', in Wolfgang J. Mommsen and Gerhard Hirschfield (eds.), *Social protest, violence and terror in nineteenth- and twentieth-century Europe* (London, 1982), pp. 13–19; Stevenson, *Popular disturbances*, pp. 303–4.

[40] Gareth Stedman Jones, 'The language of Chartism', in James Epstein and Dorothy Thompson (eds.), *The Chartist experience: studies in working-class radicalism and culture 1830–60* (London, 1982), pp. 3–58.   [41] *Ibid.*, p. 46.

since there is a 'modern' form of protest consistent with the machinery of the modern state, that is the form of protest to which groupings will proceed; deviation from that path may be seen as backward, and anachronistic. The *effect* of this approach is to make the prophecy self-fulfilling: since riotous protest should barely exist in the modern state, examples of its occurrence (or, as importantly, near occurrence) are not actively sought out; and, when they do crop up, they are dismissed as backward. It may be no coincidence that so much attention has been focused on collective violence in the period 1780–1850. These are commonly thought to have been the years in which Britain moved from a pre-industrial to an industrial economy; it is therefore 'obvious' that the transition from pre-industrial to industrial protest should have taken place at this time also. There is far less enthusiasm to analyse the incidence of riot in the later nineteenth century. Disturbances in this period tend to be portrayed as, at best, the desperate last stand of social groupings lacking in consciousness; and, at worst, as examples of apolitical rowdyism. Cursory examination of any decade after 1850 reveals numerous examples of riotous protest, and there are doubtless many more as yet undocumented incidents. The examples that have been found are rarely subject to the same kind of scrutiny as early nineteenth-century outbreaks.

Perhaps more seriously, the insistence upon absolute, rather than partial, temporary or episodic, changes in protest methods seems to have discouraged the analysis of the supposed change. Insufficient attention has been given to the precise timing, form and context of the discontinuities to which the transition theorists allude.[42] Subsequently, a number of detailed studies have been able to question the tidiness of the transition to such an extent that the notion has almost lost its usefulness.[43] At present, contextual studies of mass protest (such as those undertaken by John Walter, Adrian Randall and Richard Evans[44]), together with attempts to analyse the pragmatics

[42] Robert J. Holton, 'The crowd in history: some problems of theory and method', *Social History*, III, 2 (1978), pp. 219, 228–32.
[43] For example: Adrian J. Randall, 'The shearmen and the Wiltshire outrages of 1802: trade unionism and industrial violence', *Social History*, VII, 3 (1982), pp. 283–304; Mark Harrison, ' "To raise and dare resentment": the Bristol Bridge riot of 1793 re-examined', *Historical Journal*, XXVI, 3 (1983), pp. 557–85; Richard N. Price, 'The other face of respectability: violence in the Manchester brickmaking trade, 1859–70', *Past and Present*, no. 66 (Feb. 1975), pp. 110–32.
[44] John Walter, 'Grain riots and popular attitudes to the law: Maldon and the crisis of 1629', in Brewer and Styles (eds.), *An ungovernable people*, pp. 47–84; Randall,

of mass campaigning (such as John Belchem's important work on the 'mass platform'[45]), are the most valuable sources for the analysis of popular protest, despite the fact that they do not fit neatly into an overall theory of 'change'.

The work of Rudé, Hobsbawm and Tilly represents perhaps the best-known transition argument. It is, however, an argument that comes in two other guises. The first might be termed the 'transition to consensus', the second the 'transition to restraint'.

The consensus approach is functionalist; its analysis is based on the premise that there exists a community of common values (a state of equilibrium) to which all sensible (or even all rational) individuals will adhere. In this line of approach, the early nineteenth century is a period of disorder and strife, with the emerging, growing industrial cities being the cause and location of alienation, resulting in disaffection. Such cities were also, it is suggested, natural homes for those in society who are beyond rational, social, behaviour; who, for one reason or another, had sunk to that level where animalistic instinct was the prime motivator. These individuals, beyond redemption, fed on, and took advantage of, the confusion of decent working people, thereby encouraging disorder, violence and tumult. The mid-Victorian years, it is argued, saw a stabilisation of urban industrial society, with the development of a number of regulatory institutions, the creation of more effective agencies for public order, a growing popular awareness of the benefits of industrial growth and the increasing confidence and prominence of socially conscious middle class reformers. The result of this set of developments was an 'age of equipoise'; an age of political and social stability which was impervious to (although periodically troubled by) deviant elements. As far as collective behaviour is concerned, this 'age of equipoise' produced a decline in violence and mass dispute, and a greater popular interest in consensual events, such as those involving the monarch. This is not to say that violent conduct disappeared: the

'Shearmen and the Wiltshire outrages'; Richard Evans, ' "Red Wednesday" in Hamburg: social democrats, police and lumpenproletariat in the suffrage disturbances of 17 January 1906', *Social History*, IV, 1 (1979), pp. 1–31.

[45] John Belchem, 'Henry Hunt and the evolution of the mass platform', *English Historical Review*, XCIII (1978), pp. 739–73; John Belchem, 'Republicanism, popular constitutionalism and the radical platform in early nineteenth-century England', *Social History*, VI, 1 (1981), pp. 1–32; John Belchem, '1848: Feargus O'Connor and the collapse of the mass platform', in Epstein and Thompson (eds.), *The Chartist experience*, pp. 269–310.

'untaught minds' were still numerous, and the mid-Victorian city could still be a dangerous place. Furthermore, those events that appealed to, and encouraged, the gloating and ignorant were not always quick to disappear: executions, for instance, remained public until 1868. The best-known exponents of this argument are W.L. Burn and Geoffrey Best; more recently it has been reformulated in less judgemental tones by J.M. Golby and A.W. Purdue.[46]

Clearly the consensus argument is an approach to history which demands a thoroughgoing critique beyond the scope of this chapter – although it will be attacked implicitly by almost everything that follows. Certainly it is inimical to the historical analysis of crowds, for two reasons. First, it supports the conflation of crowd and violence (essentially along the lines of LeBon); and second, it regards all collective behaviour that is not formally institutionalised as deviant. Nevertheless, there have been publications which both adopt a consensual point of view, and also address themselves directly to crowd events; the product is a peculiar, condescending, catalogue of 'mob' behaviour, all of which is taken only to demonstrate how slow and uneven the progress to order actually was. Examples are provided by David Cooper's *The lesson of the scaffold*, on the decline and abolition of public execution, and Donald Richter's publications, 'The role of the mob-riot in Victorian elections, 1865–85', and *Riotous Victorians*.[47] These two writers produce a vulgarisation (if such a thing is possible) of the consensus argument which describes crowds in terms of mobbish chaos, and disturbance in terms of 'rioting for fun'. It is an approach, particularly to riot, which has received support in the United States in discussion of the civil disturbances of the 1960s.[48]

The last of the transition arguments is by far the most sophisticated and the most persuasive. It is not possible to talk of a self-conscious school relating to what might be termed the theory of a 'transition to restraint'. However, it embraces the work of V.A.C. Gatrell, Hugh

---

[46] Burn, *The age of equipoise*, ch. 2; Geoffrey Best, *Mid-Victorian Britain, 1851–70* (Glasgow, 1979), chs. 3, 4; J.M. Golby and A.W. Purdue, *The civilisation of the crowd: popular culture in England 1750–1900* (London, 1984).

[47] Cooper, *Lesson of the scaffold*, esp. pp. 3, 20, 28; Donald Richter, 'The role of the mob-riot in Victorian elections, 1865–85', *Victorian Studies*, XV, 1 (1971), pp. 19–28; Donald Richter, *Riotous Victorians* (London, 1981).

[48] Notably, Edward C. Banfield, 'Rioting mainly for fun and profit', in James Q. Wilson (ed.), *The metropolitan enigma: inquiries into the nature and dimension of America's 'urban crisis'* (Cambridge, Mass., 1968), pp. 283–308.

Cunningham, Robert D. Storch and David Jones, and makes much use of the work of Gareth Stedman Jones and Allan Silver. [49] Essentially, it embraces many of those writers who would have employed a liberal conception of 'social control', before Stedman Jones declared the term unusable.[50] Like the consensus theorists, these historians are rarely concerned directly with mass phenomena; it is rather that the occurrence of mass phenomena is an important element of their work.

In broad terms, the restraint argument observes a transition from violent, unruly and crowd-bound activity in the early nineteenth century towards less violent, less crowd-based activity later in the century. So far this is no different from the other transition theories. The difference lies in the explanation, which is (again in broad terms) that the lives of working people were subject to constraints from two directions. The first came from a series of initiatives and intrusions on the part of a self-conscious, bourgeois, state, in the fields of penal, police and poor law reform, the legal system, institutional administration and labour relations. The second came from the working class itself: its demand for respect and respectability, for accommodation within the political nation; and its experience of defeat in the fields of industrial relations and radical politics. Riots declined as the police and courts became more effective, and as working people became less prepared to take part. Mass meetings declined after the defeat of Chartism, with the gradual stigmatisation of 'mass politics', and with the growing efficiency of state agencies in deploying a proscriptive legal code. Crowds at 'consensual' events, such as coronations, grew

[49] V.A.C. Gatrell, 'The decline of theft and violence in Victorian and Edwardian England', in V.A.C. Gatrell, Bruce Lenman and Geoffrey Parker (eds.), *Crime and the law: the social history of crime in western Europe since 1500* (London, 1980), pp. 238–337; Hugh Cunningham, *Leisure in the industrial revolution* (London, 1980); Robert D. Storch, 'The policeman as domestic missionary: urban discipline and popular culture in northern England, 1850–80', *Journal of Social History*, IX, 4 (1976), pp. 481–509; Robert D. Storch (ed.), *Popular culture and custom in nineteenth-century England* (London, 1982); David Jones, *Crime, protest, community and police in nineteenth-century Britain* (London, 1982); Gareth Stedman Jones, 'Working class culture and working class politics in London, 1870–1900: notes on the remaking of a working class', *Journal of Social History*, VIII, 4 (1974), pp. 460–508; Stedman Jones, *Outcast London*; Allan Silver, 'The demand for order in civil society: a review of some themes in the history of urban crime, police and riot', in David J. Bordua (ed.), *The police: six sociological essays* (New York, 1967), pp. 1–24. Also see the collection of essays: Donajgrodzki (ed.), *Social control*.

[50] Stedman Jones, 'Class expression versus social control? A critique of recent trends in the social history of leisure', *History Workshop Journal*, IV (1977), pp. 162–70.

as the authorities became better able to stage and manage them, and more confident of the message being presented. They also benefited from the growing political conservatism of working people, and the development of a working class 'culture of consolation' which, amongst other things, offered spectacle.

The 'transition to restraint' point of view is refreshingly self-critical: it is enthusiastic to accommodate the continuing autonomy of popular culture, to stress the difference between perception and reality, to question the validity of its own quantitative methods, and to eschew value laden notions of 'improvement through change'. Nevertheless, the doubts it expresses relate principally to how thoroughgoing the changes really were, and to what extent the 'moral reformers' were in fact responsible for the change. It is largely content to share with the consensus point of view the picture of early nineteenth-century England as musclebound with sturdy tradition and tumult, as a time when violence continued to be 'as English as plum pudding'.[51]

In formulating the 'transition to restraint' argument, a number of historians have been squeezed uncomfortably onto the same platform. The point of this is to suggest the existence of an intelligent and rigorous body of research, which draws conclusions about the development of certain aspects of mass phenomena, but which rarely addresses the subject head-on. Were they to do so their arguments would not in all instances be discredited, but they would be modified. Insofar as this body of writing discusses crowds, it has three sets of shortcomings. First, by maintaining the presumption that there was a marked transition in public order during the nineteenth century it has (uncharacteristically) accepted at face value some of the declarations made by contemporaries, and failed to question the objective reality of some supposed changes. Thus, was the urban environment of the early nineteenth century really as unruly as some contemporaries claimed, and as subsequent historians have maintained? With this in mind, was there in fact a dramatic decline in the incidence of riot (from a high starting point) over the century? Do crowds deserve their image as fundamentally violent phenomena, and, if not, what does this suggest about contemporary characterisations and perceptions of crowds? Second, by failing to criticise Rudé's conflation of crowd and riot, and by omitting any discussion of the crowd as a general

---

[51] The phrase is Roy Porter's: *English society in the eighteenth century* (Harmondsworth, 1982), p. 114.

organising concept, it has not developed a means of examining possible continuities in crowd behaviour and perception. In other words, should crowds at celebratory events be regarded in an entirely different light from crowds at riots? How should crowds at celebrations and ceremonials be analysed? The third set of questions which the 'restraint' approach fails to answer relates to nineteenth-century commentators' apparent concern about the masses, and their apparent concern about mass. What was the relationship between the two? Was an alarm about crowds part of a broader alarm about population growth and population density? Were distinctions drawn between the crowd in the city and the crowded city; and, if so, did attitudes towards the one influence attitudes towards the other?

These questions emphasise the need for a thorough reappraisal of 'the crowd' in nineteenth-century England. It was argued earlier that the work of the 'crowd historians' was preoccupied with riots. An important context for their arguments was the notion of a transition in popular protest in England away from violence. Much of the remaining historiography dealing (albeit less directly) with crowds also accepts the notion of a 'transition to order'. Consequently its greatest concern is with the degree to which crowds were either disruptive and violent or successfully 'managed' by those in authority; to the extent that these writers consider other crowd forms, it is in terms of their supposed contribution to the increase in public order: they regard such crowds simply as 'not-riots'.

III

It might be anticipated that sociologists and social psychologists, through their interest in 'collective behaviour' rather than 'collective bargaining by riot', would employ a broader notion of the crowd. In some respects they do; but work in these disciplines appears to break down into two fields, neither of which are especially useful to the historian.

At one level, there are studies of the interpersonal relations and psychological stresses operating within gatherings of two persons and upwards. The literature on this aspect of collective behaviour is extensive.[52] An attempt to relate such discussions to historical

[52] See, for example, Erving Goffman, *Behaviour in public places: notes on the social organisation of gatherings* (New York, 1963); Paul M. Insel and Henry Clay Lindgen, *Too close for comfort: the psychology of crowding* (Eaglewood Cliffs, NJ, 1978).

analyses of the crowd could, potentially, be exciting. But some careful thinking would have to be done before applying such literature to historical (and especially pre-twentieth-century) examples. How can the historian place him or herself in the same position as the fieldworker in the social sciences, who stands beside or among the crowd, equipped with camera, tape recorder, video camera or notepad? At present, historical research in the area of mass pheno- mena is too underdeveloped to accommodate such a departure – principally because for so long as the history of the crowd remains essentially the history of the reporter's perceptions of the crowd, any consideration of the psychological components of crowd action is largely irrelevant. It is precisely because so many remarks about crowds made by historians draw on the home-spun psychoanalysis made by crowd observers that those remarks are redundant.

The other field of sociological research concerns collective 'out- bursts'. Perhaps the best-known example in this field is Neil J. Smelser's *Theory of collective behaviour*, published in 1962, and much referred to by historians and sociologists alike. It is one of the most respected attempts to find a common causal process for all incidents of collective behaviour (or, more precisely, outbursts).[53] Smelser's definition of collective behaviour, however, once more served to emphasise the supposedly mysterious and disruptive aspects of crowds. Smelser begins by defining collective behaviour as a mobilis- ation on the basis of a belief which redefines social action. Thus, his conception of the crowd is solely as an active, goal-orientated, grouping (at the expense of a conception which might include spectating gatherings, for example). But when Smelser goes on to explain what the 'beliefs' he refers to are, his definition is narrowed still further.

They involve a belief in the existence of extra-ordinary forces – threats, conspiracies etc. – which are at work in the universe. They also involve an assessment of the extra-ordinary consequences which will follow if the collective attempt to reconstitute social action is successful. The beliefs on which collective behaviour is based (we shall call them *generalised* beliefs) are thus akin to magical beliefs.[54]

Informed by beliefs which seem magical, episodes of collective behaviour proceed, Smelser argues, by a sequential logic which he terms 'the logic of value added'. By this notion, there is a precise set of

[53] Neil J. Smelser, *Theory of collective behaviour* (London, 1962).   [54] *Ibid.*, p. 8.

necessary conditions which need to occur in a definite pattern in order for episodes of collective behaviour to take place; as each determinant becomes present, the form and type of episode becomes increasingly specific. In sequence, those determinants are: structural conduciveness, structural strain, growth and spread of the generalised belief, precipitating factors, mobilisation of participants for action and the operation of social control.[55]

Quite clearly, Smelser has very particular forms of collective behaviour in mind: ones concerned with some form of protest, distrubance, disruption or crisis. His theory is therefore of only limited usefulness for a broader conception of crowd formation. But this aside, Smelser's theory is still unconvincing. Each determinant he identifies may certainly be present at some point; it is not clear, however, that they should proceed in such a neat sequence. Neither is it obvious that the various strains and beliefs should be attributable to the selected episode of collective behaviour: in searching for evidence of 'strain', how are social tensions in general to be separated from those which are specifically appropriate to the generation of collective action? Smelser's view of the position of collective action within a process is teleological. For the historian, working backwards from an incident of collective behaviour, and with the complicating factors relating to the availability and reliability of sources, the determinants are unlikely to be clearly distinguishable. For the social scientist attempting to predict an episode, the determinants may not be clearly visible without the illumination provided by the actual occurrence of the 'outburst', and the benefit of hindsight. Furthermore, 'precipitating factors' may in any case be so unpredictable as to border on the accidental.

Among social psychologists, Stanley Milgram and Hans Toch, contributing to the *Handbook of social psychology* have provided a particularly comprehensive discussion of collective behaviour, in which they make a distinction between crowds and social movements.[56] They are in no doubt that social psychologists are the only academics suited to 'the scientific treatment of collective behaviour'. After all, 'historians devote attention to particular historical episodes involving crowds, but explicate the occurrence of single events,

---

[55] *Ibid.*, pp. 13–17.
[56] Stanley Milgram and Hans Toch, 'Collective behaviour: crowds and social movements', in Gardner Lindzey and Elliot Aronson (eds.), *The handbook of social psychology*, vol. 4 (Reading, Mass., 1969), pp. 507–610.

without seeking principles common to all crowds or social movements'.[57] Significantly, however, Milgram and Toch, like so many others, find it extremely difficult to prevent their discussion of the crowd from drifting into discussion of disturbance. Their initial definition is broad enough: 'Crowd is a generic term referring to highly diverse conditions of human assemblage: audience, mob, rally, and panic all fall within the definition of crowds. Common to these terms is the idea of human beings in sufficiently close proximity that the fact of aggregation comes to influence their behaviour.'[58] But their selection of one hundred headlines from the *New York Times* dealing with episodes of collective behaviour in 1964 soon demonstrates their overriding concern with disorder, violence, panic and protest. They conclude their examination of the headlines by observing that 'the immediate motives of crowds are often the culmination of grievances built up over time'.[59]

In short, then, the basic notions of LeBon seem to be perpetuated throughout the social sciences. There seems little possibility, at present, of a break in the trend. When Jerry D. Rose published a 'sociology of collective behaviour' in 1982, he correctly observed that such studies throughout their history 'have been overwhelmingly concerned with the form of *protest*'.[60] Rose's conception is broader than this; but he nevertheless titles his book *Outbreaks*, and proceeds from a definition of collective behaviour as 'the kind of behaviour that generates *news*', to the conclusion that 'collective behaviour appears under conditions of social dislocation', via the discussion of disasters, protests, persecutions and renewals.[61]

IV

The work on eighteenth-century food crowds was concerned in the first instance with the disruptive aspect of crowds, but it also noted the role of crowd action as an agency of 'order': the widespread recognition of the validity of such action may have effectively reduced inherent class tensions. Much of the other literature discussed so far sees crowds rather more straightforwardly as disruptive, except insofar as they are brought together for the institutional fortification of order (such as at ceremonials); and even here the issue is crowd control and management. Crowds are things which either behave

[57] *Ibid.*, p. 508.   [58] *Ibid.*, p. 509.   [59] *Ibid.*, p. 517.
[60] Rose, *Outbreaks*, p. 73.   [61] *Ibid.*, pp. 4, 294.

themselves or pursue their inherent desire not to. A more broad-minded conception would examine further the role of crowds as autonomous, or quasi-autonomous, vehicles for the expression of cohesion – for the expression of different versions of order. It would look more critically at the potential for crowd members to characterise themselves, and be characterised as, the bearers of messages.

It was, of course, Hobsbawm, one of the original 'crowd historians', who pointed out that the strength of organised protest groups sometimes lies in the fact that they do not need to resort to violence, since their opponents' fear of violence is sufficient in itself to prevent them from carrying out those acts against which the protestors object. Such moments, said Hobsbawm, escape an index which looks merely at the number of violent occurrences.[62] This is, indirectly, the first invitation to a more acute study of crowd phenomena: mass, public, dispute may not necessarily be realised through physical violence. Once this premise has been established it is possible to go further: dispute may be *concealed* by last minute reconciliation, by the constraints of social propriety, by the existence of more pressing concerns or by the ritualisation of hostility. It is not the case that all crowd phenomena conceal specific disputes; but the discussion of the public expression of dispute does necessitate the examination of *all* crowd phenomena.

This important point can be illustrated through consideration of two fields of work related to mass phenomena: first, football crowds and football hooliganism; and second, ritual and ceremonial. Football crowds are a particularly vivid example, since, despite the ways in which they are commonly characterised, such crowds cannot be placed in a classification along with protest and violence, for two reasons. In the first place, despite the fact that there have always been incidents of violence among football crowds, the vast majority of such crowds are not, and have not in the past been, violent.[63] And

---

[62] Hobsbawm, 'Political violence and political murder'; E.J. Hobsbawm, 'The rules of violence', in his *Revolutionaries: contemporary essays* (London, 1973), pp. 209–15.

[63] Wray Vamplew, 'Ungentlemanly conduct: the control of soccer crowd behaviour in England, 1888–1914', in T.C. Smout (ed.), *The search for wealth and stability* (London, 1969), pp. 139–54; Geoffrey Pearson, *Hooligan: a history of respectable fears* (London, 1983), pp. 29–31, 64–5; Ian Taylor, ' "Football mad": a speculative sociology of football hooliganism', in Eric Dunning (ed.), *The sociology of sport: a selection of readings* (London, 1971), pp. 352–77; Ian Taylor, 'Soccer consciousness

secondly, recent sociological analysis of football crowds suggests that although incidents of physical violence are rare, incidents of ritualised violence occur repeatedly. Detailed research suggests that despite the fact that some football supporters themselves claim to have violent ambitions, in actuality few seek out or desire physical violence. What they perceive as their code of violence is, in fact, for most of them, a code of aggression and ritualised violence which operates within the constraints of a complex, and identifiable, set of rules.[64] In other words, in football crowds there can be seen a ritual of violence which is integral to an essentially non-protesting, non-violent crowd form.

Football crowds also provide evidence that there is a distinction to be made between aggression and violence. Definitions of aggression can be broad: Lionel Tiger has described it as 'a process of more or less conscious coercion against the will of any individual or group of animals or men by an individual or group of people'. Aggression does not necessarily contain any element of ferocity, viciousness or destructiveness.[65] So where is the line to be drawn? Some of the literature relating to ritual and ceremonial confronts the problem. A range of coercive activity from 'soft' aggression through to physical violence has been identified in festive and carnival activity in early modern Europe. Emmanuel Le Roy Ladurie has described how in Romans, in France, in the years 1579–80, annual festivity proceeded to carnage, with the antagonists engaging at once in celebration and preparation for slaughter.[66] Natalie Zemon Davis has shown how religious violence in sixteenth-century France was clothed in the procedure of rite and derision.[67] Peter Burke has examined the progression from ritualised to physical conflict in mid-seventeenth-century Italy.[68] Such discussions are of particular significance since

and soccer hooliganism', in S. Cohen (ed.), *Images of deviance* (Harmondsworth, 1971), pp. 134–64; Peter Marsh, *Aggro: the illusion of violence* (London, 1978); Peter Marsh, Elizabeth Rosser and Rom Harré, *The rules of disorder* (London, 1978), chs. 1, 3–5.

[64] Marsh, *Aggro*, ch. 1; Marsh, Rosser and Harré, *Rules of disorder*, chs. 4, 5, and esp. pp. 70–2, 96–7, 105–13. See also, Robin Fox, 'The inherent rules of violence', in Peter Collett (ed.), *Social rules and social behaviour* (Oxford, 1977), pp. 132–49.

[65] Lionel Tiger, *Men in groups* (London, 1969), p. 158.

[66] Emmanuel Le Roy Ladurie, *Carnival in Romans: a people's uprising at Romans, 1579–80*, trans. Mary Feeney (Harmondsworth, 1981).

[67] Natalie Zemon Davis, 'The rites of violence: religious riot in sixteenth-century France', *Past and Present*, no. 59 (May 1973), pp. 51–91.

[68] Peter Burke, 'The virgin of the Carmine and the revolt of Masaniello', *Past and Present*, no. 99 (May 1983), pp. 3–21.

they point to a continuous chain of action, belief, aggression and violence which extends from the rituals of the festival calendar right through to officially sanctioned massacres. Furthermore, they are concerned both with the participants in and the spectators of ritualistic and celebratory activity.

There is, in addition, an increasing number of historical studies of ritual and ceremonial mass events not associated with the occurrence of violence. Philip Ziegler's *Crown and people*, using material from the Mass Observation archive, offers some, albeit rather anecdotal, information on popular attendance at royal events of the twentieth century. The book includes evidence that the form, mood and atmosphere of crowds at royal funerals was much the same as that at royal celebrations; implicitly it suggests that such events held numerous different meanings for different groups of people, and therefore that they cannot be regarded simply as incidents of mass consensus.[69] The second example is provided by John Brewer, whose work on eighteenth-century politics has included two pieces of research which look closely at the meaning and function, particularly for processional crowds, of political ritualism and symbolism. The first of these is his examination of the mock elections at Garrat in the later eighteenth century. Here Brewer shows how a burlesque inversion ritual initially directed at national politics became transformed by the competing attentions of radical and conservative middle class patrons and spectators. The meaning of the ritual was transformed from parody directed at the ruling class, to, at once, the expression and the derision of radical politics. Crucially, the meaning changed not merely because the content partially changed, but also because the audience changed: the ritual was, literally, viewed through new, and different, eyes.[70] The second piece by Brewer is his analysis of Wilkite ritualism and propaganda. In this instance he demonstrates how Wilkite crowds served to encourage order and organisation in a hard political campaign, and yet how, for Wilkes' followers, and in their propaganda, Wilkes represented a 'lord of misrule' – the lord of a plebeian parody of established authority.[71]

A third example is Elizabeth Hammerton's and David

---

[69] Philip Ziegler, *Crown and people* (London, 1978), pp. 55–68, 90–5, 107–15, 119–20, 176–85.

[70] John Brewer, 'Theatre and counter-theatre in Georgian politics: the mock elections at Garrat', *Radical History Review*, no. 22 (1979–80), pp. 7–40.

[71] John Brewer, *Party ideology and popular politics at the accession of George III* (Cambridge, 1976), ch. 9.

Cannadine's examination of the celebration in Cambridge in 1897 of Victoria's Diamond Jubilee. In this article they have employed a methodological ruthlessness which derives from, and ultimately exceeds, that more commonly devoted to studies of popular protest. They have, thereby, identified a history of dispute and conciliation in the planning of a ceremonial event which crude statements about 'consensus' or 'class propaganda' would, in other instances, have concealed. As a result, they have made some progress towards understanding the meaning, for the inhabitants of Cambridge, of that mass event.[72] Finally, there is Linda Colley's important article on patriotism and royal spectacle during the reign of George III. Colley examines the transformation in the public presentation and reputation of the monarchy between 1760 and 1820, and, in particular, the impact upon royal display of the attempt to promote George III in opposition to French republicanism after 1789. She makes some mention of crowds at these events, but does not portray them in terms of a simple notion of patriotism and consensus. Rather, she considers the context and content of patriotism, the 'marketing' of crowd events and the basis for mass attendance.[73]

V

The concentration in much of the literature on aggression, ritualised violence, ritual and ceremonial is upon disjunctions, ranging from differing interpretations among participants in, and observers of, mass events, to disputes resulting in physical violence. It might be argued, therefore, that emphasis remains upon crowds as a disruptive force. At one level this is the case – inevitably perhaps, given that the theoretical debate underpinning the discussion of ritual activity has tended to be in terms of social cohesion versus class conflict.[74] Of greater importance, methodologically at least, is the fact that this literature takes a critical view of apparently 'conservative', 'non-protesting', crowd forms, and does not merely regard their existence as evidence of popular rejection, or authoritarian repression, of radical mass displays. Because these studies do not attempt to fit all

[72] Elizabeth Hammerton and David Cannadine, 'Conflict and consensus on a ceremonial occasion: the diamond jubilee in Cambridge in 1897', *Historical Journal*, XXIV, 1 (1981), pp. 111–46.

[73] Linda Colley, 'The apotheosis of George III: loyalty, royalty and the British nation, 1760–1820', *Past and Present*, no. 102 (Feb. 1984), pp. 94–123.

[74] See below, ch. 10.

crowd events into a model of greater or lesser public order, they are able to direct their analysis at the meaning and context of those events. In some respects these are the real 'crowd historians'.

The relevance of a sizeable proportion of the literature concerning mass phenomena is primarily its contribution to the creation and perpetuation of a mystique. What is remarkable is the apparent unwillingness to examine the basis for that mystique: although it may be the product of the susceptibility of crowds to a certain kind of reportage, most of the literature has nevertheless taken it as an inherent quality, as one generated from within crowds themselves. To the extent that such an image has been questioned, it has been only to replace it with a new myth: that crowds are riots.

2. *The crowd in history: problems of definition and method*

It is only in a crowd that man can become free of [the] fear of being touched. That is the only situation in which the fear changes into its opposite. The crowd he needs is the dense crowd, in which body is pressed to body; a crowd, too, whose physical constitution is also dense, or compact, so that he no longer notices who it is that presses against him.

(Elias Canetti, *Crowds and power*, trans. Carol Stewart (Harmondsworth, 1973), pp. 15–16)

From a distance this crowd looked a uniformly nondescript plaster colour, a neutral tone made up chiefly of faded blue and dirty grey. Now and again some workman would stop to light his pipe, but the others tramped on round him with never a smile, never a word to a mate, pasty faces turned towards Paris, which swallowed them one by one down the gaping hole of the Faubourg Poissonniere.

(Emile Zola, *L'Assommoir*, trans. Leonard Tancock (Harmondsworth, 1970), pp. 25–6)

Even if it can be demonstrated that the existing historiography relating to crowds is selective in its attentions and deficient in its explanations, this does not in itself explain the usefulness of the historical discussion of the crowd as a general organising concept. The history of crowds is in part the history of political agitation and protest, of trade unionism and labour dispute; in part of local and national government and their response to particular and public events; in part of patriotism, ritual, ceremonial; in part of industrialisation and urbanisation; in part of violence and riot, sport and leisure, crime and policing. To this extent it could be argued that a history of 'the crowd' is unnecessary, even meaningless. It could be said that the crowd is, rather, an element of these individual, and to some extent separate, developments. The moment at which crowds form within the context of each of these aspects of English history could be said to be of greater interest and significance than the formation of crowds in general.

Certainly there is a strong case to be made for the detailed study of, for example, the dynamics of crowd formation within different spheres. Or perhaps the history of the crowd can be constructed through separate histories of the mass platform, trade unionism, popular protest, popular recreation, ceremonial and so on. In the second of these chapters concerned with theory and method, it will be argued that there are good reasons for attempting a general study – ones relating to context and perception. These reasons in themselves, however, generate problems of methodology and definition, which need to be clarified before, finally, an explanation is offered for the selection of, and approach to, the four towns which form the core of this study.

I

The first argument that can be made in favour of a general study of crowds is conceptual; the second is rather more pragmatic. Both are concerned with context and perception. The conceptual argument may be outlined as follows. The immediate context for any given crowd is the event of which it forms a part. Thus, the immediate context for a mass meeting must, in the first instance, be the issue addressed by the meeting and not the crowd as an organising concept. The meaning of that meeting for its participants, however, will in part relate specifically to the issue at stake, and in part to their experience of being in crowds. For some, of course, it will be their first experience of participating in a mass event, but this novelty is in itself important since it will alter their perception of themselves, and may alter their future perceptions of other kinds of mass event. For those observing the mass meeting, meanwhile, their attitudes towards the crowd on the one hand, and towards the issue on the other, will be conditioned by two things: first their experience of the issue at stake (or similar issues, or any movement of which the issue forms a part); and second their experience of, and attitudes towards, mass.

There are, therefore, two contexts: the event itself, and the position of the event within other mass activity. Perceptions, for both crowd members and observers, will be framed by both of these contexts. There is not, however, a simple causal relationship here: although it is possible, with a reasonable degree of accuracy, for the historian to reconstruct the context, this will not in itself predict the nature of perceptions. Stated perceptions, therefore, will offer information regarding the way in which the participant or the observer has read the contexts. If those stated perceptions are publicised, then they in turn become an important part of the context for future mass events. To give another illustration: the response of a local magistrate to a potentially threatening crowd may be conditioned in part by the issue at stake, in part by his previous experience of such gatherings, in part by his experience of crowds in general, and in part by the influence upon him of the attitudes of others (as well, of course, as by considerations relating to the law and to central government policy). The response which emerges out of this complex set of influences in turn conditions future contexts and perceptions – both from his point of view, and from the point of view of those who observed his response. What is clear from these two illustrations is that histories of the respective crowd gathering issues would not in themselves offer an adequate understanding of the crowds associated with them.

The second argument to be made in favour of a general study is rather more straightforward. Was there, or could there have been, in the early nineteenth century, a commonly held notion of 'the crowd'; or were different kinds of crowd viewed as largely unrelated phenomena? Did the crowd occupy a widely acknowledged position within the ordering and understanding of the local environment? Is it reasonable to talk of coherent notions of the crowd in this period, or does this merely force a false unity upon too broad a spectrum of historical events? There may be more than one way of attempting to answer these questions; but there does seem to be a pressing need, in the first instance, for the documentation and analysis of a wide range of crowd occurrences, in a number of locations, over a reasonably long period of time.

The invitation being made by these arguments is to pitch the stated and publicised perceptions of contemporaries against basic contextual information emerging from the examination of a number of crowd events. In other words, the attempt is both to understand what contemporaries meant when they talked of crowds or public order or masses, and to contextualise the claims being made regarding the beliefs and intentions of crowds. Is the reading of mass events offered by contemporaries the only possible reading? Where accounts of crowd events are reasonably detailed, is it possible (as Peter Burke has put it) to read from the account an alternative interpretation of events which runs against the grain of the text itself?[1] Could the alternative reading be assisted by an appreciation of attitudes towards, and patterns of activity among, crowds of very different types? Given the complex influences in the formation of attitudes towards mass events, the relevant contextual background for a riot is unlikely to be only other riots; why should the popular response to ceremonials be in terms only of other ceremonials?

II

Emphasis upon context and perception may both justify and make worthwhile a general study, but it is fraught with methodological problems. There are three that stand out. The first of these is in fact relevant to any approach, namely, how is the crowd to be defined? The second problem relates to perception: in practice it is the perceptions made by crowds' non-participants that survive. The anonymity of crowds is almost total. Documentary evidence regarding the attitudes and beliefs of crowd participants is difficult to locate: crowd members rarely leave records. Furthermore, external commentators make use of the crowd to reflect and perpetuate certain views; yet it is largely to those commentators that a crowd owes its existence. Without photographs, films and tape recordings, the historical event is effectively the creation of its chronicler: without the record written by that person, an event would often, in historical terms, fail to exist. The third methodological difficulty concerns context: a rich appreciation of context can be useful in identifying the range of meanings behind an event; the risk, however, is that such an analysis becomes self-enclosed, offering little that is of use in the formulation of a wider historical explanation. Each of these three problems, and their respective solutions, will be addressed in turn.

The definition, for contemporaries, of the crowd will not emerge, of course, until after contemporary responses have been studied. However a working definition is necessary more or less from the outset if data collection is to be effective and consistent. Most dictionaries, from Samuel Johnson's highly individualistic publication of 1755 to the rather more sober Oxford English Dictionary of

---

[1] Peter Burke, 'The virgin of the Carmine and the revolt of Masaniello', *Past and Present*, no. 99 (May 1983), pp. 6–7.

the present day, make the distinction between the crowd as a dense grouping, and the crowd as 'the people'.[2]

The second of these definitions is methodologically particularly difficult. In some respects the crowd as the people is semi-visible and ever-present: it is the working class in their sheer number. This is what Lefebvre calls the aggregate or pure crowd:

between the workshop he is leaving and the family to which he is returning, the worker, in the crowds of the street, momentarily escapes the institutions which socialize his activities.

This undoubtedly explains the feeling of joy experienced by certain individuals upon losing themselves in the crowd; and it also explains the anxiety felt by others. The former feel liberated, the latter terrified by the idea of being abandoned to themselves.[3]

Lefebvre is primarily concerned here to evoke the crowd not simply as the people, but more especially as the urban masses. Similarly for Canetti, the proletariat, multiplying in industrial societies founded upon the process of multiplication, 'come to resemble a crowd'.[4] It is this notion of crowds of people permanently representing the possibility of an organised crowd which concerns most historians when they refer to nineteenth-century anxieties about 'the crowd'.[5] Whatever the accuracy of such observations, the definition of the crowd as the people does need to incorporate the potential or threatened crowd. These non-existent crowds, feared by those in authority, had their part to play in the formation of social policy – not least since threatened crowds were almost invariably large and violent:

[2] Samuel Johnson, *A dictionary of the English language* (London, 1755); *The Oxford English Dictionary* (Oxford, 1971).

[3] Georges Lefebvre, 'Revolutionary crowds', in Jeffrey Kaplow (ed.), *New perspectives on the French revolution: readings in historical sociology* (New York, 1965), p. 176. Lefebvre does make slight modification to this notion (pp. 178–9): there is not a total absence of collective mentality in the aggregate crowd; there always exists a residual consciousness which every person has of their class. The feeling of liberation he describes is reminiscent of Albert Camus' description of Sisyphus' sense of release: Albert Camus, *The myth of Sisyphus*, trans. Justin O'Brien (Harmondsworth, 1975).

[4] Elias Canetti, *Crowds and power*, trans. Carol Stewart (Harmondsworth, 1973), pp. 225–6.

[5] See, for example, Asa Briggs, *Victorian cities* (Harmondsworth, 1963), pp. 59–64; Asa Briggs, 'The human aggregate', repr. in *The collected essays of Asa Briggs* (Brighton, 1985), vol. 1, pp. 55–83; Robert D. Storch, 'The problem of working-class leisure: some roots of middle-class moral reform in the industrial north: 1825–50', in A.P. Donajgrodzki (ed.), *Social control in nineteenth-century Britain* (London, 1977), p. 140.

I make Bold to Inform you as a thief in the Night they will come on you there is one thousand Good heroes in Kingswood as will join us 5 thousand besides: Wee will pull Down your houses and your Fine Meetings and you Manchin House . . . There is now in this city and Fear it 2000 Good fellows they collecting now together I would advise you to be prepared out [*sic*] time is long Expired.[6]

The evoked crowd, whether in the form of a potential or perceived unity of large numbers of working people, or whether conjured into existence in fears and threats, is a meaning of 'the crowd' which is to be considered when analysing the formulation of contemporary attitudes. It is, however, the other definition of the crowd, as a coherent grouping, which has been employed to identify the five hundred or so crowds which form the basis for this study. A crowd is: a large group of people assembled outdoors in sufficient proximity to be able to influence each other's behaviour and to be identifiable as an assembly by contemporaries. The definition was formed in the light of some experience of the relevant archives, and the aim was to produce a definition which conformed as closely as possible to what contemporaries of English towns in the early nineteenth century would have thought of as a crowd. The terms of the definition nevertheless require explanation.

'Large group' is of course a very vague statement of size. Early nineteenth-century commentators frequently did not make estimates of the actual numbers present in an assembly. Their conviction that a certain number of people constituted a crowd was more generally expressed through their application of a vocabulary of mass. In some instances 'a few' may nevertheless, from the context of its application, denote a crowd. Otherwise 'a number' was perhaps the basic unit, with successively larger assemblies being termed 'a considerable number', 'a large number', 'vast' and, inevitably, 'innumerable'. Legal definitions have also been taken into account: the 1714 Riot Act, which formed the basis for the legal response to disturbance, directed its provisions at 'Persons to the number of twelve or more' (although the common law was directed at just three);[7] legislation for the prevention of seditious meetings was aimed at groups in excess of fifty.[8]

[6] Anon. to Harris, LMP/BRO Box 1791, 31 July 1791.
[7] *An Act for preventing tumults and riotous assemblies*, 1 Geo. I, st. 2, c. 5 (1715).
[8] *An Act for more effectually preventing seditious meetings and assemblies*, 36 Geo. III, c. 8 (1795); *An Act for . . . preventing seditious meetings*, 57 Geo. III, c. 19 (1817); *An Act for . . . preventing seditious meetings*, 60 Geo. III, c. 6 (1819).

The specification that crowds occurred outdoors is partly a pragmatic one. A full survey of mass phenomena may wish to include indoor assemblies; such an undertaking is beyond the scope of this study, however. Certainly contemporaries themselves believed that crowds only occurred outdoors: the full vocabulary for crowd description was not applied to indoor events. Although a room might be described as crowded, the people inside it would not be termed a crowd. (This distinction has remained to the present day, with the exception of those occasions when 'traditionally' outdoor events, such as some sports, are transposed to an indoor setting.) The exclusion of indoor mass events has not been total, however. As will be suggested in chapter 7, in some towns the availability of particularly large halls meant that some crowds which might otherwise have met outdoors, gathered inside. These have not been treated as crowds in the same sense as outdoor gatherings, but they will receive attention. The general distinction between indoors and outdoors does mean that most of the crowds discussed here were essentially popular assemblies. With the exception of some recreational events, exclusive gatherings of the wealthy occurred indoors.

The final elements of the definition, that people were gathered in sufficient proximity to influence behaviour, and that non-crowd members could perceive the existence of a crowd, are an attempt to set some crude physical limits on the crowd. A crowd is seen to exist at that moment when people are brought, or bring themselves, together into a grouping which possesses the capability to act, or be acted upon, as a collective and coherent entity. This could represent a serious problem of definition; certainly crowd boundaries and crowd coherence are subjects which exercise the minds of social psychologists today.[9] In practice it is rather less of a problem, largely because (as will be shown) contemporaries frequently were themselves eager to distinguish the boundaries of crowds, and particularly to separate crowd members from spectators (the objectivity of their observations is clearly another matter).

The difficulty of formulating a very precise, and yet usable, definition of the crowd, is a problem which has largely to be accepted and worked around. The same is true of the second methodological dilemma: that of crowd perception. As was suggested above, since the

---

[9] For example, Stanley Milgram and Hans Toch, 'Collective behaviour: crowds and social movements', in Gardner Lindzey and Elliot Aronson (eds.), *The handbook of social psychology*, vol. 4 (Reading, Mass., 1969), pp. 518–24.

crowd existed through the eyes of commentators who were rarely crowd members themselves, and who frequently occupied advantaged social positions, its existence functioned largely to reflect the beliefs of the commentator. Inevitably, therefore, not only have we been handed the perceptions of observers rather than participants, but many of the contexts are framed by them also. The newspaper report (often the only documentary source for a crowd occurrence) typifies this, for it provides both the supposed 'facts' relating to the crowd, and the opinions of the reporter.

To a large extent the history of the crowd is the history of other people's perceptions of the crowd. But it is a state of affairs that can be made good use of. First, the language of crowd description can be analysed in order to determine the attitudes and preoccupations of the observer. Second, alternative interpretations may be read out of the more detailed accounts. This is made possible in part by the conclusions drawn regarding the attitudes of the author, in part by complimentary and contradictory evidence provided by other sources and in part by the knowledge (from other sources) of the meaning of those details described in the text. The most basic, some of the most useful, and the most neglected, of these details are what might be termed environmental data, such as data relating to time and place. As Alan Macfarlane has noted, in studying society through the selective attentions of individual records,

It is easy to find ourselves forgetting such basic things as night and day, hate and fear, a patterning of every moment of the day and every feature of the natural world and many other fundamental features of the past. Documents lull one into a sense that the past never *fully* existed; one can retain one's superiority and distance.[10]

There is little to be gained by the crowd reporter in masking or distorting details of time and place, even if the interpretation put upon that data by the reporter her or himself is misrepresentative. Basic information such as this, built up over a large number of events, begins to form patterns which, since they relate to the most fundamental elements of the organisation and ordering of life, can be highly revealing. Crucially, those patterns form a bedrock of what might reasonably be termed historical fact, upon which the various perceptions and interpretations are overlaid. This does not amount

[10] Alan Macfarlane, 'History, anthropology and the study of communities', *Social History*, II, 2 (1977), p. 651.

to factually accurate accounts of crowd events. It might be argued, however, that the only facts that are really necessary are those which provide a basic context for the various crowd descriptions. There is no history of the crowd; it is adequate to be able to ask questions of the various historical representations of the crowd – and close examination of the language of crowd description, together with the basic factual information those descriptions unwittingly impart, is sufficient to this end.[11]

This means of accepting the constraints imposed by handling perceptions which come almost entirely from outside the crowd also suggests a mechanism for preventing the attention to context from becoming claustrophobic; it thereby suggests a solution to the third methodological problem. The failure to acknowledge the specificity of context and time has long been a criticism levelled at sociologists by historians.[12] In recent years, however, both sociologists (such as Christel Lane and Steven Lukes[13]) and historians (David Cannadine, Richard Evans and Peter Burke, for example[14]) have stressed the importance of examining not merely contexts in general, but context as a thickly layered set of meanings. It is an approach greatly influenced by the stress placed by social anthropologists such as Abner Cohen and Clifford Geertz upon 'a *holistic coverage* of the social and cultural life of the group one would be studying'.[15] Geertz's argument that culture is a context within which social

---

[11] A study which operates along similar lines (and to great effect) is John Barrell's *The dark side of the landscape: the rural poor in English painting 1730–1840* (Cambridge, 1980).

[12] Philip Abrams, 'History, sociology, historical sociology', *Past and Present*, no. 87 (May 1980), pp. 12–13.

[13] Steven Lukes, 'Political ritual and social integration', *Sociology*, IX, 2 (1975), p. 291; Christel Lane, *The rites of rulers: ritual in industrial society – the Soviet case* (Cambridge, 1981), pp. 11–12.

[14] David Cannadine, 'The context, performance and meaning of ritual: the British monarchy and the "invention of tradition", c. 1820–1977', in Eric Hobsbawm and Terence Ranger (eds.), *The invention of tradition* (Cambridge, 1983), pp. 101–64; David Cannadine, 'The transformation of civic ritual in modern Britain: the Colchester oyster feast', *Past and Present*, no. 94 (Feb. 1982), pp. 107–30; Elizabeth Hammerton and David Cannadine, 'Conflict and consensus on a ceremonial occasion: the diamond jubilee in Cambridge in 1897', *Historical Journal*, XXIV, 1 (1981), pp. 111–46; Richard Evans, '"Red Wednesday" in Hamburg: social democrats, police and lumpenproletariat in the suffrage disturbances of 17 January 1906', *Social History*, IV, 1 (1979), pp. 1–31; Burke, 'The revolt of Masaniello'.

[15] Abner Cohen, 'Political symbolism', *Annual Review of Anthropology*, VIII (1979), p. 106; Clifford Geertz, *Negara: the theatre state in nineteenth-century Bali* (Princeton, 1980).

events, behaviours, institutions or processes 'can be intelligibly – that is, thickly – described' is perhaps the most lucid and evocative expression of the methodological approach now adopted by an increasing number of historians and sociologists.[16] A measure of the influence of this approach is the growing number of full length contextual studies, such as those by Emmanuel Le Roy Ladurie, Alan Macfarlane and Carlo Ginsburg.[17]

There is a danger, however, with contextual studies, that the layers of meaning they identify are layers which fold in upon themselves: although the narrative may be both entertaining and extraordinarily complete, the scrutiny of detail may lead the work towards mere antiquarianism. In some respects, the more detail there is, the more difficult it becomes to extract the broader historical relevance, and the less usable the study becomes. Does Le Roy Ladurie's lengthy *Carnival in Romans* have significantly more to say than Peter Burke's compact article on 'The revolt of Masaniello'? Is the main body of Macfarlane's *Justice and the mare's ale* as thought provoking as the more general discussion contained in its introduction and conclusion? The problem is one also associated with local case studies. Detailed, empirical, articles repeatedly compromise big orthodoxies; but how usable is a clutch of self-contained, idiosyncratic, case studies?[18]

In fact, a limited number of contextual studies and local case studies are vital for every field of inquiry. By asking as many questions as possible, such work enables subsequent scholars more effectively to assess which questions have the greatest pertinence; by applying an almost disproportionate amount of intellectual labour in the first instance, they serve subsequently to save labour. By

---

[16] Clifford Geertz, *The interpretation of cultures* (New York, 1973), p. 14.

[17] Emmanuel Le Roy Ladurie, *Montaillou*, trans. Barbara Bray (Harmondsworth, 1980); Emmanuel Le Roy Ladurie, *Carnival in Romans: a people's uprising at Romans, 1579–80*, trans. Mary Feeney (Harmondsworth, 1981); Alan Macfarlane, *The justice and the mare's ale: law and disorder in seventeenth-century England* (Oxford, 1981); Carlo Ginsburg, *The cheese and the worms: the cosmos of a sixteenth-century miller* (Cambridge, 1981), pp. 11–12.

[18] This is, of course, an argument that can be made in defence of the 'crowd historians' in the face of local riot studies. The history of crime, policing and punishment in England has been the subject for similar case study revisionism: see, Victor Bailey (ed.), *Policing and punishment in nineteenth-century Britain* (London, 1981), and Michael Ignatieff's level-headed appraisal of the historiographical debates: 'State, civil society and total institutions: a critique of recent social histories of punishment', in Stanley Cohen and Andrew Scull (eds.), *Social control and the state: historical and comparative essays* (Oxford, 1983), pp. 75–105.

constructing full contexts, they make it possible to assess the precise elements of context most appropriate to particular questions. The numerous questions asked of one particular location can serve to clarify the more limited questions that may profitably be asked of all locations.

This adaptation to a more general study of the methods of analysis arising out of a detailed study is the solution to the problem of the broader application of contextual approaches that will be adopted here. A thoroughgoing analysis of crowds in Bristol between 1790 and 1835 will be the cornerstone for a rather less substantial examination of crowd events in Norwich, Liverpool and Manchester between those years.[19]

III

The causes, timing, pace and location of economic growth in England in the late eighteenth and early nineteenth centuries have long been a matter for academic debate. At present the weight of opinion among economic historians portrays economic and social change in the early part of the nineteenth century as less of a revolution, and more of a hazy dialectic between the 'modernised sectors' and those sectors unaffected by steam and iron.[20] Whoever says industrial revolution nowadays no longer says simply cotton or Manchester, but instead commits themselves to a lengthy discourse that will begin with population growth, urbanisation, agricultural development and the rise in national income, and will probably end in an almost indecipherable amalgam of partial explanations.[21]

Mechanical innovations in the cotton industry did have dramatic repercussions for areas such as Lancashire, and for towns such as Manchester (with sixty-six textile factories within its boundaries by 1821).[22] Nevertheless, it remained the case that by mid-century: only around 30 per cent of the labour force was employed in activities radically transformed in technique since 1780;[23] 'the man in the

[19] The original version of the Bristol study was my unpublished PhD thesis, 'The crowd in Bristol 1790–1835', Univ. of Cambridge, 1984.

[20] In particular, Donald McCloskey, 'The industrial revolution 1780–1860: a survey', in Roderick Floud and Donald McCloskey (eds.), *The economic history of Britain since 1700*, vol. 1: *1700 to 1860* (Cambridge, 1981).

[21] See, for example, Floud and McCloskey (eds.), *Economic history of Britain*, vol. 1.

[22] François Vigier, *Change and apathy: Liverpool and Manchester during the industrial revolution* (Cambridge, Mass., 1970), pp. 88–92.

[23] McCloskey, 'The industrial revolution', p. 109.

crowded countryside' was only just ceasing to be 'the typical Englishman';[24] and 'a town like York was still a more representative example of urban England than a town like Liverpool'.[25] The application of invention was subject to great regional variation; factories proliferated, but so did small work units; wages often increased, but so did work pace; increased productivity was founded upon human sweat, brute force and manual skill as much as upon mechanical ingenuity.[26] There was a twofold increase in population in many of the Lancashire textile towns between 1801 and 1821, yet urban growth in Yorkshire was generally much less dramatic;[27] between 1821 and 1831 the fastest growing British town of more than 20,000 inhabitants was Brighton.[28]

In short, there was no typical town in England in this period. The selection of representative towns is therefore to some extent arbitrary. Bristol was, if only for its quirkiness, perhaps as typical as any: it combined size (the fifth largest English town in 1801, with a population of 61,000), and a fair rate of growth (in 1841, with a population of 124,000, it was the sixth largest city), with an almost complete absence of large-scale manufacturing, and minimal mechanisation. As a large, corporate, enfranchised city, it offered what might be regarded as the full range of potential crowd gathering events, from public displays to parliamentary elections. The economic stagnation of Bristol gave the city a comparative continuity in its basic institutions, groupings, factions and patterns of everyday life that is of methodological advantage to the researcher.

Having undertaken a detailed study of Bristol, inevitably the characteristics of that city influenced the selection of other towns. Since Bristol was a large, growing (yet economically inert), corporate

---

[24] J.H. Clapham, *An economic history of modern Britain*, vol. 1: *The early railway age, 1820–50* (Cambridge, 1926), p. 66.

[25] David Cannadine, *Lords and landlords: the aristocracy and the towns, 1774–1967* (Leicester, 1980), p. 36.

[26] Raphael Samuel, 'Workshop of the world: steam power and hand technology in mid-Victorian Britain', *History Workshop Journal*, no. 3 (Spring, 1977), pp. 6–72; John Rule, *The experience of labour in eighteenth-century industry* (London, 1981), pp. 30–1.

[27] C.W. Chalklin, *The provincial towns of Georgian England: a study of the building process, 1720–1820* (London, 1974), pp. 35–9; B.R. Mitchell and P. Deane, *Abstract of British historical statistics* (Cambridge, 1962), pp. 24–7.

[28] John Lowerson and John Myerscough, *Time to spare in Victorian England* (Hassocks, 1977), p. 11. Brighton increased by 71 per cent; Bradford, it should be pointed out, was a very close second at 69 per cent: Mitchell and Deane, *Historical statistics*, p. 24.

and enfranchised port, it seemed essential to give attention to its great rival, Liverpool: a larger, faster growing, economically sturdy, corporate, enfranchised port. And since Bristol was falling from its former position as second city, it seemed appropriate to examine another former second city, also experiencing economic difficulties, but in this instance an inland settlement, namely, Norwich. Norwich also was a corporate and enfranchised city, thus facilitating direct comparison at a number of levels with Liverpool and Bristol. This makes for a very tidy trio; but the absence from the group of a large northern textile town is unavoidably glaring. For that reason some attention has also been paid to Manchester. Obviously strong arguments could also be made for the inclusion, on various grounds, of such towns as Birmingham, Leeds, Sheffield, Hull and Bradford. The selection of Bristol for the main study, Liverpool and Norwich for secondary examination, and Manchester for a further comparative dimension is not regarded as in any sense a definitive choice.

Although these four towns have received different degrees of attention, the same principles for data collection have been applied to each. As described above, the definition of a crowd employed for this study was deliberately flexible. Nevertheless, in order to ensure that there was at least skeletal detail available for the crowds in the sample, specific criteria were employed for data collection. In no instance was a probable crowd recorded as a crowd unless contemporary reports made clear mention of mass, through either an estimate, or the terminology, of numbers. Consequently, some events, such as some official celebrations of anniversaries, have not been regarded as crowd events, even though they may have at least attracted some idle spectators.

Other basic information sought for each crowd included: date and day, time, location (or, in the case of processions, route) and weather. Of these, only date (from which day could be calculated) and location were deemed essential: crowds were not recorded in the sample unless date and place were specified or clearly implied. As regards timing, it has been assumed that crowds occurred during work hours unless evidence suggests otherwise. Non-working hours have been assumed to be, in general, Sunday, and 12 pm to 2 pm and 6 pm to 6 pm, Tuesday to Saturday; for some purposes, Monday has also been taken as a non-work day. Holidays, and what have been termed *de facto* holidays, are also regarded as non-work periods. The latter category refers to those occasions when explicit sanction has been given by either local authority or employers to popular participation in a particular event. A distinction has been drawn between a crowd and a crowd event. A crowd event is the general subject around which crowds may occur: an election, or anniversary, for example. One crowd event may be the occasion for more than one crowd occurrence. Different crowds at the same event are generally distinguishable by composition, location, timing and ideology. More than one crowd may occur on one day; but no crowd is deemed to have continued over more than one day. These various distinctions are necessary in order to make sense of complex events, and in order to facilitate some quantitative analysis. Inevitably, however, they produce some distortions, or oversimplifications, and attention will be drawn to these as necessary.

The major source for the documentation of crowds is the newspaper; and newspapers will form the basis for this study. Newspapers are, among historians, a particularly unloved primary source. Posing as the purveyors of objective truth, papers are nowadays notorious for their, sometimes scurrilous, selectivity and subjectivity. This is nothing new; newspapers of the early nineteenth century were equally disingenuous. It was a period when important changes were taking place in the newspaper press, however. The background for newspaper publication was the risk of prosecution for sedition, and a stamp tax that made for prohibitive prices.[29] Of great importance also was the changing style of newspapers, with the development, from around the end of the Napoleonic war, of the leader, or editorial, article, and a gradual increase in the attention given to local events. Although there was great variation from place to place and from paper to paper, during the first years of the nineteenth century, brief local reports written to a formula were increasingly replaced by long and (sometimes extraordinarily) detailed accounts of major local events.[30] Local crowd gathering occasions were, perhaps, the single most newsworthy subject in the eyes of most newspaper proprietors and editors. The history of crowds in this period is indirectly a history of newspapers also.

Newspapers are, therefore, a difficult source to use; but if used carefully and critically they can be of great value. Their subjecting is worthy of analysis in its own right; and they were, for all their faults,

[29] For a general history of newspapers in this period, see G.A. Cranfield, *The press and society: from Caxton to Northcliffe* (London, 1978).

[30] Donald Read, *Press and people 1790–1850: opinion in three English cities* (London, 1961), ch. 3.

the carriers of much apparently incidental information which can be profitably reinterpreted. Furthermore, the proliferation of newspapers in these years means that for most crowd occurrences there exists a number of versions of events, and a number of stated attitudes; these can be usefully compared and contrasted.

The sources which supplement the newspapers are, as the bibliography will demonstrate, numerous and diverse: from official records to personal diaries, from local histories and guidebooks to miscellaneous handbills and notices. In the case of Bristol, the archives have been scoured for anything that might be elucidatory. The search in Liverpool and Norwich was rather less thorough, and here local histories, pamphlet literature and collections of printed material are the primary supplements to the newspaper reports. The examination of Manchester has been confined to newspaper records and secondary works. The various remarks and conclusions regarding these four towns are offered with proportionate and appropriate degrees of confidence.

Part 2 *Patterns, procedures and power*

3. *Introduction: the ordering of the urban environment*

'Order' has become a value laden term. It carries associations of correctness, obedience and control, standing in opposition to disorder, turbulence and change. Inevitably, therefore, when applied by historians it takes on both conservative and deterministic overtones. Conservative because order appears to be a stable condition of harmony, thereby inferring that any disruptive or confrontational events are necessarily the harbingers of disorder and disarray. Deterministic because, in a peculiar inversion of the physicist's 'second law', the historian always seems to be looking for progress *towards* order: when a nation comes of age, order arises out of chaos. Any breakdown in order, therefore, is a step backwards in time.

There are numerous conceptual and ideological objections which could be raised to this 'functionalist' approach to orderliness.[1] Suffice it to say here that such an approach offers a fraudulent neutralism which produces moderno-centric histories not of what was or could have been, but of what is and should have been. It is the history solely of and for the powerful, influential and conservative minded. Many historians would affirm these objections, and their concern is to establish first that 'disorder' may be more orderly than it appears, and second that there is, in any case, more than one kind of order.

But despite such attacks, 'order' has not lost its meaning altogether, and the functionalist approach remains virulent – for good reason: the 'conventional' application of the term 'order' contains important truths. It would, after all, be the crassest kind of relativism that depicts Britain without a formal police force or education

---

[1] For criticism of the application of functionalist approaches in this period, see, for example: Gareth Stedman Jones, 'Class expression versus social control? A critique of recent trends in the social history of leisure', *History Workshop Journal*, IV (1977), pp. 162–70; F.K. Donnelly, 'Ideology and early English working-class history: Edward Thompson and his critics', *Social History*, I, 2 (1976), pp. 219–37. See also ch. 1 above.

system, without effective local government and the administration of public services, and with a plethora of infectious diseases and cruel sports, as 'in some sense' as 'orderly' as its polar opposite. Nevertheless, to concentrate upon this dichotomy is in one important respect to miss the point: the notion of order, whether projected in conservative or liberal terms, has been narrowly conceived. Order remains, from both perspectives, that which is opposed to disorder; the dispute, effectively, is only about which label should be applied. Neglected in all this is another kind of order, one which exists in degrees of complexity, but which is less intimately bound to an opposite condition. It is what might be termed the ordering of everyday life – and, with particular reference to the concerns here, the ordering of the urban environment.

This phrase refers to the patterns and procedures which inevitably arise out of the aglomeration of people, tasks and functions that is a town. A town is not only a collection of buildings, it is also, of course, a set of relationships and familiarities. In the early nineteenth century those might include: the hours and seasons of work; the coming and going of stage-coaches; the arrival and departure of the mail; residential patterns; public spaces and popular meeting places; favourite recreations; the repertoire of committees and their meetings; trade societies and cultural institutions; public notices and advertisements; newspapers; fairs and markets; local characters; popular inns and coffee houses; fashionable and disreputable streets; the calendar of holidays, national and local celebrations, and local governments displays; public funerals; public executions; the meetings of courts; the arrival of judges; the 'rituals' of elections.

The operation of these relationships and familiarities enables a town to function as a town. In so doing they generate patterns and routines which in time become institutionalised, and give the urban environment its character. All of human society, of course, involves such ordering. The degree of human co-operation and common understanding necessary for the operation of everyday life is to be marvelled at (and should be recalled at times when social commentators talk of innate human competitiveness and the decline of order in civil society). That co-operation and interaction, and the patterns and routines it generates, exist in varying degrees of complexity and uniformity. Clearly a large city requires an extraordinary degree of ordering: the extent to which that ordering creates broadly perceivable patterns of life, however, will depend to some extent upon the uniformity or fragmentation of economic, social and political activities within the town. To give one example, a town with a highly centralised and effective system of government is likely to show more clear patterns of public activity than one which is administered on a more or less *ad hoc* basis. In the latter case ordering and routines exist (and to a sophisticated degree), but in a less clearly discernible and publicly visible way.

These are hardly novel observations. Yet because order in the urban environment of the nineteenth century has tended to be discussed in terms solely of police forces, local government structures, crime and riot statistics and economic dislocations, the simple, commonplace and inherent routines of urban life have been ignored. But why should they be restored to our field of view; and what have they to do with crowds? The two questions are, inevitably, closely linked. The patterning or ordering of the urban environment gives the closest sense of a place, since by examining the routines, unwritten rules and normative constraints of urban life it is possible to gain an insight into the preoccupations and parameters which surround social actions, and appreciate better those instances where norms have been challenged, broken or redefined. Put more simply, if one knows what is expected and what is usual, it is easier to detect and to understand what is unexpected and unusual.

The implications for the study of crowds are obvious. Crowds are, by definition, mass, public and high profile events. The statements they actually or reportedly make are to be found not only in vocal or written declarations, but in their symbolic significance. The size, composition and tenor of, say, a particular celebratory crowd may be in line with what might be expected from previous such occasions; but if that crowd were to form at an untypical time of day, or to take an unusual route through town, then it would gain some extra symbolic significance. That significance, clearly, is in terms of the departure from established patterns and practices. Routines exist to be broken. But because crowd events are as much a creation of those that report and comment upon them as those who take part in them, the *ascription* to crowds of obedience to set routines, or deviation from such routines, can also prove significant. In other words, patterns in urban life are reflected in crowd events which in turn represent themselves, and are represented by others, in terms of adherence or otherwise to such patterns. What we have here, it seems, is a history of habits.

URBANISATION AND CONSENSUS CULTURE

Inevitably, the examination of the ordering of the urban environment, and the place of crowds within that ordering, is related to the phenomenon not only of industrialisation, but, more crucially, urbanisation. Consequently, one of the side-effects of such a study is the correction of an historiographical imbalance; as Peter Burke has pointed out, the distinctive characteristics which are often attributed to 'industrial' towns should more properly be attributed to *large* towns;[2] and, with the recent stress upon industrialisation as taking place in the second quarter of the nineteenth century, it seems all the more important that attention should be focused, for the preceding years, on the phenomenon first and foremost of urbanisation.[3]

But despite the emphasis being placed here upon the minutiae of the urbanising process, to speak of urbanisation as it relates to the late eighteenth and early nineteenth centuries is to speak of industrialisation and non-industrialisation, population growth and class. The pressures of sporadic industrialisation,[4] sustained population growth[5] and uneasy alliances between a new middle class and an established ruling class[6] combined with the development of communication systems, which both highlighted comparisons with, and independence from, the capital, and endowed regional centres with high profiles.[7] The grounds for intra-urban comparison and competition were substantial. Was Bristol still the second city? And if it

---

[2] Peter Burke, 'Some reflections on the pre-industrial city', *Urban History Yearbook* (1975), pp. 13–21.

[3] Roderick Floud and Donald McCloskey (eds.), *The economic history of Britain since 1780*, vol. 1: *1780 to 1860* (Cambridge, 1981).   [4] *Ibid.*

[5] E.A. Wrigley, 'The growth of population in eighteenth-century England: a conundrum resolved', *Past and Present*, no. 98 (Feb. 1983), p. 137; E.A. Wrigley and R.S. Schofield, *The population history of England 1541–1871: a reconstruction* (London, 1981), ch. 11.

[6] Perry Anderson, 'Origins of the present crisis', *New Left Review*, no. 23 (1964), pp. 26–53; David Cannadine, *Lords and landlords: the aristocracy and the towns, 1774–1967* (Leicester, 1980); R.J. Morris, 'The middle class and British towns and cities in the industrial revolution, 1780–1870', in Derek Fraser and Anthony Sutcliffe (eds.), *The pursuit of urban history* (London, 1983), pp. 286–306.

[7] Peter T. Marcy, 'Bristol's roads and communications on the eve of the industrial revolution, 1740–1780', *Transactions of the Bristol and Gloucestershire Archaeological Society*, no. 87 (1968), pp. 149–72; John Money, *Experience and identity: Birmingham and the West Midlands, 1760–1800* (Manchester, 1977), p. 277; H.J. Dyos and D.H. Aldcroft, *British transport: an economic survey from the seventeenth century to the twentieth* (Leicester, 1969), chs. 2 and 3; G.A. Cranfield, *The press and society: from Caxton to Northcliffe* (London, 1978), ch. 7.

was no longer second in terms of trade, then perhaps it still was 'with respect to the opulence and number of inhabitants'.[8] Had Liverpool taken over the mantle of the most important provincial city? Was Norwich, formerly a spritely subordinate to London but now with stagnating population growth and a declining economy, any longer to be taken seriously as a provincial capital? Was Manchester a shambolic upstart, or the next heavyweight? These were not, for contemporaries, idle conjectures – they mattered. And at a time when scientific and statistical inquiry had become a middle class obsession,[9] and when the development of the newspaper press more directly facilitated the spread of information,[10] such contrasts and comparisons could more readily be drawn.

There are fundamental and complicated reasons, beyond the scope of this study, why comparisons mattered. In outline, however, they may be identified as threefold: commercial benefits, status and civic pride. Potentially real commercial benefits were to be gained from maintaining that the town was important, well provisioned and secure. Economic growth was taking place at differential rates, for reasons not necessarily understood or acknowledged by contemporaries. In the case of competing ports such as Bristol and Liverpool there at least appeared to be some merit in advertising the benefits to a merchant of one port over the other. Commerical considerations did not relate solely to mercantile concerns, however. There existed a market in middle and upper class tourism of some importance, particularly for a town such as Bristol. It was important, therefore, for those who presented the town through newspapers, guidebooks and so on, that the town should have a salubrious image. This element of tourism relates directly to the issue of status. As Peter Borsay has outlined, the eighteenth century saw the development of a distinctive urban culture, which had, at its centre, leisure, conspicuous consumption, status and display.[11] To belong to the ruling class of a major provincial city, in a period of such change, carried with it considerable prestige, and seemed an attractive alternative, perhaps,

[8] Quoted in Peter T. Marcy, *Eighteenth-century views of Bristol and Bristolians* (Bristol, 1966), p. 4. The remark was made in 1788.

[9] Asa Briggs, 'The human aggregate', repr. in *The collected essays of Asa Briggs* (Brighton, 1985), vol. 1, pp. 55–83.

[10] Cranfield, *Press and society*, ch. 7; Donald Read, *Press and people 1790–1850: opinion in three English cities* (London, 1961).

[11] Peter Borsay, 'The English urban renaissance: the development of provincial urban culture, c. 1680–c. 1760', *Social History*, II, 2 (1977), pp. 581–603.

to life among the rural rich – all the more so if that rule could be administered from the comfort of the immediately surrounding countryside.[12]

Tied in turn to these phenomena, and, by a quirky route, bringing us back to ordering and patterning, is the third element: civic pride. Civic pride is commonly associated with the mid-Victorian period. Indeed, in some respects it forms part of the transition thesis: freed from political and industrial strife, and having invaded the urban *terrae incognitae*, there was now the time and space for disciples of the civic gospel to develop and enjoy the great Victorian town. But it is the way of all transition arguments that they should be smoothed out, and this one is no exception. For there was a self-conscious obsession with the presentation of civic consensus in the first years of the nineteenth century which – although it may have built few houses, sewers or swimming baths – can only be described in terms of pride in place.

As Asa Briggs argued some time ago, it would be quite wrong to associate this period with the development of the grey, formless industrial city.[13] Towns (and Briggs was writing particularly about Birmingham) developed and fiercely defended distinct identities and intense civic pride. This concern to present a distinctive but 'good' image generated constant tensions, however, for those in positions of influence. Expressions of outrage at public conduct that was anything other than supplicatory and to the greater glory of the civic image clouded understanding of pressing social and political complaints, and encouraged an obsession with the presentation of consensus which ultimately served to undermine the credibility and authority of those in power. In Bristol such tensions found expression in the response by some citizens to two years of dispute culminating in the 1831 riot, solely in terms of the disgrace this represented for 'the second city in England' – a status Bristol had relinquished some decades earlier;[14] and in Liverpool and Norwich, in the midst of civic strife, some writers were publishing panegyrics on the good character and decorum of the inhabitants, rich and poor alike.[15]

---

[12] As, for example, with the development of Brislington as a fashionable village just outside Bristol: Sheena Stoddard, *Mr. Braikenridge's Brislington* (Bristol, 1981).

[13] Briggs, 'Press and public in early nineteenth-century Birmingham', in *The collected essays of Asa Briggs*, vol. 1, pp. 106–7.

[14] *FFBJ*, 18 Sept. 1830; *Bristol Job Nott*, XLVIII, 8 Nov. 1832; *BMBJ*, 2 May 1801.

[15] Edward Baines, *History, directory and gazeteer of the county palatine of Lancaster* (1824; reprinted Newton Abbot, 1968), pp. 202–3; Thomas Kaye, *The stranger in*

CROWDS AND POWER

Crowd events took place against the backdrop of this constant image building. The facilitation, management, reception and perception of crowd events was linked to and filtered through the vanity and preoccupations of those in positions of power and influence. This is where the patterns of urban life and the procedures of urban administration and organisation become inextricably linked with the occurrence of crowds. The public, symbolic and potentially dramatic power of mass events, made comprehensible and embued with extra meaning by their place within the routines and expectations of everyday urban life, possessed the capacity either ferociously to undermine or sublimely to reinforce the status, image and prestige of those who spoke for and identified with the town.

In the chapters which follow, the integral part which crowds played in the ordering of the urban environment, and the construction of images, will be described. At the same time, however, the following argument will be developed. Crowds were central to urban life in the nineteenth century, and in some respects this was the heyday of crowd activity. Yet, despite the organisational problems and routines this imposed, there was, on the part of those in positions of power and prominence, surprisingly little close personal contact with crowd occurrences. Nevertheless, crowds remained too important to ignore or neglect – either as supporting evidence for claims of social cohesion and political ascendancy, or as a measure of the threat posed to such cohesion by the forces of chaos and destruction. Inevitably, it will be argued, this combination of personal distance and selective characterisation led to the misrepresentation of crowd events – something with both short-term consequences for crowd activity, and long-term ones for the history of the perception of mass phenomena.

The process, however, was most clearly at work in towns with well-established and identifiable elites, since in such locations it was easier to categorise crowds and crowd activities as 'friendly' or 'hostile' to certain viewpoints and groupings. It was probably also the case, moreover, that such towns were more productive of large-scale and supposedly consensual public events; there was a clearer calendar and

Liverpool; or, an historical and descriptive view of Liverpool and its environs (Liverpool, 1807), pp. 39–41; P. Browne, *The history of Norwich from the earliest records to the present time* (Norwich, 1814), p. 98.

routine of crowd activity (e.g. around certain Corporation displays, national celebrations or recreational events), and a clearer and more 'ritualised' patterning of crowd behaviour (because symbolic locations and targets were clearly established and identifiable). The overall effect was that, paradoxically, the entrenched environment of a town such as Bristol was, inadvertently, productive of crowd activity and (consequently) public and ferocious dispute, every bit as great as (if not greater than) that of a fast growing and supposedly chaotic town such as Manchester. Clear contexts and clear, widely understood and generally perceived public debates and agreements were conducive to as much crowd activity as the compartmentalised, fragmented and contingent environment of the emerging industrial city.

4. Contexts for crowds in four towns: Bristol, Liverpool, Norwich and Manchester

BRISTOL

DECLINE AND PRIDE

The city of Bristol was described by Daniel Defoe, in 1724, as 'the greatest, the richest, and the best port of trade in Great Britain, London only accepted'.[1] Yet its experience during the early years of the industrial revolution was to be one not of expansion but of relative decline. The first census, in 1801, revealed Bristol's population to be just 64,000 – far short of the 100,000 confidently and proudly claimed by many eighteenth-century Bristolians.[2] As one newspaper commented, 'Many of our readers will be disappointed in finding so small a number of persons in this city, which, thirty years ago was said to amount to near double that number.'[3] The, apparently magic figure of 100,000 was not achieved until the 1830s. Many large houses left empty or uncompleted during the building industry crash of 1793 remained unoccupied in the 1820s;[4] there was no influx of new wealth, nor of the newly wealthy. The Corporation retained a monolithic grip upon the city's administration; and the same families that had dominated Bristol life during the eighteenth century remained pre-eminent into the nineteenth: the Daubenys, Brights, Harfords, Protheroes, Daniels and Baillies. Between them, the Corporation and these wealthy families (and there was some overlap between the two), constituted what one tory termed a 'commercial aristocracy'; and he warned that unless it became 'more blended with the democracy or Plebeian interests of the place, a cold

---

[1] Daniel Defoe, *A tour through the whole island of Great Britain* (1724–6; new edition, Harmondsworth, 1971), p. 361.
[2] See Peter T. Marcy, *Eighteenth-century views of Bristol and Bristolians* (Bristol, 1966), pp. 4–6.   [3] *BMBJ*, 2 May 1801.
[4] Walter Ison, *The Georgian buildings of Bristol* (Bath, 1952), pp. 27–8; J.R. Ward, 'Speculative building at Bristol and Clifton, 1783–1793', *Business History*, XX, 1 (1978), pp. 14–15.

and chilling blight, the natural attendant upon pride, will continue to blast every exertion of the humble, but not less worthy citizen, in his attempt to restore the port to a healthy and vigorous state of commerce'.[5]

Certainly economic decline had begun well before the nineteenth century. Defoe himself had observed that the Corporation policy of allowing only freemen of the city to trade within its bounds threatened to stifle Bristol's prosperity.[6] By 1807, the *Bristol Gazette* was forced to report that the commerce of Bristol was of a 'comparatively trivial amount considering the extent, situation and capital of this city'.[7] Twenty-one years later the Bristol Chamber of Commerce lamented the fact that 'no one capitalist should have been attracted to this city or neighbourhood in recent years'.[8] The *Gazette's* reports remained dismal for long afterwards:

How does Bristol stand at the commencement of 1834? Can we fully and honestly say that we are proud of her situation in the scale of British cities? Alas! the answer must be negative. As compared with herself at former periods she may not have retrograded but not to advance is to recede, and how fearfully she has been past [*sic*] by Liverpool and other places.[9]

Liverpool had long been the yardstick by which Bristol's decline was measured. In 1788 one writer observed that 'the custom house receipts of Liverpool have for some time past exceeded those of Bristol'.[10] Ten years later the *Bristol Gazette* published a table comparing the trade of the two towns, which showed Bristol to be lagging far behind.[11] By the mid-1820s, the press was publishing weekly comparisons of prices in Bristol and Liverpool, and tables of Liverpool's dock duties and trade statistics appeared regularly. Figures printed in 1834 showed that whereas Liverpool handled 828 foreign ships with a total tonnage of 227,087 in 1832, Bristol dock in the same year handled just 29 foreign ships, with a total tonnage of a mere 4,352. Bristol now lagged behind such ports as Hull, Newcastle and Leith, and was barely ahead of Greenock.[12] It was hoped by

[5] J.M. Gutch, *Letters on the impediments which obstruct the trade and commerce of the city and port of Bristol which first appeared in Felix Farley's Bristol Journal under the signature of Cosmo* (Bristol, 1823), p. 7.
[6] Defoe, *Tour through Great Britain*, p. 302.   [7] *Bristol Gazette*, 20 Aug. 1807.
[8] Chamber of Commerce, *Report . . . to consider the facilities which the city and neighbourhood of Bristol afford for the introduction of new and the extension of the existing branches of manufacture* (Bristol, 1828), p. 5.
[9] *Bristol Gazette*, 2 Jan. 1834.
[10] Quoted in Marcy, *Eighteenth-century views*, p. 4.
[11] *Bristol Gazette*, 23 Aug. 1798.   [12] *Ibid.*, 2 Jan. 1834.

some that improvements to the docks, with the provision of a floating harbour, would arrest Bristol's decline: 'by putting this glorious enterprise to execution, Bristol will become the first, best and most commodious port of its size, not in England, nor in Europe only – but in the *World*'.[13] It was not to be. The harbour scheme, completed in 1809, was remarkable primarily for the increase in local taxation made necessary in order to pay for it. The failure of the project, and the implications it carried for the existing burden of local taxation, fuelled what was by the 1820s to become a concerted attempt to wrench the Bristol economy from the grip of the Corporation, and to make up lost ground in relation to the flourishing northern cities. Part of this campaign was the foundation in February 1823 of the Bristol Chamber of Commerce, with the object 'to protect and promote the Commercial, Trading and Manufacturing Interests of Bristol, and of its individual Members; and its views of operations shall embrace the removal of obstacles, which tend to prevent the increase of Trade'.[14]

The Chamber's attempts to bring about an inquiry into local taxation led to open conflict with the Corporation, and formed an important part of the background to the disputes with local government which were to dominate the first years of the 1830s.

Restrictive local practices were the most common explanation given by contemporaries for Bristol's poor economic fortunes, but various other interpretations were – and have since been – put forward: geographical disadvantages, over-reliance on the West Indies trade, delay in constructing the new harbour, unresponsiveness to new technology and the lack of 'entrepreneurial spirit' among an elite more concerned to enjoy than to increase its wealth.[15]

---

[13] *Bristol Spectator*, 30 Oct. 1800.

[14] Chamber of Commerce, *Rules and regulations for the establishment of a Chamber of Commerce in Bristol* (Bristol, 1823).

[15] See, 'Home truths, or the sorrowful lamentation of the merchants, tradesmen and others of the city of Bristol', in 'Bristol fragments, a collection of broadsides, 1741–1819', BRL; Gutch, *Letters on the impediments*; 'Letters to J.M. Gutch on writing Cosmo's letters', BRO 13748/5; Chamber of Commerce, *Report . . . to consider the facilities . . . of Bristol*; J.B. Kington, *City and port of Bristol: letters, essays, tracts, etc.* (Bristol, 1836); W.L. Dowding, *The story of Bristol: a brief history for young citizens* (Bristol, 1906); B.W.E. Alford, 'The economic development of Bristol in the nineteenth century: an enigma?', in Patrick McGrath and John Cannon (eds.), *Essays in Bristol and Gloucestershire history* (Bristol, 1976), pp. 252–83; S.J. Jones, 'The growth of Bristol: the regional aspect of city development', *Transactions of the Institute of British Geographers*, XI (1946), pp. 57–83; W.E. Michinton, 'Bristol: metropolis of the west in the eighteenth century', *Transactions of the Royal Historical Society*, 5th series, IV (1954), pp. 69–89; W.E. Minchinton (ed.), *The trade of Bristol in the eighteenth century* (Bristol, 1957): P.J. Corfield, *The impact of English towns, 1700–1800* (Oxford, 1982), pp. 38–42.

Table 1. *Ten largest English provincial towns, 1801–41 (figures in thousands)*

1801		1811		1821		1831		1841	
Liverpool	82	*Liverpool*	104	*Liverpool*	138	*Liverpool*	202	*Liverpool*	299
Manchester	75	*Manchester*	96	*Manchester*	135	*Manchester*	194	*Manchester*	252
Birmingham	71	Birmingham	83	Birmingham	102	Birmingham	144	Birmingham	202
Bristol	61	*Bristol*	71	*Bristol*	85	Leeds	123	Leeds	152
Leeds	53	Leeds	63	Leeds	84	*Bristol*	104	*Bristol*	124
Sheffield	46	Sheffield	53	Sheffield	65	Sheffield	92	Sheffield	111
Plymouth	40	Plymouth	51	Plymouth	55	Plymouth	66	Newcastle	70
Norwich	36	Portsmouth	42	*Norwich*	50	*Norwich*	61	Plymouth	70
Newcastle	33	Bath	38	Bath	47	Newcastle	54	Bradford	67
Portsmouth	33	*Norwich*	37	Portsmouth	37	Hull	52	Hull	67
		Hull	33					*(Norwich*	62)

Note: figures for Liverpool, Manchester and Birmingham include environs later incorporated.
Source: B.R. Mitchell and P. Deane, *Abstract of British historical statistics* (Cambridge, 1962), pp. 24–7.

Perhaps one reason why observers have found it difficult to agree upon the precise causes of Bristol's economic decline, and perhaps one reason why that decline was relative and not total, has to do with the diversity of Bristol's economic base. In addition to activities associated with the docks, Bristol was well known for glassmaking, sugar-refining, soap-manufacture, distilling and brewing, and chocolate. But other sources of employment included iron, lead, copper and brass works, pottery, and a large floor cloth factory, as well as a plethora of trades and services.[16] An important further dimension was domestic service – an inevitable adjunct of Bristol's status as a 'fashionable' middle class city.[17]

The side-effect of such diverse activity was that, although Bristol suffered as did other towns during depressions such as those of 1799–1801, 1810–12 and 1816–17, and periodically experienced food rioting and the need for soup kitchens and charitable relief, it did not, unlike many other towns, suffer the calamities associated with the total collapse of a major individual trade. It is important to keep Bristol's 'decline' in perspective. Its population grew steadily in the early nineteenth century; in 1801 it was the fifth largest English town, behind London, Liverpool, Manchester and Birmingham; and by 1841 had been overtaken only by Leeds (see table 1). Throughout the nineteenth century Bristol's economic performance remained mixed, and wages relatively low; yet it had performed better than many of the other 'old towns', such as Norwich, Exeter and York.[18]

---

[16] W. Mathews, *Mathews's Bristol guide and directory, 1793–4* (Bristol, 1794); J. Mathews, *The Bristol guide* (Bristol, 1815, 1819 and 1829); *Work in Bristol: a series of sketches of the chief manufactories in the city: reprinted from the Bristol Times and Mirror* (Bristol, 1883); B.W.E. Alford, 'The flint and bottle glass industry in the early nineteenth century: a case study of a Bristol firm', *Business History*, X, 1 (1968), pp. 12–21; Joan Day, *Bristol brass: a history of the industry* (Newton Abbot, 1973); I.V. Hall, 'Whitson Court sugar house, Bristol 1665–1824', *Transactions of the Bristol and Gloucestershire Archaeological Society*, no. 65 (1944), pp. 1–97; Z. Josephs, 'The Jacobs of Bristol, glassmakers to King George III', *Trans. of Bristol and Glos. Arch. Soc.*, no. 95 (1977), pp. 98–101; Arthur Cecil Powell, 'Glass-making in Bristol', *Trans. of the Bristol and Glos. Arch. Soc.*, no. 47 (1925), pp. 211–57; Bryan Little, *The city and county of Bristol: a study of Atlantic civilisation* (London, 1954), pp. 166–75.

[17] H.E. Meller, *Leisure and the changing city, 1870–1914* (London, 1976), pp. 37–9.

[18] Meller, *Leisure and the changing city*, ch. 2; Alan Armstrong, *Stability and change in an English county town: a social study of York, 1801–1851* (Cambridge, 1974); Robert Newton, *Victorian Exeter, 1837–1914* (Leicester, 1968).

THE PERSONNEL OF POWER

The government of the city and county of Bristol was based upon numerous royal charters. It was the charter of Anne, granted in 1710, however, which formed the effective basis for the administration of Bristol in this period.[19] The Corporation in theory consisted of 'the Mayor, Burgesses and Commonalty of the City of Bristol', which totalled around 5,300 people in 1835;[20] in practice it comprised its governing body: the forty-three members of the Common Council of Bristol. This discrepancy formed the basis for wrangles regarding the legitimacy of the Corporation, which reached a climax in the 1820s. For most contemporaries, however, 'the Corporation' and 'the Common Council' were synonymous, and this common usage of Corporation to mean the city's governing body will be employed here also.

The full title of the governing body was the 'Mayor, Aldermen and Common Councillors'. The mayor was elected annually on 15 September by the Common Council from among the Common Councillors. He was sworn in at the Guildhall on 29 September, and his period in office began from that date. On leaving office, the mayor returned to the status of Common Councillor. The aldermen numbered twelve, including the recorder, and were elected for life. The recorder was elected by the Common Council;[21] the other aldermen were elected by the mayor and aldermen from among the Common Councillors. Each alderman was a magistrate, or justice of the peace, and each was appointed to one of Bristol's twelve wards.[22]

---

[19] Detailed descriptions of the structure of local government in Bristol are provided by: Graham Bush, *Bristol and its municipal government, 1820–1851* (Bristol, 1976), ch. 2; J.S. Moore and M. Williams, 'Local administration and politics', in J.S. Moore (ed.), *Avon local history handbook* (Chichester, 1979), pp. 70–3; Sidney and Beatrice Webb, *English local government from the revolution to the municipal corporations act: the manor and the borough*, part II (London, 1908), pp. 443–75; *Report from the commissioners on municipal corporations in England and Wales*, (hereafter, *MCR*), 3, appendix part I, vol. XXIII (1835), pp. 53, 114; *ibid.*, appendix part II, vol. XXIV (1835), pp. 1151–228. The charters are detailed in R.C. Latham, *Bristol charters, 1509–1899* (Bristol, 1947). Bristol was made a separate county in 1373.

[20] *MCR*, 3, app. pt I, XIII, p. 53. The Commissioners arrived at this figure from the number of freemen registered as voters.

[21] The position of recorder was as presiding judge at the new court of gaol delivery, and legal adviser to the Corporation. The office was held by a succession of leading legal figures resident in London.

[22] The twelve wards were: All Saints, Castle Precincts, St Ewen, St James, St Mary-le-port, St Mary Redcliff, St Michael, St Nicholas, St Stephen, Temple, St Thomas and Trinity.

The recorder always served Trinity ward, but, since he was not resident, the mayor would discharge the function on his behalf. The thirty Common Councillors were elected for life by the Common Council from among freemen. Two of the Councillors, usually the newly elected, were appointed as sheriffs. The sheriffs were also sworn in for one year on 29 September. Common Councillors had few duties, other than attendance at Common Council meetings. The sheriffs, however, did have specific responsibilities, including the superintendance of the Newgate gaol and the Bridewell house of correction, and the administration of parliamentary elections.[23]

The Corporation's participation in the government of Bristol was broad: there was a marked overlap in membership between the Corporation and the other local government bodies. The mayor and aldermen were represented *ex officio* on the Corporation of the Poor, the Turnpike Trustees and the Dock Company. Although the mayor and aldermen no longer attended the meetings of the Corporation of the Poor (which administered St Peter's hospital and workhouse, and provided outdoor relief), they nevertheless maintained an *ex officio* post among the eighty guardians who elected the managing officers. The entire Corporation were members of the Board of the Bristol Turnpike Trust. The Corporation nominated one third of the directorate of the Dock Company, founded in 1803 to promote and administer the floating harbour. The magistrates made the final selection from parochial nominees for membership of the Paving Commissioners of the city. There was, in addition, a high degree of common membership between the Corporation and the remaining principal local government bodies: the Society of Merchant Venturers and the Select Vestries.[24]

This common membership between the Corporation and the various bodies of local government was but one reason for a thoroughgoing popular disdain for the personnel of power. This unpopularity has already been alluded to in the course of the

---

[23] Bush, *Municipal government*, p. 20. Bush suggests that in assigning these onerous duties to the sheriffs, 'perhaps the intention was to blood the novice councillor, municipally speaking'. There were in addition numerous other officials, ranging from the chamberlain and town clerk through to the criers and musicians. These are listed in detail in Bush, *Municipal government*, Appendix 1, and W. Mathews, *Mathews's Bristol guide and directory, 1793–4* (Bristol, 1794), pp. 45–6.

[24] Webbs, *Local government*, pp. 458–9; James Johnson, *Transactions of the Corporation of the Poor* (Bristol 1826), p. 68; E.E. Butcher, *The Bristol Corporation of the Poor, 1696–1898* (Bristol, 1972), pp. 3–4; Bush, *Municipal government*, pp. 7–11.

discussion of Bristol's economic fortunes (above), but it should be re-emphasised: all that follows regarding the structure of power within the city must be placed in the context of decades of widespread loathing for Bristol's executive.

The dislike grew out of the long-standing tendency on the part of the Corporation to obtain local acts which increased its own power and functions, but for which the inhabitants had to bear the expense. By the mid-eighteenth century:

Paving, lighting, watching and cleansing the streets, and the erection and maintenance of the prisons were all now in the hands of the Corporation, at the expense of the householders. There were still to be obtained statutory powers of suppressing nuisances, of regulating the construction of new buildings, of widening and improving streets, of making regulations against the outbreak of fires, of licensing hackney coaches and many other regulative powers. All these the Common Council managed to acquire for the Corporation between 1760 and 1800 by successive Local Acts.[25]

In the early 1790s, the surreptitious introduction of a Bill for the building of a new gaol, to be paid for almost entirely out of the county rate, produced a storm of protest.[26] Shortly after, a dispute on Bristol Bridge regarding the payment of tolls culminated in a violent encounter between Corporation, troops and populace, with serious loss of life.[27] The legacy of hatred from that riot, further fuelled by the Corporation's perceived role in the mismanagement of the Bristol economy, and a number of further disputes, underpins much of the crowd activity in Bristol in these years.

The grounds for objection to the Corporation transcended party politics; nevertheless, the polical complexion of the Corporation did change in this period from being predominantly whig to predominantly tory, the shift beginning in 1812. Unsurprisingly, a religious transformation accompanied the political one: one third of the Corporation were dissenters in 1820, but anglicans dominated new appointments, and this proportion declined in subsequent years. Between 1820 and 1835, 85 per cent of aldermen were anglicans.[28]

The charter of 1710 contained no residence requirement for

[25] Webbs, *Local government*, pp. 457–8.
[26] *Bristol Gazette*, 7 Jan. 1790, 18 Mar. 1790, 7 June 1792, 12 July 1792, 19 July 1792, 26 July 1792. For a selection of handbills and broadsides in opposition to the bill, see Jefferies MSS, vol. VIII, BRL B7952.
[27] See below, ch. 11, and Mark Harrison, '"To raise and dare resentment": the Bristol Bridge riot of 1793 re-examined', *Historical Journal*, XXVI, 3 (1983), pp. 557–85.
[28] CCP/BRO, 1809–32; Rev. Alfred B. Beaven, *Bristol lists: municipal and miscellaneous* (Bristol, 1899), pp. 189–90; Bush, *Municipal government*, pp. 19, 24, 25.

members of the Corporation, a matter noted repeatedly by the Municipal Corporation Commissioners in 1835. In practice, however, the mayor was always resident, living in the Mansion House, and, according to the Commissioners, 'the general practice' in electing Common Councillors was to choose those that either resided, or had business, in Bristol. It was stressed, in 1835, however, that of the aldermen (or magistrates), 'Only one, or at most two, beside the mayor . . . reside in the city.'[29] Certainly absenteeism was thought to be a problem by the Corporation itself: the town clerk sent out a circular to thirty-four Corporation members in 1807 appealing for their attendance, 'there being at this time a great number of members of the Body Corporate absent from Bristol'.[30] A letter from the mayor in 1810 reported an insufficient attendance at Common Council for a meeting to take place, and announced that summonses would be issued for the next meeting.[31]

The extent of the absenteeism was not, however, as acute as the Municipal Commissioners, and other writers since, have portrayed it as being – at least not insofar as attendance at Corporation meetings was concerned.[32] The average rate of attendance of all Corporation members, excluding the recorder, over the forty-five year period, was 60 per cent. This figure was downwardly weighted by those members who never, or virtually never, attended, of which there were between five and eight at any one time. The attendance rate of aldermen was significantly higher, at 69 per cent; and the attendance rates for some individual aldermen were in excess of 90 per cent. The average number of aldermen attending varied from a low of 5.6 (1791–2), to a high of 9.9 (1822–3 and 1824–5; see figure 1).[33]

[29] *MCR*, 4, app. pt II, XXIV, pp. 1161–2.

[30] Circular from Worrall, 9 Sept. 1807, LB/BRO.

[31] Hilhouse Wilcox to Vaughan, Birch, Edye and Fripp, 15 Aug. 1800, LB/BRO. The appointment of Corporation members for life contributed to the dilemma. Henry Cruger's name, for instance, continued faithfully to be entered in the council minutes long after he had departed for America: Cruger emigrated in 1790; he was listed in the Corporation minutes until June 1827: *Bristol Gazette*, 15 Apr. 1790; CCP/BRO, 13 June 1827.

[32] John Latimer, *The Annals of Bristol in the eighteenth century* (Bristol, 1893), p. 454, and the Webbs, *Local government*, p. 474, have both highlighted the problem of absenteeism.

[33] These figures are derived from CCP/BRO, 1790–1835, based on the 425 of the 459 meetings between those dates for which information on attendance was provided. Although the full compliment of Corporation members was 43, the number of positions occupied could fall as low as 38, and was generally around 40. Similarly, the full complement of 12 aldermen was not always filled, and the highest possible attendance could in some years be as low as 10. The number of Corporation meetings varied wildly from year to year, from as few as 4 to as many as 20; the average was 10.2.

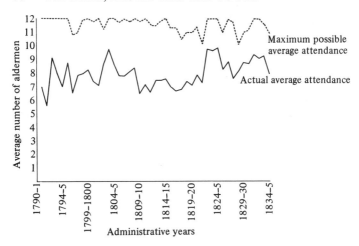

Figure 1   Average attendance of aldermen at Common Council meetings, Bristol, 1790–1 to 1834–5
Source: CCP/BRO, 1790–1835.

The most active members of the Corporation, and those with responsibility and power, were the mayor and aldermen (collectively, the magistrates), and the sheriffs. Aldermen 'licensed taverns, struck rates, supervised wards and the police force, governed charities, and served *en bloc* on more than half the Corporation's special committees'.[34] Their responsibility for a particular ward made them the subject of personal appeal. Their special status in the national machinery for the official suppression of disorder made them potentially the supervisors of military forces and the readers of the Riot Act. The character and complexion of the magistracy, and its administration of the machinery relating to public order, will now be examined in turn.

Forty-nine individuals served in the office of alderman in Bristol between 1790 and 1835. Thirty-nine individuals occupied the position of mayor, of which twenty-five also, at some time, served as aldermen. Thus, in total, fifty-seven Bristolians were magistrates at some point over the period. Of these, twenty-eight were whigs, and twenty-nine tories. For the thirty-nine for whom details of religion are known, thirty-three were anglican. Of those for whom clear

---

[34] Bush, *Municipal government*, p. 19.

details of occupation are available, 48 per cent were merchants, 11 per cent sugar refiners, 9 per cent manufacturers and 7 per cent bankers. All but sixteen of the fifty-seven magistrates held more than one of the positions of mayor, alderman or sheriff during the period; and of these sixteen, fourteen held another position pre-1790. Of the mayors serving between 1790 and 1835, 46 per cent also served as both alderman and sheriff at some time, and 64 per cent had experience as aldermen. Only one mayor, William John Struth, had no experience as either sheriff or alderman, and he, as if in compensation, served a double term, from 1814 to 1816.[35] In short, then, the Bristol magistracy was composed of men of substantial local government experience at a high level.

Economically, it was the 'established wealth' of Bristol which continued to hold magisterial power. This is to be expected, since an Act of 1744 (18 Geo. II, c. 20), stipulating a property qualification for JPs, was in force throughout the nineteenth century.[36] Even without legislative exclusion, however, it is unlikely that the economic composition of the Bristol magistracy would have been radically different. In the first place, the Bristol economy was not experiencing any radical transformation and modification. And secondly, despite the sustained attacks upon the Corporation as corrupt and illegitimate, there was little political struggle within the urban propertied classes in Bristol of the kind that has been identified in other towns by Geoffrey Crossick.[37] The Corporation's opponents had no interest in becoming magistrates (until after the 1835 reforms). Meanwhile, even those opponents, such as J.M. Gutch, editor of the tory journal *Felix Farley*, were prepared to enter into an unwritten agreement with Corporation members that the city's two parliamentary seats should be shared between whig and tory, in the

---

[35] Although election was for one year, some mayors served more than once. The principal sources for these details, and for subsequent ones concerning the magistrates and sheriffs, are: *Bristol Gazette*, 1790–1835; CCP/BRO, 1790–1835; editions of J. and W. Mathews' *Bristol guide*; Beaven, *Bristol lists*, pp. 189–90, 216–20, 227–30, 275–315; Bush, *Municipal government*, Appendix 4.

[36] This measure, combined with established prejudices against giving manufacturers positions on the bench, led, in industrial areas, to a serious deficiency in the number of magistrates: see, David Philips, 'The Black Country magistracy, 1835–1860: a changing elite and the exercise of its power', *Midland History*, III, 3 (1976), pp. 161–90; F.C. Mather, *Public order in the age of the Chartists* (Manchester, 1959), pp. 56–7.

[37] Geoffrey Crossick, 'Urban society and the petty bourgeosie in nineteenth century Britain', in Derek Fraser and Anthony Sutcliffe (eds.), *The pursuit of urban history* (London, 1983), pp. 307–26.

interests of 'stability'. When both polite culture and some new work practices were taken up in Bristol, it was largely as a result of the established city elite broadening its horizons, rather than the product of the intervention of a 'new' middle class.[38]

As regards residential patterns among the magistracy, if the definition of absenteeism is residence outside the city boundaries, then despite high attendance rates this was indeed an absentee magistracy. The jurisdiction of the Corporation was a mere 755 acres, and in this sense it is unsurprising that many magistrates lived outside the bounds.[39] Nevertheless, it was the case that an overwhelming majority of aldermen did not live in the wards for which they were aldermen, and this must have operated as a restriction upon personal appeals for judicial action. Of those for whom information is available regarding home address (as opposed to workplace address), 41 per cent lived in Clifton or Redland whilst serving as a magistrate; 12 per cent lived in Park Street or Park Row; and 12 per cent in the fashionable area between Kingsdown and Stokes Croft. An additional 12 per cent lived further into Gloucestershire or Somerset, or in another part of the country altogether, for all or part of their term as magistrate.

The trend was towards moving out of the city centre, usually late in life, probably after the accumulation of wealth, and often on passing the family business to a son or close relative. The trend towards withdrawal from active commercial life in order to enjoy the social gains brought by business profits (as described by B.W.E. Alford and captured in Sheena Stoddard's account of life in early nineteenth-century Brislington),[40] appears to be reflected in the addresses listed in the various trade directories down to 1835. It might be expected that residential trends would also reflect the domination of the magistracy by particular families. This was not, in fact, the case. Certainly all of Bristol's most prominent families were represented in the higher eschalons of the Corporation: the Ames, Baillies, Caves, Daubenys, Harfords, Protheroes, Brices, Brights, Daniels, and so on; but they were not predominant. In the list of fifty-seven magistrates who served over the period appear forty-nine different family names.

[38] Michael Neve, 'Science in a commercial city: Bristol 1820–1860', in I. Inkster and J. Morrell (eds.), *Metropolis and province: science in British culture, 1780–1850* (London, 1983), pp. 179–204.   [39] Bush, *Municipal government*, p. 17.

[40] Alford, 'Economic development of Bristol'; Sheena Stoddard, *Mr. Braikenridge's Brislington* (Bristol, 1981).

This reasonably conscientious, but socially aloof, magistracy commanded a police force which, even as late as 1835 was not extensive; indeed the Municipal Corporation Commissioners described it as 'exceedingly defective'.[41] Roderick Walters summarises it thus:

In 1835 the total police body numbered 307 men, comprising 12 chief constables, 136 petty or ward constables, 15 night-constables, 115 night-watchmen, 12 day-constables and 17 corporate officers, such as the Mayor's Sergeants and the Sheriff's Beadles, who were sworn in as Constables but whose duties were purely official and ceremonial. The 12 day-constables, were the only force appointed and financed by the Corporation to perform peace-keeping duties, and their appointment in 1832 had supposedly been on a temporary basis.[42]

Chief and ward constables were appointed each year by the mayor and aldermen. The aldermen supervised the chief constables in their respective wards. The number of ward constables appointed was dependent upon the size of each ward: St James had thirty, St Ewen's and St Thomas both had seven; the average was eleven.[43] Ward constables and watchmen acted when called upon, and were only paid for specific tasks. Night constables and watchmen were employed permanently on a weekly wage.[44] Additionally, special constables could be, and were, sworn in in moments of potential or actual crisis. Private law enforcement associations were also formed from time to time.[45]

During the last half of the eighteenth century and the first half of the nineteenth, the procedure for the suppression of riot and

---

[41] *MCR*, 4, app. pt. II, XXIX, p. 1181.

[42] Roderick Walters, *The establishment of the Bristol police force* (Bristol, 1975), p. 3.

[43] *Ibid.*, p. 3.   [44] *MCR*, 4, app. pt II, XXIX, p. 1181.

[45] For example: Association for the Protection of Property, *Bristol Gazette*, 5 Mar. 1812; Bedminster Association for the Prosecution of Felons, *Bristol Gazette*, 10 Mar. 1803; Bristol Association for the Protection of Persons and Property, *Bristol Gazette*, 19 Mar. 1818; Bristol General Association for the Prevention, Discovery and Prosecution of Burglaries and Other Offences, *Bristol Gazette*, 23 Dec. 1814; Bristol Society of Guardians for the Protection of Property and Persons from Depredators, *BMBJ*, 5 Apr. 1800; Clifton Society for the Protection of Property and Persons from all Felonies, Forgeries, Receivers of Stolen Goods, etc., *Bristol Gazette*, 14 Jan. 1976. Bedminster and Clifton were outside the jurisdiction of the Bristol magistrates. Private associations were also formed in nearby Long Ashton, Kingswood and Henbury. For discussion of such organisations, see Adrian Shubert, 'Private initiative in law enforcement: associations for the prosecution of felons, 1744–1856', in Victor Bailey (ed.), *Policing and punishment in nineteenth-century Britain* (London, 1981), pp. 25–41.

disturbance changed scarcely at all.[46] Much of the responsibility lay with the local magistrate. If, in the face of disturbance, he felt the immediately available forces for the prevention or termination of riot were inadequate, he could swear in special constables, call out the military and, if necessary, read the Riot Act. In such a situation, available military resources might include: local militia and volunteer regiments (both disbanded after the French wars), the Yeomanry cavalry (a volunteer, but well-trained and armed force, consisting principally of tenant farmers and small landowners), or the regular armed forces stationed in the district.[47] In more serious circumstances the magistrate could communicate with the Home Secretary, making a request for military reinforcements. If available, those reinforcements would be directed by the Home Secretary to the scene of the disturbance. Formally, the Home Secretary's inquiries, instructions and consultations proceeded through two layers of local authority: the Lord Lieutenants and the High Sheriffs of the counties, and the Lord Lieutenancy and justices of the peace. He would also communicate with local military commanders. On arrival, the military would be under the direction of the local magistrates, who could, if necessary, read the Riot Act and give the order to fire.[48]

The stipulated procedures for response to riot could, in practice, be simplified: the Home Secretary corresponding directly with the

[46] The machinery of public order during this period is covered by three authoritative works: Tony Hayter, *The army and the crowd in mid-Georgian England* (London, 1968); F.O. Darvall, *Popular disturbance and public order in Regency England* (London, 1934); Mather, *Public order*. The procedures described by each of these authors are strikingly similar. Perceptions of an increasing threat to public order after 1815 brought with them the belief that a barrier was needed between 'the people' and the last-resort of the military. The introduction of a professional, and centrally directed, police force, first in London in 1829, and later elsewhere under the Municipal Corporations Act of 1835, the County Police Act of 1839 and the Borough and City Police Act of 1856, although not directed entirely at problems of mass disturbance, marked the first major changes in procedures for suppressing riot.

[47] See, Mather, *Public order*, ch. 5; Hayter, *The army* ch. 3; J.R. Western, 'The volunteer movement as an anti-revolutionary force, 1793–1801', *English Historical Review*, LXXI (1956), pp. 603–14; *idem, The English militia in the eighteenth century* (London, 1965); Oscar Teichmann, 'The yeomanry as an aid to civil power, 1795–1867', *Journal of the Society for Army Historical Research*, XIX (1940), pp. 75–91 (part I), pp. 127–43 (part II).

[48] Hayter, *The army*, p. 16; Darvall, *Popular disturbance*, ch. 12; Mather, *Public order*, ch. 2; R.R. Nelson, *The Home Office, 1782–1801* (Durham, NC, 1969), chs. 6, 7. Established procedures can be seen clearly in operation in the Home Office correspondence of the period, particularly in Disturbance entry books, HO 41/1 (1816) to HO 41/11 (1834).

magistrates, for example. Certainly this tended to be the case in Bristol, although its dual status as city and county may have better facilitated this. The modification of the formal decision-making process in this way, combined with the broad responsibilities of the magistrates 'on the ground' and the inhibited operation of the Riot Act, made for great flexibility (and consequently some confusion and mishap) in the administration of public order.[49] The position of the local magistrate as arbiter between insurrection and suppression, however, necessitated a close understanding of the social parameters within which he exercised his various options.[50]

At the end of this chain of administration of public order, of course, stood the courts. Unfortunately, few of Bristol's legal records for this period have survived; it is therefore difficult to ascertain the influence upon magisterial thinking of the appearance before them in the courtroom of those accused of rioting. But even if more complete legal records had survived, the evidence provided by them would be limited. In the first place, from the calendars of prisoners which do exist for these years, it would seem that only on seven occasions between 1790 and 1835 were individuals accused of taking part in mass disturbance brought before the courts.[51] Furthermore, local magistrates rarely presided over trials concerning serious disorder: such trials were reserved for the circuit judges at the assize courts.[52]

---

[49] See, John Stevenson, 'Social control and the prevention of riots in England, 1789–1829', in A.P. Donajgrodzki (ed.), *Social control in nineteenth-century Britain* (London, 1977), pp. 27–50.

[50] The verdicts of Darvall, Hayter and Mather are that, in general, and with some notable exceptions, the magistrates carried out their difficult responsibilities with a good deal of common sense. Darvall further suggests that the magistrates of incorporated cities functioned more efficiently, with regard to disturbance, than did those of unincorporated cities: Darvall, *Popular disturbances*, pp. 234–45; Hayter, *The army*, ch. 2; Mather, *Public order*, pp. 54–65.

[51] SP/BRO, MS and printed calendars of prisoners in Newgate: 10 Nov. 1792 (November the 5th riot); 2 and 4 Oct. 1793 (Bristol Bridge riot); 15 Aug. 1804 (attack on press gang); 6 July 1812 (election riot); 11 Mar. 1820 (election riot?); 5 Aug. 1820 (riotous assault); 30 Sept. 1826 (intimidation by shipwrights). The 'riot' leading to the committal of 5 Aug. 1820 may have been carried out by only three people.

[52] A magistrate presided at summary proceedings or petty sessions, at which he would try those responsible for minor breaches of public order. He also presided at quarter sessions, which, although they might deal with rioting, would rarely cover those incidents involving physical injury or serious criminal offences: these would be tried at the assize by a circuit judge. For an explanation of the courts of criminal jurisdiction, see A.H. Manchester, *A modern legal history of England and Wales 1750–1950* (London, 1980), esp. pp. 160–6. The jurisdiction of different courts effectively institutionalised magisterial awareness of the distinctions between street order and collective violence.

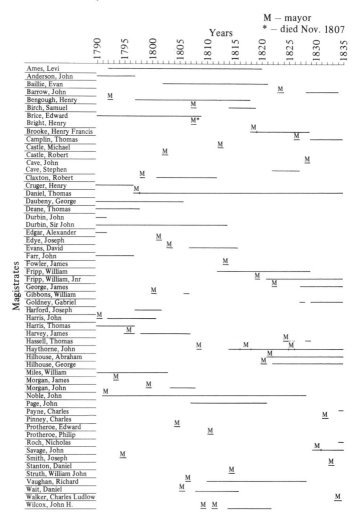

Figure 2   Periods in office of Bristol magistrates, 1790–1835
Sources: CCP/BRO, 1790–1835, and PMA/BRO, 1790–1835.

And lastly, the appearance in the dock of a supposed rioter represented a very particular aspect of the relationship between authority and public assembly: it was an end point in the collapse of the rules of conduct regarding crowd behaviour; neither rioter nor judge planned or hoped to confront each other.

In assessing magisterial experience of both the machinery of public order and the occurrence of crowds, it is also necessary to consider the 'turnover' of magistrates. Figure 2 shows that the collective experience of the magistracy will have varied considerably at different times. In years such as 1796–7 and 1821–2, for instance, there may have been less experience, and less sense of a coherent magisterial policy, than in years such as 1811–12 or 1827–8. The type of experience may also have been relevant. It may be significant that the magistrates in office in 1831 had had experience principally of recreational crowds and 'conservative' rioting.[53]

In summary, then, the Bristol magistracy, although the executive of a self-seeking Corporation, could not entirely be detached from their day-to-day concern with public order: their position in the judiciary in itself guaranteed this. Their regular attendance at meetings, their economic interests in the city and their residence near, if not in, Bristol further ensured a modicum of awareness of prevailing issues and concerns within the city. Their position within the machinery of public order brought them into contact with potential and actual mass disturbance; for most magistrates, however, this contact will have been limited. The magistrates also experienced large crowds as they processed through the streets on ceremonial occasions – as well, of course, as in their role as private citizens at elections, sporting events, and so on. The sheriffs, for their part, were particularly concerned with the management of parliamentary elections, and had the demanding task of attempting to keep order during boisterous hustings.

THE PERSONNEL OF PROMINENCE

The sheriffs and magistrates formed the *de jure* element of authority in Bristol. Attention will now be turned to the *de facto* element: the structure of influence and prominence. Clearly it is difficult to measure 'prominence'. The measure employed here is based on the newspaper press. By surveying the *Bristol Gazette* for the period, and by recording the appearance of names, as signatories to notices or petitions, as members of societies and institutions, as speakers at public meetings, and so on, it was possible to construct an index of Bristol 'personalities' (3,000 in number) from which a short-list of the

---

[53] See below, ch. 11.

most prominent could be compiled. By selection based upon the number of newspaper entries per individual, and the 'quality' of entry (attendance ten times as a member of a particular committee being deemed of less 'prominence value' than one attendance at ten different committees, for example) it was possible to compose a list of seventy-five of the most prominent individuals in Bristol society between 1790 and 1835. Clearly, the sample is biased towards individuals who lived for most or all of that period. It should also be stressed that the sample is not definitive: it cannot, with confidence, be said to represent *the* seventy-five most prominent Bristolians in these years.

Examination of the details of these seventy-five Bristolians reveals that thirty-six served at some point in the office of alderman, sheriff or mayor. A further two individuals served on the Common Council but held no higher office in the Corporation. The remaining thirty-seven held no direct links with the Corporation. Attention will be focused at this point upon those thirty-seven.[54]

In political complexion the group was 47 per cent whig and 53 per cent tory. For those for whom there is information on occupation, 53 per cent were merchants, 13 per cent clergy, 9 per cent manufacturers, 6 per cent bankers and 6 per cent attorneys. In respect of both politics and occupation, this group does not differ markedly from the magistracy. It does, however, contain members of the clergy, who were excluded from serving as magistrates. The pattern of residence is similar: 33 per cent lived for a majority of the period in Clifton or Redland; 17 per cent lived in the area between Kingsdown and Stokes Croft. The drift outwards, clearly apparent in the magisterial group, is visible here also: 31 per cent had moved out further than Clifton by

---

[54] Unsurprisingly, all thirty-seven were male. A number of women, principally the wives and daughters of prominent males, did receive mention in the newspapers for their activities in charitable organisations, particularly those orientated towards girls and poor women. That many of these prominent women were the wives of well-known men was reinforced by ascribing them their husband's forenames: Mrs Richard Ash and Mrs Richard Smith, for example. Daughters of civic notables, who were prominent in female charitable organisations, included: Mary Seyer, Mary Rowe, Elizabeth Rowe, Susanna Morgan and Ellen Estlin. For a discussion of female participation in the burgeoning of private organisations during the early nineteenth century, and middle class attitudes towards the role of women, see: Catherine Hall, 'Gender divisions and class formation in the Birmingham middle class, 1780–1850', in Raphael Samuel (ed.), *People's history and socialist theory* (London, 1981), pp. 164–75; Leonore Davidoff and Catherine Hall, 'The architecture of public and private life. English middle class society in a provincial town, 1780–1850', in Fraser and Sutcliffe (eds.), *Urban history*, pp. 327–45.

the end of the period in which they were active in Bristol life.

Many of these thirty-seven individuals received mention in the press because of their involvement in city institutions. Consequently those institutions are well represented in the sample – notably: the Society of Merchant Venturers; the Bristol Institution for the Advancement of Science, Literature and the Arts, formed in 1823; the Literary and Philosophical Society, formed at the same time; the Bristol Institution; and the Chamber of Commerce, again formed in 1823. Overlapping membership between these groups existed in various combinations.[55]

Despite the similarities between this group and the magistrates, anti-Corporation sentiments were implicitly present in two forms. One form was membership of the Chamber of Commerce, which was established in an attempt to promote new industry in direct, and specified, opposition to the economic monopoly and malpractice of the Corporation.[56]   It is here that it might be possible to detect a new manufacturing-based economic interest attempting to assert itself. Among the seven members of the Chamber in this group, are to be found three of the group's four manufacturers (Joseph Cookson, glass manufacturer, John Hare Jnr, who owned a large floor cloth works, and Christopher George, who owned a lead shot factory). Among this seven is also Thomas Stock, a sugar refiner, chairman of the Chamber of Commerce at its foundation, and President of the Chamber from 1826 to 1831. The second element of opposition to the Corporation was expressed through the refusal to serve on the Corporation, or through membership of the reformed Corporation after 1835. Seven individuals, Richard Ash, Robert Bruce, Daniel Cave, Thomas Hellicar, Philip John Miles, Thomas Stock and George Thorne, refused to serve. Five served on the reformed Corporation – Ash, Stock, Joseph Cookson, Henry Bush and Stephen Prust.[57]

Many of these prominent individuals were committee members of some of the 150 or so institutions and societies which came into existence in Bristol during these years. The direct experience, among members of this group, of the management of large gatherings was

---

[55] This confirms the argument put forward, in greater detail, by Neve, 'Science in a commercial city'.

[56] Chamber of Commerce, *Rules and regulations*. Chamber of Commerce, *Report . . . on . . . local taxation* (Bristol, 1824). It may be significant that the highest attendance rates for aldermen were from 1822–3, to 1824–5; see figure 1.

[57] Beaven, *Bristol lists*, pp. 275–315; Bush, *Municipal government*, Appendix 5.

extremely limited, however. The number of inveterate committee members was not matched by the number of public speakers. Some individuals had substantial experience of chairing the meeting of various organisations, particularly Richard Ash, Rev. T.T. Biddulph, Robert Bright, Rev. William Day, Rev. John Eden, John Scandrett Harford, Rev. Francis Randolph and Joseph Reynolds. Few ever addressed a large public meeting, however. Hugh Baillie spoke at a meeting in opposition to the Property Tax in 1816;[58] Robert Bush seconded the nomination of Richard Hart Davis at the 1820 election;[59] Andrew Pope seconded the nomination of Edward Protheroe at the October 1812 election;[60] Stephen Prust made a speech at the opening of the Cock Road school in 1816, as did Thomas Saunders.[61] The only individuals with greater experience were, on the one hand, the clergy (particularly Rev. T.T. Biddulph and Rev. John Eden), and, on the other, the politicians (Richard Hart Davis and Philip John Miles).

Thus, although these individuals held significant influence through their wealth, and through their positions within various organisations; and although their names appeared habitually in the Bristol newspapers, they appear to have had no greater contact with mass phenomena than did other Bristolians. Was the social prominence which these individuals achieved, and presumably sought, one which was also socially exclusive?

Newspapers served as a highly accessible route to social prominence: slavishly publishing the names of committee members, the names of subscribers to worthy causes, and so on, they acted as free publicity for the ruling classes. However, this form of prominence may have acted rather as an emblem of social detachment. Perhaps it was those individuals frequently to be found on the platform at crowd events, rather than those whose names frequently appeared in the press, who achieved the broadest social influence and the greatest ability to influence popular opinion and crowd action.

Such individuals do stand out. Edward Bowles Fripp, a soap manufacturer, publicly declared his opposition to slavery in 1830; chaired a public meeting in support of the whig candidate, Edward Protheroe Jnr, at the election of the same year; chaired a reform meeting in April 1831; and was a member of a committee formed to present a memorial to Lord Melbourne, requesting an inquiry into the 1831 riot.[62] William Herapath, a maltster, was a committee member

[58] *Bristol Gazette*, 22 Feb. 1816.   [59] *Ibid.*, 9 Mar. 1820.   [60] *Ibid.*, 8 Oct. 1812.
[61] *Ibid.*, 31 Oct. 1816.   [62] *Ibid.*; 15 July 1830, 28 Apr. 1831, 24 Nov. 1831.

of the Mechanics' Institution, and Deputy Governor of the Corporation of the Poor in 1828 and 1829. In June 1831 he chaired a meeting of trades expressing opposition to the coercion by employers of workers at elections. He became Vice-President of the Bristol Political Union in 1831, chairing meetings, issuing notices, negotiating with the magistrates and attempting to terminate violence, in the period surrounding the 1831 riot.[63] Thomas Jones, a merchant, was active in 1812, speaking at a public meeting in May to address the Prince Regent on the assassination of prime minister Percival, proposing Richard Hart Davis at the July and October elections and proposing a motion at a meeting opposed to concessions to Catholics, in December.[64]

Others can be identified also. Rev. John Powell, in addition to membership of numerous societies, gave speeches to the whig Independent and Constitutional Club in 1812, against the slave trade in 1814 and at a whig election meeting in 1820.[65] John Weeks, the fervently loyalist landlord of the Bush Tavern chaired a meeting of innkeepers in opposition to sedition in 1793; he was also prominent in the public reception, and celebration, of the Preliminaries for Peace in 1801, and the Proclamation of Peace in 1802. The Oxfordshire Militia presented him with a gift of silver plate after being stationed in the city in 1802. After his retirement from the Bush, he returned to make a speech from the balcony in commemoration of the death of Nelson, in January 1806.[66] Christopher George, patent shot, pipe and sheet lead manufacturer, was not only active in support of whig candidates in the elections of 1818 and 1820, a committee member of the Chamber of Commerce and of the Mechanics' Institution, and an opponent of slavery, but he was also to become an active reformer, and chairman of the reform committee in 1831.[67]

Such public prominence may have amounted to notoriety as much

---

[63] *Ibid.*, 23 June 1825, 17 Apr. 1828, 30 Apr. 1829, 2 June 1832. And, for example: ibid., 13 Oct. 1831, 3 Nov. 1831: 'Collection of newspaper extracts, reports, placards etc. relating to the riots of 1831', BRL B4782/7426; Reynolds to Herapath, 20 Oct. 1831, and Herapath to Daniel, 26 Oct. 1831, in 'MS material relating to the Bristol riots, 1831', BRL B24930.

[64] *Bristol Gazette*, 21 May 1812, 2 July 1812, 8 Oct. 1812, 24 Dec. 1812.

[65] *Ibid.*, 9 Sept. 1812, 9 July 1812, 7 July 1814, 17 Feb. 1820.

[66] *Ibid.*, 10 Jan. 1793; *BMBJ*, 3 Oct. 1801, 17 Oct. 1801; *Bristol Gazette*, 6 May 1802, 4 Feb. 1802, 16 Jan. 1806.

[67] *Bristol Gazette*, 28 May 1818, 18 Jan. 1816, 17 Feb. 1820, 2 Jan. 1823, 29 Jan. 1824, 23 June 1825, 19 June 1828, 7 Oct. 1830, 15 July 1830, 20 Jan. 1831, 20 Apr. 1831, 28 Apr. 1831, 5 May 1831; notice from George to 'Reformers of Bristol', 4 May 1831, PO/BRO.

as influence. This was certainly the case for those individuals whose names became prominent during election campaigns, such as Thomas Lee and John Agg in the 1807 election,[68] Charles Houlden Walker and Charles A. Elton in the elections of 1819 and 1820,[69] and Charles Pinney, John Hare Jnr and William Claxton in the election of 1830.[70] Thinly veiled references to a whole series of individual names sometimes appeared in election publications.[71] Local notoriety could also be achieved in other ways: John Noble became synonymous with the shooting of more than sixty people on Bristol Bridge in 1793;[72] Charles Pinney unwillingly became the best-known mayor of the period as a result of the 1831 riot; James Acland was known for his one-man campaign, waged in the columns of his newspaper *The Bristolian*, against the Corporation;[73] and J.M. Gutch (*Felix Farley's Bristol Journal*) and John Mills (*Bristol Gazette*) both achieved renown as newspaper editors and as participants in local and party politics.

THE ELITE OF PUBLIC LIFE

Three elements of power, prominence and influence in early nineteenth-century Bristol have been discussed so far: positions of power within Bristol Corporation, prominence in the press and prominence in the public eye. Presumably those individuals who can be shown to have had experience of all three of these elements could reasonably be termed some of the most broadly powerful and influential citizens in Bristol. Thirty-six men both served as magistrate or sheriff and also emerged from the survey of the *Gazette* as 'prominent individuals'. A further two were prominent in newspaper

[68] John Agg, *The lamp trimmed* (Bristol, 1807); Thomas Lee, *Election clubs* (Bristol, 1807); *idem, Eyes to the blind!* (Bristol, 1807); *idem, Trim the lamp!* (Bristol, 1807); Anon, (*idem*), *A glance at Dr. Lee* (Bristol, 1807).

[69] C.H. Walker, *An Address to the . . . electors of Bristol* (Bristol, 1819); *idem, A second address* (Bristol, 1819); *idem, A third address* (Bristol, 1819); *idem, An address to the electors of Bristol showing the ineligibility of Henry Bright Esq. the Whig candidate to represent them in the ensuing parliament* (Bristol, 1828); Charles A. Elton, *An apology for Colonel Hugh Baillie* (Bristol, 1819?); *idem, A sequel to the apology* (Bristol, 1819).

[70] 'Collection of broadsides, addresses, notices, etc.' relating to the election of 1830', BRL; Peter Marshall, *Bristol and the abolition of slavery: the politics of emancipation* (Bristol, 1975), pp. 5–17.

[71] For example, see 'Collection of broadsides, addresses, notices, etc., relating to the election of 1826', BRL; 'Collection . . . relating to the election of 1830'.

[72] See below, ch. 11.   [73] James Acland, *The Bristolian*, 1827–9.

notices and reports and served on the Common Council. Before narrowing this 'elite' further by analysing which of them had direct experience of standing before large gatherings, it is worth summarising some of the group's characteristics (see table 2).

With one exception (that of Evan Baillie), these were assiduous attenders of Corporation meetings. Whereas the average attendance rate for all magistrates over the period was 69 per cent, the attendance rate for this group was 84–6 per cent if Evan Baillie is excluded. Of this group, 45 per cent (seventeen in number) were whig, and 55 per cent tory. By occupation, nineteen of the thirty-eight were merchants. Of the remaining nineteen, four were manufacturers, three bankers, two distillers, two shipbuilders, two brewers, two sugar refiners, one barrister, one tanner and two were retired. As regards residence, 42 per cent lived in Clifton, Redland or Cotham; ten (26 per cent) had moved out further than this by the end of their active lives in the city. Thirty different families are represented in this group.

The holding of official positions in influential organisations, such as the Merchant Venturers, Corporation of the Poor, Bristol Institution, Mechanics' Institution, Literary and Philosophical Society and Chamber of Commerce, was not spectacularly high. However, the majority of the group (66 per cent) had served in the Bristol Volunteers. Insofar as they were involved with various organisations, their special prominence is reflected in their frequent status as chairmen. Richard Bright, Michael Castle, Thomas Daniel, George Daubeny, William Fripp Jnr, John Haythorne, Charles Pinney and Charles Ludlow Walker, for instance, chaired a total of ninety-six meetings between them.

However, although well known in such official capacities, and also, no doubt, as major employers of labour, few of these men can be said to have been especially prominent for their attendance at public assemblies – the two politicians in the group, Evan Baillie and Edward Protheroe, notwithstanding. Henry Protheroe (knighted in 1803) contributed some notable speeches: in favour of an address in support of the government in 1797; at a meeting opposing the local Dock Bill, in 1807; in support of resolutions at a meeting of the 'Friends to Religious Liberty', in 1811; and in opposition to the Property Tax in 1816.[74] Richard Vaughan (knighted in 1815), in addition to membership of the committees of thirty-two different

[74] *Bristol Gazette*, 9 Feb. 1797, 2 Apr. 1807, 23 May 1811, 22 Feb. 1816.

Table 2. *Thirty-eight socially prominent individuals occupying positions in Bristol Corporation*

Name	Office	Attendance rate (%)	Occupation	Politics
Ames, Levi	A	83	Banker	W
Baillie, Evan	A	14	Merchant	W
Barrow, John	A/S/M	84	Merchant	T
Bickley, Benjamin	S	83	Merchant	T
Birch, Samuel	A/S/M	63	Merchant	T
Brice, Edward	S	82	Sugar refiner	T
Bright, Richard	CC only		Merchant	W
Brooke, Henry Francis	A/S/M	72	Merchant	T
Castle, Michael	S/M	100	Malt distiller*	W
Castle, Michael Hinton	S	88	Distiller	W
Cave, John	S/M	92	Manufacturer	T
Cave, Stephen	A	53	Banker	T
Claxton, Robert	A/M	68	Merchant	W
Daniel, Thomas	A/M	89	Merchant	T
Daubeny, George	A	82	Sugar refiner	T
Edye, Joseph	S/M	89	Banker	W
Evans, David	A/S/M	81	Merchant?	W
Fripp, William	A/S	64	Soap manufacturer	W
Fripp, William, Jnr	A/S/M	92	Soap manufacturer	T
George, Christopher	CC only		Lead manufacturer	W
George, James	A/S/M	86	Brewer	T
George, Philip	S	91	Brewer	W
Gibbons, William	A/S/M	84	Merchant	T
Goldney, Gabriel	A/S/M	95	Retired	T
Hassell, Thomas	A/S/M	96	Tanner	T
Haythorne, John	A/S/M	83	Merchant	T
Hilhouse, Abraham	A/S/M	81	Shipbuilder	T
Hilhouse, George	A/S/M	80	Shipbuilder	T
Lunell, John Evan	S	100	Merchant	W
Maze, Peter	S	92	Merchant	T
Payne, Charles	S/M	100	Merchant	T
Pinney, Charles	S/M	93	Merchant	W
Protheroe, Edward	S/M	95	Merchant	W
Protheroe, Henry	S	90	Merchant	W
Protheroe, Philip	S/M	96	Merchant	W
Smith, Joseph	M	100	Barrister	W
Vaughan, Richard	A/S/M	79	Merchant	T
Walker, Charles Ludlow	S/M	94	Retired	T

Abbreviations:
A – alderman
S – sheriff
M – mayor
CC – Common Councillor
T – tory
W – whig
*Retired by 1820.
Sources: **PMA/BRO**; **CCP/BRO**; Bristol newspapers and directories (see Bibliography).

organisations over the years, may have been particularly known for his contribution to the celebrations of the Preliminary Peace with France in 1801, and the Proclamation of Peace in 1802; as captain of the 3rd company of the Bristol Volunteers; in publicly pledging his support for Charles Bathurst at the 1807 election, and later proposing his candidature; in calling out the Bristol Volunteers at the election of 1807 while serving as mayor; for his presence at the chairing of Richard Hart Davis at the July 1812 election; and in seconding the nomination of Davis at the October 1812 election.[75] Michael Castle may have held a reputation as a particularly active and vocal whig.[76] Charles Pinney's activities in forming and presiding over the Mechanics' Institute, as a prominent whig, and for chairing a meeting in support of the French Revolution of 1830 almost certainly made him well known even before his hapless role in the 1831 riot.[77]

There was, however, one individual who can indisputably be described as the single most prominent, powerful, influential and public figure in Bristol in these years: this was Thomas Daniel. He was mayor from 1797 to 1798, alderman from 1798 to 1835 (during which time he maintained an attendance rate of around 90 per cent) and went on to serve as a Councillor in the reformed Corporation from 1835 to 1841. He was also a diehard tory, a merchant with extensive West India interests, and very wealthy. On his death, in 1854, at the age of ninety-one, his estate was valued at £200,000.[78] Daniel's house in Berkeley Square, where he lived from 1803, was the one private building which popular processions would go out of their way to march past (and, on one occasion, to attack).[79]

Daniel was a remarkable man. He belonged to fifty-six different organisations and societies in Bristol between 1790 and 1835. Among the numerous public meetings he chaired were one in defence of slavery, in 1825,[80] one in opposition to parliamentary reform, in

---

[75] *BMBJ*, 17 Oct. 1801, 6 May 1802; *Bristol Gazette*, 28 Sept. 1803, 30 Apr. 1807, 7 May 1807, 23 July 1812, 8 Oct. 1812.

[76] *Bristol Gazette*, 15 July 1802, 12 July 1810, 6 Feb. 1812, 26 Mar. 1812, 9 Apr. 1812, 9 July 1812, 30 July 1812, 8 Oct. 1812, 25 June 1818, 17 Feb. 1820, 30 Sept. 1830, 20 Jan. 1812.

[77] *Ibid.* 28 Apr. 1825, 23 June 1825, 30 Mar. 1826, 6 Apr. 1826, 3 Aug. 1830, 12 Aug. 1830, 28 Apr. 1831, 9 Sept. to 23 Sept. 1830.

[78] Bush, *Municipal government*, p. 235.

[79] W. Mathews, *Complete Bristol directory* (Bristol, 1803); *Bristol Mirror*, 4 July 1812 (procession during general election attacks Daniel's house, see below, chs. 6 and 9); *Bristol Mercury*, 23 June 1832 (procession to celebrate the passing of the Reform Bill makes a detour through Berkeley Square, see below, ch. 5).

[80] *Bristol Gazette*, 15 Feb. 1823.

1831,[81] and two opposing Catholic emancipation.[82] He also chaired seven tory meetings and dinners,[83] in addition to annual celebrations of Pitt's birthday, from 1814 to 1823. His public speeches included two nominations of tory candidates at elections, two proposing declarations of loyalty to the king, and one in opposition to the 1816 West India Bill for the registration of slaves.[84] The attention paid to his residence by crowds is clear testimony that here, at least, was one man whose public prominence had a direct influence upon the conduct of popular assemblies.

AGREED PROCEDURE

The personnel that composed the structure of power and influence in Bristol society did not, it seems, possess exceptional experience of crowd phenomena, apart, perhaps from the attendance by the sheriffs at parliamentary elections, and by the magistrates at disturbances. Few individuals can have claimed special prominence as either the managers of, or the focus for, popular assemblies. The experience of crowd phenomena for those in authority was essentially *formalistic*.

That formalism, it may be argued, served only to emphasise the ambiguous relationship between crowd participant and crowd organiser. The rules for crowd organisation constrained those in authority as much as it did those in the crowd: just as there were limits beyond which crowd action was deemed, by those in prominent positions, as dangerous, subversive or bestial, so crowd participants were fully cognisant of the limits beyond which crowd management was improper, presumptuous or tyrannical.[85]

Parliamentary elections, for instance, were subject to clear procedures. At first glance it appears that it was authority that determined those procedures: the publication in the newspapers by the candidate of the time and date of his arrival; the cavalcade of the wealthy to greet him; the sheriff's conduct of the hustings and return of the votes; the dinner for the candidate's wealthy supporters. There

---

[81] *Ibid.*, 3 Feb. 1831.   [82] *Ibid.*, 19 Feb. 1829, 26 Mar. 1829.

[83] *Ibid.*, 6 Aug. 1812, 4 June 1818, 25 June 1818, 20 Aug. 1818, 28 Apr, 1831, 27 June 1833, 8 June 1835.

[84] *Ibid.*, 30 Oct. 1806, 7 May 1807, 16 Apr. 1807, 13 Feb. 1817, 22 Feb. 1816.

[85] The conduct of public executions in England up until at least the second quarter of the nineteenth century provides a graphic example of the belief in such limits; see Michael Ignatieff, *A just measure of pain: the penitentiary in the industrial revolution, 1750–1850* (London, 1978), pp. 21–4.

was a second side to such procedures, however. The announcement by the candidate – of which this one from 1802 is a typical example: 'The Friends of MR BRAGGE ARE REQUESTED To Meet Him on Durdham-Down, THIS PRESENT SATURDAY JULY 3, at ELEVEN O'clock in the forenoon precisely, *To accompany Him* to BRISTOL. WHITE LION.'[86] – was, of course, a public announcement. The wealthy would accordingly be accompanied to meet the candidate by a crowd of supporters, spectators and opponents. The route taken, despite the lead taken of the cavalcade by the 'gentlemen', was one specifically designed to pass through populous, and poor, areas of town.[87] On arrival at the hustings, the crowd both inside and outside was mainly one of the unenfranchised. They would nevertheless express their political views as the candidates delivered their speeches (which spoke of their pride at the opportunity to represent these, their fellow citizens);[88] and the crowd, by their show of hands, would force a contest.

The procedure for elections was well established. Other meetings were subject to such unwritten rules also. When, in 1803, George Daubeny, alderman of St James' parish, attempted prematurely to end a parish meeting discussing the controversial Bill for the construction of a new harbour, he was swiftly ordered to leave the chair, and replaced. The same fate befell Philip George at the corresponding meeting in St Mary Redcliff parish. Both Daubeny and George were members of the elite group of thirty-eight prominent-and-powerful individuals.[89] In 1831, Christopher Claxton called a meeting of sailors at which, under cover of a declaration of loyalty to the king, he attempted to secure their support in defence of the controversial recorder, Sir Charles Wetherell. Claxton was removed from the chair, and the sailors, while declaring their loyalty to the king, passed the resolution that they would not be 'the cat's paw of the Corporation or its agents'.[90] In June 1832, the Corporation appealed to the trades celebrating the passing of the Reform Act not to have a celebratory illumination. When there was indeed no illumination, the *Bristol Gazette* expressed pleasure at the trades' 'respect and deference' for the magistrates' appeal. The *Bristol*

[86] *FFBJ*, 3 July 1802. The White Lion was the tory party headquarters.
[87] See below, chs. 5 and 9.
[88] See, for example, *Bristol Gazette*, 30 Oct. 1806; *FFBJ*, 1 Nov. 1806; *Bristol Gazette*, 9 Mar. 1820; *FFBJ*, 31 July 1830. [89] *Bristol Gazette*, 12 May 1803.
[90] Notice of resolutions in 'Troubles in Bristol, by politicks, fire and pestilence', BRL B10112; *Bristol Gazette*, 20 Oct. 1831; *Bristol Mirror*, 22 Oct. 1831.

Mercury, however, was swift to retort that 'the trades owe them no respect, and pay them no deference in this matter. It was agreed to give up the illumination two days before the magistrates put forward their superfluous protest.'[91]

There was, then, a set procedure for the conduct of meetings, and other crowd events, which included a popular insistence against such an inflated sense of its own importance on the part of authority. The calling together of crowd events was also rule-bound. Notice of the holding of a crowd gathering was generally issued to local newspapers and handbills. The announcement might be in the form of the official publications of arrangements by the Corporation in the press, such as was the case for the celebrations of the coronations of George IV and William IV.[92] In other instances, political parties would issue handbills and posters detailing the programme for processions to the hustings,[93] for chairing processions[94] or for celebratory illuminations.[95] Such notices could also appear directed at either trades in general or to specific occupational groups.[96] Other outdoor meetings and processions were similarly advertised by means of posters and placards,[97] as was the case for sporting events.[98] The magistrates not only shared this method of publicity, requesting citizens to 'illuminate' for example,[99] but also used posters to request citizens *not* to form or attend crowd gathering events. Most dramatically:

Council House, Wednesday Nov. 2 1831. The Magistrates most earnestly desire that all Persons will Avoid Assembling in CROWDS in different parts of the City as such assemblages are likely to promote disturbances, and interfere

91 *Bristol Gazette*, 20 June 1832; *Bristol Mercury*, 23 June 1832.
92 *Bristol Gazette*, 5 July 1821, 19 July 1821, 15 Sept. 1831.
93 For example, notice from 'Friends of Protheroe', 22 July 1803, and notice to 'The friends and committee of James E. Baillie', 25 July 1830, in 'Collection . . . relating to the election of 1830', BRL.
94 'Programme of the procession for chairing Messrs. Baillie and Protheroe, May 4 1831', in 'Bristol Parliamentary Elections, 1774–1943', BRO 11944(4); 'The Chairing', undated notice (1831), in 'Collection of broadsides, addresses, notices, etc., relating to the election of 1831', BRL B10108.
95 'General illumination', 2 May 1831, PO/BRO; notice for illumination, 4 May 1831, in 'Collection . . . relating to the election of 1831'.
96 Notice for meeting of all trades to arrange 'their Triumphant Procession', 29 Apr. 1831, in 'Collection . . . relating to the election of 1831'; notice re chairing, to journeyman tailors, 30 April 1831, and to boot and shoe makers, for procession to hustings of reform candidates, 27 April 1831, in *ibid*.
97 Notice of reform meeting, 26 Apr. 1831, in *ibid*.
98 'Volume of miscellaneous sporting notices, 1822–32', BRL B22765.
99 'Illumination. Defeat of the French Fleet', 12 June 1794, PO/BRO; notice for illumination on victory over Dutch, 5 September, 1799, PO/BRO.

with arrangements now making for the recovery of Property and the Detection of Offenders. C. PINNEY. Mayor.[100]

Some crowd gathering events did not require the use of this well-developed publicity machine.[101] The organisation and procedure for public executions was well understood; their exact timing was effectively advertised by the assize reports in local newspapers. Public holidays were at fixed times, and the organisation of recreation on those days was the subject more of popular custom than of public decree.[102]

The degree of practical organisation of crowd events, as distinct from their publicity and conduct, varied greatly. For the coronation celebrations of 1821, the Corporation set up a separate committee specifically to consider organisational details.[103] A pre-arranged order and form was determined for most processional events, be they Corporation proclamations, funerals or reform processions.[104] On celebratory occasions, uniforms, banners and symbols were an essential ingredient of processions.[105] Similar in attention to detail, but very different in intent, were the magistrates' arrangements for the police and military attendance at contentious gatherings. Such arrangements were not only a categorical intrusion of officialdom into popular crowd gathering events, but also advertised clearly the location, timing and boundaries for behaviour of these events. In addition they influenced the degree and type of popular attendance.

[100] 2 Nov. 1831, PO/BRO. Other examples include: notice requesting citizens not to attend arrival of Wetherell, 2 April 1829, PO/BRO; request not to illuminate, 26 Apr. 1831, PO/BRO; request to 'masters, to restrain their servants, apprentices, and children' from attending reform meetings, Brandon Hill, Dec. 1816: *Bristol Mirror*, 21 Dec. 1816.

[101] The plethora of public notices contained in the collections relating to the elections of the later part of the period are evidence not only of vigorous popular participation in local political events, but also of the vitality (in both senses of that word) of printed communication. The extent of bill posting in the early nineteenth-century English city is perhaps difficult for us now to imagine.

[102] See, for example, Charles Phythian-Adams, 'Milk and soot. The changing vocabulary of a popular ritual in Stuart and Hanoverian London', in Fraser and Sutcliffe (eds.), *Urban history*, pp. 83–104; and Bob Bushaway, *By rite: custom, ceremony and community in England, 1700–1880* (London, 1982), ch. 2.

[103] Coronation Papers, LMP/BRO Box 1820–1.

[104] For example, on the death of George III and the accession of George IV, *FFBJ*, 5 Feb. 1820; funeral of Richard Reynolds, 19 Sept. 1816; trades procession in celebration of passing of Reform Act, *Mercury*, 23 June 1832.

[105] For example, *Mercury*, 23 June 1832; 'Greetheads panoramic sketch of the procession to the Bristol Cathedral, Thursday the 8th September 1831 on the coronation day of their majesties William IV and Adelaide', BRO 17571 MS.

In general, those events attended, organised or greatly opposed by those in authority were subject to the greatest internal or external organisation. As the popularity of the Bristol and Clifton races increased, the facilities offered to wealthy spectators improved.[106] An anti-Catholic meeting of February 1829, in Queen Square, which received the active backing of the tory notables, involved the careful erection of hustings, and the physical segregation of rival political factions.[107] Most assemblies attended by the wealthy took place indoors, of course, thus automatically facilitating a higher degree of comfort and organisation. Such facilities were offically denied to popular assemblies: the mayor could, and did, decline the use of the Guildhall by such gatherings.[108] Outdoor meetings most usually involved the erection of a speaker's platform,[109] or even the simple provision of a carriage or wagon from which the meeting could be addressed.[110] The necessity of erecting a platform on Brandon Hill, where a wagon would be of little use, was open to a devious form of semi-official subversion: the coercion by employers of local carpenters.[111] At election time, the balcony of a public house was the most commonly used platform for the calling together and addressing of a crowd.

Set procedures, then, existed for the calling together and conduct of popular assemblies; such procedures were well understood by crowd participants as well as crowd managers. The framing of these rules of conduct was, effectively, undertaken by both parties. The existence of such rules was indicative of the ordered position of crowd events in Bristol life. Because the formation of crowds was a rule-bound activity, there were strict limits upon the ability of individuals to determine or control mass phenomena.

CONCLUSION

It has been argued that in order to gain a realistic impression of power in this provincial city, it is necessary to examine not only those occupying official positions, but also those individuals prominent in

---

[106] For example, advertisements for the races, April 1827 and May 1832, in 'Volume of . . . sporting notices'.

[107] *Bristol Mercury*, 17 Feb. 1829; *FFBJ*, 14 Feb. 1829.

[108] As, for example, with the 'Peterloo' meeting in 1819, *Bristol Mercury*, 11 Oct. 1819.

[109] *Bristol Gazette*, 6 Oct. 1819.   [110] *Ibid.*, 13 Oct. 1831.

[111] This was alleged by Henry Hunt to have occurred in 1816: *Bristol Mirror*, 28 Dec. 1816.

the social life of the city. Inevitably, an overlap was found to exist between these two categories, and this overlap thereby constituted an elite of the powerful and prominent. For the most part, however, it was found that few individuals, either in official positions, in prominent social positions, or both, can be said to have held a particularly intimate association with crowd phenomena.

The perceptions and understanding of crowd events possessed by those in positions of authority were derived from three sources. The first was the common knowledge and experience available to all inhabitants of Bristol, modified and embellished by information which they gleaned from the columns of local newspapers, from pamphlets and from other publications. The second source was the occupancy of a formal position, either within the Corporation, as sheriff or magistrate, or as a member of a local organisation or interest group. This latter position could place an individual on a public platform or on a committee which was involved in arranging crowd events, such as the election committee of a political party.[112] The third source was participation in a crowd event in the role of actor: as a member, for example, of a civic procession.[113] In this instance, the individual watches the crowd watching him; his communication with them is only through the medium of ritualistic behaviour.

Misperceptions of crowd characteristics, motivation and composition were facilitated by the relative lack of direct confrontational and directional experience of mass events, by the restrictiveness of prescribed procedures for crowd organisation and by social distance. That social distance was in part geographical (a large proportion of the individuals in authority living in Clifton or beyond), and in part institutional: the devotion of large quantities of personal time to moralising, evangelical, elitist or business organisations and societies. There was far greater experience among the city's 'elite' of chairing a small meeting of wealthy individuals than of chairing boisterous and contentious mass gatherings. They knew better how to direct an assembly charged with piety than one charged with passion.

[112] The papers of the tory Stedfast Society, for example, demonstrate the extent to which such committees were concerned with the provision and management of numbers of people: 'Stedfast Society: election proceedings, 1806–1812', BRO 12144.

[113] Descriptions of such processions are contained in W. Mathews, *Mathews's Bristol guide and directory, 1793–4* (Bristol, 1794), pp. 45–6, and in J. Mathews, *The Bristol guide* (Bristol, 1815), pp. 83–5; *ibid.*, 1829 edn, p. 80.

Social and political prominence, and crowd activity, did, however, intersect. They did so, principally, in two ways. The first was when social prominence precipitated crowd attention or attack: this was the case for Thomas Daniel. It was also the case for John Hare Jnr, a major employer, and prominent supporter of Edward Protheroe at the turbulent election of 1830. His floor cloth factory was assailed by the supporters of the rival whig faction of James Evan Baillie.[114]

Intersections also occurred on occasions when crowd events held repercussions for the social standing of individuals associated with them. The reputation and credibility of Edward Protheroe Jnr, MP, was seriously undermined by his involvement with, and presence at, the hopelessly chaotic and mismanaged open-air dinner to celebrate the passing of the Reform Act, in August 1832.[115] Dr Edward Long Fox claimed that his association with the popular cause after the Bristol Bridge riot of 1793 'prejudiced his interest as a medical man, and created enemies for life'.[116] Charles Pinney's reputation was ruined by his identification with the riots of 1831 – all the more so since he had, in the months preceding the riot, shown himself sympathetic to reform.[117] This was, after all, the period of the emergence of the radical 'mass platform', and to be associated with crowd activity was, by implication, to be associated with the 'mob oratory' of Henry Hunt and William Cobbett.[118]

For those occupying positions of power, in its broadest sense, little,

---

[114] Hare MSS: 'John Hare: documents concerning the Bristol election of 1830', BRO 8033.

[115] *Bristol Gazette*, 16 Aug. 1832; *FFBJ*, *Bristol Mirror* and *Bristol Mercury*, 18 Aug. 1832; and see illustration, 'The grand reform dinner on Brandon Hill', in Daniel Vickery, 'A Bristol calendar containing brief notices of such events as have taken place in that city and its neighbourhood July 1824 to the end of the year 1835', BRL B2639 MS.

[116] Edwin F. Fox to Francis F. Fox, 4 June 1872, BRL B13064 MS.

[117] Mary Ames to Mrs Smith, undated (1 Nov. 1831?), PP/BUL R-5.

[118] John Belchem, 'Henry Hunt and the evolution of the mass platform', *English Historical Review*, XCIII (1978), pp. 739–73; John Belchem, 'Republicanism, popular constitutionalism and the radical platform in early nineteenth-century England', *Social History*, VI, 1 (1981), pp. 1–32. *FFBJ*, 9 Oct. 1819, said of Thomas Stocking, who chaired a meeting directed against the events at Peterloo, that he seemed 'to have succeeded Mr Hunt as Public Orator and Advocate'. Stocking's public career was brief, however: it began when he seconded Hugh Baillie at the 1818 election, and came to an end when, without his permission, he nominated James Evan Baillie at the election of 1820: *Bristol Gazette*, 18 June 1818, 9 Mar. 1920. In-between-times he directed his energies to the Peterloo affair, on the reformers' side: *Bristol Gazette*, 16 Sept., 23 Sept., 7 Oct. 1818; 21 Jan., 4 Nov. 1819.

in the way of social prestige, was to be gained from a familiarity with, understanding of or association with crowd events. Crowd management was on occasions necessary, either in order to present an appearance of social consensus, or as a means of bolstering political interests. It seems to have been regarded, however, as a chore which could be of little personal benefit to the individual concerned. Crowd management was not the stuff of which reputations were made; rather it represented a potential short-cut to notoriety, derision and even, perhaps, ruin.

LIVERPOOL, NORWICH AND MANCHESTER

How typical or untypical were the broad contexts for crowd events which existed in Bristol? Are comparisons with other towns possible and worthwhile, or were crowd occurrences so intimately associated with local structures and preoccupations as to make them unique? These are questions that will be answered more or less directly by all that follows. It is, however, worthwhile first to establish some basic similarities and differences between the four urban environments under consideration here. It is not possible to replicate the thorough-going analysis of the personnel of prominence and power carried out with regard to Bristol; but a number of other areas of comparison – local government, the economy and broad parameters for crowd procedure – nevertheless remain.

LOCAL GOVERNMENT

The antipathy shown towards the executive in Bristol may have been extreme, but it certainly was not unique. The structure of local government in Liverpool, Norwich and Manchester was somewhat different in each case, yet each generated its own form of hostility, and had direct influence upon crowd events.

Sidney and Beatrice Webb, in their analysis of local government before the Municipal Corporations Act of 1835, reserved particular praise for the government of Liverpool:

This close body of a Mayor and two Bailiffs, and thirty or forty Aldermen and Common Councilmen, recruiting itself exclusively by co-option, not only gave to the town its bench of magistrates, but also acted itself as Lord of the Manor, owned in fee simple a large portion of the land, governed the port, controlled the markets, and undertook with equal zeal the provision of education, the management of the churches, and defence of the estuary against the French invader.

No one, concluded the Webbs, can avoid 'being impressed by its energy, dignity, and public spirit'.[119] But benevolent or otherwise, this was clearly a corporate oligarchy; why did it not, therefore, generate the degree and type of hostility to be found in Bristol?

The explanation lies in part with attitude, part in money. Unlike Bristol where, despite having a wide sphere of influence, the Corporation seemed to be at once negligent and arrogant (particularly in the administration of the local economy), in Liverpool interventionism was more positive. The Corporation spent money on developing the docks, widening and improving the streets and providing services, governed the largest provincial police force in Britain, defended the town at its own expense and took an active part in protecting the economy – most notably by intervening in the financial crisis of 1793 by issuing its own promissory notes. Crucial to all this, however, was the income that made it possible. Half of the Corporation's money by 1833 came from property rents, and half from dues and tolls. But, unusually, there was no rate levied on the householders for police, prison or street improvement purposes.[120] On the eve of reform, Ramsey Muir and Edith Platt conclude, Liverpool stood out 'as an oasis of pure and reasonably competent government'. The Council met on the first Wednesday of the month. The quorum was set high, at twenty-five of the forty-one members. Average attendance was thirty-five, and each member served on at least one of seven committees.[121]

Such is the positive version of events, and the one put forward by the Webbs. This 'intelligent oligarchy' may have protected the Liverpool Corporation from an all-out challenge to its authority. It would be quite wrong, however, to present the executive as entirely benign or popular. The Corporation members were making money

---

[119] Webbs, *Local government*, p. 482. More precisely, there were forty-one places as Common Councillor. Aldermen constituted those who had borne the office of mayor, and consequently the number was indefinite. In 1833 it stood at sixteen. The mayor and all Councillors constituted the borough magistrates. See *MCR*, 3, app. pt I, XXIII, p. 128.

[120] Webbs, *Local government*, pp. 482–5; James Touzeau, *The rise and progress of Liverpool from 1551 to 1835*, 2 vols. (Liverpool, 1910), vol. 1, pp. 636–9; Nicholson Papers, LRO 920 NIC 9/5/6.

[121] Ramsey Muir and Edith M. Platt, *A history of municipal government in Liverpool from the earliest times to the municipal reform act of 1835* (London, 1906), p. 138.

out of their administration. As François Vigier points out: 'The investment of public funds in the development of port facilities is a particularly good example of the use of public power and resources by aldermen-merchants in an enterprise that would benefit them first as merchants, and only second as aldermen with a sense of civic responsibility and pride in a growing town.'[122] When dissatisfaction with the Corporation surfaced it was focused, as in Bristol, around issues of legitimacy and local taxation.

As elsewhere, the Corporation of Liverpool in theory consisted of all the burgesses and freemen of the city. In October 1790 a petition from 1,098 freemen requested the calling of a common hall (an assembly of the freemen), and, when it met in January 1791, challenged the closed election of Councillors, the existence of vacancies on the Council, and demanded the accounts be made available to public scrutiny. The Council managed to weather the challenge – partly by ignoring it, partly by the distracting influence of events in France (which helped to discredit the reformers leading the anti-Corporation assault).[123] Opposition to the tory dominated Council lingered on, led by dissenting whigs and radicals. Whig Unitarian and Quaker merchants were responsible for an increasing proportion of the town's trade and dues, and yet were excluded from power.[124] Also contentious throughout these years was the practice of levying town dues upon non-freemen. And in 1830 this came to a head when a number of merchants refused to pay their dues, and the matter was tried before the courts. Not surprisingly, since the practice, although unjust, was not illegal, the court found in favour of the Council.[125]

This tight control of power on the part of the tory dominated Corporation made for a clear association of tory party politics with Corporation interests (although in fact Corporation funds were not misused to sponsor party activities).[126] Any crowd event with a

---

[122] François Vigier, *Change and apathy: Liverpool and Manchester during the industrial revolution* (Cambridge, Mass., 1970), p. 54.

[123] Touzeau, *Rise and progress of Liverpool*, pp. 607–16; Ramsey Muir, *A history of Liverpool* (London, 1907), pp. 226–7.

[124] Webbs, *Local government*, pp. 489–90; Ian Sellers, 'William Roscoe, the Roscoe circle and radical politics in Liverpool, 1787–1807', *Transactions of the Historic Society of Lancashire and Cheshire*, CXX (1968), pp. 45–62; S.G. Checkland, *The Gladstones: a family biography 1764–1851* (Cambridge, 1971), pp. 29–35.

[125] Muir, *History of Liverpool*, p. 265; *MCR*, 6, app. pts IV and V, XXVI, p. 2695.

[126] *MCR*, 3, app. pt I, XXIII, p. 128, stresses the 'perfect regularity' of the Corporation accounts. See also, Webbs, *Local government*, p. 486.

political tinge was therefore more or less directly supportive or critical of the Corporation. In addition, the election of the mayor by the freemen, annually on 18 October, was one crowd event which confronted the association head on.[127] Broadly, in other words, Liverpool society was divided into a reforming, dissenting, non-Corporation, whig and radical opposition and a Corporation tory establishment. However, since Liverpool itself was tory in complexion (if partly through the more effective bribery of freemen)[128] opposition to local government was, although ever-present, never predominant.

In Norwich, local government was more directly productive of crowds, since the Corporation had a broad electoral base, and there were frequent municipal elections. Whereas the Webbs described the Corporate oligarchy of Liverpool in glowing terms, Norwich's relatively democratic system they regarded as an 'utter failure'.[129] Certainly Norwich's dualistic system seemed designed to create confusion. The Corporation, as in Bristol and Liverpool, consisted officially of all the freemen, which in Norwich numbered 3,460 in 1833.[130] The governing body comprised the mayor and aldermen (twenty-four in number), two sheriffs and sixty Common Councillors. They did not, however, sit as one body. Rather, they divided into: the Assembly, consisting of mayor, sheriffs, aldermen and Common Councillors; and the Court of Mayoralty, being the mayor, sheriffs and aldermen sitting separately. By a local Act of 1730, nothing could be done by the Assembly without the consent of a majority of the mayor, sheriffs and aldermen, on the one hand, and a majority of the Common Councillors on the other. The result: frequent disagreement, heightened still further by the effective division, from the late eighteenth century onwards, of the Corporation along political lines – Common Councillors being whig and radical, the aldermen being tories.[131]

Municipal elections during the early nineteenth century became party political affairs. Despite the Test and Corporations Act, and the attempt in Norwich to enforce it in 1801,[132] dissenters had long

---

[127] In 1819 the suspicion that tory bribery had taken place caused rioting to occur: *Liverpool Mercury*, 22 Oct. 1819.

[128] Despite the absence of official corruption, bribery, on a party basis, was rife at election time: Webbs, *Local government*, p. 486; Sellers, 'William Roscoe', p. 56.

[129] Webbs, *Local government*, p. 531.   [130] *MCR*, 3 app. pt I, XXIII, p. 126.

[131] Webbs, *Local government*, pp. 532–3, 546–50.

[132] P. Browne, *The history of Norwich from the earliest records to the present time* (Norwich, 1814), p. 73.

served as members of the Corporation, thereby opening local government office to the full range of political views – including radicalism. From 1818 onwards the local government system was in disarray. Municipal elections were violent and corrupt (even more so than parliamentary elections), admission to freedoms was conducted on party lines and the appointment of all officials (including watchmen) was dominated by political considerations.[133] Even the allocation to tradesmen of Corporation contracts was politically motivated, and in order to secure influence at elections, some employers reputedly employed workmen of one party only.[134] The Corporation was open to constant and highly personalised attack from political opponents, and the ceremonial that surrounded municipal elections was susceptible to ridicule as empty trumpery.[135] In contrast to Bristol, where party political considerations were subsumed to the disdain for local government in general, in Norwich government became merely a vehicle for party strife – and thereby also become despised. As the Municipal Commissioners put it, 'respectable persons' were deterred from offering themselves for corporate office.[136]

Manchester, for its part, was not a municipal borough. In the early nineteenth century it possessed three separate but overlapping forms of local government: the Court Leet, the parish vestry and the Police Commissioners.[137] The Manchester and Salford Police Act of 1792, however, created a new body of Police Commissioners including not only the boroughreeves (mayors) and constables of Manchester and Salford, but any owner of property within the two townships with a yearly rental equal to or greater than £30. They were also authorised to appoint a range of officials to regulate the administration of the town, thereby taking over many of the functions of the Court Leet. Consequently, the Police Commissioners became the focus for attention in the administration of public affairs in the town.[138]

The emergence of the Commissioners as the most important

---

[133] Webbs, *Local government*, pp. 552–4.
[134] *MCR*, 6, app. pts IV and V, XXVI, p. 2498.
[135] For example, Anon., *A letter to the Freemen of Norwich, containing brief remarks on the origin, loyalty and practical effects of chartered rights* (Norwich, 1833), NPL/LS; Norwich Corporation, *The guildhall bulletin; being a faithful and comprehensive account of the intended wonders of this wondrous day* (Norwich, 1800?), NPL/LS. [136] *MCR*, 6, app. pts IV and V, XXVI, p. 2499.
[137] Vigier, *Change and apathy*, p. 118.
[138] Arthur Redford and Ian Stafford Russell, *The history of local government in Manchester*, 3 vols. (London, 1939), vol. 1, pp. 201–8.

element in local government was closely linked to the role of particular individuals – a circumstance which personalised local government and local politics, and may thereby have countered the seemingly fragmented nature of the administration. The first of these prominent individuals was Charles Frederick Brandt, treasurer of the Police Commissioners from 1799 to 1810. Brandt increased the numbers and efficiency of the watchmen, and, importantly, appointed Joseph Nadin as deputy constable to superintend the watchmen, in 1805.[139] According to Archibald Prentice, chronicler and leader of middle class radicalism, as well as editor of the *Manchester Times*, the popular loathing for the local authorities in this period owed much to the personal hatred of Nadin.[140]

Between 1810 and 1820 the treasurership passed to Thomas Fleming. 'Nadin and his faction' had already been denounced by the radicals as tyrannical. Now, as Fleming solidified tory rule in Manchester, the accusations were of a corrupt oligarchy. The rise of radicalism in Manchester was simultaneously, therefore, an attack upon local government; and the massacre of 'Peterloo', carried out by a politically motivated yeomanry, solidified the radical conviction that they lived under a corrupt local administration.[141] During the 1820s, however, with the relatively broad eligibility for local government allowed by the £30 qualification, the radicals vied for power. The number of Commissioners became very high (more than 1,000 new ones were sworn in by 1826 alone), and meetings became crowd events in their own right (although taking place indoors).[142]

In 1828 a new Police Act rationalised the system. The administration of Manchester and Salford was finally legally separated (although they had in practice been for some time), and a new body of Police Commissioners for Manchester was created, consisting of the boroughreeve, constables and 240 other 'adult male persons' to be elected. The property qualification for election to office slightly favoured the tories, and they regained control of local government

[139] *Ibid.*, pp. 214–22.
[140] Archibald Prentice, *Historic sketches and personal recollections of Manchester, intended to illustrate the progress of public opinion from 1792 to 1832* (London, 1851), p. 34; Donald Read, *Press and people 1790–1850: opinion in three English cities* (London, 1961), p. 88; Asa Briggs, 'The background of the parliamentary reform movement in three English cities, 1830–32', in *The collected essays of Asa Briggs* (Brighton, 1985), vol. 1, p. 189.
[141] Redford and Russell, *Local government in Manchester*, vol. 1, pp. 240–73; Donald Read, *Peterloo: the 'massacre' and its background* (Manchester, 1958), pp. 120–33.
[142] Redford and Russell, *Local government in Manchester*, vol. 1, pp. 276–303.

from that time, operating in alliance with the whigs. With the police rate set at 18d in the pound, the radicals persistently demanded a reduction in local taxation, without success.[143]

LOCAL ECONOMY

Like Bristol, the port of Liverpool was not ideally situated; but the better access it offered to deep-sea ships than its immediate rival, Chester, together with the early improvement of the docks, ensured that, by the end of the eighteenth century it was established as the most important port in the country, aside from London.[144] The Corporation-sponsored improvement programme meant that by 1796 Liverpool had some 28 acres of docks, including five wet docks, five graving docks, three dry docks and the Duke's dock which was built to deal with traffic from the Bridgwater canal. Tonnage had increased fifteen times in fifty years; and further dock building was to take place between 1813 and 1821, and 1830 and 1836. According to Sheila Marriner, Liverpool was tied into a 'virtuous circle of expansion', with successive developments in industry and communications stimulating each other.[145]

Some Bristolians were preoccupied by rivalry with Liverpool during the 1820s. But as far as Liverpool writers were concerned the contest was all over by the 1790s.[146] The successful development of the docks and hinterland communications ensured that Liverpool was dominated by employment associated with shipping and trade to a far greater extent than Bristol. Contemporaries remarked on the relative absence of manufacturing in the town – but with no particular concern.[147] Inevitably, however, the predominance of the docks made Liverpool susceptible to depressions generated by alterations in trading conditions. Although little affected by the first years of the French wars, the Orders in Council of 1807 (which

[143] *Ibid.*, pp. 305–40.
[144] The first 'wet dock' was completed in Liverpool in 1715 – almost a century before Bristol: Vigier, *Change and apathy*, p. 37.
[145] Sheila Marriner, *The economic and social development Merseyside* (London, 1982), pp. 13, 31–2.
[146] James Wallace (?) *A general and descriptive history of the ancient and present state of the town of Liverpool* (Liverpool, 1795?), section X; Edward Baines, *History, directory and gazeteer of the county palatine of Lancaster* (1824; reprinted Newton Abbot, 1968), pp. 190–1.
[147] Baines, *History*, p. 195; Thomas Kaye, *The stranger in Liverpool; or, an historical and descriptive view of Liverpool and its environs* (Liverpool, 1807), p. 116.

culminated in the termination of trade with the United States) and the disruption of trade which followed over the next five years produced considerable distress.[148] Even in less exacting times, Liverpool was a city with a high level of casual employment and pauperism.[149]

For the most part, however, the economic context for Liverpool in these years was massive population growth and urban development, made possible by economic success but paralleled at all stages by a swelling underclass of the poor. Despite the growth of the city, many merchants continued to live centrally, although one writer observed as early as 1797 that 'men out of business' lived outside Liverpool – leaving the town itself divided into three classes: merchants, tradesmen and labourers.[150]

Norwich's fortunes were moving in the opposite direction to those of Liverpool. Norwich was largely dependent upon one industry – but an industry in relative decline. In the seventeenth century contemporaries claimed that Norwich was 'next to London . . . the most rich and potent city in England'.[151] Like Bristol, here was a former 'second city' now fast losing ground.

Norwich was built on the woollen industry. In the 1790s the city reportedly contained 6,000 looms.[152] By 1829, according to one source, there were just 1,500.[153] The reason for the decline, in essence, was competition with the West Riding; more broadly, it can be attributed to competition with cotton goods, the loss of European markets through war, geographical disadvantages compared with Yorkshire and delay in the introduction of steam power until 1838.[154] Transport developments also failed to keep pace with the local economy's needs, and there emerged in the 1820s a strong campaign

---

[148] Vigier, *Change and apathy*, pp. 74–5; B. H. Tolley, 'The Liverpool campaign against the Order in Council and the war of 1812', in J.R. Harris (ed.), *Liverpool and Merseyside: essays in the economic and social history of the port and its hinterland* (London, 1969), pp. 98–146. For an explanation of the Orders in Council and their effects, see Clive Emsley, *British society and the French wars, 1793–1815* (London, 1979), ch. 7.   [149] Vigier, *Change and apathy*, pp. 67–9.

[150] *Ibid.*, p. 52; W. Moss, *The Liverpool guide; including a sketch of the environs* (Liverpool, 1797), p. 145.   [151] Quoted in Webbs, *Local government*, p. 530.

[152] C.B. Jewson, *The Jacobin city: a portrait of Norwich in its reaction to the French Revolution, 1788–1802* (London, 1975), p. 3.

[153] M.F. Lloyd Prichard, 'The decline of Norwich', *Economic History Review*, 2nd series, III, 3 (1951), p. 375.

[154] *Ibid.*, 371–7; J.K. Edwards, 'The decline of the Norwich textile industry', *Yorkshire Bulletin of Economic and Social Research*, XVI, 1 (1964), pp. 31–41; J. K. Edwards, 'Communications and the economic development of Norwich, 1750–1850', *Journal of Transport History*, VII, 2 (Nov. 1965), pp. 96–108.

for sea-going vessels to be given direct access to Norwich – effectively to make it a port.[155] An Act in 1827 achieved this; but as in Bristol, the improvement scheme came too late to transform the city's fortunes.[156]

There is little disagreement about the cause of Norwich's decline, but some argument concerning the timing. According to Lloyd Prichard, the wool industry was well into decline by the end of the eighteenth century; the French wars merely hastened the process.[157] For J.K. Edwards, on the other hand, Norwich continued to compete until well into the nineteenth century, finally losing out in the battle against mass-produced goods from the north, from around 1830 onwards.[158] Contemporaries, however, seemed clear that a major decline had taken place during the French wars, and that by 1840 the trade was a shadow of its former self.[159]

The self-contained city of Norwich, with plenty of room within its bounds, and with a largely agricultural and remote hinterland, was the antithesis of the crowded, expanding Manchester and its industrial cluster. Between 1775 and 1800 Manchester's development was tied to the overall activity of the region. After 1800, however, with the introduction of steam power and the greater flexibility in locating factories which this allowed, Manchester grew rapidly in its own right. In 1794 there were three cotton mills sited in the town; in 1802, twenty-six; and by 1821, sixty-six. Servicing the growing textile industry were numerous engineering and foundry firms, and a fast developing communications network. Between 1791 and 1819 fourteen parliamentary Acts were passed for canal companies in the Manchester region; and thirteen road Acts were passed between 1801 and 1821.[160]

The more striking contrast in some respects, however, is with Bristol rather than with Norwich. Whereas both local government and local economy in Bristol were bound up by restriction, regulations and procedure, Manchester had few such local controls. In Manchester there were no regulations restricting trade to freemen of the town. Local government was not in itself the focus for hostility

---

[155] Edwards 'Communications and economic development', pp. 100–1.
[156] *Ibid.*, p. 101.   [157] Lloyd Prichard, 'Decline of Norwich'.
[158] Edwards, 'Decline of Norwich textile industry'.
[159] C. Berry, *A concise history and directory of the city of Norwich for 1811* (Norwich, 1810), pp. 11–13; G.K. Blyth, *The Norwich guide and directory: an historical and topographical description of the city and its hamlets* (London, 1842), pp. 59–62.
[160] Vigier, *Change and apathy*, pp. 91–2, 127–8.

regarding economic practices, although the tory manufacturers and merchants who dominated the Police Commissioners may have been the subject of dislike. However, the other side of the equation of free economic activity was unplanned urbanisation and the absence of worker protection. So, whereas industrial dispute formed a relatively minor ingredient of crowd activity in Bristol, the dependence of Manchester upon the cotton industry, its susceptibility to sudden and deep economic crisis, the existence of poor working and living conditions, and low pay made industrial crowd activity a feature of life in the town.

PROCEDURE FOR CROWD EVENTS

All of these towns exhibited set procedures for the calling together of crowd events, and those procedures were essentially the same as those to be found in Bristol. Parliamentary and local elections in Liverpool and Norwich made for an established repertoire of notices and processions. Precise times and locations, and processional routes, were advertised and adhered to, and those procedures were sufficiently well understood for the phrase 'the usual order' or 'the usual route' to be applied on occasion.[161]

The selection and availability of venues for crowd events was a matter for discussion, and was dependent, in many instances, on permissions from the mayor or boroughreeve. In Liverpool this aspect of procedure appears to have had a particularly dominant role, perhaps because the range of outdoor crowd locations used was fairly small, although there were a number of indoor locations available. This was an important ingredient for crowd occurrences in Liverpool: throughout the period, and particularly after 1813, some public meetings took place indoors. Furthermore, these meetings were not restricted to the wealthy or conservative minded. Parliamentary reformers met at the Tennis Court, Gradwell Street, in May 1813, and subsequently used not only this venue but also the Music Hall in Bold

---

[161] *An impartial collection of addresses, songs, squibs, etc. published during the election of Members of Parliament for the borough of Liverpool, October 1812* (Liverpool, 1812); *An impartial collection of addresses, songs, squibs, etc. published during the election of Members of Parliament for the borough of Liverpool, June 1816* (Liverpool, 1816); *Liverpool Courier*, 7 Jan. 1835; *Liverpool Mercury*, 7 Dec. 1832; 'Norfolk and Norwich Parliamentary addresses and squibs, relating to contested elections, from 1768 to 1830', NPL/LS.

Street, the Royal Amphitheatre in Great Charlotte Street and the Theatre Royal.[162] They seem, however, to have been denied the use of the Town Hall, which was used for meetings regarding the Corn Laws and addresses to the king.[163]

The mayor of Liverpool on a number of occasions refused requests for meetings.[164] Other restrictions seemed at times to intrude also: a meeting at the Town Hall in December 1820 to address the king could not be adjourned outdoors by the mayor 'on account of the technicality of the advertisement';[165] and in 1831 a reform meeting was forced to convene at the Music Hall because the planned venue of the area outside the Exchange was precluded by a clause in a local Act.[166] Throughout the period, such attention to organisational details, together with the availability of different kinds of meeting place, made the selection of venue a central part of the crowd gathering procedure. And by the end of the period there are signs that crowd organisation had become particularly sophisticated: the funeral of Huskisson, in 1830, was carefully organised, even down to the provision of 'crash barriers' to hold back the crowds.[167]

The possibility of even very large gatherings occurring indoors also existed in Norwich, where St Andrews Hall was used, mainly for reform meetings, from 1819 onwards. On one occasion, a reform meeting in May 1832, it was said to have been occupied by 9,000 people.[168] Advertisements appear to have been as 'binding' in Norwich as in Liverpool. During the election of 1826 William Smith had not intended to make the usual processional entry. But a notice had already been issued, without his authority, saying that such an entry would take place; a cavalcade consequently marched out to meet him, and the public entry had to be complied with.[169]

In Manchester, the Town Hall was made available for a reform meeting in January 1831 – but only after the Finance Committee had overruled the boroughreeve's refusal of the request to use the venue.[170] The use of the Town Hall for a meeting to petition

[162] *Liverpool Mercury*, 7 May 1813, 20 Aug. 1830, 29 Apr. 1831, 7 Sept. 1832, 16 Jan. 1835.
[163] *Ibid.*, 25 Feb. 1820, 29 Dec. 1820, 15 Apr. 1825, 17 Nov. 1826.
[164] *Ibid.*, 21 Feb. 1817, 27 June 1817, 4 Apr. 1817, 3 Sept. 1819, 24 Sept. 1819, 20 Aug. 1830.   [165] *Ibid.*, 29 Dec. 1820.   [166] *Ibid.*, 29 Apr. 1831.
[167] *Liverpool Courier*, 29 Sept. 1831; *Liverpool Mercury*, 1 Oct. 1830.
[168] *Norwich Mercury*, 19 May 1832.   [169] *Ibid.*, 10 June 1826.
[170] *Manchester Guardian*, 22 Jan. 1831; *Manchester Times*, 22 Jan. 1831.

Parliament on the state of the country, in February 1830, was apparently 'the first time that any meeting, for any such purpose, had been held there'.[171]

The development of the reform movement and the 'mass platform' in Manchester had very vivid repercussions for the organisation of crowd events there, since it led to military-style drilling of prospective procession members, and dispute (most importantly at Peterloo) regarding the legality of meetings. Legislation affecting popular assemblies, such as the Seditious Meetings Acts of 1795 and 1817, and the Combination Acts of 1799 and 1800, held perhaps greater significance for Manchester, dominated by crowds around the issues of industrial dispute and reform, than the other towns under examination. Reform in Manchester also generated prominent figures commonly identified with the development of mass meetings – most notably Henry Hunt. In the eyes of the Police Commissioners, to speak before a crowd in Manchester was almost by definition to be a 'mob orator'. Such oratory, however, appears, surprisingly, to have remained a largely middle class perogative. Prentice reports the speech of a spinner, Jonathan Hodgins, to a meeting of the 'Friends of civil and religious liberty', in 1825. Hodgins 'modestly stood forward and enquired if a working man might be permitted to address the meeting'; his speech, says Prentice, was 'amongst the first delivered by a working man, taking his place amongst able speakers, who held high commercial rank in the community'.[172]

In Norwich, dominated for the most part by election crowds, mass events held less pejorative associations for those in power, since the very structure of prominence was integrally linked to political, and politicised, elections, and to their associated crowds. Elections also had an important part to play in the crowd life of Liverpool, causing the prominent and powerful to take their place on the hustings, supporting their candidate. However, according to S.G. Checkland, 'contact with the electorate remained at long range', since, 'another class of men specialised in the more private forms of persuasion'; as a consequence, says Checkland, it was they who best understood the outlook of the artisan groups.[173] As in Manchester and elsewhere, public speaking in Liverpool was rarely a working class activity. The *Liverpool Mercury* reported the self-conscious apologies of working class speakers at an anti-Corn Law meeting in March 1827, as they

---

[171] Prentice, *Historical sketches*, pp. 304–5.
[172] *Ibid.*, p. 256.   [173] Checkland, *The Gladstones*, p. 66.

nervously stood forward, explaining that they were 'unaccustomed to public speaking'.[174]

CONCLUSIONS

There are important similarities to be drawn from this preliminary examination of four towns and their contexts for crowd occurrences. In all instances, although to varying degrees, local government was contentious, and this more or less directly influenced the formation of crowds. Considerable formality also surrounded the staging of crowd events in all locations: applications for the use of venues were sought, and placards, notices and advertisements were issued regarding the time, place and form of proposed gatherings. The addressing of crowds was reserved almost exclusively for the socially and politically prominent. In Manchester this was probably to invite notoriety in the eyes of those in power. In Norwich, where so much of public life was politicised, this seems less likely to have been the case. Liverpool, for its part, is more difficult to interpret without more detailed research; but the overlap between anti-tory and anti-Corporation sentiments, and the adherence to these sentiments by prominent members of the mercantile community, may have reduced the element of stigma in being regarded as a popular public speaker.

Insofar as differences between the locations emerge at this stage, Bristol and Liverpool were distinctive for their range of crowd types: they were not dominated by industrial dispute, or reform, or by electioneering. The high degree of organisation in local government and public life in both these towns may have facilitated a clearer patterning of crowd events, and, inadvertently, a greater frequency of formal (that is, planned, and reported) crowds than in Manchester and Norwich. It is only, however, through closer examination of the location and timing of crowd occurrences, the language of crowd description and the details of particular crowd events that more meaningful comparisons can be made.

[174] *Liverpool Mercury*, 9 March 1827.

5. *Time, work and the occurrence of crowds*

The version that went around was that the whole family slept until
twelve o'clock on orders from Nahir Miguel, the wise man of the
community . . . The truth is that they kept the house locked up until
very late, like so many others, but they were early-rising and hard-
working people.
(Gabriel Garcia Márquez, *Chronicle of a death foretold*, trans. Gregory
Rabassa (London, 1983), pp. 112–13)

I have sometimes, when sent to Bristol to look out ironmongery, such as
locks etc., been afraid to walk the streets, would take a rod in my hand
and walk fast, fearing I should meet the pressgang, as would be looking
out for such as they considered idlers as would be about the streets in
working hours.
('Manuscript autobiography of John Bennett, Portishead, 1853', BRO
36097 (a–b), p. 9; the year in question is 1806)

The separate subjects of crowds and time in eighteenth- and early
nineteenth-century England have been linked through the compelling
and highly regarded work of E.P. Thompson. In two well-known
articles Thompson turned historians' attention first to the work and
time patterns of pre- and early industrialisation, and then to the form
and motivation of eighteenth-century food crowds.[1] The time- and
work-discipline article examined the trauma brought about by the
imposition upon well-established work routines of the disciplines
demanded by industrial capitalism; it stressed the cultural repression
necessary to overturn the sense of permanence in the eighteenth-
century work order. The article on the moral economy of the English
crowd stressed the coherence of a popular belief in long-standing

---

[1] E.P. Thompson, 'Time, work-discipline and industrial capitalism', *Past and
Present*, no. 38 (Dec. 1967), pp. 56–97; E.P. Thompson, 'The moral economy of the
English crowd in the eighteenth century', *Past and Present*, no. 50 (Feb. 1971), pp.
76–136.

rights which provided a rationale for riotous protest; it demonstrated that food crowds were disciplined, composed of working people and possessed clear notions of the prerequisites for social order.

Thompson's articles have proved highly influential. However, the arguments they deploy have, as was argued in chapter 1, become vulgarised by repeated summary. The moral economy article has turned into (among other things) an article about 'the crowd' in the eighteenth century, despite the fact that Thompson was discussing only riots.[2] Thompson's discussion of task-orientated time- and work-disciplines, meanwhile, has been taken as further evidence of the existence in the late eighteenth and early nineteenth centuries of rollicking, haphazard and inveterately casual work patterns.[3] In fact the process of vulgarisation has produced a paradox: crowd (or rather riot) action was disciplined and ordered; work time was ill-disciplined and unordered. At face value it seems peculiar that popular culture should have been so constituted. Yet Thompson himself was making a rather different point: in both articles he was disputing any notion that the English working class undertook actions at a whim; he was arguing for the existence of a coherent, rational and assertive popular culture.

From Thompson's work, and, as importantly, from the subsequent interpretations of it, a set of intriguing questions emerge. What, in the last years of the eighteenth century and the first of the nineteenth, was the nature of, and relationship between, hours and conditions of work, and the occurrence of mass phenomena? When people took time to form crowds, where did they take it from? Did an irregular and flexible working week offer total freedom in the selection of times for the bringing together of crowds? Was it really the case that in the early nineteenth century a crowd (and, furthermore, the right kind of crowd) could be summoned up at any time, any place?

These questions are ones in the first instance about the *organisation* of crowds. They are concerned with constraints in the time-order

[2] For example, John Stevenson, 'Social control and the prevention of riots in England, 1789–1829', in A.P. Donajgrodzki (ed.), *Social control in nineteenth-century Britain* (London, 1977), p. 28; Bob Bushaway, *By rite: custom, ceremony and community in England, 1700–1880* (London, 1982), p. 64.

[3] For example, Robert W. Malcolmson, *Popular recreations in English society, 1700–1850* (Cambridge, 1973), ch. 6; R.J. Morris, *Class and class consciousness in the industrial revolution, 1780–1850* (London, 1979), p. 52; Geoffrey Pearson, *Hooligan: a history of respectable fears* (London, 1983), pp. 194–5; David S. Landes, *Revolution in time: clocks and the making of the modern world* (Cambridge, Mass., 1983), pp. 228–30.

both of a locality in general, and the life of the potential crowd participant in particular. Crowds are, by definition, constituted by large numbers of people; the availability of those people is integral to the occurrence and 'success' of a crowd event. In short, the historiographical problems which emerge from Thompson's work suggest the need to consider not only the actions which crowds carry out, or the statements that they make, but also the organisational constraints involved in their coming together in the first place. It will be argued here that the working week in Bristol was ordered, predictable and long, and that this was the result not of factory employment and mechanisation (of which there was little in Bristol), but of Bristol's status as a large town. The non-work time available in Bristol for participation in crowd events was limited. The organis- ation of crowd occurrences in the city was the product of, and reflected, the constraints of this rigorous working week. As a result, patterns of timing suggest the existence of a well-understood allocation of time to particular crowd activities. Yet the existence, in Bristol, of both ordered work time and ordered crowd forming time seems inconsistent with the received picture of an unruly popular culture and a chaotic urban environment in the early nineteenth century.

This chapter will be divided into four sections. The first will outline existing research relating to the ordering of the urban environment in the late eighteenth and early nineteenth centuries. The second will examine, in detail, trends in the timing of 245 crowd occurrences in Bristol between 1790 and 1835. The third will compare those trends with ones to be found in Liverpool, Norwich and Manchester. In the final section, conclusions to emerge from this survey will be discussed in the light of prevailing notions of crowd activity, urban order and public stability in nineteenth-century England.

THE ORDERING OF TIME

T.S. Ashton has written, with regard to the eighteenth century, that 'It would be wrong to imagine that what the ordinary man sought above all was continuity of work . . . It is true that the workers resented the imposition of unemployment . . . But leisure, at times of their own choice, stood high on their scale of preferences.'[4] The

---

[4] T.S. Ashton, *An economic history of England: the eighteenth century* (London, 1972 edn), pp. 203–4.

eighteenth century has frequently been described as a period in which 'leisure preference' dominated work experience. An Hogarthian picture is presented of the peasant-worker who, 'in moments of affluence', 'spent much of his meagre pittance in the local inn or alehouse; caroused the Saturday of pay, the sabbath Sunday, and "Holy Monday" as well; dragged himself reluctantly back to work on Tuesday, warmed to the task on Wednesday and laboured furiously to finish in time for another long weekend'.[5] Until the 1847 Ten Hours Act, the working day, Sebastian De Grazia claims, had been a 'jellylike substance'.[6] The working week, it has been said elsewhere, sometimes did not begin until Wednesday or Thursday;[7] and even if lack of money might prevent workers from being present at recreational events such as horse-racing, there was no lack of time for such activities.[8]

The process of industrialisation, it is suggested by some writers, was simultaneously a sustained attack upon irregular work routines. David Landes, in a recent study of clocks and the 'revolution in time', offers a summary of the movement towards the time-disciplined work environment.[9] During the eighteenth century, Landes argues, the conflict between the time-free attitudes of domestic workers and the time-bound attitudes of employers and their agents intensified as demand for the products of the putting-out system increased. From the employers' point of view, this problem was resolved through the construction of a workplace where the employer could directly oversee the employees' performance; this workplace was the factory. Thus, 'from the 1770s on', argues Landes, 'an increasing number of workers found themselves employed in jobs that required them to appear by a set time every morning and work a day whose direction and age were a function of the clock.[10] Workers found this difficult, partly because they 'were accustomed to work at their own pace, to take their rest and distraction . . . as and when they pleased';[11] and partly because they feared that, since the employer had control of the

[5] David S. Landes, *The unbound prometheus: technological change, 1750 to the present* (Cambridge, 1969), pp. 58–9.

[6] Sebastian De Grazia, 'Of time, work and leisure', in Michael R. Marrus (ed.), *The emergence of leisure* (New York, 1974), pp. 18–19.

[7] Alasdair Clayre, *Work and play: ideas and experience of work and leisure* (London, 1974), p. 95; J.A.R. Pimlott, *The Englishman's holiday* (London, 1974), p. 80.

[8] Wray Vamplew, *The turf: a social and economic history of horse racing* (London, 1976), pp. 19–20.

[9] Landes, *Revolution in time*, pp. 228–30.   [10] *Ibid.*, p. 229.   [11] *Ibid.*

timepiece, they were being cheated. Workers' anxiety on this score, Landes goes on to argue, prompted them to acquire watches, thus furthering the progress of time-discipline, and contributing substantially to the boom in watch manufacture in Britain during the last quarter of the eighteenth century.

Landes' summary is neat and appealing; it has internal inconsistencies, however, which demonstrate the need for a thorough reappraisal of the subjects of time- and work-discipline in this period. In the first place, the chronology suggested by Landes does not fit his explanation. It is now generally accepted that factory industrialisation was, with the exception of a few select localities, such as Manchester, a phenomenon not of the last quarter of the eighteenth century, but rather of the second quarter of the nineteenth. The boom in watch production should not, therefore, be correlated with the growth of the factory. That boom probably did reflect the existence of, and perhaps the growth in, time-discipline – but for rather different reasons.

Close examinations of the working week in various industries and different towns have now indicated not that a casual work-discipline endured far into the nineteenth century, but rather that a very disciplined, formalised, surprisingly regular, and long, working week had existed in England since at least the mid-eighteenth century.[12] Certainly the structure of this working week was different from that of the cotton mills of the industrial north-west, or from that which Josiah Wedgwood attempted to impose upon his workforce in the later eighteenth century.[13] Certainly an element of irregularity was introduced by widespread seasonal unemployment or economic depression. But it was a discipline experienced by a vast majority of the English labour force until well into the nineteenth century, and which endured even in some highly mechanised sectors.[14] Further-

[12] Monica Hodgson, 'The working day and working week in Victorian Britain, 1840–1900', M Phil. thesis, Univ. of London, 1974; M.A. Bienefeld, *Working hours in British industry: an economic history* (London, 1972); Eric Hopkins, 'Working hours and working conditions during the industrial revolution: a re-appraisal', *Economic History Review*, 2nd series, XXXV, 1 (1982), pp. 52–66. See also M. Dorothy George, *London life in the eighteenth century* (Harmondsworth, 1966), chs. 4, 6; Karl Marx, *Capital*, 3 vols. (1867–94), trans. Ben Fowkes (Harmondsworth, 1976), vol. 1, pp. 383–411.

[13] Bienefeld, *Working hours in British industry*, ch. 3; N. McKendrick, 'Josiah Wedgwood and factory discipline', *Historical Journal*, IV (1961), pp. 31–54.

[14] Roy A. Church, *Economic and social change in a Midland town: Victorian Nottingham, 1815–1900* (London, 1966), p. 41; Hodgson, 'Working day and working week in Victorian Britain', pp. 56–9, 165–6.

more, mechanisation did not in itself bring about a working week of daily or perennial regularity.[15] Uncertainty in eighteenth-century employment stemmed not from the endemic idleness of the workforce, but from the vagaries of the economy; the same continued to be true during the nineteenth century.[16]

The criteria which formed the basis for the working day during the eighteenth and nineteenth centuries were quite coherent. The hours of daylight governed the work time for most handicraft trades, for instance; the result being an average working day of 6 a.m. to 6 p.m., but with work extending to 8 or 9 p.m. in winter.[17] For outdoor workers seasonal fluctuations in the weather inevitably made for variations in work activity.[18] The elements could intervene in other respects: shipbuilding workers and boatmen were dependent upon the tides; ropemaking was better done out of direct sunlight, and ropemakers sometimes worked all night as a result.[19] There was a similarly coherent structure to the working week. Many workers in England, even as late as 1850, did not work on Monday; this, however, was a fixed arrangement and not merely a by-product of weekend inebriation. These workers worked on Saturday; their 'weekend' was consequently Sunday and Monday, rather than the present-day Saturday and Sunday. In some cases, 'St. Monday' was eventually traded off in return for a half-day holiday on Saturday; this represented a move towards the 'modern' weekend, but not a novel regularisation.[20]

For all the individual variations in work experience between different occupations and localities, however, it is safe to observe,

---

[15] Sidney Pollard, *A history of labour in Sheffield* (Liverpool, 1959), pp. 61–2, 82–3; Church, *Economic and social change in a Midland town*, pp. 85, 95, 100, 288–9; Bienefeld, *Working hours in British industry*, pp. 36–7.

[16] See, for example, David Jones, 'Crime and police in Manchester in the nineteenth century', in David Jones, *Crime, protest, community and police in nineteenth-century Britain* (London, 1982), pp. 144–77; M.E. Rose, *The relief of poverty, 1834–1914* (London, 1972), pp. 7, 17–18.

[17] John Rule, *The experience of labour in eighteenth-century industry* (London, 1981), pp. 57–8. [18] George, *London life in the eighteenth century*, ch. 6.

[19] *Ibid.*, p. 206; *Byelaws, rules and orders for the conduct, management and government of all pilots, watermen and others employed . . . within the port of Bristol*, 2 edns, (Bristol, 1810 and 1853); F.G. Webb, 'Bristol and the rope trade', Univ. of Bristol Dept of Extra-Mural Studies, Notes on Bristol History, no. 5, 1962, pp. 41–51 (BRL).

[20] Douglas A. Reid, 'The decline of St. Monday, 1766–1876', *Past and Present*, no. 71 (May 1976), pp. 76–101; Hugh Cunningham, *Leisure in the industrial revolution* (London, 1980), pp. 66, 143–7.

indeed to stress, the following: between 1750 and 1850 almost all employed people, particularly in the towns, were to be found at work between the hours of 6 a.m. and 6 p.m., Tuesday to Saturday.[21] It is most useful to see individual circumstances as deviating from, but almost invariably adding to, these hours than to emphasise the diversity of work hours between different occupational groups. The crucial point is that there were basic hours shared by a vast majority of the labour force; consequently, there was a recognisable working day and working week.

Much of the confusion generated by frameworks such as Landes', stems from the equation of industrialisation with urbanisation. It seems, from research to date, that there may have been a crucial distinction between urban and rural work time in the eighteenth century, with 'leisure preference' being, perhaps, a characteristic of the latter. The distinction is easily muddied, however, particularly if the 'regularisation' of work time is regarded as a product of factory industrialisation rather than urbanisation. Curiously, it is Landes himself who points out that without the common language of time measurement 'urban life and civilisation as we know it would be impossible'.[22] The important subject of time-disciplines related to the urban environment has received almost no attention from historians.[23] Yet from even cursory examination of newspapers published in the eighteenth and nineteenth centuries it becomes clear that these newspapers were addressing themselves to a public aware of time. Meetings, sporting events, balls, plays at the theatre, markets, the arrival of the mail, the departure of coaches, all occurred at specified, and adhered to, times. It was this urban routine far more than factory work regimes that marked the move away from rural time-disciplines.

The ordering of that urban routine and the creation of a distinctive urban calendar in the late eighteenth and early nineteenth centuries were the products of a series of continuities and discontinuities. The rural calendar, for instance, was modified, adapted and relocated for use in the urban environment. Harvest-time long continued to have some bearing upon the standard of living and public order in the

---

[21] Bienefeld, *Working hours in British industry*, chs. 2, 3; Hopkins, 'Working hours and working conditions'; Rule, *Experience of labour in eighteenth-century industry*, pp. 57–61; Hodgson, 'Working day and working week in Victorian Britain', ch. 2.

[22] Landes, *Revolution in time*, p. 2.

[23] An exception, albeit brief, is provided by P.J. Corfield, *The impact of English towns, 1700–1800* (Oxford, 1982), p. 86.

town. Some aspects of the rural calendar were directly transposed. The celebration of Guy Fawkes' Day, the ringing of church bells on secular anniversaries and celebrations, the Christmas, Easter and Whitsun holidays, although all gaining specific functions within urban life, had their foundations in the countryside.[24] The sharp physical boundaries between town and country affected the character of urban recreation: it long remained possible in densely populated cities such as Bristol and Sheffield for workers to walk out into the open country during non-work hours.[25]

The social calendar of the urban middle and upper classes held widespread implications for the allocation of work and non-work time. 'The Season' in London was important in providing employment, particularly in service occupations, during the winter; when the rich left town in the summer, on the other hand, they left behind unemployment.[26] The impact of 'the Season' in the metropolis was clearly apparent, but it is altogether more difficult to ascertain its impact upon provincial towns; the Society calendar could be highly complex and geographically diverse.[27] The increasing emphasis placed by the rich upon privacy, segregation and conspicuous consumption held rather more tangible implications not only for work structure in the major towns and resorts, but for the composition of the urban environment.[28] The proximity of the very poor

---

[24] Bienefeld, *Working hours in British industry*, pp. 19, 38–9; Bushaway, *By rite*, ch. 2 and Appendix 2; Charlotte S. Burne, 'Guy Fawkes' Day', *Folk-Lore*, XXIII (1912), pp. 409–26; Robert D. Storch, ' "Please to remember the fifth of November": conflict, solidarity and public order in southern England, 1815–1900', in Robert D. Storch (ed.), *Popular culture and custom in nineteenth-century England* (London, 1982), pp. 71–99; Douglas A. Reid, 'Interpreting the festival calendar: wakes and fairs as carnivals', in Storch (ed.), *Popular culture and custom in nineteenth-century England*, pp. 125–53; H.E. Meller, *Leisure and the changing city, 1870–1914* (London, 1976), ch. 8.

[25] Pollard, *Labour in Sheffield*, pp. 27–8; David Cannadine, *Lords and landlords: the aristocracy and the towns, 1774–1967* (Leicester, 1980), pp. 36–7.

[26] L.D. Schwarz, 'Social class and social geography: the middle classes in London at the end of the eighteenth century', *Social History*, VII (1982), p. 178; Corfield, *Impact of English towns*, pp. 73–9; David Cannadine, 'The theory and practice of the English leisure classes', *Historical Journal*, XXI (1978), pp. 461–2.

[27] See, for example, F.M.L. Thompson, *English landed society in the nineteenth century* (London, 1963), pp. 94–5.

[28] Schwarz, 'Social class and social geography'; Cannadine, *Lords and landlords*, chs. 1, 5, 16, 17; D.A. Reeder, 'A theatre of suburbs: some patterns of development in the west of London, 1801–1911', in H.J. Dyos (ed.), *The study of urban history* (London, 1968), pp. 253–71; Meller, *Leisure and the changing city*, pp. 19–24; S.J. Jones, 'The growth of Bristol: the regional aspect of city development', *Transactions of the Institute of British Geographers*, XI (1946), pp. 57–83.

to the very rich (the environmental impact of the demands of Society), and the increasing demarcation between middle and working class residential zones, almost certainly determined the location of specific urban events, and, by implication, their timing. Furthermore, the social calendar of the rich, particularly with the development of the railways and the declining influence of the rural calendar and workday, promoted the allocation of special times to specific social activities.[29]

The process of urbanisation brought about changes in leisure activities, in part because of the physical constraints of the environment, and in part through the concurrent attack upon popular (and, for that matter, aristocratic) leisure activities carried out by some members of the middle class. The changing patterns of leisure through the period may have altered the propensity of, and opportunity for, people to form crowds. The facilities for large indoor gatherings on enclosed sites, with their inevitable restraints regarding availability and location, introduced a limitation on the possible timing of crowd events not present in the case of public parks, common land or the street.[30] The siting of crowd gathering events outside the city boundaries, either as a result of increasing density of building in city centres or in order to avoid the jurisdiction of borough magistrates, inevitably entailed organisational constraints.[31]

Lastly, the ordering of time within the town was conditioned by fixed local and national events: market times, fair dates, the sporting calendar and local anniversaries were peculiar to individual localities. Their predetermined regularity would alter the structure of work time and influence the propensity of crowds to form around particular events. Similarly, the regularity or the rationale of either fixed national anniversaries (such as royal birthdays) or national events (such as parliamentary elections or military victories) might induce certain local authorities to declare a holiday or part-holiday for the occasion.

---

[29] Leonore Davidoff, *The best circles: society, etiquette and the season* (London, 1973), esp. pp. 34–5.

[30] See, for example, the case of Leicester, where the construction of a new hall and a Commercial Cricket Ground transformed the organisation of public meetings and mass recreation: A. Temple Patterson, *Radical Leicester: a history of Leicester, 1780–1850* (Leicester, 1954), pp. 173–4, 182–3.

[31] Cunningham, *Leisure in the industrial revolution*, ch. 3; Conrad Gill, *History of Birmingham*, vol. 1: *Manor and borough to 1865* (London, 1952), pp. 123–7; Pollard, *Labour in Sheffield*, pp. 5–6; Meller *Leisure and the changing city*, ch. 8.

Order in the urban environment was influenced, therefore, by what might be termed a town's time-profile. It was also influenced, of course, by the public conduct of its inhabitants, and it is this dimension of urban order which has been the subject for rather more attention from historians. Interpretations of public order as constituted by the conduct of large numbers of people on the streets have been several and, to some extent, contradictory. They all, however, take the same premise: early nineteenth-century urban society was boisterous, unruly and violent. And it is commonly agreed that this hectic state of affairs was gradually, and particularly from mid-century, calmed and tamed (see chapter 1). If it was the case, however, that work patterns between 1750 and 1850 were, in fact, far from irregular and haphazard, what does this suggest for the supposed capriciousness of other elements of pre-Victorian life? In short, the existing discussion of the development of ordered society begs the question as to just how *un*ordered the urban environment in the early nineteenth century actually was.

In summary, a study of the historiography of work, the urban environment and public order, for this period, provides a set of conflicting impressions. Work routines may have been more rigorous and predictable than was until recently thought; the process of urbanisation from about the middle of the eighteenth century appears to have facilitated the further ordering of time and the compartmentalisation of social activities; and yet, the literature suggests, 'ordered society' should be dated from the middle decades of the nineteenth century. The state of discussion so far, it seems, offers few clues as to the findings that might emerge from the detailed examination of the position of crowd occurrences in the time-structure of an early nineteenth-century English city. Perhaps from this examination it will become apparent that crowds formed at will, that time constraints were few, and that ordered society was in its infancy; or perhaps the existence of a coherent working week provided the framework for the formalistic occurrence of mass phenomena.

THE TIMING OF CROWD OCCURRENCES IN BRISTOL

An analysis of the timing trends in crowd occurrences in Bristol between 1790 and 1835 provides an opportunity to examine the structure of urban time 'in action'. The details of timing which form the basis for this analysis have been extracted primarily, although not exclusively, from newspaper sources. The definitive source for timing details, however, is the public notice which attempts to call together a crowd for a particular event. These notices have not survived for all the crowd events discussed here (and in some instances would not in any case have been issued), but those that do exist do not on any occasion contradict details provided by newspaper reports. Of course, newspapers themselves were frequently used to advertise the details for a planned gathering. For some crowd occurrences, however, no precise timing details exist. The reportage of the event may nevertheless provide certain obvious clues (such as mention that the crowd gathered at 'lunch-time' or 'in the afternoon'); but where no reliable clues are available crowds have been taken, for the purposes of this study, to have occurred *inside* work hours. In other words, the sample discussed here has an inbuilt bias in favour of figures suggesting the occurrence of crowds inside work hours. (For a detailed outline of data collection methods see chapter 2, above.)

In total, 245 documented crowd occurrences have been identified in Bristol for the years 1790–1835. The timing of these crowds create certain patterns which immediately invite the examination of them to be divided into five categories. These are: variations over the period 1790–1835; seasonal or monthly variation; the occurrence of crowds on Mondays; evening crowds; and crowds forming at mid-day. Some remarks will also be made concerning crowds that occurred during work hours.

There is no strict pattern for the annual occurrence of crowds over the period 1790 to 1835 (see figure 3). The number varies wildly from year to year. Exceptional events, such as the Bristol Bridge riots of 1793, food disturbances and the celebrations of peace with France in 1801–2, and two parliamentary elections in 1812, produce sudden peaks. But there are also years in which numbers of crowds occur for no single reason, such as 1820. In that year there were three recreational crowds, a 'radical' celebration, a disturbance, a royal celebration and three election crowds. Generally, election years do provide peaks in crowd occurrences.[32] At the end of the period the agitated events of 1830–2 produce a peak in crowd activity which quickly falls away in 1833. Despite the distorting effects of those years, there does appear to be a slight upward trend in crowd occurrences from 1815. The number of crowd *events* is more constant, however, with peaks between 1813 and 1829 being no

[32] Election years were: 1790, 1796, 1801, 1803, 1806, 1807, 1812 (June and October), 1818, 1820, 1826, 1830, 1831, 1832 and 1835.

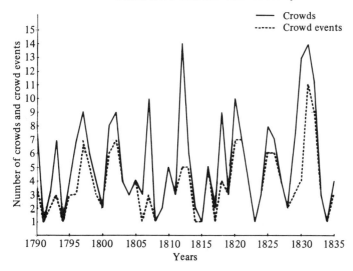

Figure 3   Annual distribution of crowds and crowd events in Bristol, 1790–1835

Note: the material for the figures and tables in this chapter is taken from the full range of sources listed in the Bibliography below. The vast majority of crowd occurrences, however, are documented in local newspapers and local government records; see particularly the following sections of the Bibliography: A2, A5, A6, B1 and B3.

higher than for 1797 to 1804. The years 1804 to 1810 were 'quieter' than average, the election of 1807 notwithstanding.

Once broken down into crowd types (table 3) fluctuations become more meaningful. The prevalence of crowds for royal and military events during the years of the French wars stands out clearly, although so does their decline as the war dragged on. Occurrences of 'patriotic' crowds fell to zero for 1825–9, but rallied during the subsequent six years both in response to a more popular monarch, and in reaction to the radicalism of those years. The number of rioting crowds (not including election riots) shows a gradual decline down to 1824, but then sharply rises during the last ten years of the period. This is due to the events surrounding the 'reform' riots of 1831, but also to anti-Catholic disturbances in 1825 and 1829.[33]

---

[33] *Bristol Gazette*, 7 July 1825, 19 Feb. 1829, 9 Apr. 1829; *FFBJ*, 9 July 1825; *Bristol Mirror*, 9 July 1825; *Bristol Mercury*, 11 July 1825, 14 Apr. 1829; Daniel Vickery, 'A Bristol calendar containing brief notices of such events as have taken place in that city and its neighbourhood July 1824 to the end of the year 1835', *BRL* B2639 MS.

Table 3. *Variations in crowd types in Bristol, 1790–1835 (percentages in brackets)*

Crowd type	1790–4	1795–9	1800–4	1805–9	1810–14	1815–19	1820–4	1825–9	1830–5	Total
Riot and disturbance	7 (35.0)	6 (20.0)	4 (15.4)	2 (10.0)	4 (13.3)	–	2 (8.0)	7 (25.0)	10 (21.7)	42
Election riots	1 (5.0)	1 (3.3)	–	2 (10.0)	3 (10.0)	2 (10.0)	–	1 (3.6)	2 (4.3)	12
Election crowds	4 (20.0)	4 (13.3)	6 (23.1)	8 (40.0)	7 (23.3)	4 (20.0)	3 (12.0)	1 (3.6)	11 (23.9)	48
'Conservative' meetings	2 (10.0)	–	1 (3.8)	1 (5.0)	1 (3.3)	–	1 (4.0)	2 (7.1)	–	8
'Radical' meetings	–	–	–	–	4 (13.3)	4 (20.0)	1 (4.0)	2 (7.1)	10 (21.7)	21
Recreational	2 (10.0)	2 (6.6)	1 (3.8)	–	4 (13.3)	4 (20.0)	14 (56.0)	10 (35.7)	2 (4.3)	39
Royal and military	1 (5.0)	15 (50.0)	8 (30.8)	6 (30.0)	7 (23.3)	2 (10.0)	4 (16.0)	–	6 (13.0)	49
Others*	3 (15.0)	2 (6.6)	6 (23.1)	1 (5.0)	–	4 (20.0)	–	5 (17.8)	5 (10.9)	26
All crowds	20 (100)	30 (100)	26 (100)	20 (100)	30 (100)	20 (100)	25 (100)	28 (100)	46 (100)	245
Crowd events	11	21	22	11	19	15	22	21	31	173

*Executions, funeral processions and miscellaneous.

Indeed, apart from some minor disturbances on the abandonment of the Pains and Penalties Bill in 1820, the only non-election riots to occur between 1813 and 1830 were those directed against the Irish.

Perhaps significantly, the same period marks the rise of 'radical' meetings and processions, the first of which took place on the arrival of Henry Hunt and Sir Samuel Romilly prior to the parliamentary election of June 1812.[34] In the 1830s the large number of mass demonstrations equalled the number of non-election riots. The other noticeable trend is the increase in recreational crowds during the 1820s.[35] This took place while other crowd events fell off. Whether the number of recreational crowds actually increased, or whether they were simply reported in compensation for the lack of other crowd events, is difficult to ascertain. It is curious that their frequency apparently declines during the increase in other crowds between 1830 and 1835. Such trends pose interesting questions relating to historical 'impressions' handed down by certain records: was it the case that these fluctuations did in fact occur; or was the recording of crowd events contingent upon the news needs of newspapers at particular times? Was it in fact the case that there was a persistently large number of recreational crowds in this period, the reporting of which was severely curtailed at times when other, more 'newsworthy', crowd events were taking place? Here, of course, the subjectivity of newspaper sources intrudes once more. But where such records provide the only available information relating to mass activity for a certain period, then the possible existence of news priorities has important implications for the image of a period gained by historians.

The seasonal, or monthly, distribution of crowds (figure 4) shows a peak in activity in the spring, which falls away over the summer, rises again in the autumn, before falling to a low over the winter. It is

---

[34] Anon. (Sir Samuel Romilly), *An account of the entry of Sir Samuel Romilly into Bristol, on Thursday April 2nd, 1812* (Bristol, 1812); Sir Samuel Romilly, *Memoirs of the life of Sir Samuel Romilly, written by himself* (London, 1840), vol. 3, pp. 21–2, 27; Henry Hunt, *Memoirs of Henry Hunt written by himself*, 3 vols. (London, 1821), vol. 2, pp. 499–505; *Bristol Gazette*, 9 Apr. 1812.

[35] Douglas A. Reid, 'Interpreting the festival calendar', in Storch (ed.), *Popular culture and custom in nineteenth-century England*, pp. 129–30, suggests that, as the routine of working life may have become more constricted, and the boredom greater, working people may have become even more keen to participate in recreational festivities. Hugh Cunningham, *Leisure in the industrial revolution*, p. 9 and ch. 1, also believes that, despite attacks on popular recreation from certain quarters, recreational events were not suffering a decline in occurrence or attendance during these years.

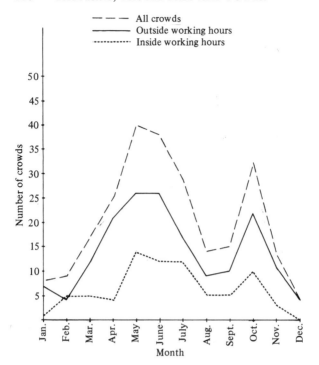

Figure 4   Monthly distribution of crowds occurring inside and outside working hours, Bristol, 1790–1835

noticeable that the occurrence of crowds outside working hours closely follows this trend, with a rapid decline in the frequency of crowd occurrences from June onwards. Although the better weather and longer days of April and May would have contributed to an increase in the staging of, and to better attendance at, crowd events, higher levels of employment, greater workloads and longer working days during the summer months may have been responsible for the subsequent decline in activity. In other words, the extension of the working day in these months may have made for fewer non-working hours in which to take part in crowd events.

The length of the working day in Bristol certainly varied with the season. Bristol Gas Light Station workers had different seasonal hours written into the rules of their employment, with hours of attendance

to be as follows (that is to say) from 14th Feb. to 5th Nov., 6 o'clock in the morning to ½ past 8, from 9 to 1 o'clock and then from 2 to 6 o'clock in the evening, from 5th Nov. to 14th Feb., 7 o'clock in the morning to 9, from $\frac{1}{2}$ past 9 to 1 o'clock and then from 2 to 7 in the evening. The bell is to be *rung* as a warning *Ten* minutes before the several Hours named for going into work and is to be *tolled* at the precise time fixed for attendance.[36]

The handsorting of tobacco leaves at the Wills factory was impossible after 4 p.m. during the winter months since gas light distorted the colours.[37] The rule books of the various institutions with working class members, which proliferated in the first quarter of the nineteenth century, showed a clear awareness of the need to alter their schedules with the season: the Loyal Union Benefit Society met between 7 and 9 p.m. in winter, and between 8 and 10 p.m. in summer; the under-secretary of the South Gloucestershire Friendly Society was available to receive members' subscriptions from 5 to 7 p.m. in winter, from 6 to 8 p.m. in summer.[38]

Broken down into crowd types (table 4), the monthly distribution for riots alone is close to the harvest-linked trend suggested elsewhere by Hobsbawm, although the occurrences in March seem high, and for June rather low.[39] These figures relate to all non-election riots, however. Of the nine riots specifically related to the price or availability of food in this period, three occurred in March, two in April, one in May, two in June and one in September. There are other variables affecting the general trend in monthly distribution. Executions tended to occur after the spring gaol delivery (but not, it seems, after the autumn one); elections were generally called in the summer months; recreational events increased in number, and were better attended, in the summer, for obvious reasons; [40] the occurrence of

---

[36] Bristol Gas Light Company Minutes, III, 28 Nov. 1821, appendix 3, BRO, 28777/1c.

[37] B.W.E. Alford, *W.D. and H.O. Wills and the development of the U.K. tobacco industry, 1780–1965* (London, 1973), p. 129.

[38] *Rules and orders to be observed and kept by the Loyal Union of Britons Benefit Society of handicraft tradesmen, commencing 8th of October 1821* (Bristol, 1821?), p. 3; *Rules and regulations of the South Gloucestershire Friendly Society* (Bristol, 1825).

[39] E.J. Hobsbawm, 'Economic fluctuations and some social movements since 1800', *Economic History Review*, V (1952), pp. 5–6.

[40] The arrival of the wealthy for the summer season at Hotwells and Clifton may have been influential. Bristol's renowned lack of social amenities might have encouraged outdoor pursuits. The entries in the *Bristol guide* under 'recreation' stressed outdoor activities: W. Mathews, 1794 edn, ch. 10; J. Mathews, 1815 edn, pp. 172–3, 1829 edn, pp. 199–201. See also, Vincent Waite, 'The Bristol Hotwell', in Patrick McGrath (ed.), *Bristol in the eighteenth century* (Newton Abbot, 1972), pp. 109–26; Kathleen Barker, *Bristol at play: five centuries of live entertainment* (Bradford-on-Avon, 1976), ch. 3; Peter T. Marcy, *Eighteenth-century views of Bristol and Bristolians* (Bristol, 1966), pp. 15–22.

Table 4. *Monthly distribution of crowd types, Bristol, 1790–1835*

Crowd type	Jan.	Feb.	Mar.	Apr.	May	June	July	Aug.	Sept.	Oct.	Nov.	Dec.
Riot and disturbance	–	3	7	7	4	2	3	1	6	4	5	–
Election crowds/riots	2	–	3	–	13	17	12	1	–	8	2	2
Meetings, radical/conservative	–	3	2	4	4	3	2	3	–	4	4	1
Royal and military	1	3	1	1	6	10	4	3	4	14	2	–
Recreational	4	–	2	2	7	4	7	5	3	1	1	1
Executions	1	–	–	10	5	–	1	–	–	–	–	–
Funeral processions	–	–	2	1	1	1	–	–	1	1	–	–
Miscellaneous	–	–	–	–	–	1	–	1	1	–	–	–
Total	8	9	17	25	40	38	29	14	15	32	14	4

royal events was distorted by the prevalence of royal anniversaries around the end of May (anniversary of the restoration of Charles II), and the beginning of June (birthdays of George III and William IV). The high number of 'patriotic' events in October is coincidental, being due to a number of military victories, the Proclamation of Peace with France in 1801, the visit of the Duchess of Kent and Princess Victoria in 1830, the anniversary of the accession of George III, and two crowd gathering displays by the Bristol Volunteers (in 1803 and 1810).

Given the size of the sample (the average number of documented crowd occurrences per year is 5.4) these qualifications to the figures for seasonal distribution are significant. They do not necessarily nullify the hypothesis that seasonal economic fluctuations and work-disciplines lessened the propensity of people to take part in crowd events, however. It seems possible that the predictable seasonal routines of work may have constrained the staging of, or attendance at, crowd events. The figures are, of course, for crowds that *did* occur, and they give no account of crowd events that 'failed'. Such events were, with the exception of unsuccessful political meetings, rarely deemed newsworthy. Of course, 'failure' is a relative term with regard to crowds: the tory newspaper *Felix Farley's Bristol Journal* believed that Henry Hunt's reform meeting on 20 December 1816 was not a success; estimates of attendance vary from 600 to 2,000.[41] Certainly the total number of *potential* crowd gathering events is likely to have been higher in the summer months. A great number of patriotic anniversaries and other events occurring in summertime failed to draw crowds.[42] Only once, for example, did the birthday of the Prince Regent, which fell on the 12th of August, succeed in attracting a popular response, and even then the public turned out primarily in the hope of another view of a triumphal arch which had been erected for Wellington's visit a fortnight earlier.[43]

The propensity of crowds to form on Mondays was extremely

---

[41] *Bristol Gazette*, 2 June 1817; *FFBJ*, 28 Dec. 1826; *Bristol Mirror*, 28 Dec. 1816.
[42] Repeatedly, in the 1790s, for instance, the anniversaries of George III's birthday and coronation, despite 'official' celebration, failed to draw crowds: *Bristol Gazette* 30 Sept. 1790, 26 Sept. 1792, 12 June 1794, 25 Sept. 1794, 9 June 1796; *FFBJ*, 25 Sept. 1790, 24 Sept. 1791, 9 Sept. 1792; *Bristol Mercury*, 6 June 1791, 26 Sept. 1791, 28 Sept. 1795, 25 Sept. 1797; *BMBJ*, 9 Sept. 1792, 6 June 1795; *SFBJ*, 8 June 1793, 7 June 1794.
[43] *Bristol Gazette*, 1, 14 Aug. 1816; *FFBJ*, 3, 17 Aug. 1816; *Bristol Mirror*, 3 Aug. 1816; *Bristol Mercury*, 19 Aug. 1816.

Table 5. *Occurrence of crowds in relation to the working day, Bristol, 1790–1835 (percentages in brackets)*

Crowd type	6–12 a.m. and 2–6 p.m.						All day Sun.	6 p.m.–6 a.m. Evening	12 a.m. 2 p.m. Mid-day	Holiday	De facto holiday	Total
	Mon.	Tue.	Wed.	Thur.	Fri.	Sat.						
Riot and disturbance	6 (14.3) (11.8)	3 (7.1) (12.0)	—	1 (2.4) (6.3)	1 (2.4) (11.1)	7 (16.6) (38.8)	4 (9.5) (66.7)	19 (45.2) (40.4)	—	—	1 (2.4) (7.1)	42 (100) (17.2)
Election riots	1 (8.3) (2.0)	1 (8.3) (4.0)	—	—	—	—	—	10 (83.3) (21.3)	—	—	—	12 (100) (4.9)
Election crowds	10 (20.8) (19.6)	11 (22.9) (44.0)	3 (6.25) (37.5)	5 (10.4) (31.3)	1 (2.1) (11.1)	6 (12.5) (33.3)	—	5 (10.4) (10.6)	6 (12.5) (17.6)	—	1 (2.1) (7.1)	48 (100) (19.6)
'Conservative' meetings and processions	1 (12.5) (2.0)	1 (12.5) (4.0)	—	—	—	—	—	—	1 (12.5) (2.9)	—	5 (62.5) (35.7)	8 (100) (3.3)
'Radical' meetings and processions	4 (18.2) (7.8)	1 (4.5) (4.0)	—	1 (4.5) (6.3)	—	1 (4.5) (5.6)	—	4 (18.2) (8.5)	4 (18.2) (11.8)	3 (13.6) (17.6)	4 (18.2) (28.6)	22 (100) (9.0)
Recreational	14 (37.8) (27.4)	4 (10.8) (16.0)	1 (2.7) (12.5)	1 (2.7) (6.3)	3 (8.1) (33.3)	1 (2.7) (5.6)	—	3 (8.1) (6.4)	1 (2.7) (2.9)	9 (24.3) (52.9)	—	37 (100) (14.7)
Executions	—	—	—	—	—	—	—	—	17 (100) (50.0)	—	—	17 (100) (6.9)
Royal and Military	13 (26.5) (25.5)	3 (6.1) (12.0)	3 (6.1) (37.5)	7 (14.3) (43.8)	3 (6.1) (33.3)	1 (2.0) (5.6)	1 (2.0) (16.7)	6 (12.2) (12.8)	4 (8.2) (11.8)	5 (10.2) (29.4)	3 (6.1) (21.4)	49 (100) (20.0)
Funeral processions	1 (14.3) (2.0)	1 (14.3) (4.0)	1 (14.3) (12.5)	1 (14.3) (6.3)	1 (14.3) (11.1)	1 (14.3) (5.6)	—	—	1 (14.3) (2.9)	—	—	7 (100) (2.9)
Miscellaneous	1 (33.3) (2.0)	—	—	—	—	1 (33.3) (5.6)	1 (33.3) (16.7)	—	—	—	—	3 (100) (1.2)
Total	51 (20.8) (100)	25 (10.2) (100)	8 (3.3) (100)	16 (6.5) (100)	9 (3.7) (100)	18 (7.3) (100)	6 (2.4) (100)	47 (19.2) (100)	34 (13.9) (100)	17 (6.9) (100)	14 (5.7) (100)	245 (110) (100)

marked. The crowds occurring during what would have been working hours on that day represent 21 per cent of all crowds (see table 5). When crowds occurring on Monday mid-day and evening, and on holidays which fell on that day, are added, the proportion of all crowds occurring on Monday rises to 31 per cent. This reinforces the impression gained from contemporary accounts. For example, a handbill which described an accident on the Rownham ferry at Hotwells included the observation that 'Monday being a day which vast numbers of persons select for taking their recreation in Leigh Woods, and the weather being fine, a large concourse of people had assembled for that purpose.'[44] The *Bristol Liberal* reported that, by the morning of the third day of the 1831 riots, 'It became evident that something should be done to quell the riotous disposition which was still by no means allayed, and especially as Monday is generally a day of idleness, and numbers of disorderly people might be expected from the surrounding country, under the plea of surveying the mischief that had been accomplished.'[45]

As these quotations suggest, there was a tendency for people not to work on Mondays. Not everyone had that day off from work, however. Visitors could watch window glass being made at the works of Vigor and Co. every Monday; and John Bennett, in his manuscript autobiography, records sending his men out to work on Monday.[46] Nevertheless, Monday did have particular significance as a rest day. Much of that significance lay in relation to the two foregoing days, and it is within these terms that the crowd gathering function of Monday is best understood: Saturday was a day of work, Sunday a 'domestic' day and Monday a day for taking to the streets. Referring to a reform meeting at the Guildhall in Bristol on Saturday 24 September 1831, 'Junius' assured reformers that 'The promoters of that meeting had a more important object than a merely numerous attendance, or they would not have convened it on a day notoriously the most inconvenient to you.'[47] An article on the evils of drink, in the conservative journal the *Bristol Job Nott or Labouring Man's Friend*,

---

44 'A dreadful accident at the Hotwells, Bristol', n.d. (1832?), in Jefferies MSS, vol. XXIV, BRL B7945 MS, p. 18.

45 *Bristol Liberal*, 5 Nov. 1831.

46 W. Mathews, *Mathews's Bristol guide and directory, 1793–4* (Bristol, 1794), p. 40; 'Manuscript autobiography of John Bennett, Portishead, 1853', BRO 36097 (a–b), p. 20.

47 'Junius to the Reformers of Bristol', handbill, Bristol, 29 Sept. 1831, in 'Troubles in Bristol, by politicks, fire and pestilence', BRL B10112.

JUNIUS

TO THE

REFORMERS

OF

BRISTOL.

THE cool but determined zeal with which you presented yourselves at the Meeting in the Guildhall, on Saturday last, is a sufficient answer to the barefaced calumny of your adversaries, that you had become indifferent to Reform. The promoters of that Meeting had a more important object in view than a merely numerous attendance, or they would not have convened it on a day notoriously the most inconvenient to you.— But they knew that you were prepared to make great sacrifices to testify your unshaken fidelity to the great measure of Reform, and your attendance on that day justified the confidence they reposed in you.

Nor have your exertions been since relaxed. In three days upwards of Eight Thousand Signatures have been attached to the Petition so unanimously adopted on that day.

But the VICTORY is not yet achieved. Sir Charles Wetherell has asserted in the House of Commons, that he used his influence to prevent you from Petitioning! Will you suffer the People of England to imagine but for a moment that HE had any influence over you? Let Twenty Thousand Signatures attest his arrogant assumption.

Your honest and enthusiastic Patriotism at the late Election gave to your City a new character. Corruption then received its death-blow in this its foulest hot-bed. The eyes of your countrymen were fixed upon you in almost hopeless expectation. Your triumph exhilarated your friends; it appalled and paralyzed your adversaries. Your example had an important influence throughout the Empire; and a House of Commons, elected under such auspices, passed the REFORM BILL.

That Bill is now passing its most dangerous ordeal. The Lords are at this moment balancing between their own interests and public opinion. They have been told, and they will not be reluctant to believe, that a re-action has taken place, and that you have become indifferent to the Measure. They must, however, be convinced that those who have circulated this report have calumniated you; and that can only be done effectively by the number of Signatures to your Petition. They must not be allowed to justify a rejection of the Bill, by the plea of the luke-warmness of the People. When the object to be attained is of such paramount importance, *the man, who neglects to sign the PETITION, neglects his duty to his Country*; he sacrifices his own and his children's rights. Should the Bill be passed, such a man will have no claim to participate in the Jubilee that will commemorate the National Triumph; he must relinquish the proudest title an Englishman can boast; — a REFORMER.

You have no time to lose,

THE PETITION

Must leave Bristol on Saturday Night.

Bristol, September 29, 1831.   **JUNIUS.**

T. J. MANCHEE, PRINTER, QUAY, BRISTOL.

1 A reform notice, 21 September 1831. Note the reference to the inconvenient timing of a recent meeting, and the emphasis placed upon local pride.

for February 1832, noted that workmen were paid on Saturday evening, after a full day's work; Saturday night and Sunday morning were for drinking; and it was on Sunday, with the week's wages, that wives did shopping and domestic chores.[48] The practice of paying workers on Saturday evening, often late, and usually at a public house, continued well into the nineteenth century. As a consequence, many spent Saturday night in the pub, as much to wait for wages as to drink them away. Sunday was for shopping, for rest, for reading and for recovery from Saturday night.[49] It was also respected as the Sabbath, and therefore as unsuitable for non-religious mass events.

The occurrence of crowd events was consistent with a weekend structured around a working Saturday, a 'domestic' Sunday and a leisured Monday. Only 2.4 per cent (six in number) of all crowds occurred on Sunday. Of these, four were riotous (and not planned by an 'organiser'), one was in any case a religious meeting and one was a celebration of the preliminary peace with France. Contemporary reports claimed that during the last of these events, the Sabbath was respected during the afternoon.[50] Generally, it was only riots or elections that brought people onto the streets during the working hours of Saturday (see table 5).[51] Saturday evening did produce slightly more crowds than most other nights, ten being recorded over the period, compared to twelve on Monday evening, eight on Tuesday, four on Wednesday, seven on Thursday and six on Friday. Saturday lunch-time produced only two crowds in these years: one election procession and one small turn-out of supposedly young men in support of the anti-Catholic recorder, Sir Charles Wetherell, in 1829.[52]

Monday, however, appears to have been deliberately selected as a day for crowd occasions. Of all crowd attended recreational events of the period, 38 per cent occurred during supposedly working hours on

---

[48] *Bristol Job Nott*, VIII, 2 Feb. 1832, LIX, 14 Jan. 1833.

[49] George, *London life in the eighteenth century*, pp. 287–9; W.B. Whitaker, *The eighteenth-century English Sunday: a study in Sunday observance from 1677 to 1837* (London, 1940), pp. 160–2; Brian Harrison, 'The Sunday trading riots of 1855', *Historical Journal*, VIII (1965), pp. 221–2; Hodgson, 'Working day and working week in Victorian Britain', pp. 161–2.

[50] *FFBJ*, 10 Oct. 1801.

[51] The Saturday market was the scene of food disturbances during working hours in 1797, 1801, 1811, 1812: *Bristol Gazette*, 11 May 1797, 28 Mar. 1811; *BMBJ*, 11, 18 Apr. 1801; Hilhouse Wilcox to Ryder, 13 Apr. 1812, LB/BRO.

[52] *Bristol Gazette*, 22 June 1826, 9 Apr. 1829; *FFBJ*, 24 June 1825; *Bristol Mercury*, 7 Apr. 1829; Vickery, 'A Bristol calendar', pp. 140–1; PO/BRO 6, 7 Feb. and 2 Apr. 1829.

Monday. The prevalence of boxing matches in particular on this day suggests a conscious attempt to cater for mass attendance. Nevertheless, it seems to have been the very rich and the very poor who attended them.[53] It may be significant that, despite a pledge in 1820 that cricket matches would become a regular Monday event,[54] they tended to be staged on other days of the week. The crowds they attracted as a result were reportedly made up of the 'fashionable', the 'beautiful' and the 'respectable';[55] their antithetical stablemates, the mobility (in this context, the unemployed) also put in an appearance on occasion.[56] If an event staged on a Monday coincided with fine weather, the crowds could be vast. Such a combination produced 'countless multitudes' at a balloon ascent in 1825, and at an ascent in 1810 it seemed 'as if the country for twenty miles around had been put in requisition'.[57] 'Extremely favourable' weather bolstered the attendance at the consecration of the Bristol Volunteers' colours in 1803, and encouraged an influx of 'strangers' for the anniversary of George III's birthday in 1804.[58]

Of all royal and military events, 28.5 per cent took place at some point on Monday. Whether this reflects careful planning by the organisers, or popular reluctance to absent from work for the sake of such occasions, is not clear. It was certainly beneficial, in crowd terms, for a royal or military anniversary to fall on a Monday. Twelve fixed royal anniversaries succeeded in drawing crowds in Bristol in these years: George III's birthday, in 1797, 1798, 1799, 1801 and 1805; Queen Charlotte's birthday, in 1805; the anniversary of the restoration of Charles II, in 1794 and 1802; the anniversary of George III's accession, in 1810; the Regent's birthday, in 1816; George IV's birthday, in 1822; and William IV's birthday, in 1832. Of these, five occurred on a Monday, six on other days but outside working hours and only one inside working hours. There were three military anniversaries which drew crowds: all were celebrations of the formation of the Bristol Volunteers. There did not appear to be a fixed date for this anniversary, however, since the crowd attracting occasions were 19 February 1798, 16 July 1810 and 23 August 1813. Nevertheless, each of those dates fell on a Monday. When the

---

[53] See comments in *BMBJ*, 23 Jan. 1802, *Bristol Gazette*, 23 Sept. 1811.
[54] *Bristol Gazette*, 1 May 1820.
[55] For example, *ibid.*, 26 Aug. 1819, 2 Sept., 7 and 14 July 1825, 12 July 1827.
[56] *Ibid.*, 2 Sept. 1824.   [57] *Ibid.*, 27 Sept. 1810, 28 July 1825.
[58] *Ibid.*, 6 Oct. 1803; *FFBJ*, 9 June 1804; *Bristol Mirror*, 9 June 1804.

Hampshire Fencibles' colours were consecrated on a Thursday in 1796, it was principally the 'fashionable' (that is, the leisured) who attended.[59]

Although parliamentary elections could draw crowds on any day of the week, nineteen of the sixty election crowds of these years (31.6 per cent) took place on Monday (including five on Monday mid-day, and three in the evening). A fifth of all non-election riots and disturbances occurred on Monday or Monday evening. The radical orator Henry Hunt was characteristically alert to the fact that Monday was a favourable time to draw a crowd. In 1813 his arrival in Bristol on Monday produced 'a larger concourse of people than we recollect to have before seen in his train'.[60] His choice of that day of the week in July 1816 resulted in 'a great concourse of people'.[61]

Next to Monday, by far the most prevalent times for the formation of crowds were in the evening and at mid-day (see table 5). Forty-seven crowds gathered in the evening in this period. It is striking that of these 62 per cent were riotous. One immediate hypothesis which comes to mind is that people sought the cover of darkness for riot action. This may have been the case at election time since although 90 per cent of non-rioting election crowds took place in the daytime, rioting was, in 83 per cent of instances, reserved for the evening.[62] It might also be argued, of course, that with the exception of celebratory illuminations, riot is the only crowd type for which darkness is not necessarily a hindrance. Reformers readily understood the need to stage meetings outside work hours, and consequently made use of summer evenings. Henry Hunt addressed a gathering at the Exchange on a Saturday evening in June 1826.[63] In the early 1830s, reformers opted for the best of all worlds by selecting the evening of Monday. A meeting was called for that time by the Bristol Political Union in August 1831, as it was for a meeting demanding the dismissal of ministers in June 1833, and one opposing compensation to West India planters in August 1833.[64] The first mentioned meeting

[59] *Bristol Gazette*, 18 Feb. 1796.　　[60] *Bristol Mirror*, 27 Mar. 1813.

[61] *Bristol Gazette*, 18 July 1816.

[62] Notable examples are the elections of 1796 and 1818: *Bristol Gazette*, 2 June 1796, 25 June 1818; *SFBJ*, 28 May 1796; *Bristol Mercury*, 30 May 1796; *Bristol Mirror*, 20 June 1818; *FFBJ*, 20 June 1818.

[63] *Bristol Gazette*, 29 June 1826; *FFBJ*, 1 July 1826; *Bristol Mirror*, 1 July 1826; *Bristol Mercury*, 26 June 1826.

[64] *Bristol Gazette*, 11 Aug. 1831, 8 Aug. 1833; *Bristol Mirror*, 8 June, 10 Aug. 1833; *Bristol Mercury*, 8 June, 10 Aug. 1833; *FFBJ*, 8 June, 10 Aug. 1833.

consisted 'almost exclusively of mechanics, and of the grade denominated by the Lord Chancellor "the humble class of society" '.[65]
The meeting in June 1833 was scheduled to begin at 6 p.m.; the
Gazette reported that 'At the time appointed . . . a very large body
assembled, which continued increasing as the men left their work in
the evening, and by eight o'clock several thousands were on the
Hill.'[66]

Mid-day was the other non-work time when crowds could be
gathered. The Bristol Political Union were again alert to this, staging
three meetings in the lunch-break during the winter months of 1831.[67]
Felix Farley reported that at the meeting of Monday 10 October, 'At
about half-past one, during the dinner hour of the mechanics, there
were from 3 to 4,000 persons assembled, men, women and children.'[68]
It is noticeable that at the funeral procession of James Bundy on
Friday 27 March 1818, which set off at 11.30 a.m., the crowds were
greatest on the return part of the procession, between 1 and 2 p.m.[69]
All seventeen executions in Bristol between 1790 and 1835 took place
at mid-day, fifteen of them on a Friday.[70] All produced large crowds;
some produced immense ones: 20–30,000 in 1828, 50,000 in 1835.[71]
The *Gazette* pointed out, in response to an inquiry in 1828, that
executions could not take place earlier since it was necessary to wait
for the London mail to arrive in case a pardon had been granted.[72]
Nevertheless, the ritualism and spectacle involved in executions, the
addresses which the prisoners and clergy frequently made to the

[65] *Bristol Gazette*, 11 Aug. 1831.
[66] *Bristol Gazette*, 16 June 1833. As the day in question was a Monday, this provides
    further evidence that not all workers observed St Monday. The quotation also
    suggests that, as it was summertime, many workers were finishing work later than
    six o'clock.
[67] On Tuesday, noon, 26 Apr. 1831: *Bristol Gazette*, 28 Apr. 1831; *Bristol Mirror*, 30
    Apr. 1831. At 1.30 p.m., Monday, 10 Oct. 1831, and at mid-day 12 Oct. 1831:
    Bristol Gazette, 13 Oct. 1831; *FFBJ*, 15 Oct. 1831; *Bristol Mirror*, 15 Oct. 1831,
    Felix Farley's Bristol Journal, in reporting an indoor reform meeting at the
    Assembly Room, in the course of the 1832 election, observed that 'The attendance
    was far from crowded throughout, and even the dinner-hour of the operatives did
    not greatly swell the numbers of auditors'. The *Bristol Mirror*, 20 Oct. 1832, in its
    report of the same meeting recorded that 'The chair was taken at one o'clock, when
    the room was about three parts full, consisting principally of the working classes'.
[68] *FFBJ*, 15 Oct. 1831.   [69] *Bristol Gazette* 26 Mar., 2 Apr. 1818.
[70] 'A list of persons executed in Bristol since the year 1741', in 'Volume, chiefly MS,
    relating to Bristol history, 1610–1873', BRL B6518; and see newspaper reports of
    these executions.
[71] *FFBJ*, 3 May 1828; *Bristol Gazette*, 8 May 1828, 16 Apr. 1835.
[72] *Bristol Gazette*, 1 May 1828.

crowd and the moral lessons which the press drew from such events suggest that the precise timing was for reasons additional to the arrival of the mail.[73] The very nature of executions demanded a large audience. 'The publicity of our executions', wrote the *Bristol Job Nott* in 1833, 'operates as a warning to the spectators, and at the same time is an important safeguard of the life of the subject.'[74] Furthermore, the infrequency of executions, as *Felix Farley* once commented, contributed much to the size of the crowds they drew.[75] Although the processional part of the event ended on the transfer of executions from St Michael's Hill to the New Gaol Drop from 1821, the attendant crowds did not diminish.[76]

Taking Monday as essentially a non-work day, and adding it to crowd occurrences in the evenings, at lunch time, on Sundays and on holidays, it becomes clear that non-work hours were extremely important in the occurrence of mass phenomena (see figure 5). For the whole period, almost 70 per cent of crowds formed outside work hours. The tendency of certain types of crowd to occur in non-work time holds important implications for their composition. For instance, 76 per cent of all riotous crowds (including elections) occurred outside work hours. The benefits of darkness notwithstanding (54 per cent of all such crowds did take place in the evening), this does seem to represent still further evidence of the 'respectability' of riotous crowds. People who took part in riots, it would seem, were not the unemployed: they were working people who, generally, could not take part in such actions during the course of the working day. A striking example of this is presented by the Bristol Bridge riot of 1793: of the five rioting crowds which that event produced, all occurred outside working hours. Activity on the bridge subsided during the daytime, with the exception of the non-working days of Sunday and Monday; and despite hostility produced when the military opened fire on the crowd late on the Monday evening, it was not until the evening of Tuesday that a large group of people convened on the bridge and then went on to attack Corporation property.

---

[73] See Douglas Hay, 'Property, authority and the criminal law', in Douglas Hay, Peter Linebaugh, J.G. Rule, E.P. Thompson and Cal Winslow, *Albion's fatal tree: crime and society in eighteenth-century England* (Harmondsworth, 1977), pp. 17–64; Michel Foucault, *Discipline and punish: the birth of the prison*, trans. Alan Sheridan (Harmondsworth, 1979), ch. 2; Michael Ignatieff, *A just measure of pain: the penitentiary in the industrial revolution, 1750–1850* (London, 1978), pp. 21–4.

[74] *Bristol Job Nott*, LXXXI, 27 June 1833.

[75] *FFBJ*, 3 May 1828.   [76] *Bristol Gazette*, 19 Apr. 1821.

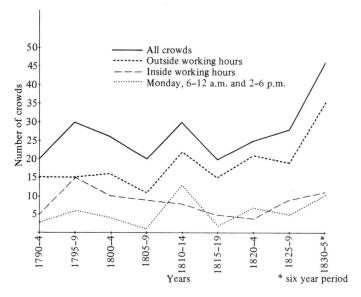

Figure 5   Number of crowds occurring inside and outside working hours, Bristol, 1790–1835

The sensitivity of reformers to the need to stage gatherings outside work time has already been mentioned; the pattern of timing of reform meetings suggests that such meetings addressed themselves primarily to the employed. The organisers of royal and military events may have had similar concerns: 65 per cent of such events took place outside working hours. These organisers tended to be individuals in positions of authority; they therefore operated under rather fewer constraints then those attempting to stage reform meetings. They could influence attendance through either intimidation or the declaration of a more or less official holiday. Nevertheless, most royal and military events did not take place on actual or *de facto* holidays, and a large number did 'fail' as crowd attracting events. The conundrum therefore remains: either organisers were forced to select times convenient for the employed, or it was only at those times that people were prepared to attend. In either instance, it seems likely that the principal crowd participants were the employed.

The trend amongst most crowd types was heavily in favour of occurrence outside work time. As table 6 shows, it was only funeral

Table 6. *Crowd occurrences inside and outside working hours,
Bristol, 1790–1835*

Crowd type	% inside work hours	% outside work hours
Executions	0.0	100.0
Election riots	8.4	91.6
Conservative meetings	12.5	87.5
Radical meetings	13.6	86.4
Recreational	27.1	72.9
Non-election riots	28.6	71.4
Miscellaneous	33.4	66.6
Royal and military	34.8	65.2
Election crowds	54.2	45.8
Funerals	71.4	28.6

processions and election crowds (but not election riots), that deviated
from such a trend.

That election crowds should occur during work time is not
altogether surprising: election time did possess a carnival element in
Bristol; there was keen interest even amongst those that could not
vote; work-based bribery and intimidation encouraged full participation; and there was workplace canvassing. Furthermore, trade
groups played an active part in electioneering. In short, election
crowds received semi-official sanction. The tendency of funeral
processions to attract crowds during work time can be less readily
explained. Such processions were the purchase of the wealthy,
influential and well known, and this may have caused employers to
regard attendance as no bad thing. If this was the case, however, it
might be expected that funerals would be staged at times more
convenient for working people to attend – particularly since such
processions did occur in the evening during the eighteenth century.[77]
It is possible that in this instance ruling attitudes had changed and
that funerals were no longer regarded as important or 'suitable'
crowd events.

For many crowds which did occur during working hours, details of
composition frequently explain timing. For example, colliers in
general stopped work in Bedminster to attend a reform meeting on a

[77] R.I. James, 'Bristol society in the eighteenth century', in C.M. MacInnes and W.F.
Whittard (eds.), *Bristol and its adjoining counties* (Bristol, 1955), p. 232.

Tuesday in 1831.[78] Striking shipwrights were able to carry out acts of intimidation against non-strikers on a Saturday in 1826 since, by definition, they were not at work.[79] Participants in food disturbances in Bristol markets were people who, through being present at the market, were already on the streets.[80] Some daytime street disturbances were described as being perpetrated by 'the rabble', a term reserved in Bristol specifically for the unemployed.[81] Durdham Down races on a Friday in 1821 were attended by the very rich and very poor: the voluntarily and involuntarily leisured classes.[82] As has been pointed out, cricket matches during weekdays were mainly attended by the wealthy.

In short, when crowds did occur during working hours they usually did so with more or less explicit sanction (as for Corporation-led processions), or because they were the acts of a specific social or occupational group acting in consort. Taking into account both those work time crowds which occurred with some degree of official sanction, and the inbuilt bias in data collection in favour of work time crowds, it would appear that on very few occasions indeed were working people in Bristol prepared, on their own initiative, to abandon their workplaces in order to take part in mass-orientated activity. Crowd events occurred within a formal framework of organisation, and within a structured, respected and constraining working week.

THE TIMING OF CROWD OCCURRENCES IN LIVERPOOL, NORWICH AND MANCHESTER

Examination of timing trends in crowd occurrences in the three other towns under discussion, although relying on small samples, confirms the impressions generated by the Bristol case. The inbuilt bias in data collection created by the presumption that crowds took place inside working hours unless there is clear indication to the contrary, may be more significant in the figures for Liverpool, Norwich and Manchester, since the information has been gathered from a smaller range of sources than for Bristol; there is therefore a greater reliance upon

[78] *FFBJ*, 15 Oct. 1831.   [79] SP/BRO, 30 Sept. 1826, info. of James Tuckfield.
[80] For example, *Bristol Gazette*, 28 Mar. 1821; Hilhouse Wilcox to Ryder, 13 Apr. 1812, LB/BRO.
[81] For example, Lewis to Gibbs, 17 Apr. 1796, LB/BRO; Serjeant's report book, 1832, St Augustine's Parish, BRO 08960/1a, 28 Feb. 1832.
[82] *Bristol Gazette*, 31 May 1821; *FFBJ*, 26 May 1821.

times being volunteered by newspaper reports. Nevertheless, in each of these towns a clear majority of crowds took place outside working hours: in Liverpool 63 per cent occurred on a Monday, Sunday, holiday, evening or lunch-time; in Norwich the figure is 58 per cent, and for Manchester 60 per cent.

The figures for Norwich and Liverpool are affected by the high proportion of election crowds in the sample. As in Bristol (and as discussed further in chapter 9), election week in these towns consisted of a great deal of semi-officially sanctioned public activity. In Liverpool half of all election crowds took place, strictly, inside working hours; the same was true for Norwich (see tables 7 and 8). If election crowds are removed from the equation, however, the proportion of crowds taking place outside work time becomes striking: in Liverpool 76 per cent of recorded non-election crowds occurred in non-work time; in Norwich it was 74 per cent. In Manchester, with only three election crowds (all occurring after 1832, of course), the figures are skewed by the occurrence of riots in work time. These, however, were predominantly associated with industrial dispute, and therefore involved specific occupational groupings.

Although it has to be emphasised that the data here is not as comprehensive as that for Bristol, some marked trends nonetheless emerge. In Liverpool, for instance, evening and mid-day crowd occurrences were particularly common, accounting for 42 per cent of all crowds. Significantly, the organisers of radical meetings and processions were reliant upon lunch-time and the evening for bringing together crowds: of the twenty-seven such gatherings recorded, sixteen occurred at mid-day and six after work; only three occurred in work time (see table 7). In Norwich and Manchester the evidence is similar. In the former case nine of the fifteen recorded radical gatherings took place at the middle or end of the day (see table 8). In Manchester, meanwhile, seven of the thirteen recorded radical crowds convened at lunch-time (see table 9). Evening-time in Manchester seems to have been a less important time for crowd occurrences: only three of the thirty-five recorded crowds took place at this time.

While again bearing in mind the limitations of the data, Manchester's distinctive profile as an unincorporated, unenfranchised, industrial town is reflected in its figures. Set dates and anniversaries for royal and military events or elections, which make for an important proportion of the crowd events in Liverpool and

Table 7. *Occurrence of selected crowds in Liverpool in relation to the working day, 1790–1835 (percentages in brackets)*

Crowd type	6–12 a.m. and 2–6 p.m.						All day Sun.	6 p.m.–6 a.m. Evening	12 a.m.–2 p.m. Mid-day	Holiday	De facto holiday	Total
	Mon.	Tues.	Wed.	Thur.	Fri.	Sat.						
Riot and disturbance	3	1	–	–	–	–	–	–	–	–	–	4 (3.3)
Election riots	–	1	–	1	–	–	–	–	–	–	–	2 (1.6)
Election crowds*	10	11	5	6	6	2	–	15	7	–	–	62 (50.4)
'Conservative' meetings and processions	1	2	1	–	–	1	–	–	3	–	1	9 (7.3)
'Radical' meetings and processions	1	–	2	–	1	–	–	6	16	–	1	27 (21.9)
Recreational	–	–	1	–	–	–	–	–	2	–	1	4 (3.3)
Royal and military	1	–	–	1	–	–	–	3	–	2	3	10 (8.1)
Industrial	–	1	2	–	–	–	–	–	–	–	1	3 (2.4)
Funerals	–	–	–	–	–	–	–	–	–	–	1	1 (0.8)
Miscellaneous	1	–	–	–	–	–	–	–	–	–	–	1 (0.8)
Total	17 (13.8)	16 (13.0)	11 (8.9)	8 (6.5)	7 (5.7)	3 (2.4)	– (–)	24 (19.5)	28 (22.8)	2 (1.6)	7 (5.7)	123 (100) (100)

Note: includes some large indoor crowds.
*Includes election crowds that developed into election riots.

Table 8. *Occurrence of selected crowds in Norwich in relation to the working day, 1790–1835 (percentages in brackets)*

Crowd type	6–12 a.m.						All day Sun.	6 p.m.–6 a.m. Evening	12 a.m.–2 p.m. Mid-day	Holiday	De facto holiday	Total
	Mon.	Tues.	Wed.	Thur.	Fri.	Sat.						
Riot and disturbance	1	–	–	–	1	–	–	4	–	–	–	6 (4.8)
Election riots	1	–	2	2	–	–	–	–	–	–	–	5 (4.0)
Election crowds*	15	8	10	9	7	4	–	11	18	–	–	82 (65.6)
'Conservative' meetings and processions	–	–	–	–	–	–	–	–	1	–	–	1 (0.8)
'Radical' meetings and processions	2	1	1	1	1	–	–	3	6	–	–	15 (12.0)
Royal and military	1	1	2	1	–	1	2	2	2	4	–	16 (12.8)
Total	20 (16)	10 (8)	15 (12)	13 (10.4)	9 (7.2)	5 (4)	2 (1.6)	20 (16)	27 (21.6)	4 (3.2)	–	125 (100) (100)

Note: includes some large indoor crowds.

*Includes election crowds that developed into election riots.

Table 9. Occurrence of selected crowds in Manchester in relation to the working day, 1790–1835 (percentages in brackets)

Crowd type	6–12 a.m. and 2–6 p.m.						All day Sun.	6 p.m.–6 a.m. Evening	12 a.m.–2 p.m. Mid-day	Holiday	De facto holiday	Total
	Mon.	Tues.	Wed.	Thur.	Fri.	Sat.						
Riot and disturbance*	1	1	1	1	1	2	–	2	1	–	–	10 (28.6)
Election riots	–	–	–	–	–	–	–	–	–	–	–	–
Election crowds	–	–	–	1	2	–	–	–	–	–	–	3 (8.6)
'Conservative' meetings and processions	–	–	–	–	–	–	–	–	–	–	–	–
'Radical' meetings and processions	3	–	1	1	–	–	·	–	7	–	1	13 (37.1)
Royal and military	1	–	–	1	–	–	–	1	–	1	2	6 (17.1)
Industrial	–	1	1	–	–	–	–	–	–	–	–	2 (5.7)
Recreational	1	–	–	–	–	–	–	–	–	–	–	1 (2.9)
Total	6 (17.1)	2 (5.7)	3 (8.6)	4 (11.4)	3 (8.6)	2 (5.7)		3 (8.6)	8 (22.9)	1 (2.9)	3 (8.6)	35 (100) (100)

*Includes industrial disturbances.

Norwich, were productive of far fewer crowds in Manchester. Less clearly institutionalised than Liverpool, Norwich or Bristol, Manchester generated crowds rather more around indigenous issues – notably industrial dispute and disturbance. A fuller examination of crowds in Manchester would undoubtedly confirm this impression.[83]

The workplace, and its discipline, encroached clearly upon non-industrial crowd events in Manchester, especially by the 1830s. Here is the conventional time-discipline picture in action: factory owners were intimately involved with the ability or otherwise of large numbers of people to attend public events. The *Manchester Guardian* characterised as 'idlers' those who, on a visit by Henry Hunt in April 1831, 'chose to lose half a day's work', and thereby half a day's pay, in order to attend.[84] When Benjamin Heywood, a reformer, won the Lancashire seat in the 1831 election, he arranged an evening-time visit to Manchester. Crowds, however, gathered from earlier in the day, because

A number of factory owners allowed their work people to cease working for the day, in order that they might be enabled to witness or join in the procession, which most people supposed would be a grand one, in consequence of a townsman being for the first time in the memory of the oldest inhabitants, elected a member for representing the country in the Common's house of parliament.[85]

An 'operatives' reform meeting' in Manchester in 1831 attracted only a few hundred during the late morning. The speakers arrived at 12.15 p.m., and it was at that point that the crowd increased to 1,500 or 1,600 people; it seems likely that this was intended as a lunch-time meeting, although that did not prevent the *Guardian* from terming the crowd members 'idlers of the lowest class'.[86] The restrictions of work time in Manchester are described more graphically by Archibald Prentice recalling the response to the news in May 1832 that the cabinet had resigned in the face of defeat over the Reform Bill. When the news arrived in Manchester on the morning of Thursday 10 May a group of 'merchants and manufacturers' called a meeting and drew up a petition. However,

The extemporaneous meeting on the Thursday had been held at an hour of the day when the working classes had not the opportunity of attending . . . It

83 See, Frank Munger, 'Contentious gatherings in Lancashire, England, 1750–1893', in Louise A. Tilly and Charles Tilly (eds.), *Class conflict and collective action* (London, 1981), pp. 73–109.   84 *Manchester Guardian*, 9 Apr. 1831.
85 *Manchester Times*, 14 May 1831.   86 *Manchester Guardian*, 18 June 1831.

was felt that a thoroughly public expression of opinion was the legitimate and safe course. A meeting was appointed to be held on the following Monday, on St. Peter's Field.[87]

The overall profile of Norwich, for its part, illustrates the importance of election activity for public gatherings in the city. The number of such crowds (even on an incomplete sample) considerably outnumbers the comparable figures for Bristol and Liverpool, with the occurrence in Norwich not only of city parliamentary but also county parliamentary and local elections clearly playing a part. It is appropriate, therefore, that contemporaries should refer to the advantages, for the bringing together of election crowds, of organising such gatherings on 'St. Monday', 'when our operatives are always disposed to holiday making',[88] or on Saturday – 'a day which generally fills the city with those who have either business to transact or pleasure to pursue there'.[89]

Liverpool, however, exhibits a spread of crowd occurrences more closely comparable to that of Bristol. Further research would probably show greater riotous and recreational crowd activity; but the general picture is of a town with clearly defined and institutionalised mass phenomena, usually (with the exception of elections) taking place outside work time. It is an organisational framework which makes typical the *Liverpool Mercury*'s complaint that 'we could have wished that a little more punctuality had been observed as to the time of ascent', when reporting a balloon display in August 1812 which had advertised the ascent as taking place at 1.00 p.m.[90] Egerton Smith, editor of the *Mercury*, reported his own speech to a meeting which had gathered on the news of the abandonment of the Bill of Pains and Penalties, during the Caroline affair. Smith proposed a procession in celebration, and suggested that 'on Friday, or some other early day, every man would either give himself a holiday, or ask one from his employer'. The crowd, however, shouted 'Monday, Monday'. And when Ottiwell Wood came onto the platform and said that 'It had been suggested to him, that Monday was the proper day for such an exhibition', he was greeted with cries of 'Yes'. His subsequent declaration that the celebrations would indeed take place on a Monday drew great applause.[91]

[87] Archibald Prentice, *Historical sketches and personal recollections of Manchester, intended to illustrate the progress of public opinion from 1792 to 1832* (London, 1851), pp. 410–11.   [88] *Norwich Mercury*, 31 July 1830.
[89] *Ibid.*, 24 Jan. 1835.   [90] *Liverpool Mercury*, 14 Aug. 1812.
[91] *Ibid.*, 17 Nov. 1820.

CONCLUSIONS

The conclusion that mass activity in early nineteenth-century England took place predominantly outside work hours may seem entirely unremarkable, at first glance. After all, a study of the timing of crowd occurrences in present-day England would reach precisely the same conclusion. This similarity, however, between the urban time-order of today and that of over 150 years ago could not immediately have been deduced from existing research. Rather, it might be expected that the similarity would date from post-1850, or perhaps later, or would be restricted to an early factory town such as Manchester.

This chapter has in part provided a static tabulation of crowd occurrences for one city in a particular period. It is the first such survey to collate information relating to crowds of all kinds, and not merely those relating to social movements. A number of patterns, of greater or lesser significance, have emerged from that process of tabulation: the decline in 'patriotic' gatherings over the course of the French wars; the development of outdoor political protest meetings; a surprising overall stability in the number of crowd occurrences between 1790 and 1835; and a striking trend in the seasonal distribution of crowds. On closer examination of the timing of the 245 Bristol crowds it becomes clear that, for example, there was a distinctive 'weekend', comprising a working Saturday, domestic Sunday and recreational Monday; the organisers of reform meetings were highly sensitive to the need to stage their meetings outside work time (using lunch-time in winter, and the evening in summer); parliamentary elections represented periods in which there were fewer constraints on the formation of crowds; the vast majority of riots took place outside working hours. As the specific details relating to time are considered more closely, the quantitative survey ceases to be static; it becomes possible to gain a glimpse of one important way in which Bristol society ordered itself. The significance of that glimpse lies in relation first to time-discipline, and second to public order.

Although the evidence presented here is by no means conclusive, it does appear that a well-understood and predictable time-discipline existed in early nineteenth-century Bristol; the timing of crowd occurrences was both the product and the reflection of this discipline. Factory employment in Bristol was, like many other provincial towns in these years, negligible. Indeed, the number of employees whose jobs were directly affected by the introduction of steam power was a matter of tens of hundreds rather than thousands. It might be expected, therefore, from the work of Landes and others, that the attitude to work time of the workforce, and perhaps some employers, would have been erratic and relaxed. It might have been possible as a consequence, to stage crowd gathering events at any time of day or week. There is nothing, however, in the timing trends which emerge from the crowd data to suggest that this was the case. Those trends instead confirm the impression gained from other Bristol evidence, and from the researches of M.A. Bienefeld, Monica Hodgson and Eric Hopkins, that the regular working week was a characteristic of the urban environment as much as of the factory of the mechanised workplace. A brief survey of crowd timing in Liverpool, Norwich and Manchester appears to confirm this view.

It is difficult to reconcile this picture of ordered time with prevailing notions of the 'disorder' of public life in early nineteenth-century England. In part, the confusion is sown by the absence of a detailed discussion of the ordering of urban life in general; but it also stems from historians' inadequate conceptualisation of 'the crowd'. 'The crowd' in pre-Victorian England has been taken to mean either a grouping of rioters and protestors, or the heterogeneous 'urban masses'. The acceptance of a broader notion of the crowd, however, in turn clarifies the perception of 'mass' in the early nineteenth century: it provides a distinction between 'the multitude' and 'a multitude'. The organisers of crowd events in Bristol were aware of the potential social grouping of the crowd they sought to draw. Contrary to some contemporary characterisations, and with the exception of some sporting activities, crowd events were rarely *designed* for those not in regular employment. Although unemployed and casually employed people almost certainly did attend crowd events, those events sought primarily to cater for those who worked a regular working day. The unemployed, for their part, rarely formed (what contempoaries would have regarded as) crowd events of their own. 'The crowd' was not, generally, the sight of large numbers of people on the streets; it was, rather, the assembly at a particular event. In attempting to understand 'public order' in pre-Victorian England, therefore, it is necessary to distinguish clearly between 'urban masses' and the organised formation of an urban mass.

The information on crowd timing offers still further evidence to counter any lingering notions of crowds as mysterious, vague and haphazard phenomena, composed of social misfits and occurring almost by chance. Furthermore, the formality of crowd occurrences, and their integral position within urban society, makes a mockery of the conceptual shorthand of crowd as riot. It seems probable that the clear-sighted members of E.P. Thompson's eighteenth-century riots were the disciplined workers in the pre-factory industry of an early nineteenth-century English provincial town. This chapter has not disproved the notion that the urban environment in England in the first years of the nineteenth century was dramatically more violent and less ordered than half a century later. But it is instructive, at the very least, to think of the workers who attended lunch-time political meetings; and to wonder if they first of all had to decide whether they could spare the time.

6. *Symbolism, ritual and the location of crowds*

There is a theatrical element in almost every large gathering of people, especially if those people happen to be chanting or carrying banners, or if they are listening to oratory projected at them from a platform. With such theatre, perhaps it is unsurprising that historians and social commentators have come to see crowds as events of high drama. Massive, disruptive, fiercely acute or wickedly capricious crowds, it is suggested, load their attention, their corporate cynicism or their mass ebullience onto a select object. That object, commentators would allow, might hold great symbolic significance: the crowd buffets the walls of Parliament during the Gordon riots of 1780, it plucks up the railings from Hyde Park in 1866 or, proverbially, it storms the Bastille.

In the apparently more ritualistic and sectarian urban environment of early modern Europe, the territoriality and symbolic weightiness of crowd locations appears to be a feature almost of everyday life. The various districts of Romans in the late sixteenth century represented both battle lines and foreign soil, to be fought for and captured;[1] youth groups in France attempted, through a sub-culture of ritual and misrule, to transpose the 'biological continuity of the village' onto urban neighbourhoods;[2] carnival in the early modern city 'may be seen as a huge play in which the main streets and squares became stages, the city became a theatre without walls and inhabitants, the actors and spectators, observing the scene from their balconies'.[3] The city-as-stage metaphor is also suggested by the ritualistic activity in English cities in this period.[4]

---

[1] Emmanuel le Roy Ladurie, *Carnival in Romans: a people's uprising at Romans 1579–80*, trans. Mary Feeney (Harmondsworth, 1981).

[2] Natalie Zemon Davis, 'The reasons for misrule: youth groups and charivaris in sixteenth-century France', *Past and Present*, no. 50 (Feb. 1971), pp. 41–75.

[3] Peter Burke, *Popular culture in early modern Europe* (London, 1978), p. 182.

[4] Charles Phythian-Adams, 'Ceremony and the citizen: the communal year at Coventry 1450–1550', in P. Clarke and P. Slack (eds.), *Crisis and order in English towns 1500–1700: essays in urban history* (London, 1972), pp. 57–85; Charles

For the nineteenth century, however, crowd events tend to be seen by the historians not so much as elements in a long (even continually) playing drama, but as isolated and melodramatic interventions in urban life. The location of crowds has been seen almost exclusively in terms either of riot action, or the supposed fear of urban hordes. It is generally accepted that riot may be aimed consciously at particular parts of a town. Little, however, is said about other crowd activity – apart, that is, from those historians who would maintain that in the turbulent environment of the early nineteenth century, crowds and gangs could assemble and roam with no rhyme or reason except their desire to be in the best position from which to gloat at whatever incident or event caught their fancy.[5]

Less controversially, it is agreed that from the second quarter of the nineteenth century English towns, and more especially their suburbs, were designed for privacy and exclusion. There were now to be places in which the individual could enjoy (considerable) personal space, away from the otherwise fearsome suffocation of urban life.[6] The design and policing of such areas attempted to ensure that mass intrusion or disturbance would not take place.

This received history of crowd activity sees a sharp discontinuity between the early modern city as an open stage for the enactment of civic mystery and dispute, and the city as a controlled set of enclosed spheres in which other than officially institutionalised mass activity was incomprehensible and alarming. Undoubtedly, striking changes in the organisation and location of mass events took place in the nineteenth century: the attempt to replace in more 'improving' form the miscellany of outdoor public spaces with halls and theatres and supervised parks has been well documented.[7] But just how sharp and neat was this supposed transition?

It is argued here that, just as the timing trends in crowd occurrence

Phythian-Adams, 'Milk and soot. The changing vocabulary of a popular ritual in Stuart and Hanoverian London', in Derek Fraser and Anthony Sutcliffe (eds.), *The pursuit of urban history* (London, 1983), pp. 83–104.

[5] For example, W.L. Burn, *The age of equipoise: a study of the mid-Victorian generation* (London, 1964), ch. 2; Donald Richter, *Riotous Victorians* (London, 1981).

[6] H.J. Dyos and D.A. Reeder, 'Slums and suburbs', in H.J. Dyos and Michael Wolff (eds.), *The Victorian city: images and realities*, 2 vols. (London, 1973), vol. 1, pp. 359–86; David Cannadine, *Lords and landlords: the aristocracy and the towns, 1774–1967* (Leicester, 1980).

[7] Hugh Cunningham, *Leisure in the industrial revolution* (London, 1980); H.E. Meller, *Leisure and the changing city, 1870–1914* (London, 1976).

suggest clear and well-understood patterns in urban life, the same is true of the location of crowds. Together, these patterns of time and place represent an important element in what might be termed the ordering of the urban environment. If the ritualistic dramas of the early modern period were less evident, they were replaced not by inchoate protest, but by more or less quietly theatrical crowd displays around elections, civic events, royal and military celebrations, political meetings and demonstrations. Those events located themselves in such a way within the urban environment as both to give and to gain from their surroundings an extra representational significance. The selection of a particular public square for a mass meeting was a strategic as well as a pragmatic decision; the intention of reformers to use a new, hitherto unpursued, processional route, could in itself induce panic among the upper classes because of the implications of a break in routine; established patterns of crowd occurrence made crowd events both more comprehensible and, as importantly, avoidable.

This chapter, therefore, analyses the spatial distribution of crowd events of all kinds in the four English towns under examination. As always, particular attention will be paid to Bristol, for which it is possible to draw reasonably firm conclusions from the comprehensive survey of crowd events between 1790 and 1835. These conclusions will then be applied in more general terms to Liverpool, Norwich and Manchester.

THE LOCATION OF CROWDS IN BRISTOL

Early nineteenth-century Bristol can be divided into four zones with regard to crowd events. The area from Queen Square to Broad Street, and slightly beyond the river Frome, formed the first. This was the commercial and administrative hub of the city, with public buildings such as the Guildhall, Mansion House and Council House; with the commercial buildings of the Exchange, Customs and Excise House, the market and the Merchants' Hall; and with the harbour-side. Residentially, this part of the town was mixed: the fine Georgian Queen Square standing adjacent to the overcrowded and poverty stricken Marsh Street. The second zone may be taken as that stretching up the hill from the docks towards Clifton, taking in College Green, Park Street, Brandon Hill and Tyndalls Park. Although the parts of this zone near the docks were poor and overcrowded, moving up Park Street it became increasingly affluent, predicting the grandeur of the third major area: Clifton. Clifton, a fashionable place to live, was carefully laid out in squares and crescents, and stood up on the hillside overlooking both the Avon gorge and the city centre. It was both physically and socially aloof. Its antithesis was the fourth zone, south of the old course of the Avon,[8] and comprising St Thomas, Temple and Redcliff parishes, and going beyond to Bedminster. Temple, St Thomas and Redcliff were populous, busy and poor. Bedminster was fast growing (with a population in 1821 of 7,979, and in 1831 of 13,124)[9] and also generally poor, 'comprising principally mechanics, shipwrights, and the families of seafaring people'.[10]

Each of these zones held a particular significance with regard to crowd events. The area of the city north of Broadmead, and east of St Peter's Street, however, experienced few documented crowd occurrences. Most of this part of town was poor, with the exception of the developing Kingsdown, which extended uphill from Maudlin Lane and King Street.

ZONE 1

The first area, stretching from Queen Square to the river Frome, was the centre for crowd activity throughout the period under discussion. The existence of Bristol Corporation buildings in Broad Street and Queen Square provided an immediate link between the two, with many formal processions passing through both districts. The annual Corporation procession on November the 5th (rarely a crowd event in itself)[11] went from the Council House, in Broad Street, to the Cathedral, and then to the Mansion House in Queen Square. Events such as the celebration of military victories during the French wars, in 1797 and 1799, the celebration of the Proclamation of Peace with France in 1801, 1802 and 1814, George III's golden jubilee in 1809 and the coronation processions of 1821 and 1831 are typical examples

---

[8] A harbour improvement scheme in 1804–9 altered the course of the Avon; see maps 1 and 2.

[9] James Johnson, *Transactions of the Corporation of the Poor* (Bristol, 1826), Appendix F; *Bristol Gazette*, 7 July 1831.

[10] *Report from the commissioners on municipal corporations in England and Wales*, 4, appendix part II, vol. XXIV, p. 1187.

[11] 1792 and 1807 are the documented exceptions: *FFBJ*, 10 Nov. 1792; *Bristol Mirror*, 7 Nov. 1807.

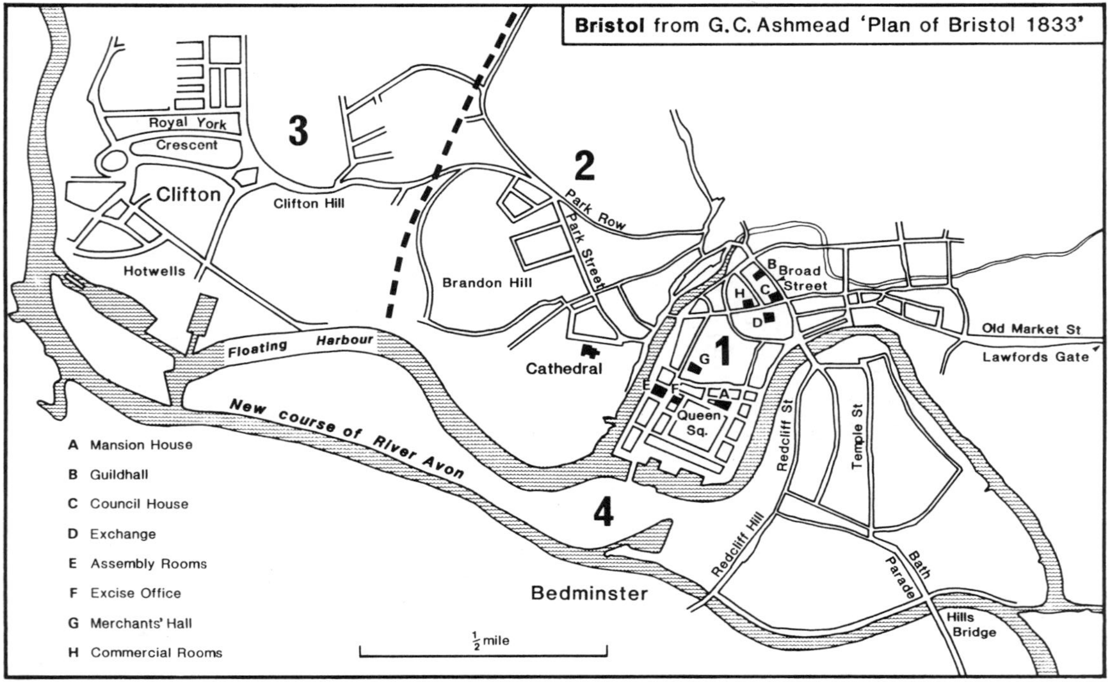

Bristol from G.C. Ashmead 'Plan of Bristol 1833'

Old Market St
Lawfords Gate
Bath Parade
Hills Bridge
Temple St
Redcliff St
Redcliff Hill
Broad Street
B
H C
D
A
G
Queen Sq.
1
Park Row
Park Street
2
Cathedral
Brandon Hill
4
Bedminster
½ mile
New course of River Avon
Floating Harbour
Clifton Hill
3
Royal York Crescent
Clifton
Hotwells

A Mansion House
B Guildhall
C Council House
D Exchange
E Assembly Rooms
F Excise Office
G Merchants' Hall
H Commercial Rooms

Map 1   Bristol

of crowd attracting formal processions which paraded through much of this zone.[12] Parliamentary elections centred on Broad Street, with the Guildhall being the location for the hustings, and the polling also, until Queen Square replaced it in 1830. The Broad Street area contained the party headquarters of the tories (the White Lion Inn) and the whigs (the Bush Inn). The chairing processions of victorious candidates frequently took in Queen Square, as in 1790, 1796, 1801, 1818, 1830 and 1831.[13] Broad Street and Queen Square were also connected by more contentious activity, such as election rioting against both the Council House and the Mansion House in 1796, assize riots in 1810 and celebrations of the liberation of an individual believed to have been unjustly convicted in 1827.[14]

That part of the zone around Broad Street, Clare Street, High Street, and Wine Street was the location for numerous crowd events since it was not only the city centre but also a cross-roads connecting the area south of Bristol Bridge with the northern part of the city, and the eastern streets with the Backs and Queen Square. Queen Square itself held a particular significance. Built in the early eighteenth century, with a character and design actively promoted by the Corporation, it represented an outpost of Clifton-like affluence located adjacent to some of the poorest parts of the city, and surrounded on three sides by water. Although it was the scene for election chairings, patriotic processions, attacks upon the Mansion House and a number of military displays during the French wars, it was not fully exploited by popular assemblies until 1831. A precedent was set in 1827 when Thomas Redding, convicted on a trifling excise charge, was, on his liberation, led as a hero through the town, and through the square. In 1830, election activity became centred on Queen Square, and the posting of thousands of placards transformed its appearance.[15] A reform meeting to choose parliamentary candidates, convened there in April 1831, confirmed the challenge to the square's hitherto exclusive image.[16]

Further reform meetings took place in June, and twice in October, 1831.[17] With the square acting as the focus for an election victory by

---

[12] Routes for these events are described in: *Bristol Mercury*, 23 Oct. 1797; *FFBJ*, 8 May 1802; *Bristol Mirror*, 2 July 1814; *FFBJ*, 28 Oct. 1809, 21 July 1821; *Bristol Mercury*, 13 Sept. 1831.

[13] For example, *BMBJ*, 26 June 1790; *Bristol Gazette*, 2 June 1796; *BMBJ*, 28 Nov. 1801; *Bristol Mirror*, 27 June 1818; *Bristol Gazette*, 29 July 1830, 5 May 1831.

[14] *Bristol Gazette*, 2 June 1796; *Bristol Mirror*, 21 Apr. 1810; James Acland's *Bristolian*, 11 July 1827.   [15] *Bristol Mercury*, 3 Aug. 1830.

[16] *Bristol Gazette*, 28 Apr. 1831; *Bristol Mirror*, 30 Apr. 1831.

[17] *Bristol Gazette*, 11 Aug. 1831, 13 Oct. 1831; *FFBJ*, 15 Oct. 1831.

2 Corn Street, Bristol, in 1829, at the junction with Broad Street and
High Street – the location of numerous crowd events.

reformers in the same year, it was as if its proprietorship was now open to question.[18] The so-called reform riots of 29–31 October 1831, in which all major public buildings and two sides of Queen Square were systematically plundered and destroyed, represented a climax to the sudden and vigorous challenge. Significantly, in immediately subsequent years Queen Square was not the scene for any popular gathering, with the exception of the election of 1832. The siting of poll booths amid the ruined houses may have contributed to the failure at that election of both the liberal candidates; certainly the tories, who now saw the ruined square as a symbol of reformism, gloried in the belief that Bristol had seemingly dissociated itself from such an evil.[19] Although in the course of the 1832 election a reform meeting was held in the square, it was otherwise shunned by the reformers. When a venue was sought for a dinner to celebrate the passing of the Reform Bill, Queen Square was discussed. The *Bristol Mercury* reported:

We are aware that, as a body, the reformers have been branded as the authors of the mischief which the ruins of the square bear witness to; but we would not, on that account, advise them to forego the use of it on the present occasion, if it should appear to be their interest to assemble there, and thus show how utterly they hold the calumny in contempt.[20]

Nevertheless, Queen Square had become too sensitive, and the meeting was eventually held on Brandon Hill.[21] The trades' reform procession of earlier in the year, although parading around most of the town, studiously avoided Queen Square.[22]

There were repeated negotiations of this kind between power and populace, between the Corporation and its opponents and between rival political parties over the symbolic control of the heart of the city. Residentially, the area represented a precarious merger of power and deprivation. Its principal buildings, meanwhile, held the ambivalent status common to all civic centres: they were monuments to commercial and Corporation exclusivity, and yet, as public buildings, they were the property of all the inhabitants. Given the restless neutrality of this part of the city, it was relatively simple for one contending group, by undertaking one well-directed and forceful action, to tip the balance of symbolic control in its favour. Since the means by which this might be accomplished were well understood,

[18] *Bristol Gazette*, 5 Aug. 1831, 12 May 1831.
[19] *FFBJ*, 15 Dec. 1832.   [20] *Bristol Mercury*, 30 June 1832.
[21] *Ibid.*, 18 Aug. 1832.   [22] *Ibid.*, 23 June 1832.

3 A contemporary depiction of the parliamentary election of December 1832 – the first crowd event to take place in Queen Square in the wake of the 1831 riot.

crowd activity and crowd targetting within the zone possessed a 'ritualistic' element.[23] For example, the popular response to conflict with the city's executive was, repeatedly, to stone Corporation property. Either the Council House or the Mansion House, or both, were attacked in this way in 1793, 1796, 1807, 1810, 1812 and 1831. Three of these occasions were parliamentary elections (1796, 1807 and 1812). The use of Corporation property for the election hustings and the conduct of the poll served to emphasise the thoroughgoing involvement of local government in the broader political process. As a result, the ritualism which surrounded elections (such as the processions of candidates to the Guildhall; the hustings; and the chairing of victorious candidates around the city centre) represented at once the sharing of 'establishment' amenities with the population as a whole, and the intrusion into a supposedly 'open' event of the power which lay behind those amenities.

It was not only Queen Square and Corporation property that were the location for regular and clearly understood acts of assertion. The headquarters of the political parties, situated around Broad Street, would expect, in the course of a contested election, to have to replace their windows after attack from the opposition.[24] The radical orator and politician, Henry Hunt, for his part, quickly made the area outside the Exchange his regular speaking place; the newspaper press, well understanding the point of such a gesture, soon began to refer to this as his 'favourite' and 'usual' venue.[25]

ZONE 2

The second zone was that of College Green, Park Street, Brandon Hill and Tyndalls Park (commonly referred to as simply 'the Park'). This area, with the Cathedral and Bishop's Palace, the prestigious Park Street, Great George Street and Berkeley Square, and, from 1823, the Philosophical Institution, was highly 'respectable'. It was not exclusive however: the road from Hotwells, and the areas around Limekiln Lane and Denmark Street, were densely populated and poor. The zone was made considerable use of during the French wars

---

[23] The term 'ritualistic' is used here in a loose sense. These were not ritual actions by the strict definition of the term, since it is unlikely that they possessed any existential element.

[24] For example: *FFBJ*, 19 June 1790; *Bristol Gazette*, 2 June 1796, 7 May 1807; *Bristol Mirror*, 4 July 1812, 20 June 1818, 10 June 1826; *Bristol Mercury*, 3 Aug. 1830.

[25] *Bristol Gazette*, 22 Oct. 1812, 14 May 1818.

for military displays, and for the firing of cannon from the heights of Brandon Hill and the Park. The Park abruptly ceased to be used for crowd events after 1799, although it is not clear why. Brandon Hill increasingly became the focus for attention although no contentious crowd gathered there until the election of 1807.[26] Its subsequent use by Henry Hunt, in 1816, by the whig candidate Colonel Baillie during the 1818 election and by radicals in 1819[27] was sufficient for the *Bristol Mirror* to comment, when a religious meeting was held there in 1820, that the Hill was 'famous' for political meetings.[28] This, together with the example of Hunt's use of the Exchange, illustrates well the speed with which a site could gain a reputation, and also indicates the importance attached to crowds and their locations by those who commented upon them.

The political use of Brandon Hill was, however, short lived, doubtless to the relief of 'respectable' inhabitants who had been made anxious by Henry Hunt's appearance there in 1816.[29] Significantly, no crowd event occurred on the Hill or on Park Street between the coronation celebrations of 1821 and a meeting of the Bristol Political Union (in self-imposed exile from Queen Square) in May 1832.[30] That interregnum, in conjunction with the events of the 1831 riots, also places in context the reform procession of June 1832. In an extraordinary symbolic assertion of power, 10,000 trade society members celebrated the passing of the Reform Bill by walking an 11 or 12 mile route from Lawford's Gate, down to Redcliffe Street and back up Temple Street, and then through the city centre to Park Street. At the top of Park Street they detoured to walk around Berkeley Square, before carrying on to Berkeley Place, down to Hotwells and back through town to Broadmead, and, finally, to Portland Square. With the notable exception of Queen Square, they had covered each significant area of the town. Their visit to the affluent Berkeley Square caused the inhabitants to board-up their

[26] *Bristol Mirror*, 9 May 1807; Henry Hunt, *Memoirs of Henry Hunt, written by himself*, 3 vols. (London, 1821), vol. 2, pp. 246–8.

[27] *Bristol Gazette*, 2 Jan. 1817; *Bristol Mercury*, 15 June 1818; *Bristol Gazette*, 6 Oct. 1819.   [28] *Bristol Mirror*, 19 Aug. 1820.

[29] *Bristol Gazette*, 2 Jan. 1817; mayor's minutes, 19 Dec. 1816, LMP/BRO Box 1816; resolutions of Castle Precincts, 21 Dec. 1816, LMP/BRO; 'A friend to good order' to Haythorne, 21 Dec. 1816, LMP/BRO Box 1816; resolutions of St Werburgh vestry, 23 Dec. 1816, LMP/BRO Box 1816; anon. to Haythorne, 23 Dec. 1816, LMP/BRO Box 1816.

[30] *FFBJ*, 21 July 1821; Serjeant's report book, St Augustine's Parish, 10 May 1832, BRO.

REFORM PROCESSION

THE COUNCIL of the BRISTOL GENERAL UNION, having a strong desire that the Pageant of MONDAY next should not be confined to any one Class of Individuals, respectfully solicit the attendance of EVERY ONE interested in the PASSING of the REFORM BILL: and it having been represented that many Citizens (*instead of Illuminating their Houses*) would prefer entering into a Subscription for the purpose of enabling the Working Classes to enjoy themselves at a Jubilee about to be held simultaneously throughout the Three Kingdoms, they beg to recommend that

No display of Lights should be made on the day of the Procession.

By Order of the Council,

WM. HERAPATH, President.

Cat and Wheel, June 13th, 1832.

Order of the Procession.

1. SONS OF REFORMERS, THREE ABREAST.
2. SHIPWRIGHTS.
3. CURRIERS.
4. UNITED GARDENERS.
5. TIN PLATE WORKERS.
6. BRUSH-MAKERS.
7. HATTERS.
8. GLASS-WORKERS.
9. COMB-MAKERS.
10. CARPENTERS.
11. POTTERS.
12. BRAZIERS.
13. SAWYERS.
14. WIRE-WORKERS.
15. BRICK-MAKERS.
16. FLOORCLOTH WORKERS.
17. CORK-CUTTERS.
18. PRINTERS.
19. SUGAR-BAKERS.
20. TAILORS.
21. ROPE-SPINNERS.
22. SMITHS.
23. CONFECTIONERS.
24. COACH-MAKERS.
25. BAKERS.
26. IRON-FOUNDERS.
27. ORNAMENTAL PAINTERS.
28. MASONS.
29. COAL-MINERS.
30. CABINET-MAKERS.
31. GLAZIERS, PLASTERERS, AND HOUSE-PAINTERS.
32. CORDWAINERS.
33. BRASS-FOUNDERS.
34. KITCHEN GARDENERS.
35. COOPERS.
36. TANNERS.
37. WHEELWRIGHTS.

TRADES NOT ENUMERATED.
TEN POUND HOUSEHOLDERS AND REFORMERS OF BRISTOL.
BATH UNION DEPUTATION.
MEMBERS OF BRISTOL GENERAL UNION, NOT IN THE TRADES.
COUNCIL OF THE BRISTOL GENERAL UNION.

ROUTE.

To meet at Trinity Church, LAWFORD's GATE, at TEN o'Clock in the Morning, then proceed through

Old Market - street; Castle - street; Bridge - street; Redcliff - street; Portwall-lane; Temple-street; High-street; Clare-street; Drawbridge; College-green; Park-street; Berkeley-square; Berkeley-Place; Jacob's Wells; Limekiln-lane; Unity-street; Denmark-street; Under the Bank; Nelson-street; Broadmead; King-street; North-street; Cumberland-street, and break up in Portland-square.

The Stewards of the Procession (Chairmen of the Trades) will be distinguished by a White Ribbon Badge; and Reformers generally, by Favours of Purple, Orange, and Pink, with Union Jacks, Medals, &c.

W. H. SOMERTON, Printer, Mercury Office, Narrow Wine-Street

4 A notice issued in June 1832 giving precise details of time, form and route of the procession to celebrate the passing of the 1832 Reform Act.

windows.[31] The single presence in the square of the much-loathed tory alderman Thomas Daniel was a permanent liability for the other residents: on the only other occasion on which a contentious crowd ventured to the top of Park Street, during the election of July 1812, it made an attack upon his house.[32]

ZONES 3 AND 4

The out-parish of Clifton, like the Park Street area, was effectively out-of-bounds for other than casual or recreational crowds. An attack upon the house of tory parliamentary candidate R.H. Davis in Clifton in 1812 consequently produced a particularly outraged response.[33] Ironically, Clifton, or more specifically the Downs surrounding it, was an area in which the very rich and very poor did both congregate, for sporting events, military displays on Durdham Down and holiday strolls. The years 1817 to 1827 saw a peak in such crowd gathering events. Boxing matches, cricket matches and horse-racing were frequent and well supported in these years.[34] They generally occurred during working hours, hence the polarised social origins of their attendants. The Downs brought together May Day and Easter holiday crowds, the participation of the young and the poor being described with benign condescension by the press.[35] It was not the case, then, that the bulk of the city population simply did not venture as far as Clifton and the Downs. Indeed, such spectacles as the so-called 'Flyingman's' two attempts to cross the Avon gorge attracted holiday crowds so large that the *Bristol Gazette* was drawn to observe that 'we never witnessed so large a share of the population collected together at one time'.[36] The absence of other than recreational crowds from this zone, therefore, appears to have been a specific policy in the organisation of such events. On the other hand, the coming together for recreational purposes of the socially disparate on the home territory of the wealthy and influential facilitated the ascription, by reporters, of a consensual meaning to these events.

---

[31] *Bristol Mercury*, 23 June 1832.   [32] *Bristol Mirror*, 4 July 1812.   [33] *Ibid.*

[34] Boxing matches: *Bristol Mercury*, 17 Mar. 1817; *Bristol Gazette*, 1 July 1822. Cricket matches: *Bristol Gazette*, 26 Aug. 1819, 1 May 1820, 14 Aug. 1824, 7 July 1825, 14 July 1825, 10 July 1827. Races: *Bristol Gazette*, 29 Mar. 1821; *FFBJ*, 25 May 1821; *Bristol Gazette*, 2 June 1823, 18 May 1826.

[35] For example, *Bristol Gazette*, 5 June 1823, 9 May 1822, 18 May 1826; *Bristol Liberal*, 9 Sept. 1831.   [36] *Bristol Gazette*, 25 May 1826, 8 June 1826.

The other principal crowd function for the Clifton and Park Street zones was as the entry point for visiting dignitaries. The Prince of Wales arrived by this route in 1807, as did Wellington in 1816 and the Duchess of Kent and Princess Victoria in 1830.[37] This contrasts strikingly with other, overtly political, entries, which were made through the fourth zone to be considered here. The road from London and Bath ran into the south-eastern part of the city, via Totterdown and Hills Bridge, and they continued to the city centre via Temple Street and Bristol Bridge. This route, through a densely populated working class area of town, was taken by all judges and non-resident parliamentary candidates, without exception. The process of entering the city possessed a ritualistic element: the fact that visitors were entering the city from outside was highlighted by the existence of an established entry point; and their popularity could be measured by the response they received from those on the roadside.

Moving south from Bristol Bridge, the suburbs seemed more and more remote and dangerous. Formal processions for official proclamations made a token journey across the bridge to Temple Street cross, at the end of Bath Street, and to the site of an old cross at the top of Thomas Street, but never beyond.[38] The long detour which the trades' reform procession took in 1832, over the bridge, down to Redcliff Hill, along the New Cut and back up Bath Parade and Temple Street, appears symbolically deliberate: the reformers were describing the physical and social extent of their constituency.[39]

The out-parish of Bedminster, a mining area, was commonly portrayed as disorderly and brutish. Some of the crowd events there were indeed wild. In 1825 a sortie was made by an anti-Catholic group against the homes of Irish people.[40] In a drawn-out incidence of intimidation, a black-leg shipwright was carried on a pole around Bristol, and south of the river to Bedminster.[41] The Bishop of Bath and Wells received a hostile reception there from reformers, in 1831.[42] The tory newspaper *Felix Farley's Bristol Journal* relished the description of a reform meeting on Bedminster Down in October

[37] *Ibid.*, 8 Oct. 1807; *FFBJ*, 3 Aug. 1816; *Bristol Gazette*, 28 Oct. 1830.
[38] Proclamation of Peace with France: *Bristol Gazette*, 6 May 1802; *Bristol Mirror*, 2 July 1814. Proclamation of accession of George IV: *FFBJ*, 5 Feb. 1820. Proclamation of accession of William IV: *Bristol Mercury*, 6 July 1830.
[39] *Bristol Mercury*, 23 June 1832.
[40] *Ibid.*, 11 July 1825; *Bristol Gazette*, 7 July 1825.
[41] SP/BRO Box 1825–7, 30 Sept. 1826.
[42] *FFBJ*, 29 Oct. 1831; *Bristol Gazette*, 26 Oct. 1831.

5 Hills Bridge: the entrance to Bristol from London, and the route by which prominent 'outsiders' entered the city.

1831, depicting the attendants as near imbeciles.[43] Bedminster, the cultural antithesis to Clifton, was, like Clifton, not made use of for organised non-casual crowd events. Crowds were found there only in exceptional instances, or as part of a barely reported autonomous sub-culture; the 'acceptable' nature of recreational events in Clifton, on the other hand, ensured that they were documented.

THE VISUAL IMAGE OF CROWDS

From the examination of crowd occurrences in these four zones it would seem that the location of crowds could be of great representational significance. Location influenced the context and presentation of crowds at a further level, however: through their visual image and organisational make-up. Spatial distribution was not only symbolic in itself but could influence a crowd's symbolic content. In general, those events attended, organised or greatly opposed by those in authority were subject to the greatest internal or external organisation. Their visual image reflected this involvement. For instance, as the popularity of the Bristol and Clifton races increased, the facilities offered to wealthy spectators improved; the staging of the races became visibly more elaborate.[44] This development served to emphasise both the fact that the races were staged in the territory of the wealthy, and the social demarcation within the event between the affluent and the indigent. When Henry Hunt addressed a meeting on Brandon Hill, in December 1816, on the other hand, it proved difficult (allegedly because of the intimidation of carpenters by employers) even to have a speaker's platform erected.[45] As the meeting was taking place, a thousand special constables and the military stood by in the adjacent streets.[46] The meeting was effectively marginalised before it even began. When radical meetings began to take place in Queen Square, they did so with minimum facilities. The speakers' platform was sometimes no more than the back of a wagon.[47] In this instance, the paucity of the facilities was juxtaposed against the grandeur of the square itself.

Most assemblies attended by the wealthy, with the exception of

[43] *FFBJ*, 15 Oct. 1831.
[44] See, 'Volume of miscellaneous sporting notices, 1822–1832', BRL.
[45] *Bristol Mirror*, 28 Dec. 1816.
[46] *Bristol Gazette*, 2 Jan. 1817; PMA/BRO vol. 1785–1820, 19 Dec. 1816; correspondence with Home Office regarding military preparations, in HO 41/2.
[47] For example, *Bristol Gazette*, 13 Oct. 1819.

6 A detail from Robert Greethead's sketch of the procession to celebrate the coronation of William IV, showing the Phoenix glassmakers and the various symbols and emblems of their trade.

some recreational events, took place indoors, thereby facilitating a high degree of comfort and organisation. Such amenities were officially denied to popular assemblies: the mayor could, and did, deny the use of the Guildhall to such gatherings.[48] Indeed, a Chartist meeting in the Guildhall in 1838 was claimed by its chairman to be 'the first meeting of the working classes ever to be held there'.[49] The very fact that a public meeting took place outdoors indicated the social group at which it was directed.

Celebratory processions (particularly those around the principal streets of the city centre) were a rather more direct declaration both of a crowd's social constituency and its symbolic control of space. The procession for a Corporation-sponsored celebration would include the military, in uniform, and Corporation officials, wearing their ceremonial robes.[50] Such a display, taking place within the civic centre, effectively identified and, at least momentarily, unified the personnel of power.[51] The supporters of a victorious parliamentary candidate, for their part, would include in their procession models and emblems of the city, and of its trade, commerce and industry; they would display colours, banners and mottos; and the presence of occupational and other societies would indicate the basis of the candidate's support.[52] The claim being made in this instance, of course, was the representation not so much of power as of Bristol. However, it was those political processions which enjoyed widespread popular support which exhibited the greatest symbolic content. Not only were banners, flags and slogans displayed, and ceremonial costumes worn, but most trades would carry emblems and symbols of their professions.[53] Furthermore, there might be the additional display of the symbols of poverty (such as the carrying of loaves on the ends of sticks), or of personalised hatred (sometimes expressed through the carrying and burning of effigies).[54]

The location in which the various devices of crowd occurrences

---

[48] Edward Long Fox, *Notice to the citizens of Bristol* (Bristol, 1793); printed poster, 20 Dec. 1816, in LMP/BRO Box 1816; *Bristol Mercury*, 11 Oct. 1819.

[49] John Cannon, *The chartists in Bristol* (Bristol, 1964), p. 2.

[50] W. Mathews, *Mathews's Bristol guide and directory, 1793–4* (Bristol, 1794), pp. 45–6; J. Mathews, *The Bristol guide* (Bristol, 1815), pp. 83–4; *ibid.*, 1829 edn, pp. 80–1; *FFBJ*, 21 July 1821; *Bristol Mercury*, 13 Sept. 1831.

[51] Abner Cohen, 'Political anthropology: the analysis of the symbolism of power relations', *Man*, new series, IV, 2 (1969), pp. 220–1.

[52] For example, *Bristol Mirror*, 24 Oct. 1812, 27 June 1818, 11 Mar. 1820.

[53] Most dramatically in 1831: *Bristol Gazette*, 12 May 1831; *FFBJ*, 7 May 1831.

[54] *Bristol Gazette*, 21 May 1812, 20 Dec. 1792, 7 Mar. 1793.

7 A detail from *The chairing of Henry Bright, March 10th 1820*, by Henry Smith, showing flags, emblems and banners, and large spectating crowds.

were deployed influenced the interpretation of those devices by non-participants. The 'right' of a successful parliamentary candidate to be paraded within the city centre was generally acknowledged and effectively institutionalised – whatever the political complexion of the party concerned. The authorities would police the event, but, nevertheless, it would rarely be regarded as posing any kind of threat to the city's social stability. Once the same ingredients of crowd display were carried into a different area, and a different context, however, their meaning was transformed. The emblems and banners of the trades which celebrated the passing of the Reform Bill became menacing, in the eyes of some of the wealthy, at the moment at which they were carried out of the city centre and into Berkeley Square and Clifton. The political tokens and colours of the tories became the insignia of xenophobic violence at the moment at which tory supporters moved off the main thoroughfares and into the back streets, for the purpose of attacking the Irish.[55]

THE LOCATION OF CROWDS IN LIVERPOOL, NORWICH AND MANCHESTER

LIVERPOOL

The themes of consistency and appropriation which characterised the spatial distribution of crowd events in Bristol similarly apply to Liverpool. They did so within the context of a city expanding rapidly, with a population of 82,000 in 1801, and 202,000 thirty years later. The river Mersey formed a boundary to the west, and Liverpool's expansion took place principally to the south-east. A striking characteristic of the city in these years was the residential mixing of rich and poor, partly caused by the reluctance of successful merchants and businessmen to move away from the city centre. During the first years of the nineteenth century, however, the new development of Toxteth Park, in the south of the city, was becoming notoriously poverty stricken and crowded.[56]

Crowd events in Liverpool fell into a very distinctive pattern. The Town Hall was the administrative focal point for the city. About half a mile south-east, however, and reflecting the direction of expansion

[55] *Ibid.*, 9 Apr. 1829.
[56] François Vigier, *Change and apathy: Liverpool and Manchester during the industrial revolution* (Cambridge, Mass., 1970).

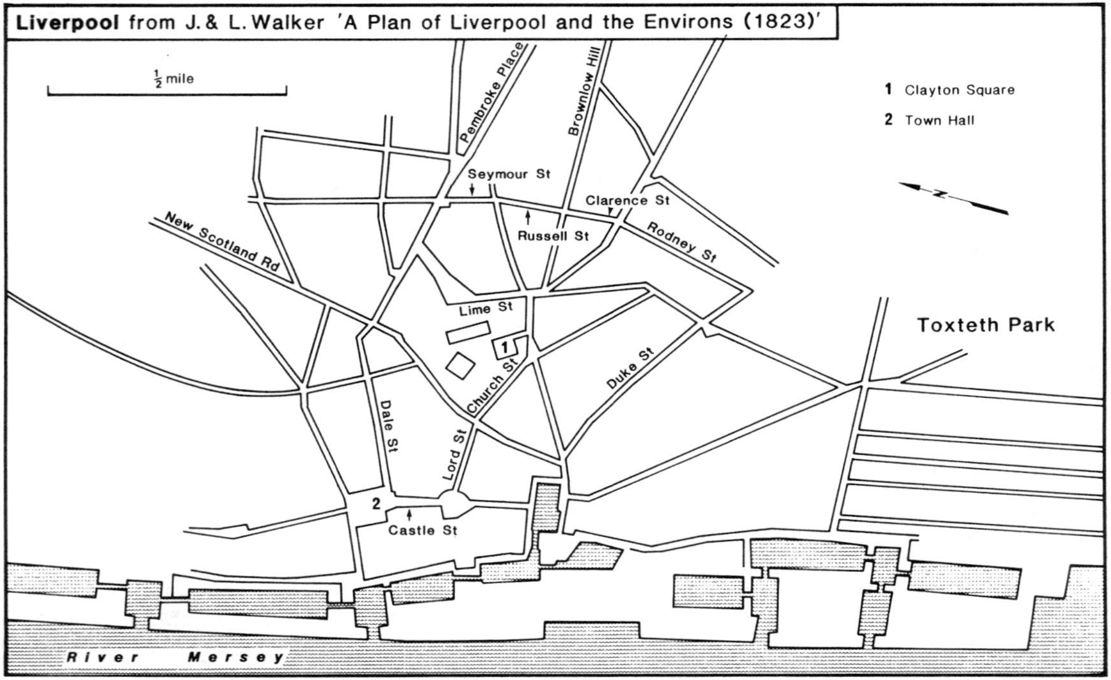

Map 2 Liverpool

of the city, Clayton Square was becoming an alternative focus. Clayton Square was developed in the later eighteenth century as a select and secluded residential area.[57] Processional crowds almost invariably 'connected' the new and old centres, and in so doing marked out a central boundary for the city, made up by the Town Hall, Dale Street, Lime Street, Duke Street, Lord Street and Castle Street. The easterly expansion of the city was acknowledged from about 1820 by major processions, which now extended the easterly boundary out to Seymour Street, Russell Street, Clarence Street and Rodney Street. These routes were so well trodden that they could safely be regarded by contemporaries as the crowd streets. Dale Street was vital in this regard, being officially recognised as the entrance to the city, and widened and improved in 1818 in line with this status.[58]

The central boundary contained a route directly connecting the Town Hall and Clayton Square, which ran along Lord Street and Church Street. This was the main passage at election time, and by 1831 could be referred to by the newspapers simply as 'the usual route'.[59] Election crowds rarely processed in from the outskirts,[60] and this confirmed the centralised nature of crowd occurrences. It may be significant that whereas in Bristol and Norwich, both of which were stagnating in this period, many inhabitants showed great interest in the symbolic significance of the city boundary, in fast growing Liverpool the emphasis was rather more upon stating and restating the outline of the core of the city.

The only two excursions beyond the inner boundary were under-taken by radical processions. The first was the celebration of the abandonment of the Bill of Pains and Penalties in 1820, when a crowd marched out to Mile End in the Scotland Road.[61] The second was the radical dominated celebration of the coronation of William IV in 1831, when the procession went out along Brownlow Hill and returned via Pembroke Place.[62] As in Bristol these deviations suggested a radical self-confidence which wanted to express as dramatically as possible its metaphorical and literal domination of the city streets.

[57] James Touzeau, *The rise and progress of Liverpool from 1551 to 1835*, 2 vols. (Liverpool, 1910), vol. 2, pp. 484–5.

[58] *Ibid.*, pp. 783–4.   [59] *Liverpool Mercury*, 28 Oct. 1831.

[60] For exceptions, see: *Liverpool Chronicle*, 6 May 1807; *Liverpool Mercury*, 9 Oct. 1812, 16 June 1826.   [61] *Liverpool Mercury*, 24 Nov. 1820.

[62] *Ibid.*, 9 Sept. 1831.

More dramatic, however, was the radical appropriation of Clayton Square. A reform meeting held there in February 1817 was the first of five such gatherings in the space of two and a half years.[63] By the early 1830s the residentially exclusive square was, for crowd gathering purposes, quite simply in the hands of the reformers. It was a powerful expression of the rise of the reform movement.

NORWICH

Crowd events in Norwich centred on the castle and market place. Although the administrative hub of the city, this area was set to the south of the main residential districts. Consequently, participants in crowd events would have travelled up to 2 miles to a no man's land of great crowd activity.

Norwich was a city dominated by elections. Its system of local government provided for ward and mayoral elections, and it was also the location for parliamentary elections not only for the city but also for the county of Norfolk. Candidates for both city and county elections frequently were non-resident; processions into the city, predominantly from the north and west, were a feature of the city's crowd activity. Such processions may have given local residents a sight of large crowds, but the destination for these processions was invariably the market place. Here, in this neutral zone, the contending parties were allocated their territories: the market place was physically divided in two by a chain. The respective groups of supporters, wearing their candidates' colours, threw abuse (or worse) across the dividing line. Sometimes they attempted to capture the opposition ground.[64] It is difficult to avoid comparison with football supporters of the present day.

Rather as in Liverpool, processional crowds of different kinds tended to share well-worn routes. Chairing processions at the end of elections took place within a tight area around the market place and castle. Effectively, crowd events in Norwich took place south of the river. Some non-election processions such as at the proclamation of George IV in 1820,[65] and the proclamation of William IV in 1830,[66]

[63] *Ibid.*, 9 Feb. 1817. For subsequent meetings see: *ibid.*, 4 July 1817, 3 Sept. 1819, 24 Sept. 1819, 3 Dec. 1819.
[64] For example, *Norfolk Chronicle*, 10 July 1802, 20 June 1818, 31 July 1830, 15 Dec. 1832.   [65] *Ibid.*, 5 Feb. 1820.
[66] *Norwich Mercury*, 3 July 1830; *Norfolk Chronicle*, 3 July 1830.

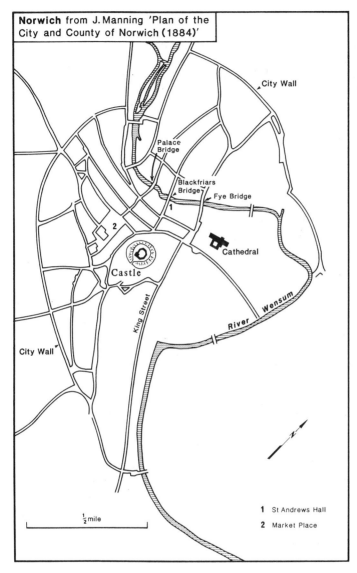

Norwich from J. Manning 'Plan of the City and County of Norwich (1884)'

City Wall

Palace Bridge

Blackfriars Bridge

Fye Bridge

1

2

Cathedral

Castle

River Wensum

King Street

City Wall

½ mile

1 St Andrews Hall

2 Market Place

Map 3   Norwich

ventured across the river at Fye bridge, but quickly crossed back and down to the market. Living north of the river in Norwich it was possible to give little thought to crowd events.

With major public meetings from 1819 taking place indoors in St Andrews Hall (also situated south of the river) the overwhelming majority of crowd occurrences were linked to elections, and centred on the entrances to the city and the market place. By 1835, and with the exception of occasional official or celebratory processions, large-scale, publicly visible crowd events in Norwich were predictable, semi-official, 'ritualised' incidents of political confrontation.

MANCHESTER

It is beyond the scope of this brief discussion to make a thorough examination of crowd occurrences in the rapidly growing town of Manchester. Two observations can nevertheless be made. First, major public meetings moved south, reflecting the pattern of growth of the town, from St Georges Road to St Peter's. This process had begun before the notorious Peterloo massacre (the trend seems to have taken place from 1816, with a reform meeting in October of that year, followed by the Blanketeers gathering at St Peter's Field in 1817, and an anti-Corn Law meeting there in January 1819);[67] but Peterloo, inevitably, made St Peter's particularly symbolically charged. Second, and perhaps indicative of the speed of change in the size and density of the town, official processions such as for the proclamation of George IV and the coronation of William IV were short, and tied to the acknowledged centre of Manchester: St Anne's Square.[68] Some processions did cut the city east to west (the coronation of George IV and the celebration of the passing of the Reform Bill),[69] or north to south (a reform procession in 1831).[70] But, unlike Liverpool, there was no regular restatement of an inner boundary.

The explanation lies in part in lack of opportunity. The absence of parliamentary elections and of a town corporation reduced the

[67] *Cowdroy's Manchester Gazette*, 2 Nov. 1816; *Manchester Mercury*, 11 March 1817; *Cowdroy's Manchester Gazette*, 23 Jan. 1819.
[68] *Cowdroy's Manchester Gazette*, 12 Feb. 1820; *Manchester Guardian*, 15 Oct. 1831.
[69] *Manchester Guardian*, 21 July 1821, 11 Aug. 1832.
[70] *Manchester Courier*, 5 Nov. 1831; *Manchester Guardian*, 5 Nov. 1831.

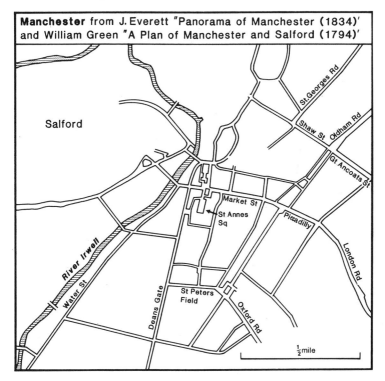

Map 4   Manchester

occasions on which such displays could take place. Large-scale
industrial dispute and riot, directed at specific workplace targets, was
as typical a crowd form as any. As Frank Munger has noted for
Lancashire in general, contentious gatherings were linked to the
demographic distribution of trades.[71] With the exception of St Peter's
Field, there was little opportunity for particular locations to gain
particular representational significance for crowd events. Furthermore, few locations were designed and built with symbolic aspirations against which crowd occurrences could be pitched.

---

[71] Frank Munger, 'Contentious gatherings in Lancashire, England, 1750–1893', in
Louise A. Tilly and Charles Tilly (eds.), *Class conflict and collective action*
(London, 1981), pp. 76–7, 81–2, 86–9.

CONCLUSIONS

This chapter has examined the representational significance of individual areas and particular buildings in the organisation and conduct of crowd occurrences in early nineteenth-century English towns. Some areas of towns were designed to have a particular symbolic impact. And in some instances patterns of crowd occurrence amplified designed symbolism. But equally, intended symbolism could be compromised: the appropriation of public space gave that space new meanings. The self-confident solidarity of Georgian squares became shaky when repeatedly occupied by shabby but sober political aspirants.[72] And repeated activity at crucial crowd venues could create a symbolic significance the architect would never have intended.

More generally, the formation of a crowd in a certain place indicated, for contemporaries, the possible composition and degree of menace of a gathering. Patterns in location invested crowd events, and crowd types, with an image. The existence of such images enabled non-participants to identify a possible and general meaning for crowd occurrences, and influenced their interpretation of the physical appearance of crowds. It was not necessarily the case, of course, that crowd participants would have shared the observer's conclusion.

Herein lies the paradox in crowd presentation. It was the observers and reporters, not the crowd members, who held the monopoly on the final presentation of the crowd. Crowds presented an image which came in part from the surroundings in which they placed themselves. As this chapter has demonstrated, there were clear patterns in crowd location which provided a common framework for the enactment of contention, and made possible and comprehensible the organisation of everyday activities. Those who commentated upon crowds well understood these patterns – clearly so, for it was they who were first to point to changes in crowd routine. Yet they also possessed the power to overlay other presentations: ones depicting crowds as fickle, capricious, haphazard. From the same sources, therefore, two histories can be read: crowds, through their locations, as comprehensible, patterned occurrences in the ordering of everyday life; and crowds, through partial reportage, as trivially subservient or

[72] Also see John Berger, 'The nature of mass demonstrations', *New Society*, no. 295 (23 May 1968), pp. 754–5.

wickedly perverse. Each, of course, emphasises crowds as things, as definable objects, rather than as collections of individuals. Ironically, however, it is the patterns generated by the susceptibility of crowds to being placed as a solid entity upon a map which, ultimately, create the evidence to counter the misrepresentations attempted by some observers.

7. Masses and masses: the language of crowd description

The mob could be dispersed: the masses were part of history.
(Asa Briggs, *Victorian cities* (Harmondsworth, 1963), p. 61)

INTRODUCTION: AMBIVALENCE AND CERTAINTY

The sheer numbers of people in nineteenth-century cities became a source for alarm among social observers. That alarm has been seen by Asa Briggs, among others, as a major explanatory component in Victorian attitudes towards the city.[1] The 'Great City' represented progress and wealth; it also represented the possibility of anarchy. Robert Storch comments: 'The vast crowds, which all domestic and foreign visitors to Manchester remarked, were deemed to possess a great potential for mischief and destruction, whatever the purpose they assembled for: a fair or wake, a Chartist demonstration, shopping or even going to and from work.'[2] At the beginning of the nineteenth century, however, civic pride in the growing town gave population increase primarily positive connotations. Bristolians longed for the population of their city to reach 100,000; in Liverpool

---

[1] Asa Briggs, *Victorian cities* (Harmondsworth, 1963), pp. 59–64; Asa Briggs, 'The human aggregate', in *The collected essays of Asa Briggs* (Brighton, 1985), vol. 1, pp. 55–83; Graeme Davison, 'The city as a natural system. Theories of urban society in early nineteenth-century Britain', in Derek Fraser and Anthony Sutcliffe (eds.), *The pursuit of urban history* (London, 1983), pp. 349–70; H.J. Dyos and D.A. Reeder, 'Slums and suburbs', in H.J. Dyos and Michael Wolff (eds.), *The Victorian city: images and realities*, 2 vols. (London, 1973), vol. 2, pp. 359–86; David Owen, *English philanthropy, 1660–1960* (London, 1965), pp. 109–13, 115, and ch. 5; Allan Silver, 'The demand for order in civil society: a review of some theories in the history of urban crime, police and riot', in David J. Bordua (ed.), *The police: six sociological essays* (New York, 1967), pp. 1–24; Gareth Stedman Jones, *Outcast London: a study in the relationship between the classes in Victorian society* (Oxford, 1971), intro. and part III; Raymond Williams, *Culture and society 1780–1850* (Harmondsworth, 1963), conclusion.

[2] Robert D. Storch, 'The problem of working-class leisure: some roots of middle-class moral reform in the industrial north: 1825–50', in P. Donajgrodzki (ed.), *Social Control in nineteenth-century Britain* (London, 1977), p. 140.

168

pride was taken that their town was second only to London in terms of size. It is in this atmosphere of delight at population growth that the emerging sense of trepidation regarding the potentially disruptive power of the 'urban masses' should be assessed.

In the first years of the nineteenth century, a sense of awe was at least as powerful as the sense of anxiety at the potential of the urban population. These were, after all, years in which the mass platform was being deliberately developed and supported by some middle class radicals, and when mass ebullition around monarchical and military celebrations was being consciously encouraged by many of those in power.[3] Here too, with the growth of urban facilities, was an opportunity for the staging of recreational events on a colossal scale: some of the largest gatherings in this period are to be found at balloon ascents and sporting occasions. Significantly, it was the specific disruptions of the Peterloo massacre and the Bristol 'reform' riots that did much to dampen the sense of wonderment and excitement, and began to encourage fear and loathing.

This chapter examines the combined sense of awe and anxiety, articulated through the language of description of crowd occurrences. It will first illustrate the expression of awe around, on the one hand, the possibilities crowds offered for the expression of social unity, and, on the other, their powerful political potential – as long, that is, as the views being expressed appeared to coincide with those of the observer. Three areas of anxiety will then be discussed: the negative implications of mass politicisation; the fear of mass disruption and disturbance; and the apparent possibilities for demoralisation inherent in the 'faceless crowd'.

Awe and anxiety, it will then be argued, while pulling in opposite directions, were confronted with the sociological reality that different crowd types were composed of the same individuals. This was a state of affairs which contemporaries found difficult to acknowledge or reconcile. The attempt to 'solve' this problem, and to express different perceptions of threatening and non-threatening crowds, is revealed in

---

[3] John Belchem, 'Republicanism, popular constitutionalism and the radical platform in early nineteenth-century England', *Social History*, VI, 1 (1981), pp. 1–32; John Belchem, 'Henry Hunt and the evolution of the mass platform', *English Historical Review*, XCIII (1978), pp. 739–73; Linda Colley, 'The apotheosis of George III: loyalty, royalty and the British nation, 1760–1820', *Past and Present*, no. 102 (Feb. 1984), pp. 94–123; Linda Colley, 'Whose nation? Class and national consciousness in Britain, 1750–1830', *Past and Present*, no. 113 (Nov. 1986), pp. 97–117.

the, sometimes very precise, application of the language of crowd descriptions. Most dramatically this could be seen in the use of the word 'mob' as the antithesis of 'crowd'. The effect, it will be concluded, was that, quite contrary to historians' conflation of the terms crowd and riot, for contemporaries a crowd was quite specifically a *non-riotous* (or at least non-threatening) grouping.

THE SENSE OF AWE

The susceptibility of crowds to description as one homogeneous entity gave the possibility for claims of passionate social unity and cohesion around crowd events. Civic and national celebrations provided the clearest opportunity. At the festivities in Norwich for the coronation of George IV, the *Norfolk Chronicle* described the presence of 'loyal John Bull and his numerous family'.[4] In reporting the celebration of George III's birthday in Bristol in June 1801, *Bonner and Middleton's Bristol Journal* claimed 'a sensation of joy was visible on every countenance' of the 'innumerable spectators'.[5] The *Liverpool Mercury* described the crowd gathered for the opening of Prince's Dock (part of the celebrations for George IV's coronations) as follows:

The operative mechanics and tradesmen of the town, united with Light Horse and several companies of a regular Regiment, backed by the mass of the male inhabitants of the town, from the highest to the lowest, and richly spangled with the gems of female beauty, all arranged in their best apparel, and in numbers exceeding the adult population of the town itself, perhaps 80,000 individuals . . . [They] formed a spectacle, calculated to arouse at once, feelings of pride and exultation and hope, in the inhabitants of a town that owes its prosperity and elevation to the daring of British seamen and the enterprise of British merchants.[6]

The possibility for mass mobilisation could be a source for delight. When a (false) report of a French landing at Fishguard reached Bristol in March 1797, 'Instead of fear or despondency, appearing in the streets, they were crowded by tens of thousands of people, all burning with the utmost zeal and impatience, to face the common enemy of their country and of mankind.'[7] The 'anxiety' which the *Liverpool Mercury* expressed, on the day of the laying of the

[4] *Norfolk Chronicle*, 21 July 1821.   [5] *BMBJ*, 6 June 1801.
[6] *Liverpool Mercury*, 20 July 1821.   [7] *Bristol Gazette*, 9 Mar. 1797.

foundation stone of the new custom house, regarding the anticipation of the 'expectant crowd' was only as to whether the arrangements would prove successful in the minds of 'all those who are fond of witnessing splendid processions and ceremonies'.[8] In fact the event passed off well enough for *Gore's General Advertiser* to report enthusiastically that 'the cheering multitude formed in "solid mass" around the immense area of the Dock – Nothing could exceed the imposing grandeur of the scene, on every side the prospect was exhilarating, but every eye was directed at the LAYING THE STONE.'[9]

The differentiation of classes that generally went along with large-scale crowd events offered a metaphor for supposed social consensus and hierarchy. *Felix Farley's Bristol Journal* described the arrival of the mail coach carrying the news of the ratification of peace with France, in October 1801:

Immediately followed the Mail-coach, a troop of the Queen's Bays, then a large number of gentlemen on horseback, and the rear of the procession was brought up by a multitude too great for us to form any estimate of its numbers. Besides the tens of thousands who were waiting in our streets to welcome the arrival of the Mail, the windows in every house near which it had to pass, were crowded with ladies, who, waving their handkerchieves, smilingly hailed the auspicious harbinger of peace.[10]

The masses offered numerical support to the more closely described celebrations of the wealthy. This is a familiar theme, and nowhere more so than in Norwich, where descriptions of the ubiquitous election processions frequently consisted of a list of names of the attending gentlemen, with the rear brought up by 'a numerous body of friends'. For the chairing procession, the following is a typical account: 'the procession entered our market-place, round which the members [of Parliament] were thrice carried, and from thence to the White Swan Inn, receiving as they passed the approving smiles and salutations of beauty and fashion from above, and the most gratifying manifestations of attachment and respect from the crowd below'.[11]

The vast turn-out for the funeral in Liverpool of William Huskisson, MP, who was killed by a train at the calamitous opening of the Liverpool and Manchester railway, just a few days earlier, facilitated the presumption that 'a universal feeling of regret . . .

---

[8] *Liverpool Mercury*, 15 Aug. 1828.   [9] *Gore's General Advertiser*, 14 Aug. 1828.
[10] *FFBJ*, 17 Oct. 1801.   [11] *Norfolk Chronicle*, 22 Nov. 1806.

pervaded all classes of the community'. The populace, it would appear, demonstrated the 'correct' response:

During the whole journey [of the funeral cortège] the assembled multitude observed a propriety of demeanour befitting the occasion, gazing upon a mournful cavalcade, as it passed by them, with feelings of the deepest interest and sorrowing sympathy; and it is a circumstance very credible to their sense of decorum, that amongst such a vast concourse of persons, which could not be computed at less than fifty thousand, not one incident should have been heard of.[12]

The ascription of corporate sentiments which the reporter believed a crowd *ought* to feel was to be found in Bristol also. For example, at the funeral of Richard Reynolds, well known for his charitable works: 'The poor . . . considered it a favour to be permitted in their turn to approach the grave of their departed Friend, and to drop the silent tear as a mark of their regard for a man whose life had been spent in DOING GOOD.'[13] Executions in Bristol also offered an opportunity to evoke appropriate deference and contrition on a crowd's behalf – as in 1805:

The procession did not reach the gallows till some time after one o'clock. There the prisoner was met by the Rev. the Ordinary and the Rev. Mr Hoare, both of whom shortly addressed the spectators; warning them to flee from the first temptations of vice, and above all to regard honesty in all their dealings – the fatal consequence of the contrary were at that moment before their eyes. They all knelt down, and joined in fervent prayer for a considerable time.[14]

The sense of a 'correct' response had its antithesis, of course, in an irritation at 'incorrect' responses, and also – revealing in terms of the positive desire for big crowds – disappointment at turn-outs deemed inadequate for some occasions. The press in Bristol expressed much anxiety that 'mischievous' individuals would celebrate the preliminaries of peace with France in 1801 with fireworks and practical jokes rather than in the 'proper' manner.[15] And, as will be described later, the occurrence of unauthorised or unofficial celebrations in all these towns could bring the application of the term 'mob' to a gathering that under official auspices would have been described as the loyal and cheerful populace. Executions, of course, were frequently open to 'incorrect' popular responses: 'In seven minutes

[12] *Liverpool Courier*, 29 Sept. 1830.   [13] *Bristol Gazette*, 19 Sept. 1816.
[14] *Ibid.*, 2 May 1805.   [15] *FFBJ*, *BMBJ*, 10 Oct. 1801.

after the culprit was turned off, a number of foolish women, with their children, ascended to the top of the lodge, for the purpose of having their disorders cured through touching the dead hands.'[16]

The expression of disappointment at the size of crowds is to be expected with regard to politicised crowd occurrences. But recreational events could also produce such complaints. Thus, although it seemed 'as if the country for twenty miles around, had been put into requisition' for a balloon ascent at Bristol in September 1810, disappointment was expressed that the number of spectators in the actual field 'from the convenience of view afforded by the adjourning hills and the openness of the ground, were less numerous than *we could have wished*' (emphasis added).[17] At a balloon ascent in Liverpool in 1824, the *Mercury* described the 'dense mass of individuals of all ranks', but then grumbled that 'the scene was not so interesting as that presented on a similar occasion'.[18]

Recreational crowds, with their mixture of social classes within large gatherings were viewed with amused and delighted approbation. The *Bristol Gazette* described the 'vast assemblage' of rich and poor at the Durdham Down races in 1823 at length. A heavy shower led many to abandon the event:

It would be almost impossible to describe the truly comic scene of the return of the cavalcade – the *dripping tails* of the female, and the adhesive *nankeens* of the male pedestrians, furnishing inexhaustible subjects of joke and gibe. Whilst the cavaliers *à cheval* came in for their share, as they thew up the dirty salutations from their horses heels. The whole procession would have been invaluable for the pencil of a Hogarth or a Rippengale.[19]

A description of May Day holiday scenes in 1822 concluded: 'The gaiety of the scene was never surpassed: here were to be seen the *well-breached swell* and the *downy coves* of Thomas market; Corinthian dames, and Marsh street *"must n't say whats"*; all assembled to see "Life in Bristol".'[20] The Bristol, Bath and Clifton races on Whit Monday, 1826, were attended by an estimated 30,000. The *Gazette* would not be distracted from its perceptions of overall unanimity.

the sport was good, the day fine, the company gay, and the whole scene most animating; of course, amidst so large a portion of the family of *John Bull*, some of its members were a little unruly, and here and there difference of

[16] *Bristol Gazette*, 19 Apr. 1821.   [17] *Ibid.*, 27 Sept. 1810.
[18] *Liverpool Mercury*, 28 May 1824.
[19] *Bristol Gazette*, 5 June 1823.   [20] *Ibid.*, 9 May 1822.

opinion was to be decided by the hardness of the knuckles, or length of the arm, but we neither saw or heard of anything which could call forth a censurable remark.[21]

However, it was the potential of large-scale public events to offer a powerful expression of political views which brought forth the most effusive rhetoric. For 'A friend to Mr Protheroe', the prospect of an election in Bristol in 1832 statutorily limited to two days, was immensely exciting: 'Eight thousand Electors awakened to the consciousness of their strength, and exercising their independent rights with dignified calmness and determination. It is *afterwards* that the burst of enthusiasm will be heard, and the shouts of "VICTORY TO THE PEOPLE" will be the reward of their virtuous exertions.'[22] The *Norwich Mercury*, reporting the celebrations of the passing of the Reform Bill in 1832, exclaimed 'who can look upon such combinations of the feeling and the strength of the people without a mingled sensation of admiration and awe!'.[23] More soberly, the same newspaper had commented a year earlier during a city election, 'there is in a mere multitudinous congregation of the people a sense of greatness which is particularly elevating or peculiarly solemn, according to the occasion'.[24] In 1835, the *Mercury* watched the popular reception of the reform candidate at the city election, and commented:

There is combined with these assemblages, in the vast masses moved by one feeling as it were, and excited to utmost bounds of enthusiasm, in the shouts and applauses, the music, the surrounding houses crowded with fair spectators who add their bright influences, in the variety of colour, and in *coup d'oeil* of thousands of eager countenances, in the intense and circling movements of the crowd, a degree of excitation which no other spectacle exhibits.[25]

The timing of these remarks may seem surprising: after Peterloo, and, with one exception, after the 1831 riots. The practice of holding large-scale outdoor meetings, and the symbolic power of popular gatherings, were regarded by some as vital political and social developments, despite the controversy that sometimes surrounded them. Dr Edward Kentish saw a Brandon hill election meeting in

[21] *Ibid.*, 18 May 1826.
[22] 'A friend to Mr Protheroe', *What has Mr. Protheroe done?* (Bristol, 1832?), p. 21.
[23] *Norwich Mercury*, 7 July 1832.   [24] *Ibid.*, 7 May 1831.
[25] *Ibid.*, 10 Jan. 1835.

June 1818 as evidence that 'we [Bristolians] are worthy descendants of our Saxon ancestors, from which we inherit our most liberal institutions'; after all, 'precedents of folkmotes, or meetings of the people, are to be found at a very early period of English history, and are as old as the constitution itself'.[26] Colonel Williams addressed a reform meeting in Liverpool in 1817, convened despite the mayor's rejection of a request that he should chair it, by saying,

Important as I think the presence of local authorities, on occasions like the present, it is of infinitely greater importance that, on the part of the people, their right should be asserted to meet to deliberate and to resolve, where and when, and as often as they please, without any hindrance, molestation or insulting precautions whatever on the part of such authorities. I am satisfied of the great advantage to be derived from frequent meetings of the people; it is proper that such a salutory practice should not fall into disuse.[27]

In 1831, referring to a reform meeting, the *Bristol Liberal* argued aggressively the merits of outdoor meetings:

The real and genuine friend of Reform – the honest politician – will be gratified in perusing an account of a meeting of THE PEOPLE, held in Queen Square, under its canopy of heaven – a meeting that, for the good sense and sound observations of its speakers, contrasts well with those assemblies held in fashionable halls and gilded rooms, where rancorous abuse and *dull* sophisms, are too often the substitutes of sound reasoning and a generous feeling of fellowship.[28]

The *Liverpool Mercury* was expressing similar sentiments when it commented on the outdoor hustings for the 1832 election: 'The proceedings were conducted in open hustings, for the first time in Liverpool within our recollection, and the proposers, seconders, and candidates spoke from a platform in front of the hustings, addressing themselves to the assembled multitude, and not to a chosen few from within, as heretofore.'[29]

These arguments were part of an awareness of the symbolic

---

[26] Edward Kentish, *A narrative of the facts relative to the Bristol election as connected with the meeting on Brandon-hill, June 13, 1818* (Bristol, 1818), pp. 16–18. The notion that there had been a Saxon 'golden age' of freedom, which had been destroyed by the Normans, was common in England from the seventeenth century. This is a late example of that notion's existence, however: Christopher Hill dates its final rejection from the 1820s. See, Christopher Hill, 'The Norman Yoke', in his *Puritanism and revolution: studies in interpretation of the English revolution of the seventeenth century* (London, 1958), pp. 50–122.

[27] *Liverpool Mercury*, 21 Feb. 1817.

[28] *Bristol Liberal*, 13 Aug. 1831.   [29] *Liverpool Mercury*, 14 Dec. 1832.

content of crowd events: the size, location and decorum of a gathering, some observers realised, could summon up a valuable emotional, as well as political, response. The *Norwich Mercury*, commenting in 1830 on rival election processions – the tories' well organised and numerous, the whigs' smaller but staffed with influential individuals – expressed a clear awareness of how powerful crowd presentation could be.

We have awarded the praise of excellent management and order to this *spectacle*, [the tory procession] and it is probably good generalship, for amongst so many, there are not a few who take their tone from outward semblances, and who . . . join . . . with the strongest. But anyone who examined the procession with the eye of experience and quiet observation could scarcely fail to perceive that its component parts had little of the elements of real power. There was youth, and zeal, and numbers, and noise; but the bones and sinews – the strength – the influences were not to be found. Yet we are bound to declare, that from time and circumstance, this procession, in the general eye, might perhaps, and probably was, in the language of the Theatre, far more *effective*.[30]

Allied to this awareness of presentation was a concern to measure the exact size of crowds. From this, inevitably, followed arguments about crowd sizes. *Felix Farley's Bristol Journal* and the *Bristol Mercury* entered into an acrimonious debate regarding the number of people who attended an anti-Catholic meeting in Queen Square in 1829. They swapped calculations not only of the city's population (and from this the adult male population as being the relevant portion), but even the precise amount of space that might have been occupied by each individual.[31] The same kind of calculations were made by *Cowdroy's Manchester Gazette*, to compute the attendance at a reform meeting in 1816.[32] In Liverpool arguments were resolved by estimates of the portion of Clayton Square that had been occupied.[33] The *Royal Magazine*, however, took on the more difficult task of trying to calculate the exact numbers taking part in the procession in Liverpool to proclaim the accession to the throne of George IV.[34]

[30] *Norwich Mercury*, 31 July 1830.
[31] *FFBJ*, 14 Feb. 1829, Feb. 1829; *Bristol Mercury*, 24 Feb. 1829.
[32] *Cowdroy's Manchester Gazette*, 2 Nov. 1816.
[33] *Liverpool Mercury*, 21 Feb. 1817.
[34] 'Proclaiming his Majesty King George the Fourth, at Liverpool', *Royal Magazine* (Liverpool), no. 1 (March 1820). See also, an article titled 'Rule for estimating the number at public gatherings', in *Liverpool Courier*, 9 Nov. 1831.

THE SENSE OF ANXIETY

It was always possible to find detractors from crowd events; and disturbance would usually be condemned and dismissed – from one quarter at least. There were, however, surprisingly few condemnations of crowds as general phenomena. This is the impression gained from the newspaper sources. But then, since newspapers generally attached themselves to a particular political cause, and since all causes had their associated crowds, they may have been unwilling to condemn crowd phenomena out of hand. It is significant that most of the evidence relating to general anxiety has emerged in relation to Bristol – the most thoroughly researched of the locations. Any conclusions that the sense of awe outweighed that of anxiety in these years may merely reflect the limitations of data collection, and therefore can only be made very tentatively.

Strikingly, and with the important exception of 'Peterloo', none of the documented non-election public meetings in these four towns in this period proceeded to disturbance. Nevertheless, some fears were expressed regarding the possibility of disorder. The *Bristol Mercury* noted, in reporting the anti-Catholic meeting of 1829 that 'when immense numbers congregate together, on any particular occasion, fears must always be entertained for the result; but in this instance the business of the day passed off without any incident happening'.[35] Days before Peterloo, *Cowdroy's Manchester Gazette*, although a pro-reform newspaper, complained about 'ranting' reformers, with their 'constant succession of meetings'.[36]

From the 1820s, some writers began to express their concern that mass meetings demonstrated an infectiousness, corporate fickleness and lack of sophistication commonly associated with 'the mob'. The *Bristol Mercury* said of a gathering brought together by Henry Hunt in Bristol in 1826,

No one perhaps possesses greater tact in managing a mob [than Hunt]; he mingles an indiscriminate abuse of the rich and the great with such an affectation of constitutional feeling and disinterested patriotism, that he never fails to carry the crowd along with him; they are led away by the enthusiasm of the moment. An indiscriminate assembly, like that which listened to Mr Hunt on Saturday night, acts on impulses; they have as little time as inclination for reflection; they listen to the professions of the orator,

---

[35] *Bristol Mercury*, 17 Feb. 1829.
[36] *Cowdroy's Manchester Gazette*, 7 Aug. 1819.

and they lose sight of his previous conduct – of each thing which has preceded, and which might enable them to appreciate the motives which influence him . . .; no efforts of human eloquence, if anyone possessed talents and nerve enough, and we might add rashness enough, to make the experiment, could have succeeded in convincing a mob under the immediate excitement of Mr Hunt's declamatory vituperation.[37]

Unsurprisingly, the 1831 riots in Bristol prompted further claims regarding the suggestibility of crowds. General Jackson, posted to Bristol in the wake of the riots, and having no long-standing acquaintance with mass phenomena in the city, felt able to assert that 'the composition of the population of Bristol is of a description very easily worked upon by mischievous persons, and the means of inflicting greater injury to property, are always at hand'.[38] The *Bristol Job Nott*, writing in 1832, explained that

A fortuitous multitude from the dregs of society without the guidance of intellect, without union or moral courage, is utterly contemptible. It is a power that may generally be crushed and dissipated almost as soon as it is put in motion. It is never formidable, unless when countenanced or joined by the operatives and more respectable classes, whom both duty and interest should urge to withdraw themselves form the beginning of tumult, to lend their assistance to suppress it.[39]

In an essay entitled 'The sign of the Times', in April 1834, the Bristol publication *A Conservative Reporter*, warned:

look at the fearful organisation, the perfect discipline, the military array, of the 150,000 Unionists, who met in London on Monday and say is it not a dangerous sign to see such a number of persons parading the streets openly in the face of day, every one of them being members of a secret, and illegal Association, and wanting but arms in their hands to constitute in an instant a rebellious army?[40]

A range of fears are being expressed in these various examples. In part there is alarm and disgust at the possibility of the residuum, the 'mobility', being treated as a political force. It is in this sense that the term 'mob' – as an abbreviation of 'mobility' – is being applied. In part also there is a fear which once more has a sense of awe at its

---

[37] *Bristol Mercury*, 26 June 1826. When, in the light of such an unflattering portrayal, the *Mercury*'s report went on to describe how the crowd expressed the 'correct' sentiments concerning Catholic emancipation, a few explanatory gymnastics were called for.   [38] Jackson to Hill, 15 Dec. 1831, HO 40/28(1).

[39] *Bristol Job Nott*, XLIX, 15 Nov. 1832.

[40] *A Conservative Reporter, or Mechanic's Friend*, 26 Apr. 1834.

centre: the prospects of a quasi-military mobilisation of the politi-cised masses. In both instances, however, the issue is one of mass politicisation, and the possibility that this could turn into mass disturbance. Destruction on a massive scale had already been evidenced by the Gordon riots of 1780, the Priestley riots in Birmingham in 1791 and the 1831 Bristol riots. Depending on one's political viewpoint, Peterloo in 1819 had also demonstrated the risks of large-scale gatherings. And onto this list need to be added reports from the French Revolutions of 1789 and 1830. The development of the provincial press, and the reporting of national news, played an important part in generalising what might otherwise have been local concerns.

Perhaps as important to everyday anxieties regarding crowds, however, was a threat of a very different magnitude; that of the seemingly incorrigible behaviour of street crowds – of the urban masses in general. In Bristol, these fears were voiced over a number of phenomena, including sporting events and fairs, and reached their most intensive pitch during the 1820s and 1830s. (This accords with Hugh Cunningham's chronology of middle class evangelical attacks upon popular culture.)[41] Attacks and insults by street crowds against the wealthy were a perennial but, it seemed at the time, growing problem. In the case of the 1818 election, 'Numerous respectable individuals of both sexes have been insulted, and had their persons and apparel injured, by the gangs of disorderly fellows there assembled, throwing stinking fish, dead cats, dogs, rats, and other offensive missiles.'[42] The journal *The Chronicle of Bristol* reported in August 1829 that

The shameful and wanton practice still continues, of destroying the silk dresses of ladies as they pass the streets: on the 2nd a lady had her dress spoiled by train oil in Old Market street; and on Saturday evening, the 25th, about 6 o'clock, some miscreants poured a mixture of oil and aqua fortis, on the dresses of two ladies in High street. A handsome reward should be offered for the discovery of the wretches, and the punishment should be exemplary.[43]

Connections were made in the minds of contemporaries between such acts of humiliation, and poverty, criminality and irreligion. There is a sense that it was essentially the same group of people, the

---

[41] Hugh Cunningham, *Leisure in the industrial revolution* (London, 1980), ch. 1.
[42] *Bristol Mirror*, 20 June 1818.
[43] *The Chronicle of Bristol*, I, 1 Aug. 1829, p. 18.

street poor (or those believed to be the street poor), that were deemed the culprits of a variety of social improprieties. 'A rate payer and neighbour' complained to chief constable Edmund Butcher about 'the number of Idle Vagabonds of Boys during the whole of Sunday playing pitch and Toss etc. etc. and using the most dreadful language in the Grove and Mr Tyndall's Park'.[44] The trading in cheap foodstuffs on Sunday was the basis for sabbatarian complaint;[45] and the fact that rioting in October 1831 occurred on Sunday, and that this was the day on which particularly dissolute scenes in Queen Square took place, was not lost on contemporaries.[46]

Disturbance, or popular celebration, was an opportunity to draw together all this moral disapprobation and fear. In 1822 the *Bristol Mirror* did so with particular clarity:

On Tuesday evening [November the 5th], a crowd of boys assembled on St James's parade, Kingsdown, and considerably annoyed the neighbouring inhabitants by throwing squibs etc. A most respectable City Magistrate, who interfered to prevent this disorderly conduct, was grossly insulted . . . It is earnestly to be wished, that the county Magistrates would devote some share of their attention to the assemblages of thieves and idle boys, who infest the outskirts of the city, particularly on Sundays. In the neighbourhood of Montpelier, the Sabbath has been for some time past constantly profaned by the disorderly conduct of such persons. There can be no doubt, but that many robberies are planned at these meetings, and many a novice is dishonestly instructed in the practice of the thieves.[47]

The one occasion on which disorderly celebration of Guy Fawkes was treated mildly by the press, and on which no pejorative terms such as 'mob' or 'gang' were applied, was when two brothels were gutted of their furniture for use in bonfires; the magistrates did not interfere.[48]

To the fears of mass politicisation and mass disturbance, therefore,

[44] Butcher MSS, 6 Apr. 1832, BRO 32955/60.
[45] Anon. to Struth, 25 Feb. 1819, LMP/BRO Box 1815; anon. to Struth, n.d. (1851?), LMP/BRO Box 1815; Address of Society for Promoting the Sabbath, to magistrates, 2 Sept. 1821, LMP/BRO Box 1821–2; *Bristol Job Nott*, VIII, 2 Feb. 1832.
[46] *Narrative of a conversation held with Christopher Davis and William Clarke* (Bristol, 1832), p. 28; *A voice from the city or the Englishman's true friend*, no. 8, 21 Jan. 1832, p. 1, in PP/BUL S-2(1); (Charles?) Kingsley, 'Letter to Lady Louise re Bristol riots of 1831, 7 Nov. 1831', BRL B28479 MS; *A voice to Bristol: the thirtieth and thirty first days of October, 1831* (2nd edn, Bristol, 1831), pp. 3–4.
[47] *Bristol Mirror*, 9 Nov. 1822.
[48] *FFBJ*, 10 Nov. 1792. The other Bristol newspapers all omitted to report the acts of destruction.

can be added a third element of anxiety: demoralisation. This concern centred around popular participation in recreational events. Boxing and horse-racing, both being gambling sports, always held an ambiguous status since they were supported by the rich as well as the poor.[49] It would be wrong, however, to associate evangelical attacks upon leisure in this period as being directed solely against the working class; the dissipated rich were equally a target. Not for the first time in English history, a peculiar alliance was thereby created between the landed wealthy and the propertyless poor.[50] Cruel sports in general could be depicted as the '*amusements* of a crowd of spectators, consisting of *gentlemen* of "the Fancy", horse-jockies, blacklegs, rogues, and vagabonds, thieves, and pickpockets'.[51] The races in particular represented a clear moral danger:

It is a well known fact, that Races are the resort of the Idle and the Dissipated – the scenes of riot and profligacy, and amongst the most powerful causes of the increase of Drunkenness, Prostitution, Theft, and other crimes!

Remember, that every individual, who by his presence adds to the Crowd, or Buys at the Booths, not only exposes himself to temptation, but does much to sanction and uphold the Races, and countenance its Vices![52]

It was fairs, increasingly given over to amusement rather than trade, that represented the quintessential 'dens of iniquity'. In Bristol it was St James' fair, in the latter part of the period which come under ferocious attack.[53] The sea of humanity which crowded into St James' churchyard (the site of the fair was ironic) could only drown the virtuous.

[49] *The Christian Guardian: a theological miscellany by a society of clergymen*, vol. IV (Bristol, 1803), pp. 108–9.

[50] Cunningham, *Leisure in the industrial revolution*, chs. 1 and 3; Storch, 'The problem of working-class leisure'; Brian Harrison, 'Religion and recreation in nineteenth-century England', *Past and Present*, no. 38 (Dec. 1967), pp. 98–125.

[51] *Bristol Job Nott*, LXXXXI, 27 June 1833.

[52] *Bristol, Bath, Gloucester, West of England and South Wales General Advertiser*, 23 Apr. 1831.

[53] The Corporation finally closed St James' fair in 1837. Bristol's other fair, at St Paul's in Temple parish, was closed in 1838. See N.F. Hulbert, 'A historical survey of the Somerset and Bristol fairs', MA dissertation, Univ. of Bristol (?), n.d., 1934 (?) (BRO 14258 (1)); F.G. Webb, 'St. Paul's fair', Univ. of Bristol Dept of Adult Education, Notes on Bristol History, 1953, pp. 15–23; Kathleen Barker, *Bristol at play: five centuries of live entertainment* (Bradford-on-Avon, 1976), chs. 2 and 3. For the history of English fairs in the nineteenth century, see: Hugh Cunningham, 'The metropolitan fairs: a case study in the social control of leisure', in Donajgrodzki (ed.), *Social control*, pp. 163–84; Douglas A. Reid, 'Interpreting the festival calendar: wakes and fairs as carnivals', in Robert D. Storch (ed.), *Popular culture and custom in nineteenth-century England* (London, 1982), pp. 125–53.

All persons who wish to discourage Vice and Profligacy are again requested to AVOID THE FAIR, and to prevent those under their influence from approaching scenes which stamp disgrace on our city, and allure multitudes to their present and eternal ruin. [Fairs] encourage persons to pursue their occupations amidst scenes of iniquity, where they attract that crowd by whom so many evils are produced.[54]

The 'Bush Houses' adjacent to the fair came in for frequent criticism as 'dens of howling riot, mad intoxication, horrible imprecations, furious discord, and brutal prostitution'.[55] 'Thousands' of people, especially the young, were attracted to the fair during the late evening, where they fell prey to 'needy adventurers' who proved 'how easily the multitude can be led by their curiosity, credulity, ignorance and folly'.[56] In one cautionary tale, William Jones joined the gullible 'crowds of men, women and children' at the fair, only to sink into drunkenness and theft; his girlfriend became a drunkard and prostitute, and met an early death. William's sister Jane succumbed also, became a destitute siphililitic and killed herself.[57]

In short, then, it was through notions of demoralisation that some people in Bristol came closest to regarding 'a mass' and 'the masses', or 'the crowd' and 'a crowded city', as one and the same problem. Nevertheless, it was through specific, identifiable, crowd events that most of the anxieties regarding the demoralising potential of crowds were discussed. Although the moral and physical condition of the poor might be a subject for concern for some observers, the question of sheer numbers of people, in these years, appears to be tied fairly firmly to, on the one hand, desirable population growth, and, on the other, the potential and size of organised crowd events.

THE MOB AND THE CROWD

The overlapping senses of awe and anxiety were directed at a wide range of crowd events, involving a large proportion of the urban

---

[54] Unsigned address in *Bristol Gazette*, 11 Sept. 1817.

[55] *An address to the inhabitants of Bristol, respecting the evils of the fairs* (Bristol, 1815), p. 4.

[56] Rev. G.C. Smith, *Bristol fair, but no preaching!* (Bristol, 1823), pp. 4, 8–14. For notions of moral contamination, see: Stedman Jones, *Outcast London*, ch. 16; Davison, 'The city as a natural system'; J.A. Banks, 'The contagion of numbers', in Dyos and Wolff (eds.), *The Victorian city: images and realities*, vol. 1, pp. 105–22.

[57] *The history of William Jones and his two sisters; with an account of their visits to the Bristol fairs* (Bristol, 1815). The other sister avoided temptation, of course, and lived a life of virtue.

population. It was not political meetings *per se* that caused either delight or disgust in the eye of the particular commentator, since the political *complexion* of the meeting was the determining factor in his or her appraisal. Recreational crowds could represent a charming intermingling of social classes, or the troublesome incorrigibility of dissipated social elements, depending on the nature, legality, timing and location of the event. Faced with such an array of crowd types and of practical and intuitive responses, how was approval or disapproval to be communicated? The answer lay in the evolution, part conscious, part unconscious, of a labelling system. Crowds could most effectively be stigmatised, eulogised or excised through the precise application of a certain word. Many words were at hand – multitude, rabble, assemblage, concourse, gathering, gang – but the most deliberately used was mob.

The unwritten rules for the description of election crowds offer the strictest example of the application of the term mob. In 199 documented election crowds in Bristol, Liverpool and Norwich over the forty-five year period, on *no* occasion, in newspaper reports, was an election crowd (as distinct from an election riot) termed a mob. (In the Bristol election of 1790 one newspaper did use the term 'the mobility'.) It was a code of language which had a useful and important role to play in an electoral system which enfranchised few yet put great store by the notion of representation, and which was resistant to the idea of true mass participation.

Elections in early nineteenth-century England belonged as much to the unenfranchised as to those with the vote. Popular involvement was a two way sham: the populace in general believed they were determining the outcome of the election, and the prospective parliamentary representatives could persuade themselves that they spoke for public opinion. Those present at the hustings were termed 'freemen', 'the electors', or so-and-so's 'friends'; that many did not in fact possess the vote is suggested by the fact that the show of hands at the hustings almost invariably produced the opposite result to that produced by the actual poll. The election crowd was reported fully; delight was expressed at the sheer numbers present; speeches were reported in full. This was the stylised format of election proceedings: elections have processions and hustings, they have banners, broadsides and bands. In short they have – must have – crowds.

But should those 'friends', 'electors' and 'freemen' riot, then immediately they are transformed: the plurality of terms applied to election crowds is replaced in favour of one, seemingly definitive, collective noun: the mob. The members of the mob were then the objects for charges of sedition, ignorance and mindlessness; of being the element which ruins elections; of being that which the authorities must show themselves capable of subduing. If the mob is reserved for such scenes of indisputable disorder, it can be depicted as that which destroys the ritual, disrupts the displays of political opinion, which shatters the consensual dream. The election mob, once perceived, is a means of distracting attention for itself. The possibility of disturbance inevitably increased during contested elections. A series of associations therefore became possible: uncontested elections meant no mobs, tranquility, and therefore free elections; contested elections meant mobs and disturbance, and an unfree election. So, in present-day parlance, greater democracy, since it arouses greater passions and induces the arrival of mobs, is a challenge to freedom.

More generally, 'the mob' could be applied wherever a gathering was unofficial or lacked approval. In the case of patriotic and ceremonial events, with their (deeply flawed) attempts to present social consensus, the term mob (and rabble) was virtually never applied. The exceptions were events in which crowd activity was independent of the authorities, or not part of the official programme of celebration. When, in Bristol in 1814, crowds of people took it upon themselves to celebrate the arrival of the mail coach which was supposed to carry news of the proclamation of Peace with France, they were described as a mob. The Proclamation had in fact arrived a day early, and officialdom was busy directing its attention towards the preparations for the Proclamation procession the following week.[58] Mob and rabble were terms used by the *Norfolk Chronicle* when the populace lit bonfires to celebrate the abandonment of the Bill of Pains and Penalties during the Caroline affair in 1820, contrary to the magistrates' orders.[59] Similarly, when the 1821 coronation celebrations in Manchester were hijacked and turned into a display of support for the queen, the offending crowds were described as 'the mob' and 'the swinish multitude'.[60]

The term mob was never applied to crowds at any of Bristol's many public executions: these after all were supposedly solemn occasions

---

[58] *FFBJ*, 25 June 1814.   [59] *Norfolk Chronicle*, 25 Nov. 1820.
[60] *Cowdroy's Manchester Gazette*, 21 July 1821.

for corporate contrition. In newspaper reports of the seventeen hangings between 1790 and 1835, the term 'multitude' was used for ten of the occasions.[61] Other words employed were 'spectators', 'crowd', 'populace', 'concourse' and 'assemblage'. This controlled language is in marked contrast to that used by David D. Cooper in his book *The lesson of the scaffold*: for him a crowd is a mob.[62] The only instance in which the entire crowd at a Bristol execution was abused by the press was when a correspondent for the *Mercury*, irritated by the apparent unconcern of the condemned M'Namara in 1790, sniped that, although the 'numerous spectators' had hitherto had the better luck to escape the same punishment', they 'cannot flatter themselves that their safety is in any degree, owing to their entertaining better principles'.[63]

At recreational events in Bristol the term mob was not usually used. There were two exceptions, however. If the sporting events were of dubious legality, then mob could be employed. The principal target was the staging of boxing matches in the city's vicinity. Thus, in 1802, when county magistrates prevented a contest, the spectators were termed 'the mob';[64] and when magistrates stopped a fight in January 1828, the *Gazette* was disparaging in its description of the would-be crowd members.[65] This was a crude adherence to officialdom's cause on the part of the newspapers, since Bristol's reputation for pugilism, particularly in competition with London,

[61] *Bristol Mercury*, 10 May 1790; *Bristol Gazette*, 15 July 1790; *Bristol Mercury*, 6 May 1793; *BMBJ*, 24 Apr. 1795; *Bristol Gazette*, 2 May 1799; *BMBJ*, 26 Apr. 1800, 2 May 1801; *Bristol Gazette*, 22 Apr. 1803, 8 May 1828; *Bristol Mercury*, 3 May 1831. Also see, *Trial, confession and execution of May Ann Burdock* (Bristol, 1835); 'Newspaper extracts relating to the trial and execution of John Horwood for the murder of Eliza Balsam', BRL B4584; *The life of Duncan M'Lachlin, written by himself, when under sentence of death in Newgate* (Bristol, 1801); *The life and confession of Benjamin Smith, who was executed at Bristol on Friday, April 24th, 1795 for forgery* (Bristol, 1795); 'Some account of John Horwood who was executed at Bristol, April 21st [1821] for the murder of Eliza Balsam at Hanham, Gloucestershire' (transcript of materials collected by surgeon Richard Smith, transcribed by George Pryce, Bristol, 1858) BRL B643 MS; 'Register of transactions in and near the city of Bristol, beginning at the year 1799 [–1810]', 26 Apr. 1805, BRL B10153 MS.

[62] David D. Cooper, *The lesson of the scaffold* (London, 1974).

[63] *Bristol Mercury*, 10 May 1790.

[64] *BMBJ*, 23 Jan. 1802. *BMBJ* approved of the magistrates' action, yet it sang the praises of boxing in immediately preceding editions: 19 Dec. 1801, 9 Jan. 1802.

[65] *Bristol Gazette*, 28 Jan. 1828.

was a piece of errant civic one-upmanship over which the press normally gloated.[66] The other exception was the use of 'the mobility', a term with fewer negative connotations than mob, but which sometimes was employed to express the antithesis of 'the gentility'.[67]

'The mob', along with other pejorative epithets such as 'gang', was principally reserved for instances of disturbance, however. Its association with riot, but its explicit distinction from 'the crowd', emphasises, yet again, the inadequacy of the synonymity of crowd and riot assumed by many historians. For contemporaries, it was not merely that only some crowds were riotous; 'crowd' was also employed specifically as a term to denote a *non-riotous* assembly. In the early nineteenth century, 'mob' was, furthermore, a term employed for *unacceptable* disturbance, rather than for all disturbance.

The obsession with tranquility during elections almost invariably cast election rioters as the mob, although (as will be argued more closely in chapter 9, below), the desire to present an election *as if* it had been tranquil, or the failure of the commentator adequately to separate rioters from election crowds in general, could prevent the term from being used. Violent assaults on press gangs, as in Bristol in 1803, were performed by 'the mob', probably because the gangs officially represented the crown, although local opinion will have held some sympathy with those resisting impressment.[68] Food disturbances could be the work of 'the mob';[69] but if there was sympathy with the rioters, the terms could be moderated to 'a few ill-disposed persons', or 'many of the poor', or just 'the populace'.[70] Disturbances amongst paupers over work rates at St Peter's Hospital in Bristol in 1832 were condemned; but it was only when non-paupers joined in the action during the evening that the term 'mob' was introduced.[71]

[66] *The Country Constitutional Guardian and Literary Magazine*, vol. I, 4 (Bristol, 1822), pp. 241–2; Rev. Samuel Seyer (the younger), 'Calendar of events in Bristol, 1820–1827', BRL B4529 MS, 11 Dec. 1821. And see, for example, *Bristol Gazette*, 7 June 1813 – a time when indoor boxing demonstrations were a common occurrence in the city.   [67] For example, *Bristol Gazette*, 24 Aug. 1824.

[68] *Ibid.*, 31 Mar. 1803, 12 May 1803.

[69] *Ibid.*, 11 June 1795; *BMBJ*, 6 June 1795; *FFBJ*, 11 Apr. 1795; Corporation notice, PO/BRO, 4 Apr. 1801; *FFBJ*, 11 Apr. 1801; *BMBJ*, 11 Apr. 1801, 18 Apr. 1801; Hilhouse to Ryder, 13 Apr. 1812, LB/BRO.

[70] *Bristol Gazette*, 11 May 1797, 25 Sept. 1800, 28 Mar. 1811.

[71] *FFBJ*, *Bristol Mirror*, 2 June 1832; Daniel Vickery, 'A Bristol calendar containing brief notices of such events as have taken place in that city and its neighbourhood July 1824 to the end of the year 1835', BRL B2639 MS, 31 May 1832.

As these examples suggest, on occasions where crowds, although riotous, did not appear to pose a major threat to the social order, or where some sympathy was held with them, they were not depicted as mobs. This was true with some food disturbances. It was also the case when hundreds of English and Irish workers began fighting after a mass dinner to celebrate the completion of the Bristol dock scheme. Since the violence was introverted, controlled and anyway directed at the Irish, the press reported it flippantly – despite arrests, injuries and the employment of press gangs to break up the battle.[72] The Bristol election of 1830 provides a particularly graphic example, since it also demonstrates the exact point at which acceptability breaks down. The *Mercury* reported how 'the people', 'conducting themselves in a peaceable manner', were listening to a speech by local radical James Acland. They were attacked, says the *Mercury*, by sixty to a hundred armed sailors and ship-carpenters; these are referred to as 'the mob'. The victims fled; but they soon returned, in greater numbers, and armed 'with a few sticks'. The sailors now dispersed – or, in the *Mercury*'s words, 'the cowardly ruffians' fled before 'the people'. 'The people', however, followed up their attack. Their physical assaults upon their initial assailants are now described by the *Mercury* as being carried out by 'the infuriated multitude'. The violence did not stop there, however. 'The multitude' smashed up the Rummer Tavern, and in so doing they now finally won themselves the label of 'the mob'.[73]

Of course, phrasing was governed by political outlook. 'Mob' was more likely to be used by a newspaper of one party against another than to be employed by all commentators. When the houses of Irish people were attacked in a protest against Catholic emancipation in 1829, the liberal *Bristol Mercury* condemned the work of the 'hired mob'; *Felix Farley's Bristol Journal*, a tory paper, preferred not to notice the disturbance.[74] When thousands of poor people invaded, and ruined, a reform dinner in 1832, the *Bristol Mercury* quickly termed them 'the mob' despite there being perhaps 15,000 of them. *Felix Farley's Bristol Journal*, on the other hand, could afford to avoid the term, and thereby avoid a differentiation between diners and invaders, since it would have preferred to have affixed the term to all reformers. It could not actually do so, of course, because the event

[72] *Bristol Mirror, FFBJ*, 13 May 1809; *Bristol Gazette*, 11 May 1809.
[73] *Bristol Mercury*, 27 June 1830.
[74] *Ibid.*, 7 Apr. 1829, 14 Apr. 1829; *FFBJ*, 10 Apr. 1829.

was not a riot. Consequently it referred to 'mobbing' as the characteristic of whig reform in general over the previous eighteen months. The official diners were called 'simple loons'; the unofficial ones, 'lookers on'; the totality, 'the multitude'. *Felix Farley* was attempting to suggest that there was no real difference between the two groups.[75]

The precise moment at which the term 'mob' is introduced can be highly revealing of contemporary attitudes. This will be seen in action in the more detailed crowd examples discussed in part 3. Nevertheless, a few examples are required here. For Bristol, the selective application of the term mob is seen most distinctly during the reform riots of 1831. In many accounts, the crowd 'became' a mob when it became active; the notion of what constituted active crowd action, however, was often reserved for fairly advanced stages of violence. In other words, for some commentators, the crowd was not threatening for so long as it whistled, threw stones or attacked constables; it was only threatening (and a mob) when it entered property. One witness was particularly precise in expressing the differentiation between the active and spectating crowd: 'There was no house lower down towards Prince's st. in flames . . . the mob extended below the Custom House (The witness explained afterwards, that he meant the crowd, and could not exactly say if the mob did extend below the Custom House).'[76]

During Bristol's other major riot of the period – on Bristol Bridge in 1793 – reporters sympathetic towards the protest against the re-imposition of bridge tolls appear to have been unwilling to apply the term mob. Indeed two newspapers, the *Bristol Gazette* and *Sarah Farley's Bristol Journal* at no point use the word. Even the magistrates' own account of the affair, issued by the town clerk, does not apply 'mob' until a section of the crowd set fire to the contents of the toll houses on the third evening of the disturbances.[77] During the Peterloo massacre in Manchester it was important for any reporter sympathetic towards the crowd to make it clear that they were the victims and not the perpetrators of the disturbance. This is seen clearly at work in *Cowdroy's Manchester Gazette* which at no point uses 'mob'. On the Monday following the massacre, however, crowds

[75] *Bristol Mercury, FFBJ*, 18 Aug. 1832.
[76] Evidence of Quarman, *Bristol riots. Trial of Charles Pinney, Esq., late mayor, for neglect of duty* (Bristol, 1832?), p. 55.
[77] *Bristol Gazette*, 3 Oct. 1793; *SFBJ*, 28 Sept. 1793, 5 Oct. 1793.

gathered in order to take reprisals and, once they had committed an assault, the word mob was used.[78]

In a leader article in the wake of the 1831 riots, *Felix Farley's Bristol Journal* exemplified the problematic application of 'mob', and demonstrated that these trends in the application of crowd terms were at least partly deliberate and conscious. First of all the article perceptively points out that,

At a Reform Meeting, the populace, consist of whom it may, are called 'the people'; but if riot ensues, the very same personages are then designated a mob. To swell the number and respectability of a Reform Meeting, every spectator is denominated a gentleman or a man of respectability; but when tumult arises, then are there always blackguards enough found to have been assembled, and they are called the mobility.[79]

As the extract implies, and as the article goes on to argue, the same people who attended the reform meetings were, in *Felix Farley's* opinion, responsible for the riots. If that was the case, and since *Felix Farley* termed those responsible for the riots 'the mob', then *a priori*, the newspaper would have been justified in calling the spectators at the reform meeting 'the mob' also. But no, it could not, no more (contrary to *Felix Farley's* argument) than could the newspaper which was the focus of the attack – the *Bristol Mercury*. It could not because the mob is almost invariably defined as active.

Felix Farley is well aware of this when, in the same leader article, it reports that Edward Protheroe Jnr, at a Queen Square meeting shortly before the riots, had said, 'Of the Bishops . . . he would speak in Mercy; their day was nearly gone by!!' At which, the article continues, 'the loud and continued cheers of the people (as we supposed we must on this day call them, no riot having ensued)' were such that Protheroe feared his words had been too inflammatory.[80] For all its sarcasm, *Felix Farley* had itself being obeying this linguistic convention over the previous forty years.

Felix Farley was attempting to expose the linguistic sleight of hand by which 'the mob' are separated from 'the crowd' and thereby made to appear as a permanent and distinct grouping which takes over an event. The *Bristol Job Nott* in considering the characteristics of 'the mob' not only introduces the notion of suggestibility and irrationality, but is at pains to portray the mob in this separate and permanent sense. 'Mob leaders', it argues

[78] *Cowdroy's Manchester Gazette*, 21 Aug. 1819.
[79] *FFBJ*, 12 Nov. 1831.   [80] *Ibid.*

flatter the *mob* as if it were the *people* at the people's expense; by a false argument, substituting the worst part of the population for the whole. The mob is a part of the people, as the chaff is part of the wheat.

The mob is an animal with many hands, but no brains. It displays collectively the worst passions of human nature, without wisdom, or mercy, or any of those qualities of which few, even of the most depraved individuals are wholly destitute.

A mob is unanimous, only while it is driven forward by a common and unresisted impulse. But when firmly opposed by a disciplined and well-directed force, it is broken and scattered like a rope of sand.[81]

CONCLUSION: CREATIVE ACCOUNTS

Whether tussling linguistically to separate the mob from the crowd, or whether pointing out, as *Felix Farley's Bristol Journal* finally did, that often spectators *become* rioters, the complexity of motive and action which informed attendance at crowd events of very different kinds was nevertheless beyond the explanatory interests or abilities of most contemporary observers.

There were good legal reasons to stress the distinction between active and passive crowd attenders – ones relating to conditions for the reading of the Riot Act, with all that that entailed. But the application of selective terminology went far beyond this, into the niceties of whether a boxing match was legal or illegal, whether a popular celebration was taking place at the 'right' time, in the 'right' manner, or whether a disturbance really mattered. The use of crowd terms in Bristol, Liverpool and Norwich, and, at least in some instances, in Manchester also, was remarkably deliberate and controlled. Mob, quite simply, was a term rarely applied: it stands out from reports, and its application says something specific about the reporter's perception of a gathering and its degree of menace.

Mobs were in observers' eyes irrational groupings. The use of the word therefore indicates the parameters of socially expected and acceptable mass activity. Comprehension breaks down (or is feigned to have broken down) only at the point at which 'mob' is introduced. A large number of large gatherings took place and were described in neutral language, or, sometimes, in the language of delight, awe and amazement. Terms of abuse were reserved and used selectively. This

[81] *Bristol Job Nott*, LIV, 20 Dec. 1832.

meant that the mob, ill-defined in itself, could become the scapegoat. The mob, by the simple use of the term, *was* the explanation; there was no need to look further or to attempt an explanation of the motives of people who would cheerfully celebrate a royal anniversary (and be termed 'the loyal populace'), but on another occasion attack property (and be termed 'the mob'). Rather, the mob could be summoned into existence at that moment when comprehension wanted to opt out – and it was no coincidence that it was the definite and not the indefinite article that prefixed the term: *the* mob, not *a* mob.

The well-understood vocabulary of crowd description also made it possible simply to dismiss or trivialise certain crowd events. Terms of abuse, when selectively applied, were all the more effective: 'a set of idlers', 'mischievous boys and women', a 'few simple loons' distracted attention from the true concerns of the crowd members.

The language of crowd description enabled observers effectively to use the same people for different ends. Those in power, and those who reported crowd events, wished to be able on occasion to claim thousands of the town's population for *their* cause, and, at another time, to be able to damn the masses for their incorrigibility, contrariness and autonomy. Language enabled them to square this circle, since it made possible the creation of groupings and sub-classifications, the separation of difficult subjects and the invention of scapegoats, all at the commentator's convenience. This labelling, and the management of this problem object – the crowd, loathed and adored – had, however, to operate in constant conflict with the object's own, essentially independent, and formidably coherent, self-definition. That coherence is to be seen in patterns of timing and location; it is also to be found when looking more closely at individual crowd events.

Part 3 *Cases, causes and contingencies*

8. *Introduction: corporate bodies*

Rise, famed Bristolia, from thine ashes rise,
And lift thy glittering turrets to the skies;
Long hast thou laid dishonoured in the dust,
The victim of fell discord and distrust.
('Bristol', by 'Poet Woodby', in *Bristol Job Nott*, XLVIII, 8 Nov. 1832)

Preceding chapters have sought to establish the patterns, procedures and routines generated by the regular formation of crowds. They have also examined the framework of reportage and power relations within which crowds occurred. It is necessary now to examine some particular crowd types and individual crowd events in greater detail: to analyse more specific aspects of the general contexts described so far.

Attention will be focused on crowd gatherings around parliamentary elections, political meetings, national celebrations and riot. In assessing the significance of each of these crowd types, the themes of timing, location and language will re-emerge. Uniting all of them, however, will be the relationship between populace and local government, and the negotiation of civic images through that relationship. It will be argued first that crowds forming for political meetings and elections occurred within distinctive local contexts, and these contexts gave those events an element of ritual. More significantly, the existence of a repertoire of activity and reportage made for the ready presentation, by local commentators, of crowd activity within a pre-determined descriptive framework. In short, actual events themselves were not the only determinants of whether an event was described in consensual or subversive terms. Such forces were also at work during national celebrations – the second crowd type to be examined here. These, however, could prove such dramatic locations for the enactment of civic contention that their apparently consensual messages were entirely lost. An external factor, such as

195

the monarchy, far from proving a unifying force, served only to point up pre-existing differences in local attitude and belief. And finally, the preoccupations which made celebratory events such complex crowd occasions could be found (in Bristol at least) occurring with equal force, but with different effects, during major disturbances. Consequently, major riots must be regarded as such multi-layered manifestations at the local level of national concerns that they cannot be crammed into the existing methodological straitjacket of 'pre-industrial' and 'industrial' collective activity.

At issue throughout these case studies is the presentation of civic image and identity within national contexts. Major crowd occurrences in Bristol and other provincial towns cannot be analysed as discrete local events. Nor can they be slotted into the kind of convenient demarcations to which historians inevitably resort: parochial versus national, conflictual versus consensual, orderly versus disorderly, pre-industrial versus industrial. The political and social culture of a town pervaded all large crowd events, and gave to them continuing feuds, reconciliations and reinvocations: a never ending story. It is important, however (particularly when dealing with a town such as Bristol which is commonly regarded by historians as the epitome of 'provincial'), not to view these all-pervading local contexts as amounting to an exclusive, idiosyncratic localism. Comparison and emulation (as it has already been argued) characterise provincial life in the early nineteenth century – at least for those who could afford such concerns. And a more general awareness of national politics and issues is what generated many of the occasions for crowd activity which, in sum, create identifiable and comparable patterns of crowd occurrence between different towns across the country.

There is a moral imperative behind many crowd events: a sense of what ought to be, of what a major town ought to be saying and doing, of how national events ought to be reflected at the local level. Conterminous with this was a sense of what ought not to be – of how a town should not be presented. This moral imperative has connections with, but is ultimately different from, the notion of the moral economy. The demand was not, in this instance, for an adherence to established practices; rather it was a demand to meet changing expectations. There is a dynamic element therefore in this sense of obligation: it is neither backward looking (in the sense of traditional rights), nor forward looking (in the sense of a model of how society might one day be), but rather reflects a view that a town should achieve certain goals in terms of status, image, size or wealth. This moralism was, perhaps, the inevitable manifestation of the prevailing political critique of the period: a critique of corruption and arbitrary authority, the abuse of power and position, the denial of rights and entitlements.

The claim to speak for the town's expectations was actively contested around major public events. This had two immediate effects: on the one hand it encouraged those who reported crowd events to present them in a certain light (notably one perceived to be favourable to the civic image); and on the other it led those without an official voice to make unequivocal statements of allegiance and belief. There were therefore contending presentations of the meaning of mass activity. The complexity of local contexts, however, makes it inadequate to describe such contentions within the terms of a straightforward conflictual class model.

For example: the obsession, on the part of Bristol's publicists, with civic image stemmed in part from a sense of the national image, and was part of a set of inter-civic rivalries within a national framework. Jonathan Barry has described how Bristol's eighteenth-century historians saw the industry and success of the city's inhabitants as paralleling similar advances for the nation.[1] Although at the turn of the century the emphasis was now on commercial failure rather than success, the concern being expressed was still about Bristol's position within the projected image of the nation. Bristol's glory enabled it to partake of England's glory; Bristol's decline detached it from the circle of privilege and prominence which surrounded national achievement. Crucially, however, the concern to locate the city centrally within the image of England promoted a sustained self-reflection which made Bristol appear remote from national developments. In short, a scampering to define Bristol's image induced insularity, and contributed to civic discord. As different groups contended the 'true' civic image and the optimum form of urban administration, the concentration was upon not national but local identity: the Bristolian.

Bristol's relative economic decline focused attention onto the Corporation. The recovery of civic status was therefore seen to be dependent upon a reform of local administration. However, there

---

[1] I am grateful to Jonathan Barry for sending me his unpublished paper, 'Civic life and urban values in eighteenth-century Bristol'.

was not a simple conflict between local government and populace. The personnel of prominence, while at times (such as in the 1820s) fiercely critical of the Corporation, retained a shared interest with the executive in staging 'consensual' public events, since these promoted a 'better' image. Thus, J.M. Gutch, the tory newspaper editor, was prominent and public in his attacks upon the Corporation, yet was the first to declare satisfaction at the occurrence of a non-contested and peaceful election; he was equally keen to proclaim that celebrations on patriotic occasions demonstrated the existence of a united, happy and loyal Bristol populace. John Mills, the whig newspaper editor, shared some of Gutch's 'consensual' rhetoric.

Many of the public, meanwhile, were determined to make it clear, on a number of occasions, that they were not lending their approval to officially staged events – despite the presence of their numbers. Consciously or otherwise, they made corporate expressions of their opposition to the civic pomposity of incompetent (even wicked) administrators, to political opponents and to those in the personnel of power seeking the presentation of consensus. Discrepancies in response were dramatically expressed around the celebration of royal events: the Corporation's enthusiasm for George IV's coronation contrasted with popular apathy; for the coronation of William IV the roles were reversed. These disagreements were connected to national issues: the Queen Caroline affair and widespread dislike of George IV in the first instance; reform and the initial popularity of William IV in the latter. But as contending groups struggled to lay claim to, or disassociate themselves from, these 'patriotic' events, the invalidity of any notion of civic consensus became so striking (and so consuming) as to eclipse any broader notion of national belief.

Such 'struggles' were overwhelmingly peaceful, however. Indeed, it would be quite wrong to see these events as 'contentious gatherings'. The framework for expression was a common one, unconsciously worked out, but tacitly acknowledged by all parties. Nevertheless, the contest over the presentation and administration of the city could and did take more violent forms. The Bristol 'reform' riot in 1831 was the most dramatic expression of this.

Bristol was never likely to gain much from the Reform Bill: it already returned two MPs, and it had one of the most enfranchised populations in the country. For Bristol the reform campaign was much more about municipal reform and the abuse of power. When the Bristol Political Union (formed in June 1831) spoke of the need 'to preserve and obtain every right which we do now possess, or may hereafter be entitled as citizens or subjects', it was speaking in the language of the national campaign – but it was also making a veiled reference to Bristol Corporation, the legitimacy of which was being questioned.[2]

Significantly, the riot was precipitated by the arrival in Bristol in October 1831 of the city's recorder, Sir Charles Wetherell, renowned for his declarations in the House of Commons that Bristol's population had no interest in reform. Once again, this had implications for the national reform campaign, but the more pressing issue was that Wetherell was *misrepresenting* the city – and this despite the fact that the reformers had just stormed to victory in the 1831 elections following huge public meetings in favour of reform. He was hated not only for misrepresenting local opinion, but for then 'coming down' to Bristol to preside as a judge. The slur had been made by an outsider; and Wetherell was forced to run the gauntlet as he entered the city along the well-established route from London.

This procedure for accepting outsiders into the city was an integral part of the parliamentary election also. Any candidate who did not establish himself as at least an honorary Bristolian was likely to find it difficult to gain support. Sir Frederick Eden, in 1802, and Sir Samuel Romilly, in 1812, both found this to be the case. At the hustings themselves, it was established procedure that candidates would express their delight at the opportunity to represent these, their fellow Bristolians and friends, and would assert their willingness to be accountable to them. Few of that audience would, in fact, have had the right to vote; but the sham satisfied both parties: the candidate could maintain a spurious sense of a popular constituency, and those in the crowd could bring some influence to bear upon proceedings from which they were officially excluded.

In summary, then, the importance of local identity, local responsibility and civic image pervaded major crowd events such as national celebrations, large-scale disturbances and parliamentary elections. Such events were, quintessentially, issues of corporate identity: the role and legitimacy of local government, together with long-standing memories and established procedures, were all tied up in mass presentations of image, belief and habit. This is not to say that all

---

[2] *Rules and orders of the Bristol General Union, established June 7, 1831* (Bristol, 1832); Graham Bush, *Bristol and its municipal government, 1820–1851* (Bristol, 1976), pp. 22–3.

major events were more or less overt confrontations – for two reasons. First, the development of established procedures, creating a framework for crowd activity and facilitating quasi-ritualistic (as well as explicit) differences of opinion, were made possible by a common and general acceptance of the importance of mass events. All social groupings benefited from, and shared in, crowd activity of one sort or another. And second, the overlapping of contexts makes it almost impossible to apply straightforward concepts of conflict or consensus. Although the coronations of 1821 and 1831 could be described as instances of covert aggression, boisterous election crowds (and even some disturbances) could paradoxically be presented as cohesive affairs with commonly understood, nonsubverting, terms of engagement. Ultimately, although the language of confrontation or cohesion provides a useful shorthand, events are better explained in terms of a notion of corporate identity.

Bristolians may have occupied a corporate universe to a unique extent. But a concern for local image and identity can be found in Liverpool, Norwich and Manchester also. In Manchester, as always, the model is less easily constructed, with a less well-defined system of local government, a rapidly growing and changing city, and a close involvement with the hinterland. This, however, did not prevent the existence of a sense of what, for the town, 'ought' to be – the moral imperative which underpins so much of the crowd activity in this period is to be found in Manchester also.

The concern for corporate identity was expressed most coherently, of course, by a town's self-appointed publicists: the newspaper editors, guidebook writers, local politicians, pamphleteers, and so on. It was a concern mobilised around particular and prominent events – such as those discussed here. It is unlikely to have consumed ordinary people to the same extent. The manuscript autobiography of John Bennett, who came to Bristol from Somerset in 1804 seeking employment as a carpenter, is a reminder of the more pragmatic and prosaic concerns of contemporary life.[3] Bennett's concerns were with finding work and getting paid, with love and marriage, with discord in his local church, and with teaching himself to read and write. In the course of his reminiscences, spanning the first half of the nineteenth century, he feels little need to recall national issues or sentiments. Yet the perennial unpopularity of the Corporation, the misery of the

---

[3] 'Manuscript autobiography of John Bennett, Portishead, 1853', BRO 36097 (a–b).

French war and the tiresomeness of official attempts to enforce public patriotism through compulsory membership of the wartime 'volunteer' forces are all clear enough. So too is the fact that Bennett, as an outsider who had 'come up' from Somerset, found it difficult to be accepted. Perpetually aware that Bristol's distinctive identity made it clearly separable even from its suburbs, Bennett, despite spending most of his lifetime in and around the city, never came to regard himself as a Bristolian.

9. Meetings and elections

> . . . popular electioneering demonstrations may be considered an
> attenuated form of rebellion.
> (Elie Halevy, *A history of the English people in the nineteenth century*, vol.
> 1: *England in 1815* (1913; this edn New York, 1949), p. 152)

From 1812, and particularly from 1819, large-scale public political
meetings became reasonably common occurrences in English towns.
Many of these meetings were directly linked to the campaign for
parliamentary reform. Crowds related to parliamentary elections
were a long-established occurrence, and part of the civic scene:
'septennial saturnalia', as the *Liverpool Courier* termed them.[1]

Election crowds contained a strong carnival element. Their
ritualised format (which facilitated maximum popular participation),
their domination of civic life and the treating and bribery carried out
by the political parties made for several days of dissipation and
disruption. As the examination of patterns and procedures demonstrated, however, election time was not simply officially sanctioned mayhem. Indeed, the comparison with carnival is made
stronger by emphasising that disportment and display took place
within well-understood rules of organisation and description.[2] The
pretence of popular representation in the electoral process required
that, in effect, a mock election took place hand in hand with the real
one. Elections emphasised both the exclusivity of political power and
its dependence upon popular participation and good humour as a
source of legitimation.[3]

At the point at which popular participation became a real and

[1] *Liverpool Courier*, 4 May 1831.
[2] See, for example, Peter Burke, *Popular culture in early modern Europe* (London,
1978), ch. 7.
[3] John Brewer, 'Theatre and counter-theatre in Georgian politics: the mock elections
at Garat', *Radical History Review*, no. 22 (1979–80), pp. 7–40.

8 A detail from *The chairing of Henry Bright, March 10th 1820*, by Henry Smith, showing the head of the procession, in quasi-military order.

PROGRAMME
OF THE
PROCESSION,
FOR
Chairing
MESSRS.
BAILLIE & PROTHEROE.
MAY 4, 1831.

TRUMPETS and BUGLES.
Royal Standard.
Shipwrights, with Emblems.
Banners: 2 Baillie's—2 Protheroe's.
BAND OF MUSIC.
Bookbinders.
Two Banners.
Tailors, with 2 Banners of Merchant Tailors' Company.
Brush-Makers.
Two Banners: 1 Baillie's—1 Protheroe's.
Carpenters, with Emblems.
Four Banners: 2 Baillie's—2 Protheroe's.
Ten Signal Colours of all Nations.
Cork-Cutters.
Banner: Baillie's.
Hatters.
Banner: Protheroe's.
Rope-Makers.
Four Banners: 2 Baillie's—2 Protheroe's.
Coopers, with Emblems.
Coopers' Flags.
Five Flags of all Nations.
Smiths, with Emblems.
Banners: Baillie's and Protheroe's.
Ten Laurel-Poles, embellished.
Tin-Plate Workers.
Two Banners.
Sawyers.
Plumbers.
Five National Flags.
Masons.
Four Banners: 2 Baillie's—2 Protheroe's.
Printers, with a *Working Press.*
Floor Cloth Workers, their Flag, and Two Banners.
Cordwainers.
Ten National Flags.
Laurel-Poles.
Potters.
Four Banners: 2 Baillie's—2 Protheroe's.
Tilers and Plasterers.
Two Banners: 1 Baillie's—1 Protheroe's.
Braziers, with Emblems.

CHAMPION, IN COPPER ARMOUR,
with his Two Esquires.
Two Banners.
BRASS BAND.
Five Shirt-Men.
Mr. BAILLIE's CENTRAL COMMITTEE,
And PRIVATE FRIENDS.
Two Banners: Baillie's.
Captain of the Chairmen.
Mr. BAILLIE's CHAIR.
Laurel Poles.
BUST OF THE KING.
REFORM COMMITTEE,
with their Banner.
Mr. PROTHEROE's PRIVATE FRIENDS.
Two Silk Banners.
The Captain of the Chairmen.
Mr. PROTHEROE's CHAIR.
Laurel-Poles.
Copper-Plate Press, *working.*
PAROCHIAL COMMITTEES.
Mr. Baillie's and Mr. Protheroe's Voters, four abreast.
Four Banners.
Sailmakers.
Ten National Flags.
Wheelwrights.
Two Banners: 1 Baillie's—1 Protheroe's.
Cabinet-Makers, with Emblems.
The Small BAND.
Four National Flags.
Bellows-Makers.
Confectioners.
Two Banners: 1 Baillie's—1 Protheroe's.
Laurel-Poles.
Glaziers.
Coachmakers, with their Arms.
Two Banners: 1 Baillie's—1 Protheroe's.
Ships' Colours.
Brass Founders.
Banners: Baillie's and Protheroe's.
Curriers, with their Emblems.
Ships' Colours.

Printed and Sold by W. H. Somerton, Mercury-Office, Narrow Wine-Street, Bristol.

9 A notice giving the order for a procession to celebrate the chairing of victorious reform candidates Baillie and Protheroe in 1831. Note the precision of the programme, and the presence of trade societies.

pressing issue, however, the carnival element became compromised. Elections had always been precarious affairs, since either the attempts of the political parties to win support could create genuine confrontations of public political opinion, or the attempt to exclude the non-electors from the political process could generate violent resentment. From around 1812, however, the determination of reformers to participate in the process increased the likelihood of contested elections, and thereby heightened the prospect of disturbance. Furthermore, it was decreasingly possible to stage an election without generating hard political and polemical confrontations, thereby providing a platform for the expression of a wide set of popular grievances.

This chapter examines these developments through four examples. First, and at some length, it will analyse the election year of 1812 in Bristol, and the impact upon the town of Henry Hunt's attempts to become its member for Parliament. Secondly, the remarkable election rituals at Norwich will be discussed, and particularly the practice of dividing the market place into opposing crowd territories, much in the manner of present-day football grounds. A third section will then look at the obsession in Liverpool, particularly around the beginning of the 1830s, with the presentation of 'orderly and respectable' political meetings. And finally, a brief examination will be made of the first parliamentary election in Manchester, in 1835, and the determination on the part of the local authorities to learn from the experience of elections elsewhere.

'HUNT AND TRUTH': 1812 IN BRISTOL

The assassination of the prime minister, Spencer Perceval, economic crisis, and disturbance in northern England made 1812 a critical year in English politics. Perceval's ministry, which had begun life precariously in October 1809, but which had survived popular opposition to the imprisonment of Sir Francis Burdett in 1810, extensive provincial unrest and the formation of the Regency, was shattered by the murder of the prime minister in May 1812. For two and a half weeks in late May and early June there was no government, until Lord Liverpool formed one by default. Motions for the consideration of parliamentary reform put to the House of Commons by Thomas Brand in May 1810 and May 1812 failed convincingly, although the extra-parliamentary campaign for reform, aided by the Burdett affair, still showed signs of life.[4]

After a boom year in 1809, economic depression set in in 1810. The French blockade, shortage of specie, bank failures, American closure of trade with Britain and poor harvests combined to ensure two years of industrial stagnation and widespread distress. The cotton industry was hardest hit, but high food prices in 1811 and 1812 affected all the working population.[5] Despite the Combination Acts of 1799 and 1800, industrial action had continued throughout the country, particularly from 1808. Luddite disturbances, beginning among Nottinghamshire stockingers in opposition to attempted pay reductions, in March 1811, reached their height in the West Riding and Lancashire in the summer of 1812. By that time, 12,000 troops were deployed throughout the midland and northern counties.[6]

In Bristol itself, the necessity for regulation in the supply and pricing of food was a primary concern. During the crisis of 1811–12, the Corporation was active, petitioning the king to request the suspension of distillation of grain, issuing requests for Bristolians to reduce their consumption of corn and prosecuting the sale of underweight bread.[7] Nevertheless, a customs officer was assaulted in March 1811, and three days later 'the populace' fixed the price of butter in Bristol market.[8] There were further food disturbances in April 1812, causing the mayor to write to the Home Office to report that peace officers were having 'some difficulty in suppressing the mob'; the Home Office declined to comply with the accompanying request for troop reinforcements.[9]

4   John Cannon, *Parliamentary reform, 1640–1832* (Cambridge, 1973), pp. 159–64; Clive Emsley, *British society and the French wars, 1793–1815* (London, 1979), pp. 147–53; Asa Briggs, *The age of improvement, 1783–1867* (London, 1959), pp. 149–58.

5   Arthur D. Gayer, W.W. Rostow and Anna Jacobson Schwartz, *The growth and fluctuation of the British economy, 1790–1850*, vol. 1 (1953; this edn Brighton, 1975), pp. 61–6, 83–7, 113–15; B.R. Mitchell and P. Deane, *Abstracts of British historical statistics* (Cambridge, 1962), pp. 486–9, 497–8.

6   E.P. Thompson, *The making of the English working class* (Harmondsworth, 1963), pp. 569–659; M.I. Thomis, *The Luddites* (Newton Abbott, 1970); E.J. Hobsbawm, *Labouring men* (London, 1964), ch. 2.

7   Hilhouse Wilcox to Gibbs, Dec. 1811, LB/BRO; HO to Corporation, 21 Dec. 1811, LMP/BRO Box 1811–12; *Bristol Gazette*, 28 Mar. 1811, 7 May 1812; printed notice, 2 May 1812, LMP/BRO Box 1811–12; *Bristol Gazette*, 4 June 1812.

8   *Bristol Mirror*, 23 Mar. 1811; *ibid.*, *FFBJ*, 30 Mar. 1811; *Bristol Gazette*, 28 Mar. 1811.

9   Hilhouse Wilcox to Ryder, 13 Apr. 1812, LB/BRO and HO 42/122; Beckett to Hilhouse Wilcox, 16 Apr. 1812, LMP/BRO Box 1811–12 and HO 43/20.

Despite their interventions in the local economy, the Corporation was a focus for hostility in these years. During an assize riot in 1810, the Mansion House, Guildhall and Council House were all stoned, amidst cries of 'Burdett for ever – No Tower!' Prophetically (in the light of events that were to occur in 1831) the recorder, Sir Vicary Gibbs, was the subject of hostility for remarks he had made in the course of the Burdett affair. Seventeen people were arrested.[10] Internal conflict also plagued the Corporation, with an unprecedented thirty-four refusals to serve on the Common Council during the period 1802–12.[11]

A parliamentary election had not been contested in Bristol since 1796. In the by-elections of 1801 and 1803 Charles Bragge was returned unopposed; and in the general elections of 1802, 1806 and 1807 the tory and whig election clubs (housed at the White Lion Inn and Bush Tavern, respectively) co-operated to ensure the return of one tory and one whig, without the expense and trouble of a contest. This state of affairs produced increasing discontent, both among the populace who contributed opinions, if not votes, at each election, and among those radically minded inhabitants who saw the electoral 'fix' as just one more example of Bristol power-magnates at work.[12] Arrangements to avoid a poll were always precarious since, although they decreased the likelihood of violence between the party partisans, the popular expectation and enjoyment of a contest was well known. Consequently, although contested elections usually involved major disturbances, as in 1790, 1796, 1818, 1826 and 1830, there was also a sense of relief expressed in the press when the election clubs succeeded in preventing a poll without precipitating a riot.

The elections of 1802 and 1806 provide two examples. During the former it seemed as though the tory, Charles Bragge, and little known outsider, Sir Frederick Eden, were to be elected without opposition. But, as local chronicler Samuel Seyer observed, 'the common people were not well pleased at this quiet manner of bringing in a new M.P.'.[13] The *Bristol Gazette* reported: 'There being a large concourse of people assembled (as there always are on these occasions) many expressed their dissatisfaction, that some other person besides Sir

[10] *Bristol Gazette*, 19 Apr. 1810; *Bristol Mirror*, *FFBJ*, 21 Apr. 1810.
[11] CCP/BRO, 1802–12.
[12] See, for example, Thomas Lee, *Eyes to the blind!* (Bristol, 1807); *idem*, *Trim the lamp!* (Bristol, 1807). Also see, Thompson, *The making*, p. 86, for discussion of popular notions of the right to participate in elections. [13] Seyer MSS, p. 55.

Frederick was not proposed.'[14] As a result, alternative candidates were hastily sought out, and Eden quitted immediately. The *Gazette* expressed its relief, since the frustrated 'lower class of the people, women as well as men' had become 'very clamorous'.[15] Seyer ended his account:

fortune [*sic*]
Such was the unexpected termination of this election.[16]

The uncontested re-election of Charles Bragge (now Bragge Bathurst) and Evan Baillie in 1806, with the usual processions and chairing, but without violence, brought delight from *Felix Farley's Bristol Journal*:

We heartily congratulate our fellow citizens on the unanimity and goodwill which has prevailed amongst us on the re-election of our late worthy respectable members . . .; and we sincerely hope that nothing may in future arise to disturb the satisfaction and harmony, which at present appear to pervade every rank and description of electors in this great commercial city.[17]

This was Bristol's fourth consecutive uncontested election, and *Felix Farley's* optimism was, in retrospect, misplaced. In the following year, 1807, yet another general election seemed set to pass off without a vote being cast. But by this time Henry Hunt was living in Bristol, and he expressed his support for Sir John Jervis, who was supposedly planning to contest the election. However, Jervis was almost certainly a decoy designed to placate the populace, and never had any real intention of standing. When he declined his nomination at the last moment, all hell let loose. Hunt was heralded as the people's friend, Corporation buildings once more were stoned, and Bathurst was, according to most reports, fortunate to escape without injury. Hunt led a crowd of 'many thousands' to Brandon Hill, and there promised to stand at the next election. Some of those at the Brandon Hill meeting argued that since the authorities had shown no mercy on Bristol Bridge in 1793, why should they be spared from attack now?[18]

[14] *Bristol Gazette*, 8 July 1803.   [15] *Ibid.*
[16] Seyer MSS, p. 57.   [17] *FFBJ*, 1 Nov. 1806.
[18] *Ibid.*, 9 May 1807; *Mirror*, 9 May 1807; *Bristol Gazette*, 7 May 1807; John Latimer, *The annals of Bristol in the nineteenth century* (Bristol, 1887), p. 30; Seyer MSS, p. 59; 'Register of transactions in and near the city of Bristol, beginning at the year 1799 [–1810]', BRL B10153 MS; Henry Hunt, *Memoirs of Henry Hunt, written by himself*, 3 vols (London, 1821), vol. 2, pp. 234–49; Thomas Lee, *Election clubs* (Bristol, 1807).

A dramatic election in 1812 seemed almost inevitable. It would have been well known, by the political clubs at least, that the Regent was due to make a decision regarding the composition of the government in February 1812 – a statutory one year after replacing his father.[19] A dissolution soon after that date was thought highly probable. In consequence, campaigning in Bristol began as early as December 1811, and was vigorous throughout the first three months of 1812.[20]

The usual sequence of events for an election in Bristol was as follows. As each candidate arrived at the city (or, if resident, as he left his house for the nominations at the Guildhall) he would be met by a large number of his 'friends'. A procession, usually involving the removal of the horses and the drawing of the candidate's carriage by the crowd, would then enter the town, and take him to a speaking place, dining place or to the hustings. The hustings at the Guildhall were invariably raucous affairs heavily attended by 'lower classes of the people'. The sheriffs, who acted as returning officers, would ask for a show of hands in favour of the candidates, and declare the result of the 'show'. If a contest was desired, the candidate or candidates who had 'lost' the show would demand a poll, which would generally then be declared to begin the next day. The poll could be kept open for a statutory maximum of fifteen days, although usually it closed when a candidate retired from the contest, or when the sheriffs felt that there had been adequate time for outvoters to come in. After the announcement of the final poll there would be speeches and then a chairing of the victors around the centre of the city.

Confusion concerning the expected dissolution of Parliament caused this electoral process to make a false start. Not only had canvassing already begun in late 1811, but by the end of March 1812 the whig Independent and Constitutional Society, who supported Sir Samuel Romilly, felt it was time their candidate left London and showed himself in Bristol. A public dinner was accordingly organised for 2 April.[21] The intention was that this should be 'merely an invitation to dine, no cavalcade or procession would be requisite'.[22]

---

[19] Emsley, *British society*, p. 148.
[20] *Bristol Gazette*, 26 Dec. 1811, *et seq.*; 'Stedfast Society: election proceedings, 1806–1812', BRO 12144, pp. 39, 44, 45–7.
[21] Samuel Romilly, *Memoirs of the life of Sir Samuel Romilly, written by himself* (London, 1840), vol. 3, pp. 21–2.
[22] *An account of the entry of Sir Samuel Romilly into Bristol, on Thursday, April 2nd, 1812* (Bristol, 1812), p. 3.

Romilly, however, was popularly regarded in Bristol as 'habitually the friend of the oppressed', and the response to his arrival was overwhelming – much to the dismay of Romilly himself.

A great number of persons came out on horseback to meet us. The crowd assembled at the distance of about a mile from the city was immense. A phaeton was brought that I might enter the city in it; and the people took off the horses, and insisted upon drawing me themselves. The weather was extremely unfavourable, and at intervals there fell a good deal of rain. An immense multitude, however, was assembled, and thronged all the streets; the windows and the top of the houses were crowded, and all the shops were shut. In this manner I entered Bristol, amidst the repeated huzzas of the people. Nothing could be more unpleasant to me than all this parade, and I had done every thing in my power to prevent it. But it was unavoidable; and I was assured that if I were to come into the city unexpectedly, it would be attended with great dissatisfaction, and might do me harm.[23]

Romilly well understood that he was obliged to go through with the procession, despite his distaste, and was the next day to be found obediently proclaiming that 'Whatever may be the event of the election, I shall always be proud of your approbation which I yesterday received.'[24]

Romilly then, however, made a serious tactical error. As he emerged to make a speech from the window of the Bush Tavern, the crowd below recognised the man that accompanied him as being Alderman Noble. Noble was popularly believed to have been the magistrate who ordered the militia to open fire on Bristol Bridge in 1793, and who had afterwards prudently chosen to move to London.[25] Immediately,

there was one general burst of disapprobation – groans, hissing, and hooting, and cries of 'No Noble! no six and eightpence! no bloody bridge! no murderers!' etc. etc. Poor Sir Samuel was astonished; but these discordant sounds quite disconcerted him, and when he began to speak, instead of his being listened to, the cries and groans were redoubled.[26]

[23] Romilly, *Memoirs*, vol. 3, pp. 21–2. In fact Romilly had, even then, understated the nature of his reception. A procession of trade societies greeted him, with flags, banners and emblems of their professions; he was also accompanied into the town by the mayor. See, *Bristol Gazette,* 9 Apr. 1812, and *An account of the entry of . . . Romilly*, pp. 3–4. For Romilly's popularity in Bristol see, *A short view of Sir Sam.l Romilly's Parliamentary conduct addressed to the electors of Bristol* (Bristol, 1812), in 'Bristol Parliamentary Elections, 1774–1943', BRO 11944(4); 'The golden days of Harry Cruger', in *ibid.*; 'Romilly and Protheroe', in *ibid.*

[24] Romilly, *Memoirs*, vol. 3, p. 27.

[25] Hunt, *Memoirs*, vol. 2, p. 501; Seyer MSS, p. 71.

[26] Hunt, *Memoirs*, vol. 2, p. 500.

Handbills and pamphlets quickly appeared attacking Noble (and thereby Romilly).[27] Hunt himself was quick to take advantage, mounting one of the copper pedestals in front of the Exchange to give an address of nearly two hours, in which he avowed himself 'the warm advocate for Radical Reform'. By his estimate there 'might have been ten thousand persons present, which was no very great number for such an occasion'.[28] The dissolution of Parliament still did not come, but Hunt kept the phoney election alive by appearing on Whit Monday and once again mounting the pedestal outside the Exchange. He had by now made this location his. As writers argued about the size of his audience, the *Gazette* was merely relieved that the day passed off without incident, noting that Hunt had fuelled popular concern regarding the 'disturbances in the North, the sufferings of the people, [and] the affair at Bristol Bridge', and that some of his followers were carrying loaves on the end of sticks.[29] As Hunt evoked memories of the 'blood-stained Bridge', the crowd cheered 'Hunt and Truth!'.[30]

When the election finally came, however, it was to be a by-election, necessitated by Bragge Bathurst's appointment to the Duchy of Lancaster, on 24 June. The tory Stedfast Society immediately initiated their campaign for the return of Richard Hart Davies. The whigs announced their intention not to contest the seat, in the interests of public peace.[31] Since the by-election was being caused by the vacation of the tory-held of the two Bristol seats, the whigs were effectively acknowledging the sharing of political power in the city.

Davis made his entrance during Saturday 27 June; Hunt arrived that evening. The minutes of the Stedfast Society demonstrate the pre-planning of the procession-in for Davis: the parish committees were called upon to supply 'able bodied decent Freemen' to act as constables, and churchwardens were instructed to arrange for the ringing of church bells.[32] Davis had only a short journey to make from his home in Clifton, less than 2 miles from the city centre. Nevertheless,

---

[27] See, Jeffries MSS, vol. X, BRL B7954 MS, pp. 236–7, 261; C.H. Walker, *An independent address to the electors of Bristol* (Bristol, 1812), p. xi.

[28] Hunt, *Memoirs*, vol. 2, pp. 504–5.

[29] *Bristol Gazette*, 21 May 1812; C.H. Walker, *An address to the electors of the United Kingdom, but in particular those of Bristol and Colchester* (Bristol, 1812), pp. 32–3; *Bristol Mercury*, 25 May 1812.

[30] *Bristol election: an account of Mr Hunt's public reception in Bristol, May 18, 1812* (Bristol, 1812), pp. 5, 10.

[31] *Bristol Gazette*, 2 July 1812.   [32] 'Stedfast Society', pp. 83–4.

A great company of his friends conducted him from his house . . . to the Council House with a large and respectable procession of carriages, horsemen, and footmen, who very generally wore the blue cockade. From there he went to the Exchange, when he declared his intention of offering himself at the ensuing election.[33]

Hunt arrived outside Bristol at 5.00 p.m.

I was met by an immense multitude, who took my horses from the carriage, and drew me into the city and through the principal streets, till they arrived at the front of the Exchange, which they had fixed upon as the theatre of my public orations . . . I left the carriage, re-mounted the pedestal, and addressed at least twenty thousand of the inhabitants, who had accompanied me thither with the most deafening shouts. I never had seen such enthusiasm in my life.[34]

Samuel Seyer commented that

At this time he [Hunt] set himself forward as a leader of the populace, and being recommended by a good figure, a ready and vulgar speech and a most abusive tongue, he gained a vast ascendancy over the mob. The ordinary subject of his discourse was the misery of the poor, the oppression of the rich, the villainy of both parties, whig as well as tories, and exhortations to the populace to rise up against their superiors.[35]

Seyer was almost certainly using 'mob' here as an abbreviation of 'mobility', but he was also reflecting the stigmatisation of Hunt's supporters (not least, as will be seen, by Hunt himself), which lasted throughout the campaign.

Over the weekend the Stedfast Society took stock of Hunt's campaigning against corruption, and wrote to their parish committees that 'As our opponent would be glad to take advantage of any inadvertent Act of Mr Davis's Friends . . . you will not give any voter a Glass of Beer or the smallest trifle or promise whatever to influence his vote.'[36] Monday was the first occasion on which the supporters of Davis and Hunt were brought into direct contact, when the two candidates were to be nominated at the Guildhall. The proceedings were conducted in uproar (although, the respective supporters not being clearly distinguishable, the newspaper reports did not apply the word mob). Two 'gentlemen' proposed and seconded Davis; two journeymen put forward Hunt. 'It was evidently a contest between

[33] Seyer MSS, p. 67.   [34] Hunt, *Memoirs*, vol. 2, p. 511.   [35] Seyer MSS, p. 67.
[36] 'Stedfast Society', p. 88. Hunt spent his journey to Bristol reading up on election law: Hunt, *Memoirs*, vol. 2, p. 512.

the rich and the poor; the whole of the former were openly for Davis, the whole of the latter, with the exception of those who were hired by the other party, were every man, woman, and child for Hunt.'[37] The show of hands was overwhelmingly for Hunt. Davis demanded a poll, which was adjourned until 9.00 the following morning.[38] The war of words now turned to physical violence. A pitched battle 'with bludgeons, brick-bats and stones' took place outside the White Lion, the windows of which were entirely demolished. The British Coffee Room, also in Broad Street, was reduced to 'a complete wreck'.[39] Several people 'were carried to the Infirmary'.[40]

Felix Farley's Bristol Journal later complained of the inactivity of the magistrates at this point,[41] but privately they were calling together the ward constables on Monday, and on Tuesday requesting 500 infantry and as much cavalry as could be spared by Severn District. It was requested that these troops be quartered in the suburbs, the magistrates being well aware that it was contrary to election procedure for the military to be present in the town.[42] A number of aldermen, and the commanding officer of the Bristol Volunteers, were called to the Council House.[43] When the poll closed for the night at 5.00 p.m. on Tuesday, 30 June, the magistrates suggested to the Davis committee that their constables be withdrawn, since their presence seemed to be creating, rather than quelling, violence; the tories agreed.[44]

The fighting in the streets did now largely subside. But it was replaced by deliberate action against specific targets. Hunt 'went riding' on Tuesday evening, accompanied by 'ten to fifteen thousand people'. He led them to the Back, where the quay was 'covered with all sorts of timber, wood, poles, faggot piles, and other rough merchandise'. Hunt had always maintained his supporters should be 'firm'. 'Though I could have wished that the weapons had been otherwise obtained, yet I must confess that I was not very sorry to see what had happened', he recorded.[45] The crowd accompanied Hunt

[37] Hunt, *Memoirs*, vol. 2, p. 517.   [38] *Bristol Gazette*, 2 July 1812.

[39] Hunt, *Memoirs*, vol. 2, pp. 517–18; *Bristol Gazette*, 2 July 1812; *FFBJ, Mirror*, 4 July 1812; Seyer MSS, p. 69; SP/BRO, Box 1809–13, Calendar 11 Jan, 1813, refers to 'two hundred and upwards' having attacked the White Lion.

[40] *Bristol Gazette*, 2 July 1812.   [41] *FFBJ*, 4 July 1812.

[42] 'Minutes of the proceedings of the election', 29 June 1812, LMP/BRO Box 1811–12; Worrall to Maj. Gen. Oswald, 30 June 1812, LMP/BRO Box 1811–12.

[43] 'Minutes of the proceedings', 30 June 1812.

[44] *FFBJ*, 4 July 1812; 'Stedfast Society', 1 July 1812, p. 93.

[45] Hunt, *Memoirs*, vol. 2, pp. 538–9.

back to the Talbot Inn, took leave of him, and made once more for Broad Street. 'Hunt's mob', as Hunt himself now referred to them, put the tory supporters to flight, smashed up public houses where Davis' committees were assembled, and headed for Clifton.[46] The destination was Davis' residence, Mortimer House. Marching up Park Street, they made a detour into Berkeley Square to destroy the windows of the house belonging to the much-hated tory alderman, Thomas Daniel, before arriving at Davis' house and giving it a thorough pelting. The rumoured approach of a group of Mr Hilhouse's shipwrights eventually caused them to flee.[47]

Whilst one crowd was attacking tory properties, another placed the Council House in a state of siege. The barrage of stones was so relentless, and the crowd increasing so rapidly, that the magistrates believed the lives of themselves and the constables to be in danger. A detachment of 100 infantry arrived, and the Riot Act was read. Nearly fifty arrests were made. Finally, at 11.00 p.m., the rioters dispersed, and the magistrates retained soldiers in the Council House and Guildhall throughout the night.[48] The worst of the violence had now passed, however. Hunt always pledged to keep the poll open for as long as a freeman could be found to vote for him,[49] and thirteen more days of polling were to follow. For the first three days of them the magistrates perceived the 'mob' to be 'riotously disposed'.[50] But for the most part this was a period of military organisation and political recrimination. Until 5 July the magistrates engaged in careful manoeuvrings of troops, bringing them into town at the close of the poll each evening, and marching them out again before the poll opened the next morning.[51] Ward constables were kept on the alert;[52] and troops were re-summoned for the final day of the poll.[53]

[46] Ibid., pp. 540–1.
[47] FFBJ, 4 July 1812; 'Stedfast Society', pp. 93, 113; Seyer MSS, p. 69; J.C. Cross to Rev. Davis, 18 May 1877, Davis MSS, BRO 16178(14) (no relation to R.H. Davis).
[48] 'Minutes of the proceedings', 30 June 1812; FFBJ, 4 July 1812; Bristol Mirror, 4 July 1812; Bristol Gazette, 2 July 1812; Seyer MSS, p. 69.
[49] Hunt, Memoirs, vol. 2, p. 514; Bristol Gazette, 2 July 1812.
[50] 'Minutes of the proceedings', 1–3 July 1812.
[51] Ibid., 1 July 1812 et seq.; MS signed WDB, 30 June 1812, LMP/BRO Box 1810; WDB to Oswald, 30 June 1812, LMP/BRO Box 1811–12. Palmerston to Hilhouse Wilcox, 3 July 1812, LMP/BRO Box 1811–12; Hilhouse Wilcox to Oswald, 5 July 1812, LMP/BRO Box 1811–12; PMA/BRO vol. 1785–1820, 5 July 1812.
[52] WBD to constables, 6 July 1812, LMP/BRO Box 1811–12; Corporation circular to constables, 7 July 1812, LMP/BRO Box 1811–12; Hilhouse Wilcox to chief constables, 11 and 14 July 1812, LMP/BRO Box 1811–12.
[53] Hilhouse Wilcox to Oswald, 14 July and 15 July 1812, LMP/BRO Box 1811–12.

The poll finally closed on Wednesday, 15 July, Davis having polled 1,907, and Hunt 235,[54] a small turn-out for an electorate of over 5,000 with two weeks in which to vote. The relief of the whigs was such that they joined with the tories to chair Davis in a formidable reassertion of power.[55] The Stedfast Society prepared the distribution of colours and the ringing of the church bells, and had around 1,200 special constables sworn in to protect the 1,600–2,000 'gentlemen' in the procession.[56] *Felix Farley* enthused,

the ceremony of chairing took place through the principal streets of the city, in one of the most elegant vehicles ever exhibited upon a similar occasion, followed by an immense number of our fellow-citizens and friends of the member, wearing blue cockades: numerous streamers and flags, models of ships, and other emblems of commerce, were exhibited in the procession, which was enlivened by the music of the Bristol Volunteers, and a private band. The windows of the different streets were crowded to excess, with beautiful females waving blue handkerchiefs and ribbons; greeting with every demonstration of joy the newly elected member, as he passed.[57]

Hunt's supporters posed no direct challenge to the procession, other than hisses and groans.[58] The tories completed their snub by ordering the treating of their voters after the poll had finished, and by publicising the names of the 235 men who voted for Hunt, together with their occupation and parish.[59]

Only two and a half months after the close of the poll at the July by-election, a general election was called, and polling was announced to begin in Bristol on 6 October.[60] There would be four candidates for the two Bristol seats. The tory, Richard Hart Davis; the radical, Henry Hunt; and two whigs. The whigs in Bristol split their allegiance between Sir Samuel Romilly, an outsider from London, a 'progressive' whig, and a lawyer; and Edward Protheroe, Common Councillor, from a well-established Bristol family, and self-confessedly an

[54] *Bristol Gazette*, 16 July 1812.
[55] Seyer MSS, p. 69.   [56] 'Stedfast Society', pp. 121, 124.
[57] *FFBJ*, 18 July 1812.   [58] Hunt, *Memoirs*, vol. 3, p. 6.
[59] 'Stedfast Society', pp. 125–6; *A list of the persons who voted for Mr Hunt at the late election* (Bristol, 1812). The list reveals the occupational bases of Hunt's support. Only four of those listed are stated to be 'gentlemen'; the remainder cover eighty-nine different occupations. Cordwainers (twenty-one), tailors (eleven), masons (eleven) and carpenters (ten) are prominent. The magistrates' list of those forty-seven people committed for rioting against the Council House offers a similar cross-section of Bristol's labour force; bakers, shoe makers and servants are prominent on this occasion.   [60] *Bristol Gazette*, 1 October 1812.

'old' whig who saw Romilly's 'democratical' principles as near revolutionary.[61]

Hunt was to arrive on Saturday 3 October. By Friday evening there were already crowds wandering the streets.[62] The arrival of Romilly on 30 September had been uneventful,[63] and Hunt's also passed off without mishap:

Mr. Henry Hunt entered this city (as previously announced by placards) on Saturday about three o'clock, in an open carriage, attended by Mr. John Allen and several other friends, from Bath, together with some of his Committee, in another carriage and on horseback, preceded by two large purple silk flags, bearing his name in gilt letters, and an arch raised upon poles covered with laurel leaves, and surmounted with carved doves, on which and its appendages were inscribed 'Plenty and Peace' 'Minority of 235' etc. Arriving opposite the Exchange, Mr. Hunt stepped from the carriage over the shoulders of the populace to one of the brazen pillars, and addressed a very crowded auditory for about two hours and a quarter.[64]

As usual, the tory and whig candidates set about canvassing the electors.[65] The magistrates made relatively low-key preparations for the security of public order, ensuring the readiness of military reinforcements, and swearing in 120 extra constables.[66] The nominations, on Tuesday 6 October, were noisy but not violent, despite controversy over the attempts to limit the capacity of the audience in the already-too-small Guildhall.[67] When the sheriffs opened the hall,

a general rush was made, and every one took such place as he was able to reach. For two hours an unusual noise and tumult continued, the galleries had been, with other parts of the Hall, boarded up, under the idea of preventing accidents but the freemen, eager to see and hear, kept destroying them.[68]

The show of hands, almost inevitably, was in favour of Romilly and Hunt.[69] In theory the polling commenced immediately, but in practice it began in earnest the next day. Almost at the outset the committees of Protheroe and Davis formed an alliance, their

[61] Seyer MSS, p. 71.
[62] Sheppard to Castle, 2 Oct. 1812?, LMP/BRO Box 1812.
[63] Romilly, *Memoirs*, vol. 3, p. 54.   [64] *Bristol Gazette*, 8 Oct. 1812.   [65] *Ibid.*
[66] Castle to Maj. Gen. Gordon, 3 Oct. 1812, LMP/BRO Box 1812; PMA/BRO, vol. 1785–1820, 3 Oct. 1812 and 5 Oct. 1812.
[67] *Bristol Gazette*, 8 Oct. 1812; *FFBJ*, 10 Oct. 1812; Hunt, *Memoirs*, vol. 3, pp. 98–103; Romilly, *Memoirs*, vol. 3, pp. 55–9; *Freedom of election: correspondence between the mayor of Bristol Mr Protheroe and Sir Samuel Romilly* (Bristol, 1812).
[68] *Bristol Gazette*, 8 Oct. 1812.   [69] *FFBJ*, 10 Oct. 1812.

supporters dividing their votes between the two conservative candidates. Romilly saw his cause was lost, and retired from the contest after eight days.[70] Hunt, true to his promise, kept the poll open, but on the tenth day, despite Hunt's protests, the sheriffs closed the poll. The tallies were, Davis 2,910, Protheroe 2,435, Romilly 1,685 and Hunt 456.[71]

The magistrates took precautions in case of violence at the close of the poll, swearing in five extra constables for each ward, but in the event they were not needed.[72] Evidence given to the committee of the House of Commons which examined Hunt's petition against the legality of the election suggests that the election was a considerably more boisterous affair than many contemporaries chose to admit.[73] Although the committee did not uphold Hunt's petition, the evidence did provide some substance for each of Hunt's claims, which included allegations of bribery, treating and intimidation.[74] Nevertheless, there had been no major or specific outbursts of collective violence.

By the time the chairing took place, commentators had already decided that this, a triumph of temperate politics, was also to be a triumph of public order. However, it seemed as if the day of the victory procession itself was to give the lie to this picture of electoral tranquility. The actual chairing of Davis and Protheroe was not disorderly; but on the same day, Hunt returned to dine at Hotwells. On his arrival 'an immense concourse of people' removed the horses from his carriage and pulled him through the centre of town.[75] As some of his supporters returned from Hotwells,

[they] broke the windows of several houses bearing the adverse colours. On approaching Messrs. Hillhouse's ship-yard on the Hotwells-road, the yard-bell rang, and one of the workmen came out shaking a *blue* riband. This was more than purple blood could bear, the blue-riband was snatched, mutual knock-down blows ensued, and the shipwrights, armed with bludgeons, followed the procession, not, as they confessed to some of Mr. Hunt's friends

---

[70] Romilly, *Memoirs*, vol. 3, pp. 60–3; *Bristol Gazette*, 15 Oct. 1812; *FFBJ*, 17 Oct. 1812; Seyer MSS, p. 71.

[71] *Bristol Gazette*, 22 Oct. 1812; Seyer MSS, p. 71; Hunt, *Memoirs*, vol. 3, p. 114.

[72] PMA/BRO, vol. 1785–1820, 15 Oct. 1812; Castle to Palmer, and Castle to aldermen, 16 Oct. 1812, LMP/BRO Box 1812.

[73] *Bristol Gazette*, 15 Oct. 1812; *An authentic report of the evidence and proceedings before the committee of the House of Commons appointed to try the merits of the Bristol election of Oct. 1812* (Bristol, 1813).

[74] *An authentic report*, p. ii, and *passim*.

[75] Hunt did not approve of his supporters pulling his coach because of its implied subservience, *Bristol Gazette*, 26 Oct. 1812.

who addressed them at the place of destination, from any political enmity towards him or his cause, but simply to avenge the attack upon their companion. However, no further mischief ensued; but nevertheless about six o'clock, the *improving* reports of this affair operated sufficiently to muster all the extra parochial constables and call out the volunteer-drums, who beat to arms for upwards of two hours; and a draft was made of 100 militia-men from the guard of Stapleton Prison, who took post at the Guildhall for the night. Fortunately, a plentiful shower damped the curiosity of the citizens to know the cause of these 'notes of preparation'.[76]

The *Mercury*'s remarks typify the self-conscious journalism applied to crowds in general and to elections in particular. Having decided, in line with other organs of public opinion, that this had been a peaceful election, the *Mercury* was determined that the closing fracas should be of no great import. The term 'riot' is not used; the actors are not called a 'mob'; the exaggerating characteristics of rumour are ridiculed; and the hasty provision of military protection, often the subject of praise in the past, is viewed almost as comic opera.

During the July election the established procedures had been disrupted first by the long expected dissolution of Parliament, and second by the appearance of Henry Hunt. Hunt's public gatherings outside the Exchange marked the beginning of a number of radical meetings to take place in the city over the next twenty years. They also upset the established election pattern, by challenging the shared-seat consensus, and by introducing an extra type of crowd event. In October, however, it was as if the local electoral system had adapted: four candidates gave the public what they wanted, namely, a good contest; yet the alliance of tory and old whig left in no doubt who would be returned. The magistrates were well prepared, and the candidates themselves were eager to prevent disturbance. Hunt's supporters could not so easily, this time, be separated from the opposition, since, with two votes per person, who was to know what shared allegiances the 'freemen' held? The end result: an election easily, and most conveniently, presented in consensual terms. The disturbances not only on the final day but at the Guildhall also, could therefore safely be reported in nonchalant terms.

The election year of 1812 in Bristol, therefore, demonstrates the

---

[76] *Bristol Mercury*, 26 Oct. 1812. See also, *FFBJ*, *Bristol Mirror*, 24 Oct. 1812; *Bristol Gazette*, 22 Oct. 1812. It was Hilhouse's shipwrights who came to defend Davis' house in July. The tory colour was sky-blue; Hunt's was purple.

part which local commentators, and established procedures of crowd occurrences, played in creating an election's image. An understanding of this process requires a great deal more knowledge about mass events than can be found in the background to a particular riot. The October election, indeed, would almost certainly escape any 'index of collective violence', and this, to speak anachronistically, was precisely the effect sought by local reporters.

There are other points to be made about this election year, however. The first is that the magistrates had a clear sense of their role when faced with disturbance. The letters to aldermen, constables and central government, the requests for military support and the careful deployment of troops within electoral rules, all suggest a firm understanding of the machinery for public order. These preparations, together with the organisation on the part of the election clubs, and the clear distinction between organised election gatherings and miscellaneous street crowds, also indicate that even during a raucous election such as that in July 1812, a discernible structure for mass events existed. For all the violence, this was not simply two weeks without rules.

The third point concerns the content of the disturbances. Hunt's great skill was his ability to link national and local issues. Nevertheless, the driving force for violence was the specifically local loathing for the Bristol establishment. The series of uncontested, seemingly 'fixed', elections appeared consistent with an establishment that had (it was popularly thought) cheated on its obligations on Bristol Bridge in 1793, and on numerous previous occasions. The electoral strength of the evocation of an event which had occurred almost twenty years earlier was remarkable. If the 1807 election had stirred considerable anger, the appearance of Alderman Noble in 1812, and the attempt on the part of the whig and tory clubs to ensure a tory return at the by-election, proved more than popular opinion could bear.

Such demands for participation – it is sometimes difficult to remember that only 5 to 10 per cent of the Bristol population had the right to vote – placed serious constraints upon Bristol's ruling class. A framework both of electoral procedure and moral obligations set the parameters for elections and their crowds. Most interestingly, however, the capacity of the establishment to impose or *generate* a sense of the *status quo* was not simply in terms of swearing in constables or ordering in the military, but also in their broader presentation of events. The July election had given vent to the most ferocious grievances; local commentators therefore seized upon October to recreate the civic consensus.

TAKING SIDES: ELECTIONS IN NORWICH

Not only was Norwich a city with frequent and partisan mayoral and ward elections, it was host to Norfolk county elections, and staged parliamentary elections with an extraordinary degree of theatre. Commentators, unwilling it seems to employ pejorative terms of description even to many disturbances, expressed a delight in the supposedly consensual aspects of large and colourful gatherings, and, by the end of the period, began to scorn the relative calm and quiet of county elections.

It was city, rather than county, parliamentary elections that produced the greatest interest in Norwich; and the central focus for city elections was the market place. This large, neutral space was divided, usually in half, with the supporters of the respective political parties, regaled in their party colours, allocated their respective sides. From behind the chain each would taunt, jeer and cheer; and, on some occasions, attempts were made to capture the opposing side's territory. Unlike Bristol where the expression of territoriality was around a number of strategic locations (with the possibility of attacks upon symbolically significant buildings), any attempts in Norwich to express domination of the city through territorial advantage were made entirely ritualistic.

A considerable degree of violence could take place within this ritualised setting without the local newspapers expressing any particular abhorrence. At the election in July 1812, the *Norfolk Chronicle* reported that early on during polling day,

a number of sailors, in uniform, with blue and white cockades, armed with bludgeons, or sticks with nails at the end of them, quitted the side of the market appropriated to their party and caused great confusion, insulting almost every person who wore the favours of the opposite party . . . About one o'clock an affray took place between these men and a party of butchers and others . . . many dreadful blows were interchanged, and many broken heads were the consequence.[77]

The disturbance was terminated by the 'spirited exertions' of the sheriffs and their *posse comitatus*.[78] The *Chronicle* had described an

[77] *Norfolk Chronicle*, 10 July 1802.   [78] *Ibid.*

election riot in 1796 in terms only of 'infuriated desperadoes' irritated by frequent appeals to their passions;[79] and in 1818 it again reported an attempt to capture ground in the market place without recourse to the word 'mob'.[80]

Although 'mob' was used to describe attacks on one of the candidates in the county election of 1826,[81] three disturbances during the city election of 1830 drew no adverse adjectives from the *Chronicle* (despite the fact that one person was killed);[82] and the *Norwich Mercury* was similarly restrained in reporting election disturbances in April 1831.[83] After particularly violent scenes during the 1832 election, with tory polling booths destroyed and paving stones torn up, one notice attempted to explain that such a riot was not the result of 'a system, or any preconceived intention. A reference to Norwich elections will prove that such encounters have raged during the memory of man, and that they arise out of the system of nature, not of politics, which has made man a pugnacious, or, according to the phrenologists, a combative animal.'[84]

Although the institutionalised confrontations in the market place did encourage disturbance, that violence was contained, and was concentrated on opposing supporters rather than public property. Perhaps this internalised nature of election disturbance explains the non-application of 'mob': crowds attacking each other did not pose any serious threat to public order, broadly conceived. Certainly this would explain the immediate application of mob when attacks were made directly upon important individuals, such as that on Edmond Wodehouse, one of the candidates, on his way home during the county election of 1826.[85] On the rare occasion when mob was applied, it was an attempt to separate out a residuum (and thereby to distract attention from the cause of the violence). For the 1826 disturbance, the *Chronicle* referred to an attack by 'some of the mob' (that is, mobility), and claimed 'only the refuse of the populace' joined in the proceedings.[86] Rioters at a county election in January 1815 were similarly termed 'three or four dozen "blackguards" – the very refuse even of a mob'.[87] Perhaps significantly, these examples

---

[79] *Ibid.*, 28 May 1796. [80] *Ibid.*, 17 June 1818. [81] *Ibid.*, 24 June 1826.
[82] *Ibid.*, 31 July 1830; Norwich Corporation, book of proceedings of the court of mayoralty, NRO, vol. XLIV, 14 Aug. 1830.
[83] *Norwich Mercury*, 7 May 1831.
[84] Notice printed in *ibid.*, 15 Dec. 1832. [85] *Norfolk Chronicle*, 24 June 1826.
[86] *Ibid.* [87] *Norfolk Chronicle*, 31 Dec. 1835.

relate to county elections, which did not possess the market place 'ritual'.

The concentration of city election crowds into one location made for a ready comparison of support for the candidates. Jonathan Peel, tory candidate at the election of 1826, achieved the great symbolic triumph of seeing his supporters allocated three sides of the market square;[88] the 'friends' of the whig candidate, William Smith, thereby 'made a secondary appearance when compared with the splendour of Mr. Peel's professional attendance'.[89] By the 1830s newspaper reports were becoming intoxicated by the site of large election crowds. The *Mercury* enthused, in 1831, at numbers which 'baffled computation', but were 'in truth ... from twenty to thirty thousand';[90] and in 1835 again expressed its 'excitation' at the spectacle of 'vast masses'.[91] As in Bristol, the fiction was generally maintained that these were the 'electors'. It was expressed particularly clearly in 1831, again by the *Mercury*, which recorded that 'MR GRANT again met his constituents at the Committee room. The number of electors far exceeded any popular assembly we ever witnessed in this city – not less than between seven and ten thousand persons being present.'[92] The Commissioners for the Municipal Corporations Report put the number of freemen in Norwich at 3,460.[93]

Such an affection for numbers and commitment was also reflected in the disparaging remarks directed towards the less dramatic county elections, despite the fact that they were well attended by the wealthy and influential. The *Chronicle* noted, in watching the chairing for the county election of 1830, that 'no contest having been fought the scene was divested of that warmth of character which opposition so naturally creates. For even the enthusiastic huzzas of friends will soon subside if there is no collision.'[94] When electoral reorganisation in 1832 made Norwich the location not for the county election as a whole, but for the East Norfolk division only, the *Chronicle* expressed disappointment that 'Norwich was shorn of much of its accustomed glory on the occasion of a contest for the county, she has at such

---

[88] *Ibid.*, 17 June 1826.   [89] *Norwich Mercury*, 17 June 1826.
[90] *Ibid.*, 7 May 1831.   [91] *Ibid.*, 30 Jan. 1835.   [92] *Ibid.*, 30 Apr. 1831.
[93] *Report from the commissioners on municipal corporations in England and Wales*, 3, appendix part I, vol. XXIII (1835), p. 126. It is odd that the *Mercury* described this as the largest assembly it had seen in Norwich.
[94] *Norfolk Chronicle*, 14 Aug. 1830.

periods been the focus of attraction, but now she plays only a fifth of the Electoral Drama.'[95]

This was not the only occasion on which reference was made to the threatre of elections. A delight in the atmosphere of performance and display characterised reports of election proceedings. That atmosphere is best conveyed by more detailed reference to one particular election; and that of July 1830 offers a good example.

The two whig (or 'blue and white') candidates, Robert Grant and Richard Harvey Gurney, made their entry into Norwich well into the evening of Saturday 24 July, greeted by their 'friends', 'with the customary assistances of flags, music, etc.'.[96] The horses were taken from their carriage, which was then drawn into the town by whig supporters. It was now very late:

To describe minutely what it was too dark to see, would be obviously absurd . . . No very accurate estimate of quality or numbers could be formed under [these] circumstances . . . but we may state that the cavalcade was headed by ANTHONY HUDSON Esq., acompanied by about fifty other gentlemen of the party on horseback. The candidates were then drawn by the populace in their carriage and there were from 10,000 to 20,000 people in the train.[97]

The *Chronicle*, despite the darkness, felt able to name six prominent individuals at the head of the procession, including the deputy mayor.[98] On the Monday it was the turn of the tories (the 'orange and purples'), Sir Charles Ogle and Colonel Peel.

The preparations for this procession, so far as we could judge from the results, were made with much more solicitude and much more care than those of the adverse party, who, in plain truth, have rarely been good at this sort of demonstration. This cavalcade was better managed, and from taking place in open day, and on the afternoon of St Monday, when our operatives are always disposed to holiday making, more imposing in its numbers and parade.[99]

Comparing the two processions, the *Mercury* concluded that what the whigs lacked in numbers and organisation, they made up for in the social significance of their supporters; nevertheless, it decided, the tory spectacle 'probably was, in the language of the Theatre, far more *effective* than that on Saturday night'.[100] The *Chronicle* also decided that 'in point of effect' the tories' entry equalled if not surpassed any

[95] *Ibid.*, 22 Dec. 1832.   [96] *Norwich Mercury*, 31 July 1830.
[97] *Ibid.*   [98] *Norfolk Chronicle*, 31 July 1830.
[99] *Norwich Mercury*, 31 July 1830.   [100] *Ibid.*

previously seen.[101] On the Thursday morning, at 9.00 a.m., the two sheriffs threw open the lower court of the Guildhall to the 'electors' for the nominations. A poll was requested without, unusually, a show of hands, and the contest began.

About half-past ten a party of the Blue and Whites entered the upper end of the market, but not content with keeping on their own half of the area, as has been the custom in order to prevent collision, and to preserve as much good order as possible, they were proceeding on to the purple and orange ground, this however was viewed as an aggression and firmly resisted, and the procession did not continue in its course.[102]

There then followed 'the ceremony of chairing and of occasionally *tossing* the respective Candidates in their chairs'. Ogle and Peel were chaired first, and then Gurney and Grant:

The two Candidates ascended their chairs, which were of an elegant description, the backs of them covered with blue and white silk and ornamented with rosettes and cockades of that material and colour. Mr. Gurney was attired in a plain black suit. Mr. Grant was in a black coat with tight trowsers [*sic*]. Their figures, manly and commanding, appeared to advantage.[103]

The streets were crowded with 'freeholders'. In the early evening, Ogle and Peel were chaired again in the market place, but this time, as they were 'passing the chain that divided the market', they were assailed by stones. The same treatment was later accorded Gurney and Grant.[104] Shortly thereafter, 'the state of things in the market place . . . became such as to beggar all description; brickbats, stones, anything in short that could be seized upon was hurled in a spirit reckless of the personal injury that might ensue'.[105] The whigs then began to demolish the tory polling booths; the tories soon retaliated in kind. The *Chronicle*, having never separated out the rioters from the freeholders, could not apply the word mob, and was restricted to terming the violence 'acts amounting to ruffianism'.[106] The *Mercury* did attempt to identify the troublemakers as 'followers of a lower order', but despite claiming the events an 'absolute outrage' seemed quite to relish its description of 'four men, stripped to their shirts, and of seemingly prodigious personal strength' who fell upon the blue and white booths. The ensuing disorder left 'two men to all appearance dead'.[107] A letter to the *Chronicle* later confirmed that one man had

[101] *Norfolk Chronicle*, 31 July 1830.   [102] *Ibid.*   [103] *Ibid.*
[104] *Ibid.*, 31 July 1830.   [105] *Ibid.*   [106] *Ibid.*   [107] *Norwich Mercury*, 31 July 1830.

indeed been killed, a 'victim of the atrocious practice of throwing paving stones'.[108]

The poll was closed at mid-day on Friday, and Gurney and Grant emerged victorious. The chairing took place in the market later that afternoon. Spectators occupied windows and roofs overlooking the market, and the square itself was crowded by spectators and by 'a cavalcade of carriages, and countless numbers on foot, with bands of music, flags, and banners, assembled in . . . regular order'.[109] The *Mercury* commented:

No pageant of the kind could have been more perfectly arranged or executed in more orderly manner than this multitudinous procession. But the great and striking effect was the display of POPULAR FEELING. By this the contest began, by this it was continued, to this it owed its triumphant termination, and whether we looked towards the windows or towards the market, whether we listened to the shouts of the multitude, or glanced at the dancing lights which were reflected from waving handkerchiefs, ribbons and cockades, we perceived only emanations of the one pervading sentiment.[110]

Certainly 'public order' became an issue in Norwich as elsewhere: placards at the chairing processions for the whig election victory in May 1831 declared 'Liberty and Public Order';[111] at the tory victory in December 1832 they called for 'Patriotism, Loyalty and Public Order';[112] and when the tories won the election of 1835, their chairing procession included the slogan 'The true liberty of the people, not the licentiousness of the mob.'[113] Commentators were always delighted to be able to report a 'warm' but disturbance-free election. But elections were clearly popular events in Norwich, in all senses, and as long as violence was restricted to the market place and to the partisans it was viewed as an inevitable, if lamentable, part of the election 'ritual'. The 'ritual' itself, with all its well-understood procedures, and the full involvement of the socially prominent and powerful, was deemed well worth the cost.

ORDERLY CONDUCT: RESPECTABILITY IN LIVERPOOL

Liverpool appears to have had a remarkably riot free history in the early nineteenth century. A riot among sailors in the docks took place

---

[108] *Norfolk Chronicle*, 21 Aug. 1830.   [109] *Norwich Mercury*, 7 Aug. 1830.
[110] *Ibid.*   [111] *Ibid.*, 7 May 1831.
[112] *Norfolk Chronicle*, 15 Dec. 1835.   [113] *Ibid.*, 10 Jan. 1835.

in 1801.[114] Orange parades in 1814 and 1819 ended in violence;[115] and there was disturbance at the mayoral election in October 1819.[116] But despite extensive treating and bribery, electoral disturbances were relatively rare, and when they did occur were on a minor scale in comparison with Norwich and Bristol. Contemporary writers liked to describe Liverpool as a particularly orderly place although such glowing characteristics may have been the product of civic image building rather than a true reflection of the state of the town. Thomas Kaye (editor of the *Liverpool Courier*), writing in his guide of 1807, and repeating the entry in later editions, claimed that 'good order prevails in almost every part of the town, and the sabbath day is observed with stricter decorum than is to be observed in many places of smaller extent'.[117] Having described the excellent character and manners of all classes, Edward Baines, in 1824, concluded that 'in no place perhaps in this free country is party feeling, either in religion or politics more chastened with liberality than in Liverpool (except during the stormy period of a contested election)'.[118]

Whether in an atmosphere genuinely less prone to riot and 'political effervescence' (as Kaye put it)[119] or not, the growing reform movement in Liverpool, particularly in the early 1830s, embraced wholeheartedly the need for 'good order' and 'respectability'. Of course, a crucial element in the reform platform everywhere was the rejection of bribery and intimidation at elections (expedient – since the tories were almost always better at it – as well as being part of an ideological tradition which associated bad governance with corruption and the abuse of power).[120] In Liverpool, however, the support given to reform by dissenting merchants gave the campaign a degree of respectability not easily achieved elsewhere. The attack was on the

---

[114] *Billinge's Advertiser*, 2 Nov. 1801; J.G. Underhill, Underhill MSS, vol. 5: 'The Liver, a MS history in three parts' (1830), LRO/942/UND5, p. 88.

[115] *Liverpool Mercury*, 16 July 1814, 23 July 1814; Underhill MSS, vol. 5, pp. 95–6; J.A. Picton, *Memorials of Liverpool, historical and topographical, including a history of the dock estate*, 8 vols. (Liverpool, 1873), vol. 3, pp. 408–9.

[116] *Liverpool Mercury*, 22 Oct. 1819.

[117] Thomas Kaye, *The stranger in Liverpool; or, an historical and descriptive view of Liverpool and its environs* (Liverpool, 1807), p. 33.

[118] Edward Baines, *History, directory and gazeteer of the county palatine of Lancaster* (1824; reprinted Newton Abbot, 1968), pp. 202–3.

[119] Kaye, *Stranger in Liverpool*, pp. 40–1, and subsequent editions.

[120] See: Gareth Stedman Jones, 'The language of Chartism', in James Epstein and Dorothy Thompson (eds.), *The Chartist experience: studies in working-class radicalism and culture 1830–60* (London, 1982), pp. 3–58.

tory establishment, and its domination, with the assistance of electoral bribery, of the political life of the city. By implication, however, and despite the fact that the Corporation was not strictly corrupt, this was also an attack on oligarchical local government. The dispute over town dues in 1830 acted as an appropriate preface to the reform campaign of the following years.[121] It was vital, therefore, that the reformers demonstrate propriety, good order and an awareness of Liverpool's public image if they were to challenge the civic and political leadership. The challenge was not straightforward, since the inevitable side-effect of the reform campaign was to generate crowd events and hotly contested parliamentary elections – thereby, it would seem to some, by definition disturbing the peace.

A burst of reform activity took place between 1817 and 1821. Reporting a reform meeting in Clayton Square in February 1817, attended by between 7,000 and 10,000 people, the *Liverpool Mercury* observed that 'according to the uniform custom of all meetings upon the same subject, the utmost order, decorum and unanimity prevailed'.[122] When disturbance looked possible during William Cobbett's visit in November 1819, the *Mercury* was careful to separate out the potential troublemakers as being non-reformers, 'for experience has fully established their character for order and decent observance of the laws; our fears arose from the opposite party'.[123] And at a pre-election meeting of reformers for the 1820 election, a large placard proclaimed 'Freedom and good order!', and this was 'borne in front of the procession, as expression of the orderly conduct which uniformly distinguishes the advocates for constitutional freedom'.[124]

With the resurgence of the reform campaign in Liverpool ten years later, and during the fierce political divides of these years, the themes of good order re-emerged. During the 1830 by-election, the *Mercury* poured scorn on the attempts to buy the ' "sweet votes" of the "free and independent burgesses" '.[125] By the end of the election, the *Mercury* echoed victorious candidate William Ewert's hope that Liverpool could now be restored to 'its usual tranquility', but then went on to comment on the good order that had prevailed throughout the election, since there had been no 'scenes of riot, hostile

[121] *Liverpool Mercury*, 7 May, 9 July 1830; 7 June 1831.
[122] *Ibid.*, 21 Feb. 1817.   [123] *Ibid.*, 3 Dec. 1819.
[124] *Ibid.*, 10 Mar. 1820.   [125] *Ibid.*, 26 Nov. 1830.

encounters, or desperate and bloody affrays'.[126] Such was the *Liverpool Courier*'s disgust at the treating and bribery of the later part of this election that it used the word 'mob' to describe the tumultuous street scenes, although there appear to have been no specific disturbances.[127] A select committee of the House of Commons, appointed to look into the alleged bribery of the 1830 election, seems to have been similarly disgusted, and declared the return of Ewart void.[128]

The contrast offered by the next election, in May 1831, therefore, struck the *Courier* as remarkable. The followers of the two pro-reform candidates, Ewert and Denison, had, allegedly, taken to heart an appeal to 'reform at home', that is, to reject the bribery and disruption that characterised previous elections, and had rendered the 1830 return illegal. The *Courier* concluded in May 1831 that,

with the exception of the immediate neighbourhood of the scene of action, 'Britain's Septennial Saturnalia' has lost its power to annoy the peaceable inhabitants of this great town by the tempestuous uproar of its noisy clang or the tumult of a riotous mob, and to offend the eye of decency by the brutal sights of shameless and disgusting intemperance.[129]

Both newspapers being sympathetic to the candidates at this time (Egerton Smith, joint editor of the *Mercury*, was a member of Denison's election committee), they had an interest in presenting the election in a positive light. However, it had been Denison and Ewert who stood at the by-election of 1830, and whose supporters were then the subject of such strong condemnation by these two newspapers. But quite apart from the reality of the situation, it is the presentation of crowd events which is the central issue here; and from 1831 the *Mercury* and *Courier* were concerned that they should, and should be able to, present the reform campaign favourably.

During the succession of reform meetings in 1831, therefore, the *Mercury* was at pains to point out the respectability and good conduct of the gatherings, and to list the 'gentlemen present', as well as the speakers and speeches. The names of the joint editors, Egerton

[126] *Ibid.*, 3 Dec. 1830. One contemporary account claimed votes were being sold for up to £40: *The poll for the election of a Member of Parliament for the borough of Liverpool taken between William Ewert, Esq. and John Evelyn Denison, Esq.* (Liverpool, 1830), p. 31. [127] *Liverpool Courier*, 1 Dec. 1830.
[128] *Report of the proceedings before the select committee of the House of Commons, appointed to try the matter of the petition against the return of William Ewert, Esq. for the borough of Liverpool* (Liverpool, 1831).
[129] *Liverpool Courier*, 4 May 1831.

Smith and John Smith, were sometimes to be found in those lists.[130] Large outdoor reform meetings left the reporters unruffled; elections, however, at least to the *Courier* were still a disruption. Faced with the fourth election in a year, and because of the clash of the local mayoral election and the parliamentary election, the second in a week, the *Courier* sighed that 'The coincidence, however, will no doubt be rather advantageous than otherwise: the bustle and interruption will be got over at once, and the usual machinery of elections answering for both occasions, may conduce somewhat to convenience and economy.'[131]

The *Mercury* regarded the reform meeting of May 1832 as 'one of the most numerous, if not the most numerous, meetings ever held in the town of Liverpool', but noted that it was 'without the least appearance of tumult and disorder'.[132] The absence of a victory procession, unlike many other towns, on the passing of the Reform Bill, denied the reformers the opportunity of a massive demonstration of orderly conduct. The occurrence instead of a reform dinner staged indoors, and for the benefit of just 350 'gentlemen', perhaps epitomises the tone and priorities of the Liverpool campaign.[133] For the 1832 election, the hustings took place outdoors, for the first time. An amendment to the polling system had been made in 1831, with the introduction of compartmentalised booths allocated without reference to party preference (that is, a freeman voted at a general polling booth, and not at a tory, whig or radical booth). For the 1832 election this was carried further, with the booths sited in a number of locations, and not all concentrated outside the Town Hall. In addition, the practice of chairing the victorious candidates was now abandoned.[134]

Mass attendance had been firmly in the service, rather than the vanguard, of the Liverpool reform campaign. The 'taming' of elections, and the reorganisation of them so as to reduce the possibility of confrontation and disturbance, was a reaction against the drunkenness and corruption of earlier elections; although these changes were not carried out by the reformers alone, they had their wholehearted support. Reform meetings, meanwhile, do not appear to have generated any particular unease among commentators. The

[130] *Liverpool Mercury*, 29 Apr., 23 Sept., 14 Oct. 1831.
[131] *Liverpool Courier*, 19 Oct. 1831.
[132] *Liverpool Mercury*, 18 May 1832.   [133] *Ibid.*, 7 Sept. 1832.
[134] *Ibid.*, 14 Dec. 1832, 16 Jan. 1835; *Courier*, 14 Jan. 1835.

domination of these meetings by prominent 'gentlemen', and the sympathy and involvement of the newspaper press ensured their 'respectability'. Anxiety regarding large-scale politicised events does not appear to have been great; the issue was rather by which means gatherings could best be marshalled and employed.

ACCEPTING DEFEAT: THE FIRST ELECTION IN MANCHESTER

Despite the absence of elections in Manchester in the early nineteenth century, politicised mass events were controversial, to say the least. Some contemporaries dated the beginning of open hostilities between tory-dominated local government and popular opinion from the Exchange riot in April 1812. On this occasion, a meeting to express support for the Prince Regent, called by the boroughreeve and constables, was called off at the last moment, when it became clear that there would be difficulty in passing the motion. (The authorities pleaded problems with access to a meeting room in the Exchange as the official reason for cancellation.) By this time, however, thousands of local and nearby inhabitants had assembled, and they expressed their irritation by entering and, later, destroying the Exchange reading room. They were finally dispersed by the Riot Act and the Scots Greys.[135] Archibald Prentice reported an acquaintance as having concluded that 'the occurrences of that day indicated a turn in the current of popular opinion. Previously to that time, "Church and King" was the favourite cry, and hunting "Jacobins" safe sport; but subsequently the old dominant party appeared to feel that they had an opposition to contend with.'[136]

Cowdroy's Manchester Gazette reported a meeting of 15,000 reformers at St Peter's Field, in October 1816, conducted by 'the labouring classes' themselves, with approval. It regretted, however, that they had not had the benefit of middle class support:

they conducted themselves in a very creditable manner, yet we could have wished for the honour of our own, that the business had been in other hands. We believe that political information is rapidly extending itself among the labouring classes but they are not generally and sufficiently enlightened, to be safely trusted with the details of the subjects they discuss.[137]

[135] *Manchester Mercury*, 7 and 14 Apr. 1812; Archibald Prentice, *Historical sketches and personal recollections of Manchester, intended to illustrate the progress of public opinion from 1792 to 1832* (London, 1851), pp. 50–2; Henry Dunckley (ed.), *Bamford's Passages in the life of a radical, and early days*, 2 vols. (London, 1893), vol. 1, pp. 240–1.   [136] Prentice, *Historical sketches*, p. 52.
[137] *Cowdroy's Manchester Gazette*, 2 Nov. 1816.

The 'Blanketeers' march of 1817 (a projected march of weavers from Manchester to London to petition the Prince Regent on the state of the cotton industry), spinners' riots in 1818 and Peterloo in August 1819 were all major confrontations with local authority; and all demonstrated the power and potential of autonomous working class mass activity. As elsewhere, the reform campaign gained a resurgence in the early 1830s, and visits by Henry Hunt, in January and April 1831, rekindled memories of Peterloo. The first of these meetings allegedly drew 5,000 people, the second 65,000.[138]

The representation of the reform movement by much of the press became hostile. The *Guardian* described the crowd at Hunt's April meeting as composed mainly of 'idlers'.[139] It then reported a reform meeting at St Peter's Field in June 1831 as taking place 'on that part of the field usually occupied by Mr. Hunt, when he visits it for the purpose of haranguing the mob', and thought 'the spectators or auditors composed of idlers of the lowest class'.[140] 'Mob', 'thieves' and 'pickpockets' were all labels attached to a reform meeting in October 1831;[141] another meeting, two weeks later, was said by the *Courier* to have been attended by 'the lowest rabble'.[142]

When the Reform Act was passed, and the celebrations took place, however, the *Guardian* now declared itself to have 'seldom witnessed a more exhilarating sight than . . . nearly the whole population of the town joining in the celebration of those great legislative measures'.[143] Now that the campaign was over, the pejorative terms were dropped. One of the immediate effects of the victory was a parliamentary election – the first in Manchester's history. The authorities, and the newspapers, quickly adjusted. The staging of the election was clearly designed to demonstrate that lessons had been learnt from elsewhere. And good order and good organisation, rather than the fruits of the reformers' campaign, were to be presented as the focus of the event.

Nominations of the candidates took place in St Anne's Square, but the polling booths were positioned in eight separate locations around the town. It was agreed in advance with the election committees that

---

[138] *Manchester Courier*, 8 Jan. 1831; *Manchester Guardian*, 8 Jan. 1831, 9 Apr. 1831; *Manchester Times*, 9 Apr. 1831.

[139] *Manchester Guardian*, 9 Apr. 1831.   [140] *Ibid.*, 8 June 1831.

[141] *Ibid.*, 15 Oct. 1831; *Manchester Courier*, 15 Oct. 1831.

[142] *Manchester Courier*, 5 Nov. 1831.

[143] *Manchester Guardian*, 11 Aug. 1832. Despite the tone of the earlier reports, the *Guardian* had been a supporter of 'practical reform' from the mid-1820s: see, Donald Read, *Press and people 1790–1850: opinion in three English cities* (London, 1961), pp. 82–5.

'no flags, banners, or music should be used by any of the candidates, or their committees, and that no chairing of the successful candidates should take place'.[144] The *Manchester Guardian* was 'quite sure' this would 'conduce to the preservation of the peace'.[145] It was further agreed that each candidate should deposit £100 with the returning officers against the cost of the arrangements.[146] There were no grand entries or processions to the hustings. As if for the convenience of the reporters, the non-electors (who, of course, had a point to make) stood under a banner proclaiming themselves as such, and cheered for their favourite candidate, William Cobbett.[147] The polling, with five candidates, lasted for two days, presided over by local constables. Apart from the visible cockades of Cobbett's supporters, the remainder of the 'vast assemblage' (estimated at 40,000) consisted of 'an indiscriminate class of other inhabitants, not distinguished by cockades, favours, or other badges, as belonging to any party'.[148] Just as there were no processions-in, neither was there any chairing ceremony.

The newspapers regarded the event as successful, and adjusted their reports of any disturbance accordingly. The *Manchester Courier*, despite its disappointment at the outcome of the election, concluded its editorial:

It now only remains for us to congratulate our fellow townsmen on the tranquility which has prevailed during this contest; for we scarcely consider the few disorders which took place yesterday as breaches of the peace. Whether this absence of riot is attributable to the excellent arrangements of the municipal officers; or, which we are inclined to think was the case, to the good sense of the people, it is a circumstance which cannot but be regarded as an auspicious commencement of the electioneering proceedings of Manchester.[149]

The individuals responsible for the 'few disorders', were carefully separated out by the reports from the main body of the electors. The *Courier* termed them 'a mob', 'chiefly of young men and boys'; the *Manchester Times* saw them as 'blackguard fellows' who had 'assumed' Cobbett's colours, before smashing the windows of the two pubs which served as headquarters for one of the candidates.[150]

Officials in Manchester had clearly identified the ingredients in

[144] *Manchester Guardian*, 1 Dec. 1832. [145] *Ibid.* [146] *Ibid.*
[147] *Ibid.*, 8 Dec. 1832. [148] *Manchester Times*, 15 Dec. 1832.
[149] *Manchester Courier*, 15 Dec. 1832.
[150] *Ibid.*; *Manchester Times*, 15 Dec. 1832.

elections which made for potential disturbance, or 'excessive' jubilation, and had done their best to eliminate them. This then offered local reporters the straightforward task of presenting a well-organised, successful, low-key, mass event. They did have the option of presenting the disturbance as the work of reformers, and as evidence that they were not fit to take part in that for which they had been working. But such a presentation would have both raised issues regarding the franchise created by the Reform Act, and stigmatised the whole electoral process. There was no need for that, since elections could be controlled, and disturbance so readily marginalised.

10. *Celebration and ceremonial*

[The Bristol coronation celebration of 1821] was from sun-rise to sunset a continued ebullition of loyalty, rejoicing and good humour.
(*Felix Farley's Bristol Journal*, 21 July 1821)

A more spiritless pageant we never witnessed.
(*Bristol Mercury*, 21 July 1821)

The single most straightforward argument in favour of a broad study of crowd events between 1790 and 1835 is that this was a period not only of radical mass meetings and major riots, but also of unprecedented mass mobilisation around 'patriotic' events. The war with France, and the determination of British politicians to concentrate patriotic display around the monarch, generated what Linda Colley has termed 'the apotheosis of George III'. That deification was made possible, in large measure, by provincial towns eager to emulate and compete in the sponsorship and organisation of loyalist display.[1]

Celebrations of military victories and royal anniversaries, and the participation in these events of local authorities and local employers, facilitated the frequent exhibitions of mass loyalty throughout the years of the war. Once the war was over, the precedent had been set, and although anniversaries and spontaneous celebrations died away, the coronations of 1821 and 1831 produced some of the largest crowds in England in this period.

So is this where, in the words of Geoffrey Best, we are forced to register 'that flag-saluting, foreigner-hating, peer-respecting side of

---

[1] Linda Colley, 'The apotheosis of George III: loyalty, royalty and the British nation, 1760–1820', *Past and Present*, no. 102 (Feb. 1984), pp. 94–123. See also: David Cannadine, 'The context, performance and meaning of ritual: the British monarchy and the "invention of tradition", c. 1820–1977', in Eric Hobsbawm and Terence Ranger (eds.) *The invention of tradition* (Cambridge, 1983), pp. 101–64; Hugh Cunningham, 'The language of patriotism 1750–1914', *History Workshop Journal*, no. 12 (1981), pp. 8–33.

the plebian mind'?[2] Is this, above all, where local authorities could marvel at the sight of 'vast masses all in sympathy'? Certainly there was flag-saluting, and certainly there were displays of mass solidarity, but, as this chapter will demonstrate, there was a great deal more to these corporate expressions of loyalty than meets the eye. As Linda Colley points out, the attendance at royal events of large crowds, made easy and tempting by the declaration of a public holiday, and the provision of fireworks, food and drink, could not necessarily be taken as evidence of national or local consensus.[3]

It will be argued here that discrepancies between official and popular perceptions of the political content of 'patriotic' events, and disagreements regarding the appropriate form for jubilation, made seemingly consensual occasions highly contentious. Three examples illustrate the case: the celebration of the peace with France in 1801, the celebration of the coronation of George IV in 1821 and the coronation of William IV ten years later, in 1831. As always, it will be events in Bristol that are examined in greatest detail, but the experience of the other three cities will be outlined also. The issues arising from these cases will then be assessed in the light of recent discussions of the conceptualisation of ritual, ceremonial and 'consensus'.

1801: PEACE WITH FRANCE

The 1790s, for the vast majority of people, was an exceptionally miserable decade. When the preliminary peace with France was announced in October 1801, it was to almost audible relief: 1801 was a year of critically high prices, and a drastic decline in real wages. When peace finally (and, as it turned out, temporarily) came, the displays of delight and loyal devotion concealed tensions and frustrations regarding the conduct and effects of the war which, only months earlier, had produced scenes of riot.

In Bristol, and nationally, food prices steadily increased from 1789 to crisis levels in 1795–6,[4] provoking price-fixing riots in Bristol

---

[2] Geoffrey Best, a review of E.P. Thompson, *The making of the English working class*, in *Historical Journal*, VII, 2 (1965), p. 278.

[3] Colley, 'Apotheosis of George III', p. 122.

[4] James Johnson, *Transactions of the Corporation of the Poor* (Bristol, 1826), Appendix I; Bristol Corporation assize of bread records, BRO 04350/4a–6a. For national trends see: Arthur D. Gayer, W.W. Rostow and Anne Jacobson Schwartz, *The growth and fluctuation of the British economy, 1790–1850*, vol. 1 (1953; this edn Brighton, 1975), pp. 10–12, 27–31; B.R. Mitchell and P. Deane, *Abstract of British historical statistics* (Cambridge, 1962), pp. 469, 486–9, 497–8.

market in June 1795, and again in 1797.[5] The newspapers offered rather token outrage at the disturbances: both they and the Bristol magistrates well understood the demands of the moral economy, and had been repeatedly seeking measures to improve supply and reduce prices.[6] *Felix Farley's Bristol Journal* recommended the posting of names of individuals prosecuted for selling underweight provisions, and in so doing inadvertently subscribed to a belief in public punishment of the kind held by the rioters.[7]

Also in common with the rest of the country, the 1790s in Bristol produced a number of industrial disputes.[8] These were concentrated in the period 1791–5, but the city also experienced conflicts involving journeyman tailors and boot and shoe makers in 1796, and carpenters and tobacco pipemakers in 1799; there was a major rising of the nearby Kingswood colliers in 1795, and a disturbance at a Bedminster distillery in 1799.[9] In 1800, 7,000 Bristol workers signed a petition in oposition to the Combination Acts.[10]

The local authorities in Bristol had grounds for unease on three further fronts. The first was popular opposition to impressment: naval press gangs, increasingly desperate for men during the French wars, were notorious for their ruthless operations in ports such as Liverpool, London and Bristol.[11] The second was a number of

---

[5] *Bristol Gazette*, 11 June 1795; *Bristol Mercury*, 8 June 1795; *BMBJ*, 6 June 1795; CCP/BRO, 10 June 1795; *Bristol Gazette*, 11 May 1797, 1 June 1797.

[6] Regarding corn shipments: Portland to Smith, 11 July 1795, HO 43/6; petition to Privy Council, LMP/BRO Box 1794, 4 July 1795. Setting the price of bread: *Bristol Gazette*, 23 July 1795; PO/BRO, 21 June 1796. Requests for reduction in consumption: *Bristol Gazette*, 21 and 28 June 1796. Notice against forestalling: PO/BRO, 21 June 1796. Requests for reduction in consumption: *Bristol Gazette*, 21 and 28 June 1796. Notice against forestalling: PO/BRO 1 Feb. 1796. Newspaper reports against forestalling: *Bristol Gazette*, 11 Feb. 1796, 14 Apr. 1796. Seizing of 'light' butter by magistrates: *Bristol Gazette*, 23 Nov. 1797, 27 June 1799, 1 Aug. 1799. Moral economy notions are discussed by: E.P. Thompson, 'The moral economy of the English crowd in the eighteenth century', *Past and Present*, no. 50 (Feb. 1971), pp. 76–136; R.B. Rose, 'Eighteenth-century price riots and public policy in England', *International Review of Social History*, VI, 2 (1961), pp. 277–92; Sidney and Beatrice Webb, 'The assize of bread', *Economic Journal*, XIV (1904), pp. 196–218.   [7] *FFBJ*, 6 June 1795.

[8] C.R. Dobson, *Masters and journeyman: a prehistory of industrial relations, 1717–1800* (London, 1980), p. 26.

[9] *Bristol Gazette*, 31 Mar. 1796, 7 Apr. 1796, 13 May 1796, 13 June 1799, 11 July 1799, 19 Mar. 1795, 26 Mar. 1795, 23 Apr. 1795, 4 May 1795; LB/BRO, 17 Mar. 1795, 8 May 1795; unsigned letter dated 'Council house, 15 May 1799', LMP/BRO Box 1797–8(2).   [10] Dobson, *Masters and journeyman*, p. 147.

[11] J.R. Western, *The English militia in the eighteenth century* (London, 1965); John Stevenson, *Popular disturbances in England, 1700–1870* (London, 1979), pp. 35–40; Clive Emsley, *British society and the French wars, 1793–1815* (London, 1979), pp. 52–6, 72–3.

anonymous letters addressed to the magistrates, particularly in 1800, threatening violence if food shortages were not remedied. On one occasion the letters were affixed to bloody loaves, and to the Mansion House itself.[12] The third area for concern, as the anonymous letters suggest, was continuing dislike for the Corporation, in the wake of the 1793 Bristol Bridge affair, and despite the magistrates' attempts to intervene in the supply and pricing of food. An attack was made on the Mansion House and Council House in the course of the 1796 election;[13] and the Corporation's problems were reflected in its difficulty in filling Council vacancies, despite an increase in the fine for refusing to serve.[14]

In the face of such disturbance, dispute and discontent, the local establishment could appeal to the seemingly unifying values of patriotism and loyalism, expressed through royal and military anniversaries, the threat of invasion, hostility to political sedition and the raising of local volunteer regiments. Popular celebration of royal anniversaries was not a mere formality, however. *Official* celebrations were frequent – and were expressed by flags, military displays, the ringing of church bells, Corporation processions and balls – but only rarely did newspapers clearly specify the presence of a crowd. On only four occasions was popular response mentioned: the anniversary of the restoration of Charles II, in 1795, when the trades joined the Corporation procession to the Cathedral; George III's birthday in 1797 when a 'vast concourse' spent Monday in the sunshine watching a military display on College Green; and George's birthday in 1788 and 1799, when 'spectators' were reportedly present at military displays.[15]

During the second half of the 1790s there does appear to have been a lull in loyalist enthusiasm, at a time when support for the war was at

[12] Anon. to Harvey, 31 Oct. 1795, LMP/BRO Box 1794; Anon. to John Jarritt, 19 Feb. 1800, LMP/BRO Box 1799; Morgan to Portland (with copies of notes enclosed), 26 Feb. 1800, LB/BRO; Portland to Morgan, 18 Feb. 1800, LMP/BRO Box 1799; Anon. to Morgan, 19 Sept. 1800, LMP/BRO Box 1801. And see: E.P. Thompson, 'The crime of anonymity', in Douglas Hay, Peter Linebaugh, J.G. Rule, E.P. Thompson and Cal Winslow, *Albion's fatal tree: crime and society in eighteenth-century England* (Harmondsworth, 1977), pp. 255–344.

[13] *SFBJ*, 28 May 1796, 5 June 1796; *Bristol Gazette*, 2 June 1796; *Bristol Mercury*, 30 May 1796.

[14] CCP/BRO, 13 Apr. 1796. Refusals to serve, post-1793: CCP/BRO, 2 Oct., 16 Oct. 1794; 5 Sept., 10 Sept., 29 Sept. 1795; 8 Sept. 1798; 12 Sept. 1801 (two); 1 Oct. 1801 (two).

[15] *Bristol Gazette*, 5 June 1794; *Bristol Mercury*, 2 June 1794; *FFBJ* and *BMBJ*, 31 May 1794; *Bristol Mercury*, 12 June 1797; *Bristol Gazette*, 8 June 1797, 7 June 1798; *FFBJ, BMBJ, SFBJ*, 9 June 1799.

Council-Houſe,

BRISTOL.

Thursday, September 5, 1799.

THE MAGISTRATES being diſpoſed to ſhew every Demonſtration of Joy on the glorious News contained in the Two Extraordinary Gazettes of the Third Inſtant, are deſirous that a

General Illumination

ſhould take Place this Evening.

They however earneſtly requeſt their Fellow-Citizens not to fire Guns or Piſtols, or ſet off Fire-works in any of the Streets of this City. And they alſo caution them againſt committing any Outrage on well-diſpoſed, peaceable Perſons who rejoice equally with their Neighbours, but who, from reli-gious Principles may not be diſpoſed to testify their Joy by Illuminations.   *Worrall*

ANN BRYAN, PRINTER.

10 An official notice from September 1799 calling for an illumination, but placing restrictions upon 'unofficial' jubilation.

a low ebb everywhere. Newspaper reports of loyal events became shorter and more formal, and celebration became centred around George III's birthday. Nevertheless, celebration of November the 5th, and of various military victories, ensured that no year passed in Bristol in the 1790s without at least one, and sometimes several, public displays of patriotism.[16] Additionally, there was a steady flow of loyal addresses and dedications, reinforced by public subscriptions, including one for the defence of the country, in 1798.[17]

There was concern throughout the second half of the decade regarding the possibility of a French invasion. When a landing was made in Pembrokeshire in February 1797, it sparked a nationwide run on the banks, and fears that the French would make a second attempt. Indeed, a rumour that they had done so brought 'tens of thousands' onto the streets of Bristol in March 1797 to send off the Sussex Fencibles and Royal Berkshire Militia to meet the enemy.[18] It was a false alarm, but the threat of invasion seemed to emphasise the need for a strong local volunteer force. In practice, however, such forces during the French wars were used more to suppress domestic disturbance than to guard against the French.[19] A 'Loyal Bristol Regiment' was formed in 1794; in 1797 the Bristol Volunteers were created; and a year later a Yeomanry regiment was added.[20]

Loyalism in Bristol had only fleetingly to encounter an indigenous radical movement. (The Bristol Constitutional Society made a brief appearance in 1794.)[21] Immediately after the rumoured French

[16] For example: Anniv. 5 Nov.: *Bristol Gazette*, 11 Nov. 1790; *Bristol Mercury*, 7 Nov. 1791; *FFBJ*, 10 Nov. 1792; *SFBJ*, 9 Nov. 1793; *Bristol Gazette*, 6 Nov. 1794 and 8 Nov. 1798; *FFBJ*, 9 Nov. 1799. Consecration of the colours of the Hampshire Fensible Cavalry: *Bristol Gazette*, 18 Feb. 1796. Duncan's victory over the Dutch, *Bristol Mercury*, 23 Oct. 1797. Visit of Sir Sidney Smith, *Bristol Gazette*, 31 May 1798. Nelson's victory at the Nile, *Bristol Gazette*, 11 Oct. 1798. Victory over the Dutch fleet, *Bristol Gazette*, 12 Sept. 1799.

[17] *Bristol Gazette*, 22 Feb. 1798, *et seq.*; mayor to Portland, 17 Feb. 1798, LB/BRO.

[18] *Bristol Gazette*, 9 Mar. 1797. And see, Emsley, *British society*, pp. 56–7.

[19] J.R. Western, 'The volunteer movement as an anti-revolutionary force, 1793–1801', *English Historical Review*, LXXI (1956), pp. 603–14; Oscar Teichmann, 'The yeomanry as an aid to civil power, 1795–1867', *Journal of the Society for Army Historical Research*, XIX (1940), pp. 75–91 (part I), 127–43 (part II).

[20] CCP/BRO, 11 June 1794; 'The mock volunteers, or Bristol heroes; a satire by Peter Pickle, Junior, 1794', BRL B26635 MS; PO/BRO, 1 Feb. 1797; *Rules and Regulations to be observed by the Bristol Volunteer Association* (Bristol, 1797); James Brown, *The rise, progress and military improvement of the Bristol Volunteers* (Bristol, 1798); *Bristol Gazette*, 16 Nov. 1797, 12 Apr. 1798.

[21] *Journals of the House of Commons: report of the Committee of Secrecy*, 1794, vol. XLIX, pp. 726–7; Bristol Constitutional Society for a Parliamentary Reform, *Address to the people of Great Britain* (Bristol, 1794); *Bristol Gazette*, 9 Oct. 1794.

landing, in 1797, two supposed 'Jacobins' were attacked, reportedly with the tacit approval of the magistrates and 'well dressed persons'.[22] Despite hostility towards the Corporation, and rather patchy demonstrations of public loyalism, therefore, there was little interest in radical politics. At the turn of the century the overriding issues were frustration at the continuation of the war, and hunger.

During 1800 food prices soared. Soup-kitchens were in operation during the winters of 1799–1800 and 1800–1.[23] Parish meetings organised relief measures for the poor.[24] The Corporation issued proclamations against high quality bread throughout 1800 and into 1801, and a notice against forestalling in May 1800.[25] The press fuelled popular hostility towards forestalling and regrating.[26] Rioting broke out in the market in September 1800 (it is not clear how many people were involved, although the military were twice called out), but it produced a low-key response from both magistrates and newspapers.[27] Over the winter disturbances occurred in the surrounding countryside,[28] and further relief measures were taken in the town.[29] By the spring of 1801 provisions were, according to contemporary chronicler Samuel Seyer, 'at an enormous price'.[30] Between 1799 and 1800 the Bristol Corporation of the Poor suffered an increase in the price of food of nearly 100 per cent; wheaten bread increased in price by 200 per cent between March 1798 and March 1801.[31] 'These evils', mused Seyer, 'could scarcely fail to produce tumults.'[32]

---

[22] *A statement of facts relative to the riot . . . in Union street . . . 27th and 28th March 1797* (Bristol, 1797); *Bristol Gazette*, 24 Aug. 1797; Lewis to Gibbs, 3 Mar. 1797, LB/BRO.   [23] *Bristol Gazette*, 5 Dec. 1799, 16 Oct. 1800.

[24] *Ibid.*, 21 Nov. 1799, 4 Jan. 1800; *BMBJ*, 11 Jan. 1800, 18 Jan. 1800.

[25] *Bristol Gazette*, 16 Jan. 1800, 26 Apr. 1800; *BMBJ*, 26 July 1800, 23 Aug. 1800, 6 Dec. 1800, 10 Jan. 1801, 11 May 1800.

[26] *Bristol Gazette*, 15 Feb. 1800; *BMBJ*, 26 July 1800, 2 Aug. 1800, 16 Aug. 1800, 27 Sept. 1800, 3 Oct. 1800; *FFBJ*, 20 Sept. 1800.

[27] *Bristol Gazette*, 25 Sept. 1800; *FFBJ*, 13 Sept. 1800, 20 Sept. 1800; *BMBJ*, 20 Sept. 1800.   [28] *BMBJ*, 25 Oct. 1800, 1 Nov. 1800, 14 Feb. 1801.

[29] *Ibid.*, 17 Jan. 1801, 24 Jan. 1801, 7 Feb. 1801, 21 Feb. 1801, 7 Mar. 1801, 21 Mar. 1801.   [30] Seyer MSS, p. 51.

[31] Calculated from assize of bread records, BRO 04350/5–6a.

[32] Seyer MSS, p. 51. Riot in these years was a nationwide phenomenon. See: Stevenson, *Popular disturbances*, ch. 5; Alan Booth, 'Food riots in the north-west of England, 1790–1801', *Past and Present*, no. 77 (Nov. 1977), pp. 84–107; Roger Wells, 'The revolt of the south-west 1800–1; a study in English popular protest', *Social History*, II, 1 (1977), pp. 713–44; Adrian J. Randall, 'The shearmen and the Wiltshire outrages of 1802: trade unionism and industrial violence', *Social History*, VII, 3 (1982), pp. 283–304.

On Saturday 4 April, the sheriffs of Bristol reported to Lt Gen. Rooke that 'a very large Mob are assembled on the Brislington, Bedminster and Ashton roads taking away Butter and other articles of food'.[33] 'A large body of men, women and boys' gathered in the market and forced the sale of meat, butter and potatoes at fixed prices. 'A number of inflammatory bills' were also posted on the walls. The mayor called out the Bristol Volunteers and the other military forces garrisoned in the town, and the Riot Act was read.[34] The attention of the reports of the event now shifted: the riot ceased to be about the grievances of the poor, and became the scene for a display by the Volunteers:

Several of the most riotous (some of whom had taken meat and other articles from the market) were conducted by the Volunteers, to Newgate and Bridewell, by order of the Magistrates; and we have the satisfaction to state, that by these prudent and spirited measures, peace and tranquility were restored – The Volunteers, consisting of a Captain's guard, remained on duty, at the Exchange, till nearly one o'clock on Sunday morning; before they were dismissed, Gen. Rooke, in the most handsome manner, returned them his warmest thanks for their conduct on that day, and said that 'the safety of the city could not be entrusted in better hands' – A picquet guard has been mounted every day since, and both the horse and foot soldiers quartered here have held themselves in readiness to suppress any outrages that might happen.[35]

The recorder, at the opening of the assizes, derided the 'absurdity of the deluded mob', and stressed the duty of the magistrates, peace officers, soldiers and citizens 'to unite together to suppress all such illegal and ruinous proceedings'.[36] A meeting of parish deputies resolved to assist the magistrates against any such further obstruction to provisions.[37] In September, with a good harvest, bread prices at last began to fall. Now, as outrage against the rioters faded, the press returned to its condemnation of 'the sinful hand of Monopoly', and complained of continuing 'exhorbitant prices'.[38]

Peace negotiations had been going on in secret since 1800, and were completed on 1 Oct 1801. Improvement in British military and diplomatic fortunes in 1801, and a renewed invasion threat, combined with the secrecy of negotiations, created a mood in national

[33] Ireland and Brice to Rooke, 4 Apr. 1801, LB/BRO.
[34] *BMBJ*, 11 Apr. 1801; Seyer MSS, pp. 51–7.   [35] *BMBJ*, 11 Apr. 1801.
[36] *Ibid.*, 11 Aug. 1801, 18 Apr. 1801.   [37] *Ibid.*, 25 Apr. 1801, 6 June 1801.
[38] *BMBJ*, 20 June 1801, 22 Aug. 1801. For prices, see assize of bread records; and Seyer MSS, p. 53.

opinion first of patriotic vigour, and then of sudden, surprised and immense relief as peace was announced.[39] During 1800 and 1801, royal anniversaries were again publicly celebrated in Bristol. The birthday of George III in 1800 was marked by a military display, although reports do not specify crowds of spectators.[40] The public response to the king's birthday in June 1801, celebrated on a Monday, was less equivocal. *Bonner and Middleton's Bristol Journal* claimed 'never was more loyalty and affection evinced towards our well-beloved sovereign'.[41] The military, including the Volunteers, once more turned out, in front of 'innumerable' spectators, 'and a sensation of joy was visible on every countenance'.[42]

When the news that the preliminaries of peace had been signed on 1 October was communicated by Charles Bragge MP to Bristol's notorious patriot-publican, John Weeks, at the Bush Tavern, 'this city experienced a shock (we may be allowed the expression) of joy words cannot describe; no sooner was it known than the bells of every church began firing incessantly, and thousands flocked around the Bush tavern to hear the glad tidings'.[43] For a week the city awaited the news of the ratification of the treaty with France; and *Felix Farley* voiced fears that mischievous individuals would ruin the proceedings by their practical joking.[44] The mail coach carrying the news of the ratification approached around 2.00 p.m. on Sunday 11 October,

when, with colours flying and covered with ribbons and laurel, it entered, drawn by eight horses, having diadems on their heads, preceded by a party of the Queen's Bays, a city-officer on horse-back bearing the British flag; and then Mr Weeks in his curicle, and accompanied by a musical gentleman, the delightful sound of whose trumpet announced the joyful tidings. Immediately followed the Mail-coach, a troop of the Queen's Bays, then a large number of gentlemen on horseback, and the rear of the procession was brought up by a multitude too great for us to form any estimate of its numbers. Besides the tens of thousands who were waiting in our streets to welcome the arrival of the Mail, the windows of every house near which it had to pass, were crowded with ladies, who, waving their handkerchieves, smilingly hailed the auspicious harbinger of peace. But amidst the general joy, it was gratifying to observe, that public testimonies of it which were manifested did not trench upon the duties or decencies of the Sabbath; for during divine services in the afternoon, all was stillness and propriety; but afterwards, the bells of the parish-churches were merrily rung until a late hour.[45]

[39] Emsley, *British society*, ch. 4; Albert Goodwin, *The friends of liberty: the English democratic movement in the age of the French revolution* (London, 1979), pp. 451–4.
[40] *FFBJ, BMBJ*, 7 June 1800.   [41] *BMBJ*, 6 June 1801.   [42] *Ibid.*
[43] *BMBJ*, 5 Oct. 1801.   [44] *FFBJ*, 10 Oct. 1801.   [45] *Ibid.*, 17 Oct. 1801.

At dawn on Monday, celebrations continued. The streets were crowded, bells were ringing, and the military were drawn up on Brandon Hill to fire 'three vollies and a *feu de joie*, upon which occasion the precision of the Volunteers was highly and deservedly complimented'.[46] Mr Weeks displayed himself once more before a 'numerous assembly of the populace', and in the evening there was an illumination. The illuminated 'transparencies' decorating the houses of the 'principal inhabitants' and principal buildings were described in the press at great length.[47]

As in the case of the April riot, events were 'appropriated'. The ladies, the Volunteers, the eccentric Mr Weeks and the illuminated houses of the wealthy drew the attention of the newspapers. The populace, 'numerous' and 'inestimable', were, by the very function of turning out in the thousands which the Bristol establishment hoped for, rendered anonymous. *Bonner and Middleton* once more directed attention towards the magistrates, and away from the populace:

The evening [of Monday] was remarkably serene and fine, and better order and decorum we believe we never observed on a like occasion. There was a universal cheerfulness displayed in the countenance of the people, and but few thoughtless, mischievous persons in the streets, with their guns or fireworks, either to frighten or annoy the peaceable inhabitants; this we greatly attribute to the very judicious caution of the Magistrates, who ordered public notice to be given through the city to prevent such dangerous, foolish and unmanly proceedings.[48]

But the sharp-eyed Samuel Seyer recorded:

it was very observable, how much more pleasure the poorer classes seemed to receive from the prospect of peace than the richer: the former supposed peace would necessarily produce plenty and cheapness, whereas the richer had made great and unusual profit by the war, and moreover probably foresaw that the peace would not be of long duration.[49]

At first glance, the food riots of April 1801 and the celebrations of a few months later may appear to have little in common. In fact they were intimately connected. The first was the product of despair at economic hardship; the latter the product of hope that such hardships were now to end. October 1801 was a month in which the recently abundant harvest, combined with imports, had triggered an increased supply and decreased price of wheat, and a fall in prices

[46] *Ibid.*   [47] *Ibid.*; *BMBJ*, 17 Oct. 1801.
[48] *BMBJ*, 17 Oct. 1801.   [49] Seyer MSS, p. 53.

generally.[50] The sense of relief must have been immense; and amongst those celebrating will have been those who had either actively rioted, or held sympathies with the rioters, six months earlier. Those in power, and those who reported such events, discouraged such connections. In both instances the *content* of crowd activity was subsumed to the *form* of events. For all the dedication to the moral economy, and for all the displays of loyalty, the crowds in both instances are presented as vague and fickle: as that which tests the local authorities or supports them, which makes public order precarious or patriotic display sublime. It is the prominent, the wealthy, the 'respectable', who emerge, clearly visible, detached and untainted, from out of the crowd.

A similar concern that the peace celebrations of 1801 should only take place within official, prescribed boundaries can be found elsewhere. Despite the *Manchester Gazette*'s sympathetic conclusion that 'the reception that the Peace has met with, is a more correct standard of the general unpopularity of the war than any other evidence that can be adduced', complaint was still made about the 'frequent and dangerous conduct of many *grown children* discharging guns and pistols in public'.[51] In Norwich there were military displays and a dinner for the magistrates and military, but the mayor ordered that celebratory bonfires lit in the market place should be extinguished, and issued a formal notice against unofficial illuminations.[52] The Corporation waited until London had 'set the example' of illuminating before ordering one in Norwich. The result – the illumination of public buildings and the houses of wealthy inhabitants and major employers – occupied several newspaper columns, but the *Mercury* confessed it was 'disappointing to public expectation'.[53] This was not surprising since official notification and spontaneous celebration had by that time occurred ten days earlier. In Liverpool, *Billinge's Advertiser* prefaced a lengthy report of the celebrations of the wealthy by noting:

Great honour is due to the magistrates for the precaution they published, to preserve the safety and quiet of the town, as well as the liberal injunctions in favour of those who might scruple to comply with the mode of rejoicing,

[50] Gayer, Rostow and Schwartz, *Growth and fluctuation*, pp. 61–6; 'Manuscript autobiography of John Bennett, Portishead, 1853', BRO 36097 (a–b), p. 2.
[51] *Manchester Gazette*, 17 Oct. 1801.
[52] *Norwich Mercury*, 10 Oct. 1801.   [53] *Ibid.*, 24 Oct. 1801.

which were generally adopted; nor can we pass over the temper and manners of the populace, who received the requisitions of authority with respect and submission.[54]

1821: CORONATION OF GEORGE IV

If the motivation and sentiment of popular celebration in 1801 was easily subsumed by contemporary reporters to the official version, twenty years later the discrepancies in sincerity between plebeian and patrician celebration were less readily concealed. The effective mobilisation of public display on 'patriotic' occasions had been a hallmark of the latter part of George III's reign. When the French wars were over, and when George III was replaced by his son, the Regent, some of the momentum of that mobilisation was carried over; the content of it, however, changed considerably.

At least part of the reason for the popularity of George III after 1789 was his relative dignity and morality when compared with the profane conduct of his sons, including the Prince of Wales.[55] Of all the royal anniversaries celebrated in Bristol, the king's birthday was the most likely to draw crowds – until 1810 that is, when overt celebration of such anniversaries went into decline. The timing may be significant, for the king was replaced by the Prince of Wales, as Regent, in February 1811. Only once did the Regent's birthday elicit a popular response to Bristol, in August 1816, and that was when crowds turned out in the hope that a triumphal arch, illuminated during Wellington's visit two weeks earlier, would be given a second showing.[56] In the year of the first major scandal involving Queen Caroline, in 1805, an 'immense crowd of spectators' turned out to watch military displays in celebration of her birthday.[57] When the Prince of Wales visited in 1807, there were large crowds, but these may have been the product of his notoriety rather than popularity (and it also happened to be outside working hours).[58]

The golden jubilee of George III, in 1809, and the celebration of the anniversary of his accession, in 1810, both provided different responses from the public and the authorities. It was a discrepancy to be amplified in later years. In the first instance, the Corporation's

---

[54] *Billinge's Liverpool Advertiser*, 19 Oct. 1801.
[55] J.H. Plumb, *The first four Georges* (London, 1959), pp. 143–5.
[56] *FFBJ*, *Bristol Mirror*, 3 Aug. 1816.
[57] *FFBJ*, 19 June 1805.   [58] *Bristol Gazette*, 8 Oct. 1807.

lack of interest in the event contrasted with the parishes who, deliberately eschewing illuminations as a waste of money in austere times, concentrated on providing the poor with food and money. Not surprisingly, while the Corporation received widespread criticism and processed quietly to the mayor's chapel, parish churches, such as St Paul's were 'crowded beyond description'.[59] In the second instance, it was officially decreed that there should be no public celebrations, out of sympathy for the 'afflicting state' of Princess Amelia. But popular celebrations took place just the same. As far as *Felix Farley's Bristol Journal* was concerned, the anniversary was not celebrated in the usual sense;[60] and the *Bristol Gazette* also reported that the anniversary 'was not celebrated in this city by any *public*, municipal or military demonstrations of joy' (emphasis added).[61] What took place in the evening was not a display of patriotism by a loyal and devoted populace, as would have been claimed had events been official, but rather 'the rabble and the boys partaking to the full extent of their accustomed indulgences in bon-fires, squibs and crackers'.[62] The *Gazette* observed that whilst Amelia's condition prevented 'proper' celebrations, 'The mobility . . . in the evening, was restrained by no such delicacy, and squibs, crackers, pumps, and blazing tar barrels on the very Exchange satisfied their appetites for mischief, and disgraced the police of the city.'[63]

This disjunction between official and unofficial perceptions of royal celebrations was undiminished ten years later, on the Regent's accession to the throne, following the death of George III. By this time popular sympathy for reform, and antipathy towards the prince (now to be George IV), was felt nationwide.[64] In Bristol, the ceremonial proclamation of George's accession, on 3 February 1820, brought an 'immense concourse' onto the streets, assisted by fine weather, a large procession and a partial holiday. But it was an 'establishment' event: a Corporation procession with no trades presence, and a Corporation reception for 240 invited guests.[65] The

---

[59] *Ibid.*, 12 Oct. 1809 to 2 Nov. 1809; *FFBJ*, 7 Oct. 1809 to 28 Oct. 1809; 'Register of transactions in and near the city of Bristol, beginning at the year 1799 [–1810]', BRL B10153 MS, 25 Oct. 1809.

[60] *FFBJ*, 27 Oct. 1810.   [61] *Bristol Gazette*, 1 Nov. 1810.

[62] *FFBJ*, 27 Oct. 1810.   [63] *Bristol Gazette*, 1 Nov. 1810.

[64] Stevenson, *Popular disturbances*, pp. 190–218; Plumb, *First four Georges*, pp. 184–216; E.P. Thompson, *The making of the English working class* (Harmondsworth, 1963), pp. 660–780.

[65] *FFBJ, Bristol Mirror*, 5 Feb. 1820; *Bristol Gazette*, 3 Feb. 1820, 10 Feb. 1820; *Bristol Mercury*, 7 Feb. 1820.

tory, and deeply loyalist, *Felix Farley* claimed that 'the enthusiasm and shouts of the populace were as warm and loud as the most loyal of his Majesty's subjects have even witnessed'.[66] But the *Bristol Mirror* reported that, although the streets were crowded, 'the populace, on this occasion did not join cordially in the acclamations of the higher classes'.[67] These disagreements were to be amplified still further by the Queen Caroline affair.

The Prince of Wales had made a marriage of convenience with Caroline, Princess of Brunswick, in 1795. From the outset, it was a hopeless union, and they separated immediately. In 1814, after years of rumour surrounding her sexual exploits, Caroline left the country. She had already, however, gained the support of a number of whigs and radicals who saw her as a helpless princess used and abused by a morally degenerate and selfish prince. With the accession of the prince to the throne in February 1820, Caroline stated her intention to claim her title as queen. Whigs and radicals rallied behind her, seeing the opportunity to precipitate a crisis for both the tory ministry and the much-loathed new king. Her return to England, in June 1820, produced a display of popular support in London unequalled since the days of Wilkes. The government attempted to disprove her claim to the title by introducing a Bill of Pains and Penalties: in effect, the queen was to be tried by the House of Lords. In the face of massive support for the queen, the Bill was dropped in November 1820, to scenes of great jubilation. The government did not fall, however, and after this climax, interest in Caroline waned. Her attempt to attend the coronation uninvited proved farcical, and only her subsequent death, in August 1821, rekindled public affection.[68]

From the return of Caroline in England in June 1820, the Bristol press was obsessed with her cause. The tory *Felix Farley's Bristol Journal* greeted her arrival with dismay, fearing for public order, and went on to act as a rallying point for supporters of the king and government. The *Bristol Mirror* attempted a neutrality tempered by a conservative scepticism. But both the *Mercury* (openly radical since the editorship of Thomas Manchee in 1818)[69] and the *Gazette* (pro-reform whig) came out in vociferous defence of Caroline. Editorials

---

[66] *FFBJ*, 5 Feb. 1820. [67] *Bristol Mirror*, 5 Feb. 1820.
[68] John Stevenson, 'The Queen Caroline affair', in J. Stevenson (ed.), *London in the age of reform* (Oxford, 1971), pp. 117–48; Plumb, *First four Georges*, pp. 167–77.
[69] Harold Lewis, *The history of the Bristol Mercury 1715–1886* (Bristol, 1886?), in 'Bristoliana', BRL B21964. In 1818 the circulation of the *Mercury* was only 300

and leader columns now became a feature of these newspapers. Barely a week passed during the remainder of 1820 when the *Mercury* and *Gazette* did not report the state of royal play, and pass judgements of their own. In July the *Gazette* claimed 'The QUEEN is still the only topic of public interest.'[70] The newspapers, through their overt politicisation of the issue, were sponsors of a controversy which split Bristol society in two.

An address in support of the queen in August 1820 was reputedly signed by 24,640 Bristolians.[71] *Felix Farley* retaliated by attacking the social status of the signatories.[72] The social divide was widened by the news of the abandonment of the Bill of Pains and Penalities. As the main coach approached,

> a waving of hats was the signal of the affirmation when the 'welking rang' [*sic*] with loud huzzas from an immense concourse of people – on Monday there was a partial illumination, which would probably have been more general, if the magistrates, fearful of disturbance, had not advised their fellow-citizens to restrain their *loyalty*.[73]

The *Mirror* claimed the failure of the illumination demonstrated the lack of public support for the queen, and cited as evidence the fact that illuminations were only widespread in poorer areas such as Broadmead. In fact, of course, this only emphasised the divisiveness of the issue.[74] The tory-dominated select vestries subsequently pledged their loyalty to the monarch; and a request for a public meeting to offer a loyal address represented a roll-call of Bristol's wealthy tories. The list of names included three aldermen, both the sheriffs, three Common Councillors and prominent individuals such as the bible-thumping John S. Harford, and veritable tory institutions George Daubeny and Thomas Davies. The prominent Bristol family names of Hilhouse, Hassell, George, Daniel, Vaughan and Harford dominate the list.[75]

During 1821 concern for Caroline was largely replaced by

copies a week, although by 1840 it was to become the foremost newspaper in the west of England. The circulation of the *Gazette*, *Mirror* and *FFBJ*, were all around 1,000 weekly. All Bristol newspapers at this time were voraciously perused in taverns and club rooms: 'Under five monarchs – Bristol in old days – veteran citizen's reminiscences' (extract from *Bristol Mercury*, 1902?), BRL B3630; Charles A. Elton, *An apology for Colonel Hugh Baillie* (Bristol, 1819), p. 4.

[70] *Bristol Gazette*, 20 July 1820.
[71] *FFBJ*, 23 Sept. 1820; *Bristol Mercury*, 9 Oct. 1820.
[72] *FFBJ*, 9 Sept. to 30 Sept. 1820.   [73] *Bristol Gazette*, 16 Nov. 1820.
[74] *Bristol Mirror*, 10 June 1820.   [75] *Bristol Gazette*, 30 Nov. 1820.

speculation regarding the form of the forthcoming coronation celebrations, and by the efforts of George IV's supporters to ensure the occasion was a success. In February the *Gazette* complained that the tories had attempted to appropriate the celebrations of the anniversary of George IV's succession.[76] As the day approached it reflected that some good had come from the Caroline affair, namely that

The people will become better informed of the nature and use of a Coronation; it is a solemn ceremony at which the compact between sovereign and subject is completed, the antiquity as well as design of the ceremony render it worthy of veneration and respect; with these feelings we regretted to see it stigmatised in some Journals as a ridiculous and useless pageantry.[77]

One of those journals was the *Mercury*. An editorial in June contrasted the sufferings of the poor with the continuing and conspicuous comfort of the rich. The coronation was an unjustifiable expense. 'The most splendid robe with which the Prince can invest himself', declared the *Mercury*, 'is in our estimation, sympathy with the wants, wishes, and distresses of the people.'[78] The argument was sustained in the following edition, the coronation now being termed 'this splendid gewgaw'.[79] In July an editorial condemned 'the performance of a useless, but enormously expensive ceremony'. 'Whose eyes,' the *Mercury* asked, 'do they [the government] think this pageant is to blind?'[80] Two days before the coronation the pro-reform Concentric Society joined in the resurrection of the queen's cause, supporting her 'just claims' to be present at the coronation.[81] But the *Gazette*, by this time, was unqualified in its determination to stem divisiveness. On the eve of the coronation, it proclaimed that

We hail the occasion with pleasure; because it is one of the few opportunities when all party distinctions are lost in general feeling and good fellowship – The King is Monarch of the beggar as well as the noble; he is king of the Whig and the Tory; of the Royalist and Radical; and when the Crown is placed on his head so weighty is the burthen, that all should unite and shout – *'God bless him.'*[82]

Others, with different political views, shared the *Gazette's* desire to see the celebrations succeed. The Corporation set up a committee

[76] *Ibid.*, 1 Feb. 1821.   [77] *Ibid.*, 12 July 1821.
[78] *Bristol Mercury*, 11 June 1821.   [79] *Ibid.*, 23 June 1821.   [80] *Ibid.*, 7 July 1821.
[81] Notice dated 17 July 1821 in *Bristol Gazette*, 19 July 1821.
[82] *Ibid.*, 19 July 1821.

specifically to plan the festivities. They announced the proposed form of celebrations as early as 25 June[83] (unlike the authorities in Bath, who asked Bristol what they should do),[84] and added further details to their plans during July.[85] These arrangements were almost exclusively for the elite, however, with the only gestures towards popular festivity being the pledge *not* to have a bonfire and the issuing of the notice prohibiting the discharge of firearms and fireworks in the streets.[86] Individual inhabitants expressed opinions as to how the celebrations might be improved, requested they be well publicised and that the present route should take in populous areas.[87] The Bristol Military Pensioners Society observed that 'should their services ever be required in quelling any disturbance they will feel it a duty incumbent on them to rally around the Union and the Laws for the protection of which they consider as duty they owe to their Sovereign and their Country'.[88]

At 1.00 a.m. on Thursday 19 July, cannon on Brandon Hill announced the commencement of celebrations. The salute was repeated at 4.00 a.m., and at intervals throughout the day. Around 8.00 a.m., 'gentlemen with parties of well-dressed females were seen escorting them to the different houses of their friends through which the intended Procession was to pass; and the Parish bells were all ringing merry peals'.[89] The weather was 'the finest we have enjoyed this summer'. At 9.00 a.m., 'the Ministers, Churchwardens, and Vestries of the different parishes began to walk in procession to the Guildhall, most of them proceeded with a Royal Blue Banner, made for the occasion, there to wait till the other parties had assembled at the Council House, from which the procession to the Cathedral was to commence'.[90] This set off at 12.30, was generally agreed to have taken precisely thirty-seven minutes in passing,[91] and reached the Cathedral at 2.00 p.m. for a religious service; 120 'Ladies' were allowed to attend the Cathedral with tickets. The Dean spoke on the subject of 'Love the Brotherhood, fear God, honour the King.' To his dismay, a 'general admission' to the Cathedral after the arrival of the

[83] Circular from coronation committee, 25 Jan. 1821, LMP/BRO Box 1820–1.
[84] P. George Jnr, Bath to Town Clerk, Bristol, 19 June 1821, LMP/BRO Box 1820–1.
[85] 'Coronation papers', July 1821, LMP/BRO Box 1820–1.
[86] *Ibid.*
[87] Letter from 'A member of the White Lyon Club' (*sic*), July 1821, LMP/BRO Box 1820–1; 'A citizen' to Hilhouse, 13 July 1821, LMP/BRO Box 1820–1; 'A Freeman' to Hilhouse, 16 July 1821, LMP/BRO Box 1820–1.
[88] Christopher Ford, secretary, to magistrates, July 1821, LMP/BRO Box 1820–1.
[89] *FFBJ*, 21 July 1821.   [90] *Ibid.*   [91] *Ibid.*, and *Bristol Gazette*, 26 July 1821.

11 A handbill detailing the order of procession for the celebration of the coronation of George IV. Note the absence of all but a few trades.

official procession was prevented. After the service the procession, which had approached the Cathedral via High Street, the Back, Princess Street, the Quay and St Augustine's Back, now returned to the Council House via Clare, Wine, Dolphin, Bridge and High Streets. At the Assembly Rooms, there was a coronation dinner for around 250 invited 'gentlemen', the names of all of which were listed by *Felix Farley*.[92] The evening was marked by fireworks on Brandon Hill, and a general illumination.[93]

Popular participation in the celebrations was minimal. The procession, dominated by the Corporation, the military, merchants and the freemasons, contained only a marginal trades presence.[94] *Felix Farley*, after two closely written columns describing the procession and the Assembly Room dinner, with its toasts and speeches to the government, the king, constitution, and to Bristol's mercantile prosperity, could only muster a note that 'The poorer orders of society in our city and neighbourhood were not forgotten on this interesting occasion. It is impossible for us to enumerate or collect particulars for this day's publication.' The following week, in keeping with the *Gazette*, the varying degrees of parish philanthropy in handing out bread, cheese and money to the poor received limited attention.[95] In terms of festivity, the fireworks on Brandon Hill were the full extent of official arrangements for the poor. The reports of the subsequent illumination consisted of a list of well-known buildings and personalities.[96]

Despite *Felix Farley*'s assertion that 'Never since we have had the honour of putting upon record a description of passing events, have we felt such unmixed gratification as we do in detailing the events of this day in Bristol. It was from sun-rise to sun-set a continued ebullition of loyalty, rejoicing, and good humour',[97] the coronation celebrations seem to have been met by very little public enthusiasm. Unsurprisingly, the *Mercury* was the first to point this out. In its leader of 21 July it stated regret that the maltreatment of Caroline should have produced a coronation 'of a King of England exciting a spirit of bitter disappointment throughout the country'. This was reflected in Bristol, where,

[92] *FFBJ*, 21 July 1821.   [93] *Bristol Gazette*, 26 July 1821.

[94] *FFBJ*, 21 July 1821; *Order of procession on celebrating the coronation of his Majesty King George the Fourth in the city of Bristol, on Thursday, the 19th of July, 1821* (Bristol, 1821), BRO 32079(224)d.

[95] *FFBJ*, 21 and 28 July 1821; *Bristol Gazette*, 2 Aug. 1821.

[96] *Bristol Gazette*, 26 July 1821.   [97] *FFBJ*, 21 July 1821.

A more spiritless pageant we never witnessed ... From the time the procession started from the Council-House till it returned, no one cheer of approbation from *the people* marked its progress, and yet there were myriads assembled to witness it: not a handkerchief waved from the crowded windows of the streets through which it passed – and yet the windows of this city were never graced with a more numerous and respectable assemblage of female beauty: the pageant passed through the streets in all the silent dullness of a funeral procession.[98]

Even the illumination, although it had its moments, was not in fact 'general': 'The public feeling was most unequivocally expressed; "the Queen, the Queen" was the universal cry through the street; and though there were so many houses without lights, we have not heard of a single broken pane of glass.'[99]

The *Gazette* believed the *Mercury* overstated the case, but confessed that 'There was an absence of martial music, particularly of trumpets, the heralds being the most *silent* we ever witnessed; nor was there much popular applause,' and added, revealingly, 'yet the Procession was gay, and in other eyes than those accustomed to a Bristol Election pageant, would have been thought splendid.'[100] The *Mercury* pounced on this admission:

What! a procession in honour of the coronation of a patriot king, which occurs only once in his life, to add to the splendour of which the whole influence of the city was put forth, and yet to be admitted inferior to an election pageant, – a mere party ebullition in honour of a private individual, of every five or six years occurrence![101]

The *Mercury* took its accusation of the event's failure as far as to argue that it was only the scandalous treatment of the queen that gave the 'great body of the people' in England any interest in the coronation at all.[102]

The news of the queen's death was first reported in the later editions of the *Gazette* on 9 August. In the following black-edged edition the editorial rediscovered its earlier attachment to Caroline's cause: 'THAT event, which defeats all human calculation and blasts the expectancy of all human hopes, has taken place in the instance of CAROLINE, Queen of England.'[103] The bells of the parish churches tolled, flags on public buildings and on a number of ships were at half-mast, some shops closed, and the Council (perhaps as a sign of

[98] *Bristol Mercury*, 21 July 1821.   [99] *Ibid.*   [100] *Bristol Gazette*, 26 July 1821.
[101] *Bristol Mercury*, 28 July 1821.   [102] *Ibid.*   [103] *Bristol Gazette*, 16 Aug. 1821.

grief, but more probably in self-protection) shut up its shutters.[104] The *Mercury* claimed that amongst the 'impatient assemblage' that awaited confirmation of the news, 'every face was sorrow'.[105]

The barely concealed antagonisms in the Bristol celebration were far from unique. In Liverpool there was a similar background of support for George III and Caroline. An estimated 50,000 people watched the celebrations of George III's jubilee in 1809 – celebrations taken very seriously by the *Liverpool Courier*, which believed that 'holding so high a rank in the empire it was a consideration of great importance how its [Liverpool's] affection for our venerable sovereign should be expressed'.[106] The turn-out for the proclamation of George IV's accession was even larger – 100,000 was the *Liverpool Mercury*'s claim – and does seem to have passed off with little dissent, assisted no doubt by the beef and ale with which employers regaled their workers throughout the afternoon and evenings. The *Mercury*, however, was careful to point out that the participation of all political parties in the procession indicated a respect for 'one of the branches of the constitutional government', and should not necessarily be understood as 'paying any homage' to the new monarch 'as an *individual*'.[107] The signs of political difference were to emerge soon afterwards, however, with 35,000 taking to the streets to celebrate the abandonment of the Bill of Pains and Penalties.[108]

As in Bristol, the Caroline affair dominated the Liverpool press throughout 1820. During the first half of 1821 the issue died down. In July, however, the *Mercury* was questioning the 'mummery' and 'propriety of a gorgeous ceremony' at a time when the money could have been better used for charitable purposes.[109] It was also making mention of the 'peculiar' arrangements planned in Liverpool. The Corporation, through its select finance committee, was making preparations for the grand opening of Prince's dock, which had been under construction since 1811 – a celebration 'judiciously reserved for the day of his Majesty's coronation'.[110] It was an ingenious idea, typical of Liverpool Corporation's pragmatism, which enabled all trades and political parties to take part, and could divert some attention from support for the queen. Furthermore, at a time of

---

[104] *Ibid.*   [105] *Bristol Mercury*, 11 Aug. 1821.
[106] *Liverpool Courier*, 1 Nov. 1809.   [107] *Liverpool Mercury*, 25 Feb. 1820.
[108] *Ibid.*, 24 Nov. 1820.   [109] *Ibid.*, 6 July 1821.
[110] Liverpool Corporation, select finance committee minute book, LRO, vol. IV, 7 July 1821; Liverpool Corporation, town books, LRO, 17 July 1821; *The Imperial Magazine*, vol. III (Liverpool, 1821), p. 772.

complaints regarding the profligacy of such celebrations, the final preparation of the dock provided some temporary employment. Editor of the *Liverpool Mercury*, Egerton Smith, withdrew from the coronation committee in light of political differences;[111] but on coronation day confessed that 'those whose political opinions urged them to condemn the expensive pageant of a coronation, were, at least, pleased to celebrate the opening of a magnificent basin for the more substantial purposes of commerce'.[112] The opening of the dock 'was calculated to rouse the most cheerful feelings of civic gratulation and national pride'.[113]

The celebrations themselves, however, showed evidence of the discontent which the Corporation was, presumably, attempting to contain. Although pro-Caroline banners were omitted from the official procession, spectators carried flags proclaiming 'Queen Caroline'. As the procession moved off from the dock, the band at its head struck up 'The girl I left behind me', and, 'as the evening closed, the streets were enlivened with cries of "the Queen", "the Queen" from hundreds of men who had during the day maintained the most respectful silence as a mark of coincidence on the objects of the splendid pageant'.[114] 'Perhaps 80,000 individuals' were in the streets during the day. The opening of the dock 'was unmarked by any tincture of politics – all eyes being fixed, and all minds absorbed in the more worthy (because of the two, the only profitable) pageant, of opening the new dock for the purposes of commerce'. But as for the procession, 'it appeared to us to move along self-cheered and self-elated, and altogether unmarked by those hearty rounds of general applause and enthusiasm, which we have so often witnessed in the processions of the independent freemen of *Liverpool*'.[115]

In Norwich the plans to celebrate George III's jubilee in 1809 with the roasting of a bullock in the market place, the distribution of beer, and a bonfire, were overturned by the Court of Aldermen. A Corporation procession and a private dinner were the final extent of festivities, with all popular participation effectively excluded.[116] The proclamation of George IV was similarly a Corporation-dominated event, with no trades involvement or general public celebrations.[117] With the news of the abandonment of the Pains and Penalties Bill, the Corporation issued notices forbidding popular celebration, and

[111] *Liverpool Mercury*, 20 July 1821.
[112] *Ibid.*   [113] *Ibid.*   [114] *Ibid.*   [115] *Ibid.*
[116] *Norfolk Chronicle*, 14 and 21 Oct. 1809.   [117] *Ibid.*, 5 Feb. 1820.

swore in 1,000 special constables – an act which led one anonymous correspondent to accuse the mayor of wishing 'to get up a Manchester riot'.[118] The *Chronicle*, a copy of which was allegedly burned in the course of the celebrations, poured abuse upon the crowds which defied the Corporation's orders and marched with torches and placards, describing them as 'the rabble' and like 'a political mob'.[119] A profusion of handbills and broadsides were published in support of Caroline.[120] On the coronation day, the Corporation again issued restrictive notices, but this time, after a procession once more without trade participation, distributed beef, beer and bread in the market place. The *Chronicle* delighted in the sight of 'loyal John Bull and his numerous family' scrambling for the food; but the day's celebrations were nevertheless once more geared to the Corporation.[121]

The proclamation of George IV in Manchester was made with almost no public support. After the reading of the proclamation by the boroughreeve in St Anne's Square, only 'a very small portion of the people assembled joined the authorities of the town and the soldiers in giving nine cheers'.[122] The abandonment of Pains and Penalties allegedly brought thousands onto the streets, although there were no organised celebrations – a state of affairs *Cowdroy's Gazette* considered shameful when compared with the rest of the country.[123] Rather like the *Bristol Gazette*, however, when coronation day arrived, *Cowdroy's Gazette* shifted its weight behind the desire for a consensual display. It heaped praise upon the preparations of the coronation committee, and claimed that 'the long period that has elapsed since the same ceremony was performed for George the Third, nearly two generations of man, has whetted the curiosity of all, to witness the scene'.[124] *Cowdroy's* delight turned to disgust, however, as the populace, regaled with food and drink, began to express their true allegiance. Bribed by one of the yeomanry (who were jeered throughout the day, in memory of Peterloo) to cheer for the king in return for a barrel of beer, 'while the beer lasted the mob shouted; but as soon as it was done, they, ungratefully, forgetting the lessons just taught them, sent up a spontaneous chorus of God save the Queen'.[125] The *Guardian* believed it was 'the rabble without

---

[118] *Ibid.*, 25 Nov. 1820; Norwich Corporation, books of proceedings of court of mayoralty, NRO, vol. XLI, 16 Nov. 1820.   [119] *Ibid.*
[120] 'Collection of handbills, broadsides etc. relating to Queen Caroline', NPL/LS.
[121] *Norfolk Chronicle*, 21 July 1821.
[122] *Cowdroy's Manchester Gazette*, 12 Feb. 1820.
[123] *Ibid.*, 18 Nov. 1820.   [124] *Ibid.*, 21 July 1821.   [125] *Ibid.*, 28 July 1821.

conduct or fixed principles which is always to be found amongst the population of an immense town' which was responsible for the worst scenes of dissipation.[126] It also claimed, more generally, that 'the show was splendidly got up and the whole went off very well, but . . . we observed no symptoms whatever of enthusiastic feeling'.[127]

1831: CORONATION OF WILLIAM IV

Ten years later the position was reversed. As *The Times* of London noted in 1831, whereas 'the cold, fastidious, selfishness of . . . George IV repelled the "sweet voices" of the commonalty whenever he condescended not to spurn them',[128] William IV, with his sympathy for reform, was an extremely popular new monarch. Local Corporations, however, felt rather less affection for him. As the *Bristol Mercury* was to observe on coronation day:

the conduct of the Monarch, which has rendered him so popular in the estimation of his subjects, and which had in this city so unequivocally elicited their approbation, is opposed to the polity of that body [the Corporation] in their collective capacity, as, indeed, it unquestionably is to the practice of every close Corporation in the United Kingdom.[129]

In Bristol, the proclamation of the new king in July 1830, shortly after the death of George IV, had produced large crowds, despite poor weather and the limitation of Corporation celebrations to the bare minimum of the proclamatory procession.[130] As the coronation approached, the Corporation did not, this time, form a committee to plan the day's events; indeed, the Corporation records show no signs of any official preparations. In the face of such official uninterest, the trades took over the event, adding their numbers, banners and symbols, unsolicited, to what would otherwise have been a routine Corporation procession.[131] Despite the pouring rain, and the absence of many of the 'principal inhabitants', the *Mercury* was delighted with the spectacle:

From what we had witnessed of the public spirit of the mechanics and artizans of this city, we felt confidence in stating that the procession would be

126 *Manchester Guardian*, 21 July 1821.   127 *Ibid.*
128 *The Times* (London), 9 Sept. 1831.   129 *Bristol Mercury*, 13 Sept. 1831.
130 *Ibid.*, 6 July 1830; *Bristol Mirror, FFBJ*, 3 July 1830.
131 *Bristol Mercury*, 13 Sept. 1831; 'Greetheads panoramic sketch of the procession to Bristol Cathedral, Thursday the 8th September 1831 on the coronation day of their majesties William IV and Adelaide', BRO 17571 MS.

a splendid one; but in reality our expectations were greatly exceeded by the magnificent spectacle which graced our streets and gratified the immense concourse of spectators who crowded them.[132]

The number of Bristolians was reportedly swelled by the presence of 50,000 of the population of the surrounding towns and villages.[133]

The *Mercury* was nevertheless disappointed by the lack of Corporation interest:

we cannot conclude our report of the proceedings on this memorable day without regretting that the authorities should have manifested, comparatively, a degree of apathy with regard to its celebrations, ill according with the much vaunted loyalty of this ancient city. As it was, however, we rejoice to say, the ardent feelings of the people more than compensated for the falling off of the usual observances, though we have reason to know that our fellow-citizens would have been better pleased had there been a Public dinner and a Ball, as at the former Coronation.[134]

Felix Farley's Bristol Journal, in the difficult position of opposing the implicit political sentiments expressed through a nevertheless royalist event, contented itself with insisting that political differences were '*almost* entirely excluded' from the celebrations.[135] It also chose to highlight differences among the trades themselves by reprinting a notice issued by the cordwainers, in which they explained their intention to boycott the celebrations because

idle pageantry cannot add anything to the dignity of the SOVEREIGN, but only afford the rich and powerful of an opportunity of displaying the wealth that they have wrung from the pockets of a suffering people. And they believe that idle show has a tendency to abstract the mind from the considerations of higher import. And they further declare their decided objection of following in the train of the high Tories.[136]

That reform was the motivating factor in popular support of the 1831 coronation was demonstrated by events nine months later. On the anniversary of William's birthday, in May 1832, at a time when the king was showing reluctance to create new peers and thereby enable the passing of the Reform Bill, and in the wake of the 1831 riots, public opinion in Bristol showed a reversal. When a military officer called to 'the people' for a 'huzza for the king',

[132] *Bristol Mercury*, 13 Sept. 1831.
[133] Daniel Vickery, 'A Bristol calendar containing brief notices of such events as have taken place in this city and its neighbourhood July 1824 to the end of the year 1835', BRL B2639 MS, p. 243.   [134] *Bristol Mercury*, 13 Sept. 1831.
[135] *FFBJ*, 10 Sept. 1831.   [136] *Ibid.*

not a hat moved – not a voice was raised; and an attempt having been made by three gentlemen who were stationed in a car to get up a cheer, the effect of their combined voices proved so ludicrous, that it was speedily stifled in a general laugh, and an universal cry of 'It won't do', from the assembled crowd.[137]

The *Mercury* was correct in 1831 to suppose that a similar situation pertained elsewhere. One week before the coronation celebrations in Liverpool, the *Liverpool Mercury* was complaining that, unlike 1821, 'not a word was heard of corporate preparations'.[138] In the absence of Corporation interest, a succession of meetings were called to arrange independent preparations, and a deputation met the mayor to request a meeting to consider the best mode of celebration. The mayor declined to comply with the request.[139] A meeting of trades was planned for 15 September 1831, but their leaders failed to turn up; the editors of the *Mercury*, Egerton Smith and John Smith, who *were* present therefore took the opportunity to address the crowd from a balcony in Queen Square. Egerton Smith declared that since the Corporation might fail to 'do honour' to the rendering of 'God save the King', 'the people should remind them of their duty by assembling around the Town-hall in thousands and sing the national air in full chorus (Roars of applause, and cries of "we will, we will".)'.[140]

When it came to coronation day Liverpool Corporation took their apathy further than their Bristol counterparts by taking no part at all in the celebrations. They abandoned the proceedings entirely to the reformers, who duly organised a procession made up of trades and friendly societies, and formed a meeting in Clayton Square, attended by 15,000 people, to address the king and queen. In the evening there were fireworks, with the *Mercury* (having a strong interest in the success of the proceedings) declaring that it had 'not heard of any accident or the slightest breach of the peace throughout the day'.[141]

There was a similar story in Manchester:

Although the preparations in this town to celebrate the Coronation of William IV, received no such encouragement from the authorities as was given to those for the coronation of George IV, the loyal spirit of the people, grateful for the measures of reform which his Majesty has sanctioned, was abundantly manifested. The day by tacit but universal consent was,

---

[137] *Bristol Mercury*, 2 June 1832.   [138] *Liverpool Mercury*, 2 Sept. 1831.
[139] *Ibid.*, 9 Sept. 1831.   [140] *Ibid.*   [141] *Ibid.*

throughout all parts of the town observed as a holiday, and probably nineteen twentieths of the inhabitants were collected into the streets through which the procession passed.[142]

The procession, which was attended by the local authorities, was dominated by trade societies, marching in costume, carrying symbols of their occupations. One group of weavers did, however, stage a demonstration to draw attention to their distress.[143]

In Norwich, it was inevitable that the political element of the coronation would divide the city. 'The spirit of party, which infuses itself more or less into everything appertaining to public transactions in this city,'[144] split the Corporation, and the tory-dominated Court of Aldermen would not agree to any official celebrations. In the event a committee of 'gentlemen' combined with the mayor and some members of the Corporation to stage a procession to the Cathedral. A foundation stone was then laid at the new Bazaar in St Andrew's Street (perhaps a small-scale version of the tactics employed by Liverpool Corporation in 1821), and in the evening there was a private dinner, and a general illumination.[145]

THE PRECARIOUS CONCEPT OF CONSENSUS

The depiction by historians of patriotic events such as coronations as 'consensual' stems from the work of Emile Durkheim, and has, more recently, been developed by sociologists such as Shils and Young.[146] All societies, they argue, require rituals which state commonly shared values and beliefs, and which reflect a moral consensus. The symbolic elements of ceremonial provide a corporate means both of making sense of, and expressing, reality. Consequently, national ceremonial events such as coronations possess a quasi-religious significance; or, put another way, secular and religious ceremonials may hold similar functions and employ similar devices.[147] In the elements of the present-day coronation ceremony, Shils and Young contend, it is possible to locate specific statements about the position and function of the monarch in British society.[148] Their perception of a conscious

---

[142] *Manchester Times*, 10 Sept. 1831.   [143] *Ibid.*
[144] *Norwich Mercury*, 19 Sept. 1831.   [145] *Ibid.*, 3 Sept. 1831, 10 Sept. 1831.
[146] Emile Durkheim, *The elementary forms of the religious life*, trans. Joseph Ward Swain (London, 1915; this edn, London, 1976); E. Shils and M. Young, 'The meaning of the coronation', *Sociological review*, new series, I, 2 (1953), pp. 63–81.
[147] Durkheim, *The religious life*, p. 427.
[148] Shils and Young, 'The coronation', pp. 73–5.

symbolism is borne out, in part at least, by close examination of royal and civic spectacle in England from the fifteenth to the seventeenth centuries, and by the deliberate invention of royal and civic ritual during the last quarter of the nineteenth century.[149]

Although it might be agreed that national events represent an opportunity for at least some sections of the population to assert or create a sense of social consensus, some sociologists, anthropologists and historians have questioned whether these events contain such uniform and clearly understood significance as would seem to be suggested by Shils and Young.[150] Steven Lukes and N. Birnbaum have both pointed out that ceremonial occasions may facilitate the presentation only of propaganda for the dominant value system (the expression of *a* reality, not *the* reality); and that conflictual events may be as much at work in social integration and cohesion as is supposed 'value consensus'.[151]

It has been emphasised by Jack Goody that the existence of common norms does not necessarily depend upon the existence of general assemblies;[152] it could also be said, of course, that the

---

[149] D.M. Bergeron, *English civic pageantry, 1558–1642* (London, 1971); Charles Phythian-Adams, 'Ceremony and the citizen: the communal year at Coventry 1450–1550', in P. Clark and P. Slack (eds.), *Crisis and order in English towns 1500–1700: essays in urban history* (London, 1972), pp. 57–85; Gerard Reedy, 'Mystical politics: the imagery of Charles II's coronation', in Paul J. Korshin (ed.), *Studies in change and revolution: aspects of English intellectual history, 1640–1800* (Menston, 1972), pp. 19–42; Roy Strong, *Splendour at court: renaissance spectacle and illusion* (London, 1973); David Cannadine, 'The transformation of civic ritual in modern Britain: the Colchester oyster feast', *Past and Present*, no. 94 (Feb. 1982), pp. 107–30; Cannadine, 'Context, performance and meaning of ritual'.

[150] Robert Bocock, *Ritual in industrial society – a sociological analysis of ritualism in modern England* (London, 1974), ch. 3; N. Birnbaum, 'Monarchs and sociologists: a reply to Professor Shils and Mr Young', *Sociological Review*, new series, III, 1 (1955), pp. 5–23; J.G. Blumler, J.R. Brown, A.J. Ewbank and T.J. Nossiter, 'Attitudes to the monarchy: their structure and development on a ceremonial occasion', *Political Studies*, XIX, 2 (1971), pp. 149–71; Cannadine, 'Context, performance and meaning', p. 111; Abner Cohen, 'Political symbolism', *Annual Review of Anthropology*, VIII (1979), p. 102; Jack Goody, 'Against "ritual": loosely structured thoughts on a loosely defined topic', in Sally F. Moore and Barbara G. Myerhoff (eds.), *Secular ritual* (Amsterdam, 1977), p. 31; Hugh Cunningham observes that although there was working class attendance at 'patriotic' events in the last quarter of the nineteenth century, the reasons for attendance were related to an enjoyment of the show of conservative patriotism, rather than to outright approval of the ideology itself: Cunningham, 'The language of patriotism', pp. 25–7.

[151] Steven Lukes, 'Political ritual and social integration', *Sociology*, IX, 2 (1975), pp. 289–308; Birnbaum, 'Monarchs and sociologists'.

[152] Jack Goody, 'Religion and ritual: the definitional problem', *British Journal of Sociology*, XII, 2 (1961), p. 146.

existence of general assemblies on ceremonial occasions does not in itself indicate the existence of common norms. Equally, the occurrence of those assemblies is unlikely in itself to *create* the existence of common norms. In other words, the display of a corporate agreement as to generally held values and beliefs presupposes the prior existence, in embryonic form at the very least, of those values and beliefs, in order that their display in public and corporate form may be possible. The only prominently held common norm in Bristol society which was relevant to the local celebrations of 1821 was the acceptance of the monarchy as an institution. There was not even, however, a general acceptance of particular monarchs.[153] A substantial body of opinion in Bristol thought George IV to be an unworthy king. Similarly, although it may have been the case that most Bristolians believed in the existence of municipal government in some form, the particular form of government which ruled the city in 1821 was not universally accepted. On the particular occasion of the coronation celebrations, that 'unacceptable' embodiment of local government was to be found parading its support for an 'unacceptable' king: George IV.

The local authorities and the populace were to be found present at the same celebratory events, but they nevertheless held quite contrary points of view. Those differences of opinion were further emphasised, in the course of the ceremonial, first by the lack of provision of formal means of popular participation, and secondly by the inherent tendency of ceremonial to identify and unite the personnel of power.[154] The performance of the celebrations, building on pre-existing disagreements, thereby solidified conflicts rather than generating consensus. Such conflicts, rooted in long-established grievances, overshadowed the ritualistic component of the celebrations. The order and costume of the Corporation procession, the service in the Cathedral, the processional route, the illuminated emblems and decorations in the windows of private houses and public buildings were understood not as quasi-mystical expressions of the moral order, but rather as just one more example of civic discord. Thus: the

---

[153] Max Gluckman, in *Rituals of rebellion in south-east Africa* (Manchester, 1954), pp. 11–24, observes that criticism of the king, in ritual form, among the Swazi, is *facilitated* by the general acceptance of kingship and the established order. He suggests that the very real opposition to monarchy in modern Europe in fact precludes the expression of hostility to the monarch on a ceremonial occasion.

[154] See, Abner Cohen, 'Political anthropology: the analysis of the symbolism of power relations', *Man*, new series, IV, 2 (1969), pp. 220–1.

scarlet gowns of Bristol Corporation (or Corporations elsewhere) possessed perennial meaning as symbols of wealth and the unity of power; but more importantly they were symbols of a hopeless separation from public opinion.[155] Although the Cathedral might ring with the Dean's call to 'love the Brotherhood, fear God, honour the King', only the wealthy were there to hear it; the general public were both literally and metaphorically excluded. The processional route marked out the already well-understood boundaries of the civic centre; the illuminations seemed designed to draw attention to prominent individuals rather than to display corporate sentiments.

Local authorities almost certainly believed 'successful' spectacles to be in some respect beneficial; after all, those celebrations which received official approval, such as for the coronation of 1821, were the subject of considerable organisation.[156] It is difficult, however, to quantify what 'success' could mean in this context – particularly when the aims of the event are not clearly stated.[157] There are a number of possibilities: a formal and undisturbed expression of power and dominance; an enhancement of the civic image and an appropriate display of civic pride; the staging of a complex event without disturbance or disarray; or the discovery that a consensual evocation was possible. But even if this last possibility appeared in the minds of contemporaries to offer itself, the celebrations discussed here could never *in fact* fulfil such a wish. This is because the ritualism of the celebrations was too weak to unify and express common beliefs on an existential level. Consequently, those crowd events could never attain the 'bivocality' between their organisational and existential elements identified by Abner Cohen as essential to the mystical element in ceremonial.[158]

If ceremonial is to be anything other than a series of formal gestures, it requires total orientation.[159] That orientation was

---

[155] The appearance of Corporation officials on ceremonial occasions is described in W. Mathews, *Mathews's Bristol guide and directory, 1793–4* (Bristol, 1794), pp. 45–6; J. Mathews, *The Bristol guide* (Bristol, 1815), pp. 83–4; *ibid.*, 1829 edn, pp. 80–1.

[156] An example of the organisation of a major spectacle (the Imperial Assemblage, in India, 1876–7), with the explicit hope of giving additional legitimacy to authority, is discussed in Bernard S. Cohen, 'Representing authority in Victorian India', in Hobsbawm and Ranger (eds.), *Invention of tradition*, pp. 165–209.

[157] See Moore and Myerhoff (eds.), *Secular ritual*, pp. 12–15.

[158] Cohen, 'Political symbolism', pp. 102–3.

[159] See Erving Goffman, *Behaviour in public places: notes on the social organisation of gatherings* (New York, 1963), p. 199.

precluded in these cities on these occasions. Indeed, so weak was the ritualistic element that, unless a meaninglessly broad definition of ritual is employed, it could be said that the events were not, in fact, ritualistic at all.[160] It is tempting to use the term nonetheless, because no other word as well conveys the element of formalism and the public display of symbols of power. For the same reason, it is inviting to term such events 'ceremonials'. Indeed, historians and many anthropologists have regarded the terms 'ceremonial' and 'ritual' as synonymous.[161] To break out of these linguistic confusions, therefore, it seems that a clear and distinct terminology for 'empty ritualism' needs to be developed if formal, symbol-carrying, mass display is to be distinguished from corporate, mystifying symbolism.

The participation of distinct social groupings with distinct outlooks in the celebrations of 1801, 1821 and 1831, therefore, represent the formulation not of 'consensus', but of autonomous expressions of group (or class) solidarity. These expressions coincided (occurred in the same location) at celebratory events; different social groupings attended the same events for different reasons, and used these events for the expression of different beliefs. The *form* of celebrations, however, does not necessarily in itself disclose the preconceptions, compromises and contentions that may lay behind an event.[162] And certainly it is hopelessly inadequate to draw from a portrayal of people enjoying themselves the conclusion that here was evidence of people sharing common social and political assumptions. It is only through consideration and identification of the relevant context for a celebratory or ceremonial event that an accurate 'reading' of seemingly ritualistic behaviour becomes possible.[163]

That reading will not be gained merely from the fact of crowd presence. A number of writers have observed that the active quest for, or feeling of, group solidarity is an important feature of popular

---

[160] For discussions of definitions of ritual, see: Bocock, *Ritual in industrial society*, intro. and ch. 2; Goody, 'Religion and ritual'; Goody, 'Against "ritual"'; Peter Marsh, Elizabeth Rosser and Rom Harré, *The rules of disorder* (London, 1978), p. 121; Moore and Myerhoff (eds.), *Secular ritual*; Christel Lane, *The rites of rulers: ritual in industrial society – the Soviet case* (Cambridge, 1981), ch. 1.

[161] Lane, *Rites of rulers*, pp. 14–15.

[162] Elizabeth Hammerton and David Cannadine, 'Conflict and consensus on a ceremonial occasion: the diamond jubilee in Cambridge in 1897', *Historical Journal*, XIX, 1 (1981), pp. 111–46, present a detailed argument to this effect.

[163] Clifford Geertz, *The interpretation of cultures* (New York, 1973), ch. 1; Clifford Geertz, *Negara: the theatre state in nineteenth-century Bali* (Princeton, 1980), ch. 4.

participation on ceremonial occasions.[164] The orientation in this instance, therefore, is towards companions in a mass event, and not the message of the ceremonial itself. In the crowd events discussed here, a sense of solidarity may well have been achieved – particularly for reformers in 1831. But the simple fact of numbers present at an event such as a coronation is insufficient evidence for the existence of such solidarity. Similarly, Philip Zeigler has recorded that, apart from the actual moment of the passing of the coffin, the 'flavour' of the crowd presence at the funeral of George VI in 1952, was remarkably similar to that of his coronation twenty-five years earlier.[165] In short, it is possible to mistake crowd presence for a collective comprehension of, and participation in, the specific ritualism of an event.[166]

Just as it is important not to inflate the 'consensual' element in celebratory and ceremonial crowd events, neither can they straightforwardly be termed 'conflictual'. Conflict is perhaps a less value laden term than 'consensus', suggesting for most purposes simply disagreement. It can also be applied, however, to indicate the existence of an alternative, subversive social framework – a model *for* society. Clearly in the examples discussed here, although popular domination of the 1809 jubilee or William IV's coronation facilitated the presentation of an alternative form of celebration and of different attitudes, it cannot meaningfully be said to have represented the presentation of an alternative *social order*. It has been suggested by Christel Lane that the precondition for the ritualised enactment of conflicting relationships is that the conflict should only be latent at the everyday level. In other words, the ritual event expresses (in an acceptable form) that which cannot be, or is not normally, expressed.[167] But in early nineteenth-century British ceremonial it would appear that precisely the opposite situation pertained: actual

---

[164] Eric Hobsbawm, 'Mass producing traditions: Europe, 1870–1914', in Hobsbawm and Ranger (eds.), *Invention of tradition*, pp. 282–7; Goffman, *Behaviour in public places*, pp. 131–9; Goody, 'Religion and ritual', pp. 146–7; Goody, 'Against "ritual"', p. 31; Philip Zeigler, *Crown and people* (London, 1978), pp. 46–68.

[165] Zeigler, *Crown and people*, pp. 94–5.

[166] Compare, for example: direct participation of spectators in agricultural ceremonies in south-east Africa, described by Gluckman in *Rituals of rebellion*, pp. 14–15; crowd participation in state ceremonials in Bali, analysed by Geertz, *Theatre state in Bali*, pp. 118–19; and Zeigler's discussion of evidence from the British Mass Observation Archive, in *Crown and people*. The relative emptiness of British royal ceremonial quickly becomes apparent.

[167] Lane, *Rites of rulers*, pp. 11–13.

conflicts became, for the most part, latent conflicts for the duration of the ceremonial.

To summarise: celebratory events in these towns in this period were frequently more than they might at first appear. Effusions of loyalism at one level *concealed* disagreements; but, on a closer analysis, it would seem that they more commonly *demonstrated* disagreement. The deliberate mobilisation of large numbers of people around loyalistic events, although effective inasmuch as people were brought into the streets, cannot simply be seen as evidence of popular conservatism, quiescence, effervescence or, indeed, radicalism. Meanwhile, the conceptual language of ritual is helpful primarily in demonstrating the mystical *emptiness*, rather than richness, of these occasions.

Analysis of local and specific contexts and concerns is the most effective means of gaining a meaningful reading of such events. What such analysis shows is that a broad range of crowd events – not only political meetings or riots, but ceremonials and celebrations also – were shot through with local antagonisms, and politicised at a complex level. Crowds could be organised to portray common norms; but their appearance in the street without official sanction or organisation just as powerfully portrayed autonomous sets of preoccupations.

Above all, civic ceremonial was precarious. Fine lines separate the quasi-ritual violence of elections, the quiet antipathy of ceremonials, the good humoured co-mingling of public recreation and the physical violence of riot.[168] It would be a mistake, however, to take this

---

[168] For discussion of the narrow, but distinct, boundaries between aggression and violence, see, for example: E.J. Hobsbawm, The rules of violence', in E.J. Hobsbawm, *Revolutionaries: contemporary essays* (London, 1973), pp. 209–15; E.J. Hobsbawm, 'Political violence and political murder: comments on Franklin Ford's essay', in Wolfgang J. Mommsen and Gerhard Hirschfield (eds.), *Social protest, violence and terror in nineteenth- and twentieth-century Europe* (London, 1982), pp. 13–19; Robin Fox, 'The inherent rules of violence', in Peter Collett (ed.), *Social rules and social behaviour* (Oxford, 1977), pp. 132–49; Peter Marsh, *Aggro: the illusion of violence* (London, 1978); Marsh, Rosser and Harré, *Rules of disorder*. Authorised public gatherings may become the opportunity for the expression of collective grievances; see, for example: Michel Foucault, *Discipline and punish: the birth of the prison*, trans. Alan Sheridan (Harmondsworth, 1979), pp. 57–68; Charles Tilly, 'The web of contention in eighteenth-century cities', in Louise A. Tilly and Charles Tilly (eds), *Class conflict and collective action* (London, 1981), pp. 37–8; Orlando Patterson, 'The cricket ritual in the West Indies', *New Society*, no. 352 (26 June 1969), pp. 988–9. More dramatically still, carnival and violent insurrection may be embodied in one crowd gathering episode: Emmanuel Le Roy

continuity to suggest that all crowd events were points on a finely graded scale of violence; it is as much the case that overt violence was the end of a scale of ritualised and routinised conflict, co-operation and exchange. Certainly contemporaries knew this: there was as much shock borne of a crowd event which fell into violence as there was trepidation created by the potential for havoc of a large and peaceful gathering.

Ladurie, *Carnival in Romans: a people's uprising in Romans, 1579–80*, trans. Mary Feeney (Harmondsworth, 1981); Peter Burke, 'The virgin of the Carmine and the revolt of Masaniello', *Past and Present*, no. 99 (May 1983), pp. 3–21.

11. *Riot and revolt*

O what misery power in bad hands.
(Anon. to Pitt, 3 Oct. 1793, HO 42/26/673)

There was . . . a hangover from the past . . . in the Bristol riots of 1831.
(George Rudé, *The crowd in history 1730–1848: a study of popular
disturbances in France and England* (New York, 1964; revised edn
London, 1981) p. 149)

This book began with the observation that the tendency to see crowds
as essentially violent gatherings has dominated historical discussion
of mass phenomena. The emphasis has been, throughout, on riots as
non-typical in the contemporary experience of crowds: the formulation of attitudes towards large gatherings was conditioned only in
part by popular disturbance. However, if attention is nevertheless
now turned specifically towards the subject of riotous crowds, then a
number of the themes which have emerged in the course of this study
are thrown into sharp relief.

The first of these is also the broadest, namely, the inadequacy of the
division by historians of both popular protest and public order into
categories of industrial and pre-industrial, forward and backward,
traditional and modern. The second is the importance of local
contexts in the reinterpretation of national issues, and the provision
of local imperatives and contingencies. The third theme concerns the
language of crowd description in demonstrating the preconceptions
and preoccupations of contemporary observers. The fourth, related
closely to the third, is the precise distinctions made between crowd
and riot. And the final theme reflects the general sense of shock and
disruption which often accompanied an outbreak of mass violence.

In developing these themes, attention will be concentrated upon
just two examples of riot, both occurring in Bristol: the Bridge riot of
1793 and the reform riot of 1831. This exclusive concentration on
major riot in Bristol does not deny (indeed it recognises) that riots in

other towns were similarly complex in their contexts and repercussions. The two Bristol riots, however, were connected, as it will emerge, in some important regards; and this strong continuity gives Bristol a particularly interesting place in the discussion of 'traditional' and 'pre-industrial' forms of popular protest.

THE METHODOLOGY OF RIOT STUDIES

The radical reappraisals of English rioting crowds made by Hobsbawn, Rose, Rudé and Thompson more than twenty years ago established new premises in the discussion of popular protest.[1] They demonstrated that if the composition, organisation, objectives and beliefs of eighteenth-century rioting crowds were examined closely, then those crowds would be found to have been informed, disciplined and in possession of broad notions of the necessity and legitimacy of their action. To regard such crowds simply as 'rabble', 'mobs' or 'the criminal residuum' was both conceptually misleading and factually wrong.

These formulations have never been seriously challenged. Although numerous riot studies have followed from the new respectability these historians accorded to the discussion of mass violence, criticism of the 'new orthodoxy' has been rare.[2] There is a good reason why the observations of Rudé *et al.* have stood the test of historiographical time: inasmuch as the claims of any historical

---

[1] E.J. Hobsbawm, *Primitive rebels: studies in archaic forms of social movement in the nineteenth and twentieth centuries* (Manchester, 1959); R.B. Rose, 'Eighteenth-century price riots and public policy in England', *International Review of Social History*, VI, 2 (1961), pp. 277–92; George Rudé, *The crowd in history, 1730–1848: a study of popular disturbances in France and England* (New York, 1964; revised edn London, 1981); E.P. Thompson, *The making of the English working class* (Harmondsworth, 1963); E.P. Thompson, 'The moral economy of the English crowd in the eighteenth century', *Past and Present*, no. 50 (Feb. 1971), pp. 76–136.

[2] E.P. Thompson's discussion of the riots of 1766 has been queried by Dale Edward Williams, 'Morals, markets and the English crowd in 1766', *Past and Present*, no. 104 (Aug. 1984), pp. 56–73 (and see, in defence of Thompson, the comment by Andrew Charlesworth and Adrian J. Randall in *Past and Present*, no. 114 (Feb. 1987), pp. 200–13). Thompson was more generally criticised by Geoffrey Best in his review of *The making of the English working class*, in *Historical Journal*, VIII, 2 (1965), pp. 271–81; this, and other criticisms, invoked, much later, a fierce reply by F.K. Donnelly, 'Ideology and early English working-class history: Edward Thompson and his critics', *Social History*, I, 2 (1976), pp. 219–37. The only thoroughgoing critique, however, has remained unanswered and, seemingly, unnoticed: Robert J. Holton, 'The crowd in history: some problems of theory and method', *Social History*, III, 2 (1978), pp. 219–33.

model can survive the scrutiny of the local case study, they have proved to be correct. What is surprising, therefore, is not that the model has been largely unchallenged, but that it has remained largely *undeveloped*. Such has been the influence of the 'crowd historians' that in the subsequent work of other writers, the subjects of composition, organisation and sense of legitimacy have remained the pre-eminent considerations; and 'crowd' and 'riot' have, almost invariably, been used as interchangeable terms. It is only the separation of popular protest into categories of pre-industrial and industrial that has been effectively called into question.[3]

When studying a specific outbreak of mass violence, it is axiomatic that the study should have three simple elements: the context in which the riot occurs, the events of the riot itself and the riot's repercussions. It is tempting, however, thereby to give the riot 'solipsistic' qualities: that is, everything around the riot becomes defined in terms of that riot. Thus, context is seen as consisting of previous riots and disturbances; the event is discussed in terms solely of the activities of the rioters and the forces of suppression; and the repercussions are seen either to relate to further riots or to clearly identifiable claims and issues made in the course of the disturbance. Few riot studies, in practice, fall right into all these traps; but there is a neatness and compactness to the 'riot study' which makes it the perfect case history for publication in article form, and which has perhaps contributed to its conceptual compartmentalisation.[4] It is ironic that one of the clearest examples of such 'solipsism' relates to one of the riots discussed here: Philip D. Jones' examination of the 1793 Bristol Bridge riot.[5]

Perhaps something new could be found to say about riots if this solipsism was challenged. Contexts can be more than just previous disturbance; the examination of crowd activity could go beyond those actually rioting; and repercussions may be far from straightfor-

[3] Holton, 'The crowd in history'; Adrian J. Randall, 'The shearmen and the Wiltshire outrages of 1802: trade unionism and industrial violence', *Social History*, VII, 3 (1982), pp. 283–304; Richard N. Price, 'The other face of respectability: violence and the Manchester brickmaking trade, 1859–70', *Past and Present*, no. 66 (Feb. 1975), pp. 110–32.

[4] See the list of 'riot articles' in ch. 1, fn. 30, and the bibliography below. Many of these, of course, are excellent and important pieces of research.

[5] Philip D. Jones, 'The Bristol bridge riot and its antecedents: eighteenth-century perceptions of the crowd', *Journal of British Studies*, XIX, 2 (1980), pp. 74–92. For detailed summary and criticism of Jones' approach, see: Mark Harrison, ' "To raise and dare resentment": the Bristol Bridge riot of 1793 re-examined', *Historical Journal*, XXVI, 3 (1983), pp. 557–85.

ward. Perhaps also it is necessary now to look beyond the (admittedly still important) notions of crowd discipline, legitimation and the 'moral economy'. It seems all the more appropriate that new perspectives should be sought through two riots which have hitherto been regarded as archetypically 'pre-industrial' and 'backward looking'.

THE BRISTOL BRIDGE RIOT OF 1793

CONTEXTS

Bristol experienced a number of serious riots and disturbances in the eighteenth century. If the riotous and nearby Kingswood colliers, with their periodic 'invasions' of Bristol, and their opposition to turnpikes, are included, then the tally is considerable: 1709, 1714, 1727, 1728, 1740, 1749 and 1753 were all years of well-documented and major disturbance.[6] However, in assessing the consciousness of riot which may have informed the actions of the Bristol magistrates in 1793, it would be stretching the point to make 1753 the last point of reference.[7] Their experience of riot was probably second-hand – through reports of a number of West Country riots in the second half of the eighteenth century, the Wilkite and Gordon riots in London, the Priestley riots in Birmingham and events in France.[8]

[6] *The Bristol riot* (London, 1714); Anon., *The tryals of the rioters at Bristol* (London, 1714); Anon., *A full and impartial account of the late disorders in Bristol* (London, 1714); Samuel Seyer, *Memoirs historical and topographical of Bristol and its neighbourhood*, vol. 2 (Bristol, 1823); J.F. Nicholls and John Taylor, *Bristol past and present*, vol. 3 (Bristol, 1882); W. Hunt, *Bristol* (London, 1887); John Latimer, *The annals of Bristol in the eighteenth century* (Bristol, 1893); Robert W. Malcolmson, '"A set of ungovernable people": the Kingswood colliers in the eighteenth century', in John Brewer and John Styles (eds.), *An ungovernable people: the English and their law in the seventeenth and eighteenth centuries* (London, 1980), pp. 85–127.   [7] As Philip D. Jones does in his 'Bristol bridge riot'.

[8] For major disturbances in the south-west in the eighteenth century, see: William Albert, 'Popular opposition to turnpike trusts in early eighteenth-century England', *Journal of Transport History*, V, 1 (1979), pp. 1–17; Dale Edward Williams, 'Midland hunger riots in 1766', *Midland History*, III, 4 (1976), p. 258; Robert F. Wearmouth, *Methodism and the common people of the eighteenth century* (London, 1945), pp. 27–8, 30–6, 39, 43–5; John Stevenson, *Popular disturbances in England, 1700–1870* (London, 1979); R.S. Neale, *Bath: a social history, 1680–1850* (London, 1981), pp. 90–2, 310–13. For Wilkite, Gordon and Priestley riots, and the influence of France, see: Stevenson, *Popular disturbances*, ch. 4; Rudé, *The crowd*, chs. 3 and 4; John Brewer, *Party ideology and popular politics at the accession of George III* (Cambridge, 1976), ch. 9; P.A. Brown, *The French revolution in English history* (London, 1918), ch. 4; *Bristol Gazette*, 8 June and 15 June 1780, 21 and 28 July 1791.

Of more immediate concern to the local authorities will have been local distress and industrial dispute. Nationally, these were years of steadily rising prices. In Bristol, the price of meat increased 20 per cent between 1789 and 1795; malt prices rose 48 per cent, cheese 65 per cent and flour 116 per cent.[9] Not surprisingly, there were a number of wage demands in the city – most strikingly in 1792, with disputes involving journeyman pipemakers, basket-makers, shoe makers, bakers, farriers, tailors and dressers and weavers.[10] In the building trade a crisis was generated by the collapse of a speculative building boom in Bristol. In 1792 journeymen were taking advantage of the boom to make wage demands.[11] However, the trade crashed in February 1793 with the declaration of war with France.[12] There followed widespread unemployment and a record number of ban-kruptcies.[13] During the second quarter of the year, 'There was scarcely a tradesman in the city who did not feel the common calamity in his own circumstances.'[14] In this economic climate local taxation is likely to have been a sensitive issue. One historian has claimed that the tolls on Bristol Bridge at this time 'cost some citizens about £2 a week'.[15] Two of the masters who signed protests against the wage demands of their employees in 1792 were to be wounded in the 1793 riot, and a third, William Powell, was killed.[16]

In addition to the tensions created by economic crisis, there were continuing, and long-established, tensions between the inhabitants

---

[9] James Johnson, *Transactions of the Corporation of the Poor* (Bristol, 1826), Appendix I (the figure for flour is distorted by the dramatic price increases during 1795).

[10] *Bristol Gazette*, 12 Jan. 1792, 16 Feb. 1792, 16 May 1792, 21 June 1792, 26 July 1792, 23 Aug. 1792, 30 Aug. 1792, 25 Oct. 1792.

[11] Noble to Dundas, 13 Aug. 1792, LB/BRO; *Bristol Gazette*, 12 Apr. 1792, 3 May 1792.

[12] J.R. Ward, 'Speculative building at Bristol and Clifton, 1783–1793', *Business History*, XX, 1 (1978), pp. 3–18; Walter Ison, *The Georgian buildings of Bristol* (Bath, 1952), pp. 25–6.

[13] 1793 accounts for more than 25 per cent of all Bristol bankruptcies between 1784 and 1800. Only twenty-three of the ninety-four bankruptcies in this year were directly linked to the building trade. I am grateful to Julian Hoppit who kindly provided me with these bankruptcy figures. See also Ward, 'Speculative building', pp. 13–16. There was a run on the Bristol banks: see William Dyer, 'Memorable events, extracted from memorandums and diarys commencing 1744', BRL B20095 MS, pp. 275–6.   [14] Seyer MSS, pp. 39–41.

[15] Charles Wells, *Historic Bristol* (Bristol, 1902), pp. 66.

[16] *Bristol Gazette*, 23 Aug. 1792; *A list of persons killed and wounded (at the late riots in Bristol respecting the Bridge tolls) on the memorable evening of the 30th of September* (Bristol, 1793).

and the Corporation. And it was these tensions that were to dominate Bristol in 1793. The procurement of local Acts, giving greater powers to the executive, but financed by local taxation, had generated hostility throughout the eighteenth century; the Lighting and Paving Bill of 1749 and the Nightly Watch Bill of 1754 encountered particularly strong opposition.[17] In February 1790 the Common Council resolved to apply for powers to build a new gaol, to be paid for almost entirely out of the county rate. In the face of popular opposition, they were forced to withdraw the Bill; and an attempt to revive it in 1791 was unsuccessful. In June 1792, however, readers of the local newspapers found themselves faced with an 'Abstract of Bristol Gaol Bill now lying before the Lords': the Bill had already been through the Commons. Parish petitions and a subscription were raised in opposition, and, although the protests were in vain, there was a private assurance from some members of the Corporation that the Act would be allowed to expire in seven years.[18] One letter to the *Gazette* complained that 'the Corporation have centred in themselves an authority too unlimited for the possession of any body of men; utterly incompatible with the rights of the people'. Another warned: 'In its present shape it is hoped and presumed the Corporation will not attempt to put in effect the authority they are possessed of.'[19]

During these years criticism of the Corporation was relentless. A group of citizens questioning the constitutional basis of the Common Council examined Bristol's charters.[20] Broadsides and pamphlets attacked the mayor, aldermen and Common Councillors.[21] In 1789–90 and 1791–2 there were refusals to serve as mayor – a symptom of internal discontent which was to become a major problem in future years.[22] Nevertheless, the Corporation's power

---

[17] P.T. Underdown, 'The political history of Bristol, 1750–1790', MA dissertation, Univ. of Bristol, 1948, p. 23; Sidney and Beatrice Webb, *English local government from the revolution to the municipal corporations act: the manor and the borough*, part II (London, 1908), pp. 456–7.

[18] *Bristol Gazette*, 7 Jan. 1790, 18 Mar. 1790, 7 June 1792, 12 July 1792, 19 July 1792, 26 July 1792, 2 Aug. 1792, 9 Aug. 1792, 27 Aug. 1792. Latimer, *Annals . . . eighteenth century*, pp. 488–9. For a selection of handbills and broadsides in opposition to the bill, see Jefferies MSS, vol. VIII, BRL B7952.

[19] *Bristol Gazette*, 26 July 1792.   [20] *Ibid.*, 10 Nov. 1791.

[21] *Speech of Balaam's beast* (Bristol, 1792); *Free thoughts on the offices of mayor, aldermen, and common council of the city of Bristol with a constitutional proposition for their annihilation* (Bristol, 1792); Jefferies MSS, vol. VIII.

[22] CCP/BRO, 9 Mar. 1791, 15 Sept. 1791, 14 Mar. 1792, 13 Sept. 1792; Latimer, *Annals . . . eighteenth century*, p. 507.

base was broad, and not easy to upset. There was considerable overlap in membership between the Common Council and other principal bodies of power in the city, including, significantly, the Bridge Trustees. Of forty-one Corporation members in late 1793, fourteen were members of the Merchant Venturers. Of the forty-nine Bridge Trustees, the mayor and aldermen comprised thirteen, *ex officio*, and a further thirteen were Common Councillors. Of the remaining twenty-three, eleven were members of the Venturers, and two had recently held high positions in the Corporation of the Poor. Only nine of the Bridge Trustees had no link with the city Corporation, Venturers or Poor Corporation.[23]

Trade dispute, economic crisis and criticism of the Corporation may all have made life uncomfortable for Bristol's broad power base. But its security was certainly not threatened by radical politics. Radicalism was spectacularly absent from Bristol in these years. Secretary of State Henry Dundas wrote to mayor Noble in September 1792 seeking information on 'the number and extent of seditious Associations which have formed in Bristol'. There is, however, no evidence of a reply from Noble.[24] Even the notoriously recalcitrant Kingswood colliers, far from adopting Tom Paine, burnt him in effigy. And they were not the first to do so around Bristol.[25]

If public radicalism was absent, public expression of loyalism was abundant. A number of loyal addresses were presented to the king by the Corporation and the 'Inhabitants' during 1792.[26] In December 1792 and January 1793, the Benefit Society, Quakers, True Briton Society, Union Society of Carpenters and the Innkeepers and Victuallers all made loyalist declarations.[27] Such loyalism, from such social groups, is unsurprising. Nevertheless, their resolutions were not a foregone conclusion. In Norwich, for example, a resolution to the king in May 1792 was rejected by the Common Council.[28]

---

[23] CCP/BRO, 1793; Merchants Hall books of proceedings, vol. XII, BRL; W. Mathews, *Mathews's Bristol guide and directory, 1793–4* (Bristol, 1794), p. 3. W.W. Minchinton (ed.), *Politics and the port of Bristol in the eighteenth century: the petitions of the Society of Merchant Venturers, 1698–1803* (Bristol, 1963), pp. xiv–xvii; 'A list of the present Bridge Trustees', *Bristol Gazette*, 24 Oct. 1793; Johnson, *Transactions*, pp. 26–9.

[24] Dundas to Noble, 12 Sept. 1792, LMP/BRO Box 1791.

[25] *Bristol Gazette*, 20 Dec. 1792, 7 Mar. 1793.

[26] *Ibid.*, 21 June 1792, 13 Dec. 1792, 20 Dec. 1792.

[27] *Ibid.*, 13 Dec. 1792, 10 Jan. 1793, 7 Feb. 1793, 13 Dec. 1793, LMP/BRO Box. 1792; 11 Dec. 1792, LMP/BRO Box 1793.

[28] *Norfolk Chronicle*, 23 and 30 June 1792.

Bristol's public loyalism, meanwhile, went beyond resolutions and into loyalist songs at the theatre and celebrations of royal anniversaries.[29]

THE RIOT

Controversy had surrounded Bristol Bridge ever since the plans for its rebuilding in the late 1750s. The publication of the Trustees' annual accounts had helped to keep the issue alive, and the attempt to obtain a Gaol Act re-awakened protest about 'that heavy and approbious Tax the *Bridge Tax*'.[30] In the early 1790s, the press openly discussed the state of the bridge debt.[31]

The new Bristol Bridge was completed in 1768 and was to be paid for by means of a house tax, wharfage tax and a toll.[32] By the Bridge Act tolls were to be collected until an excess of £2,000 had accumulated, and were then to cease immediately. The interest from this £2,000 would then, it was said, pay for subsequent maintenance costs. From 1787 onwards the tolls were leased every Michaelmas (29 September). John Rose, a writer and printer, Abraham Hiscoxe, the collector of tolls for 1792–3, and George Webb, a witness, were all to claim that the Trustees' broker declared in 1792 that the tolls would cease on Michaelmas 1792.[33] Just before the lease was due to expire, Hiscoxe was asked by the clerk of the Trustees to collect the tolls again for 1793–4. Hiscoxe refused, saying he had been assured that the tolls would cease in September 1793 and he was not prepared to suffer the consequence of their continuing.[34] The Trustees went ahead with their plan: the tolls were advertised for another year.[35] It was, however, believed by many, including Hiscoxe, that if the tolls were not collected for nine days then it would require an Act of

---

[29] *Bristol Gazette*, 6 Dec. 1792, 29 Sept. 1791, 27 Oct. 1791, 1 Nov. 1792, 24 Jan. 1793, 6 June 1793.

[30] *To the citizens and inhabitants of Bristol, from a citizen* (Bristol, 1792), in Jefferies MSS, vol. VIII.   [31] *Bristol Gazette*, 5 Apr. 1792 and 4 Apr. 1793.

[32] *An act for rebuilding and enlarging the bridge over the Avon (Bristol Bridge)*, 33 Geo. II, c. 52 (1759).

[33] John Rose, *An impartial history of the late disturbances* (Bristol, 1793), p. 6; *To the public, a notice from Abraham Hiscoxe* (Bristol, 1793); deposition of Abraham Hiscoxe, in 'The minutes of the committee for investigating the Bridge affairs' (hereafter, 'C'ttee of investigation'), BRL 13065 MS, pp. 5–8; deposition of G. Webb, 'C'ttee of investigation', pp. 19–20. Unfortunately the broker had since died.

[34] Deposition of Hiscoxe, 'C'ttee of investigation'.

[35] *Bristol Gazette*, 5 Sept. 1793; *SFBJ, FFBJ, BMBJ*, 7 Sept. 1793. The advertisement appeared for three consecutive weeks.

Parliament to re-introduce them. Hiscoxe was assured by acquaintances that they could regain by subscription the money lost through discontinuing the tolls prematurely. The intended removal of the toll gates became public knowledge, and they were removed and burnt by 'a large number of people' on 19 September.[36]

The Bridge Trustees intervened by producing a notice denying that they held sufficient profits to discharge the Bridge debt, and outlining punishments for assaulting or threatening toll collectors or destroying the toll houses and gates. A reward was offered for the prosecution of those responsible for the actions of 19 September.[37] The Trustees' yearly accounts appeared but, as always, their complete accounts did not. At their meeting of 23 September they resolved to erect new gates and 'support and protect' the new lessee, Wintour Harris, in the collection of the toll.[38] On 28 September new gates were erected.

Accounts of what happened over the next few days inevitably vary. From an examination of a number of sources, the following picture emerges.[39] On Saturday evening 28 September a 'very considerable number of persons' destroyed the newly erected toll gates. Later that evening the Herefordshire militia were summoned to the bridge with the magistrates and perhaps a few ward constables. (Of eleven chief and petty constables, representing eight of the twelve wards, later interviewed by the 'Committee of investigation', only three were officially summoned on the 28th and 29th. All refused to attend because their sympathies lay with the protestors.)[40] The Riot Act was read, without effect. The militia opened fire. One man, John Abbott, generally held to have been either looking-on or passing-by, was killed; two or three were wounded. The crowd still did not disperse, but they were left to their own devices overnight.[41]

---

[36] *Bristol Gazette*, 26 Sept. 1793; *SFBJ*, 28 Sept. 1793; *FFBJ*, 21 Sept. 1793; *BMBJ*, 21 Oct. 1793.   [37] *Bristol Gazette*, 26 Sept. 1793.

[38] 'Minutes of the Bristol Bridge Trustees, 1763–1794', 23 Sept. 1793, BRL B5014 MS.

[39] The main sources are: *A plain and circumstantial narrative of the proceedings of yesterday in the city of Bristol*, published by order of the mayor and aldermen (Bristol, 1 Oct. 1793), in PO/BRO; *BMBJ*, 5 Oct. 1793; *The Times* (London), 2 Oct. and 3 Oct. 1793; Seyer MSS, pp. 41(1)–43(3); Anon., *An impartial history of the late riots* (Bristol, 1793); John Rose, *A reply to a Bridge Trustee* (Bristol, 1793); 'C'ttee of investigation'; 'Minutes of the Bristol Bridge Trustees'; *Annual Register*, XXXI (London, 1793), pp. 45–6; *FFBJ*, 5 Oct. 1793; Dyer, 'Memorable events', 19–30 Sept. 1793.   [40] 'C'ttee of investigation', pp. 26–9, 43–4.

[41] There is little evidence of what happened after the shooting; according to the *Annual Register*, XXXI (London, 1793), pp. 45–6, 'the city was in a ferment the whole night'.

The next day, Sunday 29 September, the crowd was even larger than that of Saturday evening.[42] The new rentor, along with the magistrates and the soldiers in support, endeavoured to collect the tolls. Several persons attempted not to pay and a number were reputedly taken to the Bridewell.[43] The Riot Act was read but there was no shooting. The mayor reported the situation to the Secretary of State and requested more troops.[44]

On Monday 30 September, the scene continued. The Riot Act was read three times, the last at 11.00 a.m., and the crowd told that if they did not disperse by 12.00 the magistrates would return with the civil power and, if necessary, the military, to 'do their Duty'.[45] They returned to much the same situation but did not, in fact, 'do their Duty'. Around 6.00 p.m. it was decided to close up the toll houses for the night and abandon the scene. But immediately after the militia and magistrates had gone a small crowd began to set fire to the contents of the toll houses.[46] A small group of soldiers hastily returned, but were beaten off. Soon afterwards the mayor marched to the bridge accompanied by five aldermen, one sheriff, 'peace officers' and the militia.[47] The Corporation allege the crowd were ordered to disperse. When they did not do so, the military opened fire, leaving ten dead and around fifty wounded.[48] The crowd stampeded away

---

[42] *The Times* (London), 2 Oct. 1793, estimated 10,000. This is almost certainly a gross exaggeration. From the range of figures given by other sources it seems there were hundreds rather than thousands of people present.

[43] There is a lack of evidence of arrests, only five are recorded: 29 Sept. 1793 and 2 Oct. 1793, quarter sessions records, BRO. Only one of these was committed: 12 April 1974, Court of Oyer and Terminer, gaol delivery, BRO. Some reports claim there were attempts to free prisoners on their way to gaol.

[44] Bengough to Dundas, 29 Sept. 1793, LB/BRO.

[45] An excellent example of the confusion over the Riot Act. The magistrates were, in fact, obligated by common law to take action at any time if they believed the crowd were acting violently. Tony Hayter, *The army and the crowd in mid-Georgian England* (London, 1978), esp. ch. 1, explains the popular, magisterial, and governmental confusion over the law of riot. See also Leon Radzinowicz, *A history of English criminal law*, 5 vols. (London, 1948), vol. 1, pp. 619–20; and *An Act for preventing tumults and riotous assemblies*, 1 Geo. I, st. 2, c. 5 (1715).

[46] Rose, *Reply to Bridge Trustee*, claims it was 20 boys with 200 onlookers singing 'God save the king'. *An impartial history of the late riots* put the crowd at 100. Other estimates claim up to 12,000 (*The Times* (London)).

[47] Seyer MSS, p. 41(5), suggests 40 or 50 troops. Others suggest a full force (unlikely, since it was 500 at this time – 'proposed distribution of troops in south Britain, January 1793', HO 41/24/307), with Lord Bateman in attendance.

[48] *A list of killed and wounded*. Seyer MSS, p. 41(6), suggests bodies were carried away, and puts the total dead at around forty. Some sources suggest that the military threw bodies into the river, e.g. *Cain and Abel Tavern, near Bristol bridge* (Bristol, 1 Oct. 1793), *Extraordinary gazette, published by authority* (Bristol, 2 Oct.

from the bridge, and some claimed a few individual soldiers picked off stragglers as though 'trying their skill at a flying shot'.[49]

There was a dramatic change of atmosphere the next day: 'A rage and indication, on the following morning, were apparent in the countenance of the multitude; the Bridge became a secondary consideration; and revenge, alone, dwelt in the breast of the people.'[50] The Guildhall was the obvious target for such revenge: a Corporation building, it was also the temporary barracks for the militia (now unable to return to their lodgings because of public hostility) and the meeting rooms of the Bridge Trustees. A crowd smashed its windows. The military made one attempt to disperse them but did not open fire. The Council House, the main Corporation building, was the next target: it too had its windows broken.

The Herefordshire militia, reduced to walking the streets in groups for fear of attack, hastily left the city. Around midnight on Tuesday 1 October the Monmouthshire and Brecon militias marched in, followed the next day by a party of Dragoons. The Corporation and Trustees grudgingly accepted an offer by four individuals to take assignment of the lease and to raise the money by voluntary subscriptions.[51] There was no more disturbance; and tolls were never again collected on Bristol Bridge.

Such is the generally accepted account. It is, however, one which gives little sense of the popular experiences and perceptions of the riot. Some of these, recorded in the depositions to the independent committee of investigation at its hearings of late 1793 and early 1794, convey a more vivid sense of the trauma of the events on Bristol Bridge. Although the accuracy of recollections made weeks after the event is questionable, there is no reason to suppose that they were any more or less reliable than many of the other, 'established', accounts. Furthermore, people's possession of, and belief in, those memories (apocryphal or not) is in itself important to any understanding of consciousness formed as a result of the riot.

An apprentice, Robert Lee, testified to the good behaviour of the crowd on 28 September. He reckoned half of those present to be spectators. Mr Stone, who was present at the bridge on Saturday night, said he saw no rioting, and, with the fire around the toll gates

1793). *Annual Register*, XXXI (London, 1793), p. 46, reported that three bodies were retrieved from the river.
[49] 'C'ttee of investigation', pp. 15–16.   [50] *An impartial history of the late riots.*
[51] *Bristol Gazette*, 10 Oct. and 17 Oct. 1793.

nearly extinguished, he went home to bed. He was awoken at 11.00 p.m. by the sound of gunfire, which he assumed was merely intended to disperse people still lingering around the bridge. What exactly happened at the time of the shooting is unclear. David Sawyer relates seeing John Abbott (who was killed that night) on the pavement, with three soldiers 'using him very cruelly'.[52] The inquest on Abbott's body suggests he may have been shot in the back.[53] Thomas Vaughan, a cabinet maker, was returning home with his child on the 28th. As he crossed the bridge an officer commanding the militia came on to the pavement and said 'Damn your eyes go back', and pushed him. Vaughan said he wanted to go home. The officer repeated his remark, and Vaughan retreated to the bridge railings. One soldier separated off from the others, and said to Vaughan 'You are one of the rioters', whereupon he wounded Vaughan in the leg with a bayonet, and hit him.

On the 29th, Mr Ring and Mr Thomas went to the Council House to ask to see the mayor in order to request that some plan be adopted to avert the violence that was likely to ensue if the trustees continued to collect the toll. They were refused an interview. The next day, Monday, John Chandler, a relation of John Abbott, was carrying Abbott's coffin over the bridge with the assistance of his employees. They were about to put the coffin down so that they could rest, when alderman Noble told them they did so at their peril. One of the militia officers asked 'who that coffin was for'. Chandler said it was for the man murdered on the bridge on Saturday night. On this, Noble came up and said, 'that's your expression Chandler, is it?'. Chandler replied, 'it is'. 'Then sir,' said Noble, 'I am determined to mark you, I know you very well.'

John Sircom put the number involved in burning the contents of the toll houses on Monday evening at only six, with a 'considerable' number present as spectators. Mr Viney was one of the constables ordered to the Council House on the news of the attack upon the toll houses. He went with the soldiers to the bridge. As they were approaching they were pelted with stones. The magistrates arrived, and the military, which Viney numbered at around 100, formed up into two columns, two ranks deep. The drums ceased and the soldiers fired without any apparent orders. At first they fired high, and the

[52] This might explain the belief of some, including Samuel Seyer (Seyer MSS, p. 41(3)), that Abbott was 'killed by a bayonet'.
[53] A ball was found lodged firmly in his backbone, 'C'ttee of investigation', pp. 29–30.

crowd continued to hurl missiles; but immediately officers called out to fire low.

A number of depositions relate to the shooting. Viney claimed to have heard two peace officers say, as they came from the Council House, that now they had orders to fire they would disperse the crowd. Dennis Sullivan deposed that Blackwell, a drummer in the Herefordshire militia, told him that he had asked 'one of the Corporation', 'for what purpose they should go to the Bridge'. The Corporation member replied that 'it was of no use to go there without doing execution'. Sullivan examined the musket of militiaman Richards (who was lodging with Sullivan's father) after Richards returned home on Monday night. The musket, which had come from the Guildhall, contained 'one leaden ball cut into four equal quarters, and after this a cartridge of a peculiar kind, after this another Ball, jagged or notched with some instrument'.

On that evening George Adkins, a tobacconist, was on his way to Temple Street (the main street leading from the south of the bridge) when he noticed a noisy but peaceful crowd on the bridge, and soldiers 'parading down High Street'. He walked 'leisurely forwards' to where the toll gates had stood. The troops arrived at the middle of the bridge, and he immediately heard the order to fire. A man walking beside him fell, and he himself had a shot pass through his hat. He then heard an order to fire low, upon which he turned and ran. John Hannum, a twenty-year-old apprentice who had been with William Powell and Anthony Gill (both killed), deposed that he heard Lord Bateman give the orders to fire. The soldiers asked how they were to fire, and Bateman replied 'fire low, breast high'. John Sircom saw the soldiers fire with their muskets resting against their thighs. Constable Viney described the soldiers as seeming confused. He saw one soldier deliberately shooting a man, and an officer say 'Damn ye, Tom has killed that man', but not reprove the soldier. Viney saw a Mr Snow pass over the bridge after the firing had ceased. One of the military said to Snow, 'Damn ye, what do you want here?' Snow said 'I am going on my business being an Exciseman.' 'Then Damn ye make haste', said the officer, and beat Snow about the back with his sword.

Mr Higgs saw a soldier 'bend upon his knee, and aim at a man and fire, and the man immediately fell'. Mr Vinning, a broker, heard Horler, 'the Mayor's officer', give orders to fire at James Bennet, who fell dead. Bennet's father came up, and Horler asked who the dead man was. Bennet said it was his son. Horler replied, 'Damn ye, take him away directly or I'll assure you worse will ensue.' Sarah Wilcox, returning from work, went to the bridge to look for her husband. While passing the Bell public house at about 8.15 p.m. she was shot. A ball passed through her hip and out through her groin. She 'was lamed for life, and will not be able to work again'. Thomas Knotley, a saddler, arrived at the corner of Bath Street having abandoned his attempt to cross the bridge, and suddenly 'found himself wounded in both thighs'. He had not been at the scene more than thirty seconds. Henry Knotley was crossing the bridge with his wife when he saw a man on the ground. As he bent down to help him he too was shot. He was so badly wounded that he had to have an arm and a leg amputated.[54]

REPERCUSSIONS

Bristol Corporation, already ill-respected and disliked, became further isolated in the aftermath of the riot. This isolation can be seen operating in three areas: the attempt by the magistrates to legitimise their actions by claiming they were faced with revolutionary insurrection; the breakdown in the Corporation's relations with central government; and the local hostility expressed both immediately after the riot and in the long-term corporate memory.

The tendency on the part of those in power to attribute disturbance to the work of outsiders, agitators and revolutionaries, despite all evidence to the contrary, could with some justification be termed one of the few hard rules identifiable by the social sciences. It is almost impossible, to this day, to find a major riot about which claims regarding the presence of outside agitators have not been made.[55] Bristol in 1793 was no exception. In attempting to explain their behaviour, the magistrates reported their fear that 'some person or persons who are certainly at the bottom of this Business, and who must undoubtedly have been all along inciting the common people . . . should under cover of the Night, be guilty of outrages'.[56] But, like

---

[54] *Ibid.*, pp. 10–11, 16–19, 23–4, 28–41, 44–51, 53–4, 66–7, 71.

[55] For a few modern examples, see: 'Hunt for "the four horsemen"', *The Daily Telegraph* (London), 11 July 1981; 'Sri Lanka blames foreign plotters', *Guardian* (Manchester and London), 1 Aug. 1983; 'Tunisia declares emergency after 25 die in bread riots', *Guardian*, 4 Apr. 1984; 'Morocco disorder is blamed on outsiders', *Guardian*, 23 Jan. 1984; 'Civil rights group saying ruling Congress Party was behind anti-Sikh rioting', *Guardian*, 30 Jan. 1985.

[56] *A plain and circumstantial narrative.*

all the assertions of seditious motivation, this claim occurred *well after the riot was over*. One week after the riot, the mayor wrote to Dundas that 'the magistrates are using their best endeavours to discover and bring to Justice the Instigators of the Disturbance who (there's too much reason to fear) had other objects besides putting a stop to the collection of the Bridge-Toll'.[57] In fact, there is no evidence to support these assertions. At the time of the riot no radical slogans were reported; indeed the crowd (admittedly perhaps for reasons of self-protection) sang 'God save the King'.[58] Nowhere in the minutes of the committee of investigation does a witness make even passing reference to radical agitation or radical politics. Not even the contemporary chronicler, John Evans, in his self-confessed attempt to put the Corporation case in a book dedicated to (and paid for by) them, bothered with such claims.[59]

Did the magistrates *at the time they marched down High Street* towards Bristol Bridge on 30 September believe they were about to put down a revolutionary insurrection? It seems unlikely. Even the Home Office, at a time when it sought close co-operation with provincial magistrates in containing riot and sedition, was unresponsive to such suggestions. The Bristol magistrates did not communicate their unease to the Home Office concerning the possibility of violence until the evening of the 29th itself, when military assistance was requested;[60] further communication then followed, including, ultimately, the claim of insurrectionary motives.[61] There is, however, no evidence that the Home Office responded to any of these letters. All that exists is a copy or draft of a letter from Dundas to mayor Morgan, dated simply 'October 1793', which begins: 'Reports having been circulated in Town since I heard from you last that Riots of an alarming nature have taken place in Bristol, I could have wished that you had sent me the earliest intelligence of the extent of the same.'[62] For a ministry supposedly obsessed with insurrection, the response was decidedly cool. Even

[57] Morgan to Dundas, 7 Oct. 1793, LB/BRO and HO 42/26/685.

[58] Rose, *Reply to Bridge Trustee*.

[59] John Evans, *Chronological outline of the history of Bristol* (Bristol, 1824), pp. 299–301. Evans was paid a 'token of esteem': Evans to Bristol Corporation, 18 Aug. 1825, LMP/BRO Box 1825.

[60] Bengough to Dundas, 29 Sept. 1793, LB/BRO.

[61] Morgan to Duke of Beaufort, 1 Oct. 1793, LB/BRO; Morgan to Dundas: 4 Oct. 1793, LB/BRO; 7 Oct. 1793, LB/BRO; 11 Nov. 1793, LB/BRO and HO/42/27/102; 19 Nov. 1793 LB/BRO and HO/42/27/207.

[62] Dundas to Morgan, Oct. 1793, HO 42/26/900.

Morgan's suggestion of 'wider motives' elicited no interest. Significantly perhaps, correspondence from the Corporation to the Home Office over the next two years was infrequent, terse and unhelpful. In May 1794, in response to an inquiry from Dundas, Morgan (that great discoverer of sedition) reported that no seditious societies existed in Bristol – curious since the Bristol Society for Constitutional Information was in existence at that time.[63] During a riot by Kingswood colliers in 1795, the Corporation's requests for troops went direct to the military at Chippenham, Devizes and Warminster, contrary to the accepted procedure of making all such requests through the Home Office.[64]

With the justifications for its actions half-hearted and incredible, and its relations with central government in disarray, the Corporation faced the music of local recrimination. That all the magistrates were *ex officio* Bridge Trustees placed them, in popular perception, at the centre of all aspects of the dispute. A stream of ferocious broadsides attacked them both individually and collectively.[65] The broadsides refer to a number of elements in the affair: the Gaol Act, the plans for a floating harbour, the order to troops to fire low, the unpopularity of the military, the bias of the press, and so on. But most persistent is the sense of shock, illustrated by one of the mildest publications:

> to commit overt acts of usurpation – to raise and dare resentment of the Populace – to defy with Military force, and proceed to the Horrors of a bloody Tragedy – which nothing but the extremity of violence against the most righteous cause could justify – are imputed crimes, my fellow citizens, over which we should not slumber![66]

The language of murder and butchery pervades the post-riot publications; the bridge becomes 'the Slaughtering House'.[67] The

---

63 Dundas to Morgan, 20 May 1794, LMP/BRO Box 1794; Morgan to Dundas, 21 May 1794, LB/BRO; Bristol Constitutional Society for a Parliamentary Reform, *Address to the people of Great Britain* (Bristol, 1794); *Bristol Gazette*, 9 Oct. 1794.

64 Smith to Windham, 22 Dec. 1794, LB/BRO; King to Smith, 16 Mar. 1795, LMP/BRO Box 1794 and HO 43/6; Smith to King, 17 Mar. 1795, LB/BRO; *Bristol Gazette*, 26 Mar. 1795; Smith to Duke of York, 8 May 1795; LB/BRO.

65 E.g., *The speech of alderman Twig Pigeon concerning the late riot; Cain and Abel Tavern near Bristol Bridge; Extraordinary gazette, published by authority; A capital selection of Bristol worthies; Tragedy called cowardice and murder; Plain truth; A chapter out of the book of Morgan; The lamentation of Bristolia; Daniel's dream; Inquisition for blood shall be made; Lord B[ateman] otherwise Lord Bodadil; About 400 couples of bloodhounds, the property of L[or]d B[atema]n; Statement of bridge account by Civis.* All publications Bristol, Oct. 1793.

66 *Inquisition for blood.*   67 *About 400 couples.*

magistrates, one writer claimed, had 'insinuated the *Citizens* wished for a revolution', in the hope of sanctioning 'the late murders, and (if possible) wipe off the foul stain of BLOOD'.[68]

The magistrates, it was argued, had set themselves up for their own fall. Their ill-judged reliance on grandeur – their 'Haughty and Imperious Countenance'[69] – had led them to deploy 'their proudly commanded force'. This only drew a larger crowd of sightseers, however, and the magistrates were now forced 'to disperse the crowd which their own measures had increased, and to quell a riot which their appearance had renewed'.[70] The presence of a respectable *spectating* crowd became a crucial issue. William Dyer recorded: 'my nephew George Dyer stood as a spectator [at] the upper end of high street and providentially escaped unhurt, but a Gentleman by his side had two fingers shot off, another Gentleman near had a Bullett pass through his thigh'.[71] The magistrates themselves did not dispute the fact that not all the crowd were rioters: 'several persons have been killed and wounded, some of them, it is very probable, may have been innocent without any evil intentions themselves'.[72] *Bonner and Middleton's Journal* reported that most of those killed and wounded were 'innocent spectators';[73] *The Times* (of London) noted the death of 'respectable tradesmen';[74] and the death of well-known local employer William Powell occasioned particular attention.[75] The list of sixty-three killed and wounded shows a cross-section of Bristol's trades: a shoe maker, three master bakers, an auctioneer, carpenter, mason, accountant, saddler, and so on. Of the sixty-three, eight were women; the average age was twenty-nine.[76]

The Corporation's attempts to regain control all backfired. They dominated the Trustees' meeting of 7 October which gave their version of events; but the chairman, William Grosvenor, refused to sign the minutes.[77] Their appeal for expressions of support from the 'respectable inhabitants' of the wards led to some obedient but lukewarm addresses in the newspapers. The original manuscript

---

[68] *Plain truth.*   [69] *Book of Morgan.*

[70] Anon., *Strictures on a pamphlet called Impartial History* (Bristol, 1793), p. 9.

[71] Dyer, 'Memorable events', p. 279.   [72] *Plain circumstantial narrative.*

[73] *BMBJ*, 5 Oct. 1793.   [74] *The Times*, 3 Oct. 1793.

[75] N.J. *Elegy on the late riots in Bristol* (Bristol, 1793?); 'Prose and poetry on religious, moral and entertaining subjects by Mrs Rueful', MS in Bristol Bridge Collection, BRL B11539; 'Diary of Betty Bishop, 1779–1801', BRL B22250 MS; Dyer, 'Memorable events', p. 279.   [76] *List of killed and wounded.*

[77] 'Minutes of the Bristol Bridge Trustees', 7 Oct. 1793.

copies of the addresses received by the Corporation a week earlier, however showed even less enthusiasm; it was doctored versions that were finally published.[78] The attempt was also made to head off criticism by preventing the meeting of the independent committee of investigation led by local physician, Edward Long Fox. Fox was refused the use of three venues before the committee finally succeeded in meeting on 20 November 1793. The depositions they collected suggested gross mismanagement by Corporation and Trustees, and gave further weight to reports that the mayor and coroners had interfered with juries' verdicts of 'Wilful Murder' at the inquests on the dead.[79]

Ironically, the riot may have been a catalyst for the development of radicalism in the city. In 1794 the Bristol Constitutional Society was formed,[80] and a radical candidate, Benjamin Hobhouse, stood, unsuccessfully, at the parliamentary election of 1796.[81] The riot remained in the corporate memory for many years. The Hereford militia were requested to cancel their planned visit to Bristol in 1797 because of continuing hostility.[82] In July 1799 they did pass through the city, and were duly 'insulted and pelted by some women and rabble, who called them the *bloody* regiment in remembrance of the affair at the bridge'.[83] The riot was repeatedly invoked during the 1807 and 1812 elections (see above, chapter 9). In the course of the 1807 election, the *Gazette* expressed its fear that the calling out of the military during a disturbance might draw together 'the mob' and 'a repetition of the Bridge scene' might ensue.[84] The 1815 edition of Mathews' *Bristol guide* openly recalled the riot in which 'about 40 or 50 persons were vindictively killed and wounded by the Military, at the command of the Magistrates of the City'.[85] In 1828, the radical

[78] 2 Oct., 3 Oct., 4 Oct., 1793, LMP/BRO Box 1793; *Bristol Gazette*, 10 Oct. 1793.
[79] *Bristol Gazette*, 24 Oct. 1793; 'Notice from E.L. Fox to the citizens of Bristol', MS draft, BRL B13088 MS, and printed version BRL B13090; Edward Long Fox, *Notice to the citizens of Bristol* (Bristol, 1793). Little is known about the twelve man committee. Two were tobacconists, one a linen draper, one a stationer and one a tea dealer.
[80] Bristol Constitutional Society for a Parliamentary Reform, *Address to the people of Great Britain* (Bristol, 1794); *Journals of the House of Commons: Committee of Secrecy*, 1794, vol. XLIX, pp. 726–7.
[81] (Benjamin Hobhouse), 'Mr Hobhouse', extract from *Public characters of 1807* (London, 1807).   [82] Harvey to Duke of York, 19 Sept. 1797, LB/BRO.
[83] Seyer MSS, p. 49.   [84] *Bristol Gazette*, 14 May 1807.
[85] J. Mathews, *The Bristol guide* (Bristol, 1815), p. 61. The 1829 edn, although it still claimed the magistrates gave the order to fire, is more moderate in tone (see p. 58). *Mathews' complete Bristol Guide*, 7th edition (Bristol, 1829), p. 58.

James Acland could still invoke the events and the personalities of 1793.[86] And as late as 1887, a history of Bristol concluded its account of the riot by noting that 'The remembrance of this riot is still preserved in the cry "Give 'em Bristol Bridge!" which is still raised by the roughs of the city when they mean mischief.'[87]

CONCLUSIONS

In three important respects the Bristol Bridge riot conforms with the established historiographical model for provincial disturbance in this period: the rioters were disciplined and had specific objects for their protest; their violence was directed against property and not people;[88] and the rioting was essentially localist in its concern, with the local authorities selecting their own means for dealing with the disturbance.[89] It is a mark of the efficacy of the 'new orthodoxy' model that these conclusions are entirely to be expected. The significance of this riot, for contemporaries, however, almost certainly did not lie in these elements. The central response to the riot was one of shock – a shock, crucially, borne out of the magistrates' unsure handling of a very specific protest.

This mixture of confusion and certainty operated at a number of levels. First there was the question of the statutory power which the magistrates possessed in their command of the military. Their actions on Monday 30 September illustrate the common confusion regarding the use of the Riot Act. The Act in fact supplemented but did not supersede the common law obligation to take action at any time it was believed that a crowd might proceed to violent action. Had the magistrates taken military action more promptly that Monday, it is not clear that there would have been any less sense of popular outrage. However, the to-ing and fro-ing of the military that day

---

[86] *The Bristolian* (new series), I, 1 (15 Nov. 1828), pp. 9–10.

[87] Hunt, *Bristol*, p. 202.

[88] This point is particularly emphasised by Joyce Ellis, 'Urban conflict and popular violence: the Guildhall riots of 1740 in Newcastle upon Tyne', *International Review of Social History*, XXV, 3 (1980), p. 346.

[89] In particular, see: Williams, 'Midland Hunger riots', pp. 256–97; Roger Wells, 'The revolt of the south-west, 1800–1: a study in English popular protest', *Social History*, II, 4 (1977), pp. 713–44; Norman McCord and David E. Brewster, 'Some labour troubles of the 1790s in north east England', *International Review of Social History*, XIII, 3 (1968), pp. 366–83; David V.J. Jones, 'Law enforcement and popular disturbance in Wales, 1793–1835', *Journal of Modern History*, XLII, 4 (1970), pp. 496–523.

almost certainly led to the belief that the Riot Act in each instance had not been acted upon (and would therefore have to be re-invoked before the military could open fire), and that military action was therefore unlikely actually to occur.

From one point of view the crowd action was clearly identifiable. The location of the activity was fixed around the bridge; indeed, it was even there that the crowd gathered on the Tuesday before moving off to pelt the Guildhall.[90] The largest and most active crowds formed at specific times: during the non-work hours of Saturday evening, Sunday, Monday and Tuesday evening. From another perspective there was room for confusion. Bristol Bridge was a major thoroughfare for the city (indeed that was why the tolls had become such an issue). The crowds present during the dispute will therefore have been constantly changing, and supplemented by passers-by. So, when did a crowd composed of both the active and spectating, and both the ever-present and passing, constitute a riot? For the magistrates there was a riot at the moment the Riot Act had been read. But those people present at the bridge on Monday evening who had not heard the Act read that morning had no reason to consider themselves rioters. The sense of shock when the troops opened fire will therefore have been immense: suddenly all those present had been officially designated as rioters; they had no right to be there, and were liable to be arrested or shot.

Lastly, the issue itself was highly specific. It is tempting to see this riot, as Philip D. Jones has, as another example of the moral economy, with the perceived illegality of the Bridge Trustees' actions being the 'legitimising notion'.[91] This, however, would be to overuse the moral economy model. Bristolians may have had ideas regarding the obligations of local government not to hinder them economically by exacting unjustified taxes, but this is a weak element in the dispute. There was no moral economy in force on Bristol Bridge – for two reasons. First, there was no evocation of long-established rights. The demand being made was for the termination of a toll which it was believed under the terms of the bridge's administration (and not under some ancient common right) should cease *that* Michaelmas. This was what justified the action: it was a legitimation only in the sense that all gatherings possess explanations for their actions; it had little to do with the quite specific notion of legitimation introduced by

---

[90] *Impartial history of the late riots.*   [91] Jones, 'Bristol bridge riot', pp. 84–5.

Thompson, and meaning 'that the men and women in the crowd were informed by the belief that they were defending traditional rights and customs'.[92] And second, the magistrates had a simple choice: stand up, or back down. There was no well-established procedure for compromise: no price to set, or commitment to intervene as a third party; no ritualised sequence of intimidation and accommodation. There was no room for negotiation: this was confrontation, not collective bargaining.

The specific nature of the dispute gave the magistrates one simple way out of the crisis: they could suspend the bridge toll as demanded. That, however, would have been to admit defeat. If that option was not to be adopted, then they were tied into confrontation which, for the reasons already outlined, was almost bound to end in disaster. The shock created by the outcome of that confrontation is expressed in the depositions to the committee of investigation; it is also expressed by the semi-literate, semi-legible, anonymous letter which arrived at the Home Office on 3 October, addressed to William Pitt, and which pleaded:

My Dear Sir

help help us to have Justice our streets are filled with the Murdered bodyes of the Hinabitants the Most Wanton Cruelty have been exercised by Lord Batman's soldiers . . . we should have ad no disturbance wase it not for the Coporation help us help us kind Gracious Sir we shall all be murdered . . . for God sake send us some help or some person that is human George daubeny as brought this misery on a people peaceably inclined and firmly attached to his Majesty and the present constitution by a show of Justice Yes I will wrigh to the King we want him yes I have wrote to the King and long may he live . . . We shall be murdered indeed Sir we shall They have so enraged the people can it be wondered at O what misery power in bad hands[93]

Power being in bad hands was a problem not to be remedied by an appeal to the moral obligations of local government (the moral economy model), but by a major reform. Firm hostility towards the Corporation, and conviction of the need for its full reform, was to underpin social relations in Bristol for the next thirty-eight years, before finding expression in another, more terrible, conflict.

---

[92] Thompson, 'Moral economy of the English crowd', p. 78.
[93] Anon. to Pitt, 3 Oct. 1793, HO 42/26/673.

THE 'REFORM' RIOTS OF 1831

CONTEXTS

Hostility towards the Corporation enjoyed a hitherto unprecedented breadth of support during the mid-1820s. By that time the city's economic decline relative to the flourishing northern cities was glaringly apparent. At the forefront of the assault not only on the atrophied Corporation but on its associated bodies – the Merchant Venturers and the Dock Company – was J.M. Gutch, tory editor of *Felix Farley's Bristol Journal*. Writing under the pseudonym of Cosmo he located local taxation (including harbour dues up to twice that of other ports) and a lack of imaginative schemes for the revival of the local economy as the root of the problem.[94] Gutch was engaged in a carefully orchestrated campaign with Loudon M'Adam, R.L. Pearsall, John Mills (the whig editor of the *Gazette*) and the newly formed Chamber of Commerce. One letter from Pearsall ends: 'I am glad you like my essay – Do what you will with it but get it published if you can. It is of importance to our cause that the Corporation should be brought into public contempt.'[95] Mills meanwhile was continually publishing comparisons between the trade of Liverpool and that of Bristol;[96] and the Chamber of Commerce attempted to bring about an inquiry into local taxation.[97] Critical and satirical publications fuelled the attack.[98]

Over the previous decade, the composition of the Corporation had changed from predominantly whig to predominantly tory. Of the sixteen aldermen appointed between 1812 and 1821, thirteen were tories; of eighteen Common Councillors appointed, only six were

[94] J.M. Gutch, *Letters on the impediments which obstruct the trade and commerce of the city and port of Bristol which first appeared in Felix Farley's Bristol Journal under the signature of Cosmo* (Bristol, 1823).

[95] Pearsall to Gutch, 5 Feb. 1824, in 'Letters to J.M. Gutch on writing Cosmo's letters', BRO 13748/5.   [96] *Bristol Gazette*, 24 Aug. 1826, *et seq.*

[97] Chamber of Commerce, *Report . . . on . . . local taxation* (Bristol, 1824); Chamber of Commerce, *Further reports . . . on local taxation* (Bristol, 1824); Chamber of Commerce, *Report . . . to consider the facilities which the city and neighbourhood of Bristol afford for the introduction of new and the extension of the existing branches of manufacture (Bristol, 1828)*.

[98] E.g. *Reasons for objecting to the proposed bill of the common council for the reduction and alteration of the town and mayor's dues* (Bristol, 1825); *A small token of admiration at the talents and acquirements of the Corporation of Bristol . . . by two schoolmasters* (Bristol, 1824).

whig.[99] The Corporation, however, retained a striking facility for being out of sympathy with public opinion on all occasions. Despite their tory support for popular hostility towards Catholic emancipation, the Corporation's policies backfired in April 1829 when they tried to prevent public acclamation on the arrival of the anti-Catholic Sir Charles Wetherell (ironic in view of the events to occur two years later).[100] From the opposite political perspective, they found themselves left behind by popular enthusiasm for William IV, expressed on his accession in July 1830 and his coronation in September 1831.[101]

In 1830, however, the battle cry issued by *Felix Farley* was taken up by Bristol's radicals, causing Gutch to retreat into embattled defence of the *status quo*. In September 1830, a public meeting at the Guildhall, chaired by one of the Corporation's few whigs, and future mayor, Charles Pinney, declared its sympathy with the French Revolution of July.[102] The following April, a 'large concourse' spent the lunch-hour standing in the rain in Queen Square to express support for parliamentary reform.[103] One month later two reform candidates, James Evan Baillie and Edward Protheroe, Junior, were returned unopposed at the general election – at a total cost of an unprecedentedly meagre £200. In the chairing procession, 10,000 took part.[104] Twenty-seven trade societies published declarations, all with the unifying theme of 'the King and reform'. 'How the mighty have fallen', proclaimed the smiths; 'Reform – who'd have thought it' gloated the sail-makers.[105]

In June a meeting of trades led to the formation of the Bristol General Union (subsequently generally referred to as the Bristol Political Union).[106] Early in August, a BPU meeting in Queen Square, attended by 'a very numerous assemblage', almost exclusively of 'mechanics', expressed concern at the slow progress of the

[99] CCP/BRO, vols. 1809–14 to 1827–32; Graham Bush, *Bristol and its municipal government, 1820–1851* (Bristol, 1976).
[100] *Bristol Gazette*, 6 Apr. 1829; *Bristol Mercury*, 7 Apr. 1829; Daniel Vickery, 'A Bristol calendar containing brief notices of such events as have taken place in that city and its neighbourhood, July 1824 to the end of the year 1835', BRL B2639 MS, pp. 140–1; PO/BRO, 6 Feb. 1829, 7 Feb. 1829, 2 Apr. 1829.
[101] See above, ch. 10.
[102] *Bristol Gazette*, 9 Sept. 1820 to 23 Sept. 1830; *Bristol Mercury*, 7 Sept. and 14 Sept. 1830; *FFBJ*, 11 Sept. and 18 Sept. 1830.
[103] *Bristol Gazette*, 28 Apr. 1831, *Bristol Mirror*, 30 Apr. 1831.
[104] *Bristol Gazette*, 28 Apr. 1831 to 12 May 1831; *FFBJ*, 7 May 1831; *Bristol Mercury*, 10 May 1831; Ellen Sharples, 'Diary, 1803–1836', BRL B23783, 4 May 1831.
[105] *Bristol Gazette*, 5 May 1831.
[106] *Rules and orders of the Bristol General Union, established June 7, 1831* (Bristol, 1832).

Reform Bill.[107] When the House of Lords rejected the Bill on 8 October 1831, the campaign stepped up its urgency. The rejection in itself provoked rioting in Derby and Nottingham.[108] Two hastily convened lunch-time meetings in Bristol brought several thousand of the 'labouring population' into Queen Square to condemn the House of Lords' decision.[109] A Guildhall meeting two weeks later launched a petition calling for the Lords to pass the Bill – within a week 26,000 people had signed.[110]

Some Bristolians were now expressing anxiety not only at the size and tone of the reform meetings, but at the prospect of the impending visit of Sir Charles Wetherell.[111] Although Wetherell, the city's recorder and *ex officio* alderman of Trinity ward, had been welcomed in 1829, his opposition to parliamentary and municipal reform had made him notorious. The *Gazette* had been reporting his declamations since March 1831.[112] And when Wetherell came to preside over the Spring gaol delivery in April he was greeted with 'emphatic demonstrations of popular disapproval'.[113] By August, the *Gazette* declared itself to be 'sick of Wetherell';[114] both press and handbills continued to cite his opposition;[115] and reform meetings ended with 'three groans for Sir Charles Wetherell'.[116] Wetherell meanwhile continued to declare that there was little interest in Bristol for reform.[117]

As the date for the gaol delivery, and Wetherell's arrival as

[107] *Bristol Gazette*, 11 Aug. 1831.

[108] R.A. Preston, 'Nottingham and the Reform Bill riots of 1831: new perspectives, Part I', and John Wigley, 'Nottingham and the Reform Bill riots: new perspectives, Part II', *Transactions of the Thoroton Society of Nottinghamshire*, LXXVII (1973), pp. 84–103; John Cannon, *Parliamentary reform, 1640–1832* (Cambridge, 1973), pp. 224–7; George Rudé, 'English rural and urban disturbances on the eve of the first reform bill, 1830–1831', *Past and Present*, no. 37 (July 1967), pp. 97–8.

[109] *Bristol Gazette*, 13 Oct. 1831; *FFBJ* and *Bristol Mirror*, 15 Oct. 1831.

[110] Requisition for meeting, 21 Sept. 1831, and 'Junius to the Reformers of Bristol', both in 'Troubles in Bristol, by politicks, fire and pestilence', BRL B10112; *Bristol Gazette*, 29 Sept. and 6 Oct. 1831; PO/BRO, 24 Sept. 1831.

[111] E.g., Claxton to Melbourne, 17 Oct. 1831, HO 40/28 (1); Claxton to Pinney, 16 Oct. 1831, PP/BUL, S-2(1); Lamb to Claxton, 17 Oct. 1831, PP/BUL, S-2(1); broadsides in 'Collection of newspaper extracts, reports, placards etc. relating to the riots of 1831' (hereafter, 'Riots collection'), BRL 4782, pp. 17, 20.

[112] *Bristol Gazette*, 10 Mar. 1831.

[113] John Latimer, *The annals of Bristol in the nineteenth century* (Bristol, 1887), p. 146; J.C. Cross to Rev. C.H. Davis, May 1877, in Davis MSS, BRO 16178(15); *Bristol Gazette*, 14 Apr. 1831.   [114] *Bristol Gazette*, 4 Aug. 1831.

[115] E.g., *Bristol Gazette*, 24 Sept. 1831; 'Junius to Reformers'.

[116] *Bristol Gazette*, 11 Aug. and 13 Oct. 1831.

[117] *Hansard's Parliamentary debates*, vol. VI, 17 Aug. 1831, p. 189, 27 Aug. 1831, pp. 698–9.

recorder, loomed, the BPU were requested, without success, to provide assistance against disturbance.[118] Christopher Claxton made an abortive attempt to raise a force of sailors to protect Sir Charles – they vowed instead that they would not be 'the cat's paw of the Corporation or its agents'.[119] The magistrates first made a vain attempt to dissuade Wetherell from coming, and then sent a delegation to Home Secretary Lord Melbourne to seek assistance.[120] Consequently, two troops of the 14th Light Dragoons, and one of the 3rd Dragoons, arrived at Clifton on the 27th of October.[121] The magistrates called for order on Wetherell's arrival,[122] but disturbance had already occurred. On the arrival of the Bishop of Bath and Wells (who had voted against the Bill in the Lords) to consecrate a new chapel at Bedminster on the 24th of October, he was hooted and pelted by a waiting crowd.[123]

THE RIOT

By Saturday 29 October, the magistrates had already been deserted. Their appeal for citizens to come forward to act as constables fell on deaf ears, and they were compelled carefully to deploy a relatively meagre force of 300 hired constables and 'bludgeon men'.[124] On the Saturday, shops were closed, troops had been noticed assembling in the cattle market and at the New Gaol, and the drawing-up of constables outside the Exchange attracted crowds and made nonsense of the magistrates' plan to beat the populace by bringing in Wetherell at 10.00 a.m. instead of the usual 4.00 p.m.[125] The events of the following seventy-two hours were complex, dramatic and copiously documented. Individual incidents were the source for great

[118] Reynolds to Herapath, 20 Oct. 1831; Herapath to Daniel, 26 Oct. 1831 in 'MS material relating to the Bristol riots of 1831', BRL B2436 MS.
[119] 'Troubles in Bristol, by politicks, fire and pestilence'; *Bristol Gazette*, 20 Oct. 1831; *Bristol Mirror*, 22 Oct. 1831.
[120] Town clerk's statement, CCP/BRO, 18 May 1832; Fripp to Pinney 20 Oct. 1831, PP/BUL S-2(1); Pinney to Melbourne, 4 Nov. 1821, CCP/BRO, 18 May 1832; Jefferies MSS, vol. VII, p. 187.
[121] *Bristol Gazette*, 27 Oct. 1831.   [122] PO/BRO, 27 Oct. 1831.
[123] Notice from 'A Churchwarden', in 'Riots collection', p. 22; Vickery, 'A Bristol calendar', p. 255; *FFBJ*, 29 Oct. 1831; *Bristol Gazette*, 26 Oct. 1831.
[124] Arrangements of constables, Butcher MSS, BRO 32955/50a; *Bristol Gazette*, 3 Nov. 1831; *FFBJ*, 29 Oct. 1831.
[125] W.H. Somerton, *Narrative of the Bristol riots on the 29th, 30th and 31st of October, 1831* (4th edn, Bristol, 1831), p. 9; *Bristol Liberal*, 5 Nov. 1831; Vickery, 'Calendar', p. 258.

debate, of course, but it is nevertheless possible to present a narrative which accords with, and combines, a wide spectrum of contemporary accounts. They have formed the basis for the narrative which follows. Less well-substantiated assertions or descriptions are referenced individually.[126]

As the constables marched out to meet Sir Charles Wetherell at 10.00 a.m., the streets were crowded, and they were followed by something between 400 and 2,000 people, variously described as 'chiefly labourers', 'unemployed youths and women' and 'vagabonds and low women'. The sight of Wetherell's coach produced 'astounding yells and groans'.[127] As he proceeded into town from Totterdown, the constables protecting him were themselves the subject of attack.[128] As the carriage passed over Hill's Bridge, it was hit by three or four stones, and the crowd, which choked the route through Temple Street, Bridge Street and High Street, became increasingly hostile. Nevertheless, the procession succeeded in reaching the Guildhall in Broad Street, and Wetherell alighted and took his place at the bench. The hall was crowded, and there were shouts for reform. Indeed, such was the disruption that Wetherell announced an adjournment until 8.00 a.m. Monday, returned to his carriage and set off for the Mansion House.

The route was lined with hostile people (except for a brief cheer that went up as the carriage passed the Commercial Rooms). Many who had been at the Guildhall took short-cuts to Queen Square, arriving there ahead of the procession.[129] Stones were thrown as

---

[126] The main sources are: November 1831 editions of *Bristol Gazette, Bristol Liberal, Bristol Mercury, Bristol Mirror, FFBJ*; Lant Carpenter, *Letter to the editor of the Monthly Repository on the late riots in Bristol* (Bristol, 1831); 'Riots collection'; John Eagles, *The Bristol riots, their causes, progress and consequences* (Bristol, 1832); (W.H. Somerton), *A full report of the trials . . . of the Bristol rioters before the special commission* (Bristol, 1832); Thomas John Manchee, *The origin of the riots in Bristol and the causes of the subsequent outrages* (2nd edn, Bristol, 1831); Jefferies MSS, vol. VII, p. 187; Latimer, *Annals . . . nineteenth century*, pp. 146–87; 'MS material relating to the Bristol riots of 1831', BRL B24136 MS; *Bristol Riots. Trial of Charles Pinney, Esq., late mayor, for neglect of duty* (Bristol, 1832?); Somerton, *Narrative*; 'Troubles in Bristol'; 'Court martial of Lt. Col. Brereton', and 'Court Martial of Capt. Warrington', both in *Full report of the trials*; town clerk's statement, CCP/BRO, 18 May 1832; PB/BRO; Bristol riots correspondence, HO 40/28(1); Bristol riots: depositions re prisoners, HO 40/28(2); 'trial of Lt Col Brereton', HO 52/12; Disturbance entry book, vol. X, HO 41/10; entry book, Sept. 1831–Feb. 1832, WO 3/83; PP/BUL, S-2(1); and R-5.

[127] Somerton, *Narrative*, p. 10.

[128] Jefferies MSS, vol. VII, p. 187; Somerton, *Narrative*, pp. 7–8; evidence of Hare, *Trial of Pinney*, p. 21.   [129] *Bristol Liberal*, 5 Nov. 1831.

Wetherell and the mayor alighted and went into the Mansion House. As a crowd developed outside the Mansion House, the constables – young, undisciplined and 'over-zealous' – attempted to arrest individuals. In response a group, perhaps of fifty, and perhaps mainly of youths,[130] went to the Back to find sticks and other weapons and missiles. On their return the constables again went on the offensive, making sorties into the crowd and attempting to 'snatch' perceived ringleaders.[131] There were around 10,000 in the square now, of which 100 to 150 were involved in violence.[132] Skirmishes went on from 12.30 p.m. to 4.00 p.m. The constables' aggression had heightened the sense of irritation among both the active rioters and the spectators. As dusk fell, the Mansion House was stoned. Mayor Pinney emerged, and addressed the crowd, calling for order. He was met only with missiles and derision and, amid verbal and physical assaults, read the Riot Act, to no effect.[133]

In fact, the response of the rioters was to attack the constables (in the course of which 'some limbs were broken'),[134] break into the Mansion House and ransack the ground floor. Their fear that the military might arrive reputedly led them to construct barricades at the entrances to the square.[135] Meanwhile Wetherell was making his escape, in disguise, across the rooftops. Around 6.00 p.m., half an hour after the reading of the Riot Act, the 3rd Dragoons arrived along with the commander of military forces, Lt Col Brereton.[136] They were greeted with cheers, and shouts of 'God save the King', and 'King William and reform'. Brereton, whose approach throughout the subsequent events was one of conciliation, chatted with the crowd, urging them to disperse. The arrival of troops had been enough in itself to bring the rioters out of the Mansion House, but the constables, imbued with new courage, made further assaults. At 9.00 p.m. the 14th Light Dragoons came into the square. They held a reputation for putting down riots throughout the West Country, and

---

[130] *Bristol Gazette*, 3 Nov. 1831.
[131] Interestingly, especially since this was supposed to have been an ill-disciplined group of constables, the 'snatch' method of riot control is used to this day.
[132] Anon., *Particulars of the dreadful riots in Bristol on Saturday and Sunday, Oct. 29 and 30, 1831* (Bristol, 1831), p. 3; *Trial of Pinney*, p. 8.
[133] Alexander Baharie, 'An awful brush with the "old fourteenth" ', BRL B16727 MS, pp. 5–6, provides a vivid, perhaps embroidered, description of this scene.
[134] *Bristol Liberal*, 5 Nov. 1831.
[135] Somerton, *Narrative*, p. 15; Latimer, *Annals . . . nineteenth century*, p. 152.
[136] *Trial of Pinney*, p. 6; 'Trial of Brereton', p. 103.

had gained the nickname of 'the Bloody Blues'.[137] They were jeered as they arrived. Throughout the evening the crowd grew, including many new spectators, and the 14th bore the brunt of the hostility, three or four of them being injured. By 11.00 p.m. the crowd was 'immense', perhaps 8,000 or 10,000,[138] although it was also around this time that some of them began to disperse.[139]

At midnight some of the crowd moved out of the square and attacked the Council House, smashing its windows. The cavalry charged, using the flat of the sword, but causing some injuries nevertheless.[140] As troops pursued stragglers, an innocent bystander, Stephen Bush, was shot dead. Although the streets were fairly well cleared by 1.00 a.m., the death of Bush was generally believed to have heightened the tension, particularly towards the military. During the night the Mansion House was boarded up. In the early hours of Sunday morning, 30 October, many of the constables drifted away, and the troops were withdrawn for refreshment. At 7.00 a.m. a new assault was made on the Mansion House by around 200 people.[141] The boards were torn down, the building smashed up with stones and iron railings, and twenty or so of the rioters attained access to the upper floor, where Wetherell's ceremonial wig and robe were found and destroyed. The Mayor, along with Major Mackworth, made his escape out onto the roof. As the wine cellars were plundered and around 1,000 bottles of wine consumed or destroyed,[142] Alderman Abraham Hilhouse read the Riot Act three times, amid a volley of stones. At 10.00 a.m. the 14th arrived, to hisses, boos and shouts of 'down with the bloody blues', 'murder the buggers'.[143] Brereton decided to pull them out, and replace them with the 3rd.

As the 14th retreated a group pursued them, hurling stones. At the Drawbridge, on the Quay, the military turned and fired, killing one man. It had little impact on the assailants, however, who followed them to College Green, where they were again fired upon, and then to the 14th's headquarters at the Boar's Head, where yet again they came under fire. In addition to the original fatality, a further seven or eight were wounded. Brereton returned to the square, amid cheers, and promised the crowd that there would be no more firing, and that

[137] Susan Thomas, *The Bristol riots* (Bristol, 1974).
[138] 'Trial of Brereton', p. 110; *Trial of Pinney*, p. 54.
[139] 'Trial of Brereton', p. 109.
[140] Baharie, 'An awful brush', pp. 9–10.   [141] *Trial of Pinney*, p. 10.
[142] Somerton, *Narrative*, p. 18.   [143] 'Trial of Brereton', p. 112.

12 The Bristol riots on the night of 30 October 1831, looking towards Queen Square and the Cathedral, from Bedminster.

the 14th would be sent out of town if they promised to disperse. Accordingly the 14th were sent to Keynsham, but, although the level of violence in the square declined, the size of the crowd did not. By now a tri-coloured cap of liberty had been posted on the statue of King William III, at the centre of the square.

In the early afternoon, a group of rioters made off for the Bridewell to release those captured the previous day. On their way, they raided a smith's for hammers and other tools. The gaol was broken into with little difficulty by around 50 to 100 people, the prisoners were released and the building set on fire. A number then marched through the centre of town towards the New Gaol, situated on the island in the floating harbour, again procuring tools along the way. Around 2.00 p.m. they reached the gaol, where first a small group of magistrates and 'gentlemen', and then William Herapath and others from the BPU attempted, without success, to persuade them to turn back. Three or four hundred broke open the gaol, the 170 prisoners were liberated, the caravan for conveying prisoners to the gallows, and the gallows equipment itself, were thrown into the water and the buildings were fired. As many as 10,000 to 12,000 watched from the opposite bank. Twenty soldiers from the 3rd Dragoons arrived, were cheered, reputedly cheered back, and, to the astonishment of most subsequent chroniclers, rode off.

The rioters now held a 'council of war', discussing what to attack next. The house of Alderman Daniel in Berkeley Square was suggested, but the toll houses were finally selected.[144] The toll houses and gates on Princes Street Bridge and Cumberland basin were subsequently destroyed. Around 7.00 p.m., an assault upon the Gloucestershire County prison at Lawford's Gate liberated the prisoners there, and added another set of buildings to the catalogue of destruction. A group of forty or so also attacked and destroyed Lawford's Gate lock-up, and raided a liquor shop.[145] The Bishop's Palace (the Bishop of Bristol had voted against the Reform Bill[146]) in College Green was the next target. Fifty or a hundred 'men and boys' forced an entry, destroyed books and documents and attempted to set fire to the Palace. As some magistrates made their way to the scene, they requested help from members of the public, all of whom refused.[147] The mayor wrote to the commanding officer at Cardiff,

[144] Carpenter, *Letter*, p. 848; Vickery, 'A Bristol calendar', p. 262.
[145] *Bristol Liberal*, 5 Nov. 1831.
[146] *Hansard's Parliamentary debates*, vol. VIII, 7 Oct. 1831, p. 342.
[147] Town clerk's statement, CCP/BRO, 28 May 1832.

requesting assistance.[148] Meanwhile, the troops' attempts to break up the groups in Queen Square failed, and a renewed attack on the Mansion House brought about its total destruction. One prominent citizen in desperation suggested to the magistrates that they try to placate the crowd by burning Wetherell in effigy. The idea was not taken up.[149]

Throughout Sunday the magistrates had issued notices warning people that the Riot Act had been read,[150] and informing them that Wetherell had left the city.[151] The second of these was torn down, and the bill poster assaulted.[152] The BPU also issued notice that Wetherell had gone, and that violence only harmed the reform cause; these remained unmolested.[153] The magistrates appealed to citizens to assemble at the Guildhall to discuss what measures to take to resolve the crisis.[154] The meeting, at mid-day, attracted only 200 people, and produced nothing but argument and recrimination. There was an adjournment till 3.00 p.m., but even fewer, around 150, came to the second meeting.[155] Matters now seemed entirely out of control. With the 14th out of town, the magistrates scattered and confused, the constables gone and the Mansion House in flames, the firing of the Bishop's Palace was at last accomplished, and the systematic destruction of Queen Square began. Having destroyed the Custom House, groups of rioters moved from one house to the next, giving up to half an hour's notice to the inhabitants to quit, and then plundering and setting fire to the buildings. They progressed in this fashion along two sides of the square from the Mansion House, taking in the Custom House and Excise Office. Whilst some plundered, others sprawled on the grass, or sat on the stolen furniture, and consumed wine from the Corporation cellars, and food from the houses. For many witnesses it was a scene of indescribable depravity.

As if to emphasise the desperate state of the civil and military forces, Captain Codrington arrived about 10.00 p.m. with fifty or sixty of the Dodington Yeomanry, believed he could not act without the reading of the Riot Act, failed to find a magistrate, and led his troops back out of town.[156] The rioters were in undisputed control of

---

148 Pinney to commanding officer, Cardiff, 30 Oct. 1831, HO 40/28(1).
149 Evidence of Samuel Waring, *Trial of Pinney*, p. 8.
150 PO/BRO, 30 Oct. 1831.   151 *Ibid.*, 31 Oct. 1831, two versions.
152 *Trial of Pinney*, p. 55.   153 'Riots collection'.
154 PO/BRO, 30 Oct. 1831.   155 *Trial of Pinney*, p. 35.
156 Yet another incidence of ignorance surrounding the law of riot. See Hayter, *The army*. Hayter, pp. 9–10, cites the Bristol riot as an example of continuing confusion

the square all night. Some groups extended their action to attack
liquor shops and pubs. As dawn approached, people were to be found
sleeping on pilfered mattresses, or sprawling, hopelessly inebriated,
on the grass. The estimates of the number present vary wildly from
1,000 to 10,000. At 3.00 a.m. the mayor wrote to Brereton commanding him to take vigorous measures to suppress the riot. The note got
as far as Captain Warrington, at about 4.00 a.m., and he dithered
such that Brereton was not located until nearer 5.00 a.m. At that
point, however, Brereton led a detachment of twenty-one men into
the square, and began to disperse the crowd. Earnest repression was
yet to come. Major Beckwith (whom the popular histories delight in
describing as a real soldier, unlike the part-time and vacillatory
Brereton)[157] was sent to bring back the 14th. He returned ahead of
them, at 7.30 a.m., and sought the magistrates for their assistance.
Beckwith later related that 'They [the magistrates] all refused to do
so, stating that it would make them unpopular, and cause their
property to be destroyed. They also said none of them could ride on
horseback, except one, who was pressed to accompany me, but he
stated he had not been on horseback for eighteen years.'[158] Beckwith
abandoned them, and at 10.00 a.m. led a charge of the 14th and a
small detachment of the Bedminster Yeomanry.

Warrington had by now arrived with a reserve of eleven men from
the 3rd, and, with the addition of the 14th and perhaps 4,000
constables enlisted with the help of the BPU, a ferocious suppression
began. Although the mayor was active in correspondence during the
night and into Monday, informing Melbourne of events, and
requesting troops,[159] less attention was given to informing inhabitants of the military action that was about to take place. Notices that
the *posse comitatus* had been called out, and that people were to stay
indoors, did not appear until after the mopping-up operation.[160]
Innocent individuals were consequently caught up in the military's
action. Between 120 and 250 were killed and wounded in the

more than a hundred years after the introduction of the Act. Indeed, it was
following the 1831 riot that Lord Chief Justice Tindal made what was intended to
be a definitive ruling clarifying the law of riot. Nevertheless, confusion continued
during the disturbances of the Chartist period.

[157] Geoffrey Amey, *City under fire: the Bristol riots and aftermath* (London, 1979), p.
96.   [158] 'Court martial of Capt. Warrington', p. 12.
[159] Pinney to Melborne, 31 Oct. 1831, HO 40/28(1); Pinney to Codrington, 31 Oct.
1831, HO 40/28(1); Melbourne to Pinney, 31 Oct. 1831, HO 40/28(1).
[160] PO/BRO, 31 Oct. 1831.

Council House
Wednesday, Nov. 2, 1831.

The Magistrates most earnestly desire that all Persons will

Avoid Assembling in CROWDS

in different Parts of the City as such assemblages are likely to promote disturbances, and interfere with arrangements now making for the Recovery of Property and Detection of Offenders.

C. PINNEY, *Mayor.*

MILLS & SON, PRINTERS.

13 A Corporation notice issued in the wake of the 1831 riots, showing an awareness of the distinction, but potential connection, between 'crowds' and 'disturbance'.

operation, which was to draw criticism for its lack of discrimination.[161] (The official figures for the entire riots were much lower, at twelve killed and ninety-four injured.) No further rioting took place. Although in the evening Prince's Street again burst into flames, now fire engines were on hand to bring the blaze under control. The BPU formed night patrols, and at 8.00 p.m. the 11th regiment arrived from Cardiff.[162] Almost immediately the task of attempting to retrieve stolen property was begun. It was alleged that vast quantities of

[161] E.g., Carpenter, *Letter*, p. 850; *Bristol Liberal*, 5 Nov. 1831; Manchee, *Origin*, pp. 36–7.
[162] Despite having played no active part in the suppression of the riot, the 11th regiment suffered popular hostility on their return to Wales: see Gwyn A. Williams, *The Merthyr rising* (London, 1978), p. 220.

goods were subsequently recovered from the poor areas of town. Total damage was estimated at £4,000 to £8,000, although actual claims for compensation were to total £150,000 (of which £56,000 was paid).[163]

ANALYSIS

There has been little attempt, either by contemporaries or by historians, to look closely at the composition, actions or form of the crowds that dominated Bristol during these three days.[164] Most publications, including those of recent years, have portrayed embattled, desperate citizens and military fighting a faceless mob in much the same way as they might deal with a natural disaster. Contemporaries depicted the rioters as rabble, as outsiders, as the unemployed, or the Irish, as partly made up of 'low women', and almost entirely made up of young boys. Nor was this presentation of the rioters as the criminal residuum confined to the conservative minded. Clearly it was in the interests of the reformers to present this as the work of 'the mob' – and therefore entirely out of their hands.[165] Yet it is the very language of these contemporary accounts, as part of a broader language of crowd description, which does much to contradict these pejorative characterisations.

At the centre of the accounts of the riot was the careful and

---

[163] *Bristol riots 1831. Report of the commissioners appointed under the Bristol Damages Compensation Act* (Bristol, 1835).

[164] There have been three thoughtful examinations of the 1831 riot: Susan Thomas' useful pamphlet, *The Bristol riots*; Alphonsus Bonner's idiosyncratic article 'Catholics and the Bristol riots of 1831', *The Month*, CLX (1932), pp. 426–33; and a well-researched radio play, which concentrates on Brereton's role as commander of military forces: Elizabeth Holford, 'A man of too much honour', broadcast BBC Radio 4, 14 Dec. 1981. There have been numerous other less considered accounts. The fullest is Amey's *City under fire*. Other include: Henry Graham, *The annals of the yeomanry cavalry of Wiltshire. Being a complete history of the Prince of Wales' own royal regiment from the time of its formation in 1794 to October, 1884* (Liverpool, 1886), ch. 8; Latham Browne, *The burning of Bristol: a reminiscence of the first reform bill*, reprinted from *National Review* (Sept. 1884), pp. 45–62; Alfred Harvey, 'The Bristol riots', in P.H. Ditchfield (ed.), *Memorials of old Gloucestershire* (London, 1911), pp. 219–32; H.G. Brown and P.J. Harris, *Bristol England* (Bristol, 1946), ch. 25; Bryan Little, *The city and county of Bristol: a study of Atlantic civilisation* (London, 1954), ch. 11; Mary Gibson, *Warneford. Being a life and times of Harriet Elizabeth Wetherell Warneford* (Bournemouth, 1965), ch. 8; Herbert Payne, *Bristol riots 1686–1831* (Bristol, 1974) (despite its ostentatious title, this booklet is almost exclusively devoted to the 1831 riot).

[165] Reformers in Nottingham adopted a similar attitude after the riots there: Preston, 'Nottingham and the Reform Bill riots', p. 84.

selective application of the term 'mob'. Almost invariably it is used to denote active violence: actual rioters. As action ebbed and flowed, so the writers slipped from 'crowd' to 'mob', to 'multitude', to 'spectators', back to 'mob', and so on. In some instances that differentiation was particularly deliberate. In Lant Carpenter's account, with the removal of the troops on Sunday morning, 'the worst part of the population' began forming plans, and 'about half-past one the worst began. They were the mob of destruction, without personality.'[166] For Thomas Manchee, during Sunday afternoon,

The character of the crowd became gradually changed, many respectable people, anticipating mischief, left the Square; desperate wretches, to whom scenes of turmoil and confusion are sources of profit and enjoyment, supplied their places. Men and women joined in the most horrible imprecations of vengeance; the crowd degenerated into a mob, reckless of danger, and capable of the most daring excesses.[167]

Manchee insisted, in opposition to others, that those caught in the suppression of Monday morning were not 'A MOB' but 'respectable persons'.[168] The *Liberal* applied similar differentiations: a 'crowd' and 'the multitude' greeted Wetherell and threw stones at his carriage, and even the early violence in Queen Square was carried out by 'the multitude' and also, by implication, 'the spectators'. It is only when the Mansion House is finally entered that the term 'mob' is introduced.[169] Rev. Thomas Roberts, giving evidence at the trial of Pinney, believed that 'the mob' was composed of two separate classes, although both of the same grade of society. One class was riotous, one spectating.[170]

This differentiation, between the active and spectating crowd, was commonly made. Generally, the former was 'the mob', and the latter the 'crowd', 'multitude', 'populace' or 'people': 'There was no house lower down towards Prince's street in flames . . . The mob extended below the Custom-House (The witness explained afterwards, that he meant the crowd, and could not exactly say if the mob did extend below the Custom-House).'[171] Such differentiations on the part of witnesses during the trial of Charles Pinney are marked. John Walker Newcombe stressed that during the attack on the Mansion House on Saturday, 'the persons collected were some thousands. The rioters were not fifty.' He reserves the term 'the mob' for those who actually

---

[166] Carpenter, *Letter*, p. 847.   [167] Manchee, *Origin*, p. 23.
[168] *Ibid.*, pp. 36–7.   [169] *Bristol Liberal*, 5 Nov. 1831.
[170] *Trial of Pinney*, p. 15.   [171] Evidence of Quarmen, *Trial of Pinney*, p. 55.

broke into the Mansion House (the same distinction as was made by the *Liberal*). But Newcombe later applies 'the mob' to all those in Queen Square that the magistrates wished to disperse – a number, from all accounts, of some hundreds at least.[172] In Samuel Waring's evidence, he specifies 100 to 150 as active against the mansion House on Saturday. These were 'the mob', and generally he continues to term them such after they ceased to be active.[173] Samuel Selfe differentiated the 100–150 mainly 'women and boys' active in destroying the New Gaol from the thousands of spectators. Selfe also pointed out that only three were active in destroying the toll house at Prince's Street Bridge, although 100 were present.[174]

A number of further distinctions were made in the course of the apportioning of blame and stigma. For instance, and as will already be evident, 'the mob' was commonly believed to have been composed of young males. Rev. Francis Edgeworth claimed that 'the mob' that attacked the Bridewell was composed of around 150 lads of less than twenty years old.[175] One source put the active youths at less than twelve years old.[176] The *Liberal* claimed Queen Square was destroyed by boys aged ten and eleven.[177] The Irish were similarly supposed to have been prime culprits: the *Gazette* reckoned thirty to forty of them were the driving force behind the whole event.[178] Most accounts of the recovery of stolen property emphasise that it was retrieved from the Irish quarter of town. 'Low women' were another group reported to have been active, particularly in the turmoil of Wetherell's arrival, and in the destruction of Queen Square.[179] And finally, as ever, a conspiracy theory developed around the Kingswood colliers – promoted by Mackworth, and hotly rebuffed by two prominent Kingswood inhabitants.[180] Brereton had continually feared their arrival;[181] but General Jackson was looking for an excuse to 'give a lesson' to the colliers.[182] The more general belief that the riots were the work of outsiders was oft-stated.[183]

---

[172] *Trial of Pinney*, pp. 5–6.   [173] *Ibid.*, p. 8.   [174] *Ibid.*, p. 11.
[175] *Ibid.*, p. 19.   [176] *Old Jonathan*, Feb. 1883, p. 20.
[177] *Bristol Liberal*, 5 Nov. 1831.   [178] *Bristol Gazette*, 3 Nov. 1831.
[179] E.g., *Bristol Liberal*, 5 Nov. 1831; 'Riots at Bristol. By an eyewitness', extract from *New Monthly Magazine*, vol. XXXII (1831), p. 58; Manchee, *Origin*, p. 23; Sharples, 'Diary', 30 Oct. 1831; Somerton, *Narrative*, pp. 11, 30.
[180] Mackworth, *Personal narrative*, in 'Riots collection', Whittuck to *Bristol Gazette*, 10 Nov. 1831 and 24 Nov. 1831.
[181] Brereton to Somerset, 30 Oct. 1831, HO 40/28(1), and 31 Oct. 1831, HO 40/28(1).
[182] Jackson to Somerset, 2 Nov. 1831, HO 40/28(1).
[183] E.g., Beckwith to Home Office, 2 Nov. 1831, HO 40/28(1); Brereton to Somerset, 30 Oct. 1831, HO 40/28(1); Cross to Davis, 8 Dec. 1877, Davis MSS.

The evidence, of course, contradicts all the common assertions regarding the dominance of proceedings by particular groupings. Since boys were deemed to have been the most active, it might be supposed they would have suffered badly at the hands of the military. Yet the average age of those wounded in the cavalry charges was 30.3 years old. And the average age of those admitted to the Infirmary (excluding William Protheroe, injured while acting as fireman, and Mr Wilcox, hurt defending his property), was 23.2 years old; 97 per cent of casualties were male.[184] Of the sixty-five for whom details are provided, fifty-seven came from Bristol, and eight from nearby locations: two from Westbury, three from Horfield and one each from Bath, Stapleton and Clifton. As Susan Thomas points out, the trial of the prisoners shows them to have been reasonably well-known citizens: generally they were able to bring forward local witnesses to testify to their good character.[185]

Examination of the list of prisoners also counters the received picture. Only 8.8 per cent were female;[186] and only 10 per cent under the age of eighteen, of which only one was convicted of a major offence.[187] Just two prisoners were described as Irish,[188] and of the twenty-five for whom parish of residence is given, only three came from the Irish-dominated parishes of St Stephen and St Werburgh. Occupations are given for thirty-two prisoners: just two were unemployed. Seven of those brought to trial were servants, four sailors, two firemen, two carpenters, and among the remainder were a sawyer, milk-carrier, lime-kiln worker, book-keeper, accountant, butcher, stonemason, methodist preacher and a wagon-warehouse keeper.

But even if it can be shown that the attempt by contemporaries to distinguish particular social groupings as responsible for the riots had little or no foundation, the broader distinctions that were drawn between active and passive crowd members remain important. It was a distinction not without its problem. For many writers, 'the mob' was both a permanent and active entity; yet 'the people' *turned into* 'the mob' on becoming active. That supposed transition remains largely unexplained. Nevertheless, the presence of large numbers of non-rioters gives particular significance to the fact that the city was, for a

---

[184] Returns of killed, wounded and injured admitted to the Infirmary, in *Bristol Gazette*, 3 Nov. 1831. The list states ninety-four as wounded, and twelve as killed, but details are provided for only sixty-seven.

[185] Thomas, *Bristol riots*, p. 23.   [186] *Full report*, pp. 103–4.

[187] *Ibid.*, pp. 17–20.   [188] *Ibid.*, pp. 29, 62.

long period, in the rioters' hands: it was not so much grasped as placed there. Three questions arise from this: to what extent were the spectators responsible for the riots; what was the attitude towards the apparent control of the town by rioters; and if the military had not finally stepped in, would the whole town eventually have been destroyed? All these questions may be addressed through examinations of the scenes in Queen Square on Sunday night.

THE DESTRUCTION OF QUEEN SQUARE

The gradual demolition of Queen Square – proceeding along two sides, from house to house – was the first damage inflicted on private property; and it did not commence until after all major *public* buildings had been destroyed. It was to be the final phase in the rioting: no other public or private property was attacked once the systematic destruction of the square had begun (with the possible exception of the theft of alcohol from shops and pubs). During the destruction there were two types of crowd (presumably with some overlap): one attacking houses, the other lounging on the grass in the square drinking, laughing and cheering.

Operations probably began around 8.00 p.m. following the final attack on the Mansion House, a raid on its cellars and the destruction of the Customs House.[189] Some now retired onto the grass to drink the plundered wines, and to watch, as other groups entered the houses, giving the occupants half an hour to remove themselves and some valuables before moving in and smashing window frames, removing furniture and starting fires.[190] Of the twenty-seven houses successfully entered, twenty-four were effectively burnt out.[191] Estimates of the numbers involved vary, but it seems groups ranging from 15 to 100 were active in the housebreaking. Most of those in the square were engaged in either revelry or destruction; few were merely standing and watching. Spectating crowds, then, were a phenomenon of the early stages of the riot, when public buildings were under attack. At that point their apathy was crucial.

There was a bond, during the early stages, between spectators and

---

[189] *Bristol Gazette*, 3 Nov. 1831; *Full report of the trials*; Somerton, *Narrative*, pp. 29–30.

[190] *Trial of Pinney*, pp. 8, 11, 14; Ham to Place, Aug. 1835; 'MS material'; Somerton, *Narrative*, pp. 30–1.

[191] *Bristol riots 1831. Report of the commissioners appointed under the Bristol Damages Compensation Act.*

14 A contemporary representation (almost certainly exaggerated) of the debauched scenes in Queen Square on the night of 30 October 1831.

activists: a common loathing for the Corporation. Contemporaries acknowledged this rift between the public and the executive. Somerton, and others, saw the riots as a product not only of a rift but of outright vengeance on the part of the inhabitants.[192] The magistrates themselves were aware of this: their inactivity was in part due to direct fear of reprisals.[193] When citizens were gathered in the Guildhall and their aid requested by the magistrates, many retorted 'Why should we protect the Corporation's property? Let them protect their own property.'[194] Rev. James Bulwer claimed he heard many say that 'it served the Corporation right for bringing that arrant villain, Sir Charles, down to insult the inhabitants of Bristol'.[195]

It was the attack upon the private property in Queen Square, however, that altered the public mood: 'as various parts of the Mansion-House fell in when in flames, I heard cheers from among parts of the crowd. There were no cheers when the private property was destroyed . . . I know there is a dislike entertained towards the Corporation on account of the government they exercise.'[196] The fear that private property might suffer had first come when the rioters were rumoured to be discussing the possibility of destroying Alderman Daniel's house in Berkeley Square. Individuals began to fear that their houses would be singled out for destruction.[197] Ellen Sharples recorded in her diary the sudden burst of activity among the wealthy of Clifton in the early hours of Monday, as they armed themselves with 'guns, pistols, swords rusty and bright'.[198]

When political apathy turned to social outrage it was not only at the sight of the destruction of private property, but at the reputedly licentious scenes in the square, which generated a fascinated moral horror. Ellen Sharples recorded the sight of 'horrid monsters', and scenes that were 'too revolting' for description.[199] Somerton similarly felt 'the scenes of brutality . . . [and] the obscenity of conduct and language was revolting to every feeling of decency'.[200] But he went on:

---

[192] Somerton, *Narrative*, p. 5 and *passim*; Jefferies MSS, vol. III, p. 191; *Remarks suggested by recent events, and on the necessity of an efficient police in this city, by a householder* (Bristol, 1831).
[193] 'Court martial of Capt. Warrington', p. 12.
[194] Latimer, *Annals . . . nineteenth century*, p. 157.
[195] *Trial of Pinney*, p. 53.   [196] Evidence of Selfe, *ibid.*, p. 12.
[197] Cross to Davis, May 1877, Davis MSS.
[198] Sharples, 'Diary', 30 Oct. to 1 Nov. 1831.
[199] *Ibid.*, 30 Oct. 1831.   [200] Somerton, *Narrative*, p. 30.

At one spot, three of the incendiaries, who seemed exhausted with their fatigues, were joined by two females, and, seating themselves in chairs, the whole group gave themselves up for a while to refreshment. Whilst they were eating, and drinking wine, each one from a separate bottle, they revelled in delight at the scene before them. 'I'm d—d,' said one of them, 'if we arn't been b—y hard at work, and now I think 'tis time to rest a bit.' Another, with an oath at every word, said, 'I'm cursed if this bean't very funny: Charley com'd down here to try the prisoners; but Charley funk'd, and so he cut and run'd away. Well, we turn'd judges, and so we found all the pris'ners not guilty; and I'm d—d if we arn't made a reg'lar gaol deliv'ry.' It is almost needless to add that his wretched companions testified their pleasure by sending forth the most horrid yells of laughter.[201]

The debauched scenes held a sexual suggestiveness few writers could resist. There was also, unsurprisingly, outright religious condemnation: previous habits of drunkenness, bad company and Sabbath breaking were deemed a causal factor in this ultimate violation of the Sabbath, 'led by Satan'.[202]

When the riot no longer represented an opportunity to teach the Corporation a lesson, but became instead the supersession of established authority by an alien counter-culture, then the shock induced sufficient military and civilian activity for large-scale and violent reprisals. The British Association believed that 'Had magisterial action been suspended 30 days instead of only during three, all Bristol would have been burnt to the ground.'[203] They were wrong: the scenes in the square, taking place in a location which was a well-defined symbol of power and influence standing both physically and symbolically aside from the rest of the city, were more a *charivari*, a celebration of misrule, than a calculated challenge to established order.[204] Rather than ritualised conflict turning to physical violence

---

[201] *Ibid.*, p. 31.

[202] *A voice to Bristol: the thirtieth and thirty first days of October, 1831* (2nd edn, Bristol, 1831), pp. 3–4; Rev. W. Thorpe, *A report of the lecture . . . upon the riots of Bristol* (Bristol, 1832), p. 11; *Narrative of a conversation held with Christopher Davis and William Clarke* (Bristol, 1832), p. 28; *Lamentation of those unfortunate men now lying under sentence of death in Bristol goal* (Bristol, n.d., 1832?).

[203] British Association, *Bristol and its environs, historical, descriptive and scientific* (London, 1875), p. 64.

[204] In December 1832, the conservative journal *Bristol Job Nott*, playing on the centuries old occurrence of 'lords of misrule' ceremony at Christmas time, and turning it to the recent prominence of reform, commented: 'let [this] be a season of order. Our popish ancestors had their *lords of misrule*, and their seasons of *topsy turvy*; in which, by way of sport, the servants ruled the masters. But there is no need of playing at that game, this Christmas. *We have been playing at it too long*' (20 Dec. 1832). Actions of misrule and inversion can be said to confirm and reinforce

(a process which has been described in a variety of contexts by a number of writers), here was physical violence returning to ritualised conflict.[205] Those that rioted in Bristol in 1831 demonstrated the *precise* limits to which they were prepared to go; having reached those limits, the only way was back. The burning of the square was not a dramatic climax but a parting gesture. The action, carried out slowly, stopped half-way through; and it did so well before the military arrived.[206] It was the lack of threat, and of opposition, posed by the crowd at this point that caused many to view the military suppression as needlessly brutal.

CONCLUSION

The riots did nothing to alter hostility towards the Corporation. Demands for local government reform continued.[207] And, most significantly, despite the apparent demonstration by the rioters of the inadequacy of Bristol's police forces, ensuing proposals for police reform brought public hostility. The grounds for opposition were familiar: the cost, and concern at the prospect of placing further powers in the hands of the Corporation.[208] Even the proposal to levy

the existing order by acknowledging its form, functions, importance and cohesion; the more potent an opposite, the greater potency attributed to the reality. But just how far statements about dramatic (literally), institutionalised or carnival presentations of inversion may be applied to more spontaneous, less institutionalised and more ambiguous manifestations of misrule and mockery requires further discussion. See: Joseph Strutt, *The sports and pastimes of the people of England* (London, 1801), book IV, ch. 3; Barbara A. Babcock (ed.), *The reversible world: symbolic inversion in art and society* (Ithaca, 1978); John Brewer, 'Theatre and counter-theatre in Georgian politics: the mock elections at Garrat', *Radical History Review*, no. 22 (1979–80), pp. 7–40; Natalie Zemon Davis, 'The reasons for misrule: youth groups and charivaris in sixteenth-century France', *Past and Present*, no. 50 (Feb. 1971), pp. 41–75; E.P. Thompson, ' "Rough music": le charivari anglais', *Annales ESC*, XXVII, 2 (1972), pp. 285–312.

[205] Peter Burke, The virgin of the Carmine and the revolt of Masaniello', *Past and Present*, no. 99 (May 1983), pp. 3–21; Emmanuel Le Roy Ladurie, *Carnival in Romans: a people's uprising at Romans, 1579–80*, trans. Mary Feeney (Harmondsworth, 1981); Robin Fox, 'The inherent rules of violence', in Peter Collett (ed.), *Social rules and social behaviour* (Oxford, 1977), pp. 132–49; Peter Marsh, *Aggro: the illusion of violence* (London, 1978).

[206] Evidence of Selfe, *Trial of Pinney*, p. 11; 'Holograph letter from W. Capper re. riots of 1831', BRL B23542 MS, SR134.

[207] Somerton, *Narrative*, p. 38; Manchee, *Origin*, p. 40; Bristol Chamber of Commerce, to Corporation, 5 Mar. 1832, LMP/BRO Box 1832, and 15 Mar. 1832, LMP/BRO Box 1832.

[208] *Bristol Gazette*, 22 Mar. 1832, *et seq.*; Roderick Walters, *The establishment of the Bristol police force* (Bristol, 1975), pp. 6–8.

15 A cartoon drawn shortly after the 1831 riots, mocking Sir Charles Wetherell's misrepresentation of reform opinion in Bristol.

a new local rate to pay for the riot compensation prompted hostility from the parish committees, as well as from one of the magistrates' most loyal chief constables.[209] By the time of the executions of the rioters on 7 January 1832, public opinion had already moderated: a petition, signed by 10,000 people, including many 'respectable inhabitants', and even two of those whose houses had been burnt down, called for a pardon for the condemned.[210] The executions themselves were effectively boycotted, about 7,000 turning out, instead of the 20,000 or more such occasions could draw.[211] And in June 1832, 10,000 were processing in celebration of the passing of the Reform Act.[212]

The riots may indeed have hastened the passing of the Reform Bill – certainly they influenced the subsequent form of the reform campaign, creating a polarisation of attitudes towards agitation on the streets.[213] According to Gwyn Williams, news of the Bristol riots 'threw the whole of the South Wales coalfield into crisis';[214] and there was apprehension of sympathy riots in a number of other towns.[215] Just as the Gordon riots in London in 1780 (although apparently reactionary in motivation) profoundly influenced perceptions of urban crowd activity, the responsibilities of the magistracy and the potential of extra-parliamentary pressure,[216] so the Bristol riots seemed, for many outside Bristol, to prove the case for provincial police reform, and for municipal reform, as means towards improvement in public order.[217]

The discrepancies and overlaps between local and national responses, however, serve to emphasise the glib inadequacy of dismissing these disturbances as 'a hangover from the past'.[218] E.P.

---

[209] Butcher to Daniel, Butcher MSS, BRO 32955/5b; Latimer, *Annals . . . nineteenth century*, pp. 181–2; *Bristol Gazette*, 15 Mar. 1832, *et seq.*
[210] *Full report of the trials*, pp. 85, 117.   [211] *Bristol Gazette*, 2 Feb. 1832.
[212] *Bristol Mercury*, 23 June 1832; *Bristol Gazette*, 20 June 1832.
[213] Asa Briggs, *The age of improvement, 1783–1867* (London, 1959), pp. 253–60; Cannon, *Parliamentary reform*, p. 227; Stevenson, *Popular disturbances*, pp. 221–7; Rudé, 'English rural and urban disturbances', p. 102.
[214] Williams, *Merthyr rising*, p. 218.
[215] Rudé, 'English rural and urban disturbances', pp. 98–9.
[216] See J. Paul De Castro, *The Gordon riots* (London, 1926), and Stevenson, *Popular disturbances*, pp. 76–90. After the 1831 riots the *Gazette*, 13 Nov. 1831, reprinted its 1780 report of the Gordon riots.
[217] *Hansard's Parliamentary debates*, vol. IX, 6 Dec. 1831, pp. 4, 11, 38; Derek Fraser, *Power and authority in the Victorian city* (Oxford, 1979), pp. 3–4.
[218] Rudé, *The crowd*, p. 149.

Thompson commented that 'Bristol in 1831 exemplifies the persistence of older, backward looking patterns of behaviour, just as much as Manchester in 1819 exemplifies the emergence of the self-disciplined patterns of the new working-class movement.'[219] But to reject the significance of riots bound up in the campaign for parliamentary and local government reform simply because recourse was made to direct action is to miss important points about extra-parliamentary protest, perceptions of public order, popular crowd activity and reform itself.

Manchester in 1819 and Bristol in 1831 had more than a little in common. Behind both events was a popular dislike for local government, and an alienation of that government from popular opinion and its espousal of radical politics. Both events solidified this mutual hostility and suspicion. And both, therefore, have their part to play in the process of municipal reform. Secondly, the repercussions of the brutal intervention of local forces in Manchester fed into existing confusion among the provincial magistracy regarding their rights and role in suppressing popular demonstrations and disturbances. That events in Bristol in 1831 could escalate was due in part to the fact that the precipitous actions of the Manchester magistrates had produced national outrage (reinforced by the memory of Bristol's own 'Peterloo', in 1793). The context for thorough reappraisal and reform of local administration and social organisation represented by the 1829 Metropolitan Police Act, the 1832 Reform Act, the 1834 Poor Law Amendment Act and the 1835 Municipal Reform Act was contributed to by both these famous disturbances: the fact that one concerned a well-organised working class mass demonstration and the other a keenly targeted outbreak of mass violence is, in this regard, of secondary importance.

More importantly for this study, however, the labelling of popular protest as 'backward' or 'forward', carrying pejorative overtones of, respectively, 'irrelevance' and 'relevance', has done much to hinder the broader analysis of crowd activity. Crucial to the context for the 1831 riot were the coronation celebrations in 1821 and 1831 (which demonstrated a gulf between local government and populace, as they did in other towns); the sequence of carefully organised reform meetings taking place outside work hours and inside Queen Square; and the well-understood repertoire of crowd activity over a number

---

[219] Thompson, *The making*, p. 81.

of decades, which established the symbolic language of the urban environment, and facilitated the perception of different crowds as representing different degrees of menace. The 'crowd historians', having constructed a transition thesis, dismissed numerous large-scale crowd events, involving thousands of working people, because they could not be fitted neatly into a mould of industrial and political organisation. This is quite aside from whether the ideological content of the northern reform campaign was in fact so different from that of the south, or from that of the eighteenth century.[220]

The concepts of pre-industrial and industrial crowd activity are entirely useless in drawing attention to these important contexts for crowd activity, which not only illuminate social relations in the early nineteenth-century provincial city, but provide an insight into contemporary attitudes towards mass. To give just one example: the distinction between spectating and active crowd members, central to both the 1793 and 1831 riots in Bristol, was an important element in the formulation of a policy of restraint in the handling of disturbances sought by the first Municipal Police Commissioners. The Commissioners' aim was to ensure that the sympathy and assistance of spectators was with the police and not those engaged in disturbance or provocation.[221] There is almost nothing in the existing historiography of riot-dominated crowd studies to explain the background to such a policy. More grandly, fear of mass 'contagion' of spectators by rioters, expressed in the early nineteenth century, was a precursor of the theories of crowd psychology to be developed at the end of the century by LeBon and others.

Similarly, the industrial and pre-industrial duality shows no interest in the language or crowd description carefully deployed in the chronicling of the 1831 disturbances, and which reflects a (perhaps growing) concern to differentiate and classify crowd activity and composition. Such differentiations were also to be found, of course, in the concurrent obsession with the 'deserving' and 'undeserving' poor, which was the focus for poor law reform, and at the heart of notions of incorrigibility, habituality and reformability which were to inform social policy for decades to come.

---

[220] See Gareth Stedman Jones' important article, 'The language of Chartism', in James Epstein and Dorothy Thompson (eds.), *The Chartist experience: studies in working-class radicalism and culture 1830–60* (London, 1982), pp. 3–58.

[221] Wilbur R. Miller, *Cops and bobbies: police authority in New York and London, 1830–1870* (Chicago, 1977), pp. 13–14.

It is the sense of a contemporary attempt to comprehend the acceptable limits of public and mass expressions of commitment, support or disapprobation, and a confusion over the point at which these uncertain limits were nevertheless demonstrably transgressed, which the established historiography of mass cannot adequately address. The co-existence of broadly supported campaigns for parliamentary and municipal reform, with different but overlapping constituencies; organised and orderly protest meetings and shambolic scenes of revelry; passive spectators and active crowd members; inept and provocative local authority and the need for disciplined public policy was as baffling for contemporary observers as it might respectably be for historians.

12. *Conclusions*

To other poeple, we also are masses. Masses are other people.
(Raymond Williams, *Culture and society 1780–1950* (Harmondsworth,
1963) p. 289)

Crowds in early nineteenth-century English towns were at once
essential and invisible. Essential because of their potential powerfully
to illustrate and validate an action, exhibition, celebration or cause.
Invisible because without the self-interested presentations of observers and chroniclers, crowds and crowd events would not, in
historical terms, exist. This important duality both compromises the
received historiographical picture of mass tumult and disarray and,
paradoxically, ensured that contemporaries left a record of crowd
activity and patterning which contradicted their own assertions
regarding the terrifying potential of the urban masses. Like them or
not, most sizeable crowd occurrences had to be reported, even if those
reports misrepresented the motives and appearance of the crowd
members. And most sizeable crowd occurrences were not riotous.

The emphasis within the historiography of this period has been
upon the problems posed for social order and public administration
of massive population growth tied to rapid industrialisation. A
sequence of major disturbances – the Gordon riots, Priestley riots,
food riots, Luddism, Peterloo, the Merthyr rising and the reform
riots – appear in this historiography to fuel and confirm broader
concerns regarding the supposed incorrigibility and incomprehens-
ibility of the masses. Those concerns found statutory expression in
penal, police and poor law reform, and in the remodelling of the
structures of public administration and public order.

The close examination of crowd occurrences at the local level does
not necessarily overturn this overview. It does, however, add a series
of further considerations which, when taken in conjunction with
existing research, suggest the need for a thorough reappraisal of the

315

history of public order and attitudes towards mass in the nineteenth century.

The first of those considerations is that rapid population growth and urbanisation created, for late eighteenth- and early nineteenth-century observers, at least as much a sense of awe and delight as of fear. The immediate response to the prospect of urban growth was the potential for greater competitiveness with other urban areas, both in the economic and the social sphere. Civic pride, rivalry and emulation are neglected elements in the existing account of early nineteenth-century towns; they were attributes not of the late Victorian period alone. Nor were they restricted to those towns developing at the fastest rate, such as Manchester and Liverpool. In Bristol, and perhaps to a lesser extent in Norwich, civic pride motivated a near obsession with rejuvenation – a rejuvenation which it was hoped would take place at the expense of their rivals. 'The ancient and honourable city of Bristol' had to be defended against all detractors, 'in spite of all the pretensions of such a modern upstart as Liverpool'.[1]

Secondly, although issues of policing and public order were raised and discussed, they were not seen as overwhelmingly important, or necessarily defined in terms of the suppression of mass activity. Precisely for the reasons of civic pride already mentioned, commentators were as eager to emphasise local tranquility, public safety and good order as to vocalise unease about the potential of the urban mob. Furthermore, insofar as local and national disturbance did generate questions of the official response to violence, a professional police force was by no means regarded as the obvious answer. Indeed, discussions of overall police reform are surprisingly absent from the local press and pamphleteers. Rather the attention was focused on the form and conduct of existing local government forces. Consequently, the Bristol Bridge riot, the Peterloo massacre and the Bristol reform riot all produced concern, in the first instance, regarding the ability of existing local forces to manage crowd events. There was local hostility in Bristol in the wake of the 1831 riots to the prospect of police reform, since it was thought that this would invest an already incompetent body with even greater power. Furthermore, crowd activity was overwhelmingly non-violent in character; its occurrence was not automatically associated with the need for strong

---

[1] *The Chronicle of Bristol*, V, 1 Dec. 1829.

policing. Boisterousness was common enough, but actual riot was not.

The third consideration is that although the prominent and powerful did not generally hold crowds in especially high esteem, they did frequently support and sponsor their mobilisation. The prevalence of large-scale crowd events in this period should not simply be equated with population growth or with campaigns for radical reform. Insofar as population increase had a direct influence upon crowd occurrences it was in reinforcing the potential for the organisation of mass exhibitions of social consensus. Just as population increase was viewed positively as an expression of social and commercial progress, so large crowd events could elicit expressions of wonderment and awe at their potential as powerful statements of unity and solidarity. Mass attendance at recreational and celebratory events was therefore actively encouraged. In addition, of course, political events reflecting the ideological preoccupations of those in positions of power and prominence were also seen as worthwhile occasions for mass mobilisation. Nevertheless, such crowd 'management' was precarious: the messages sought were not always those actually communicated by the gathering itself; the unequivocal expression of social concensus was an elusive goal.

Fourthly, most major crowd events were immediately connected to local concerns, and particularly what might be termed corporate identity. That is to say, the aspirations and beliefs of various social groupings regarding not only national issues but also representations of the town, coincided around prominent crowd events. This could on some occasions make for violence; on others for dramatic public expressions of differences of perception (as during royal celebrations); and on still others a complex amalgam of meanings and expectations around a well-established public spectacle (such as at elections, executions or public funerals). All crowd events therefore, although not necessarily idiosyncratically localist in concern, were intimately connected to the expression of local identities, contentions and practices.

The final consideration to emerge from the detailed examinations of provincial crowd activity in this period is perhaps the most significant of all: namely, that analysis of the trends in crowd occurrence and the established forms for describing those crowds produces clear patterns of procedure, location, timing and language. These patterns, it can be argued, are not only visible to the historian;

they were also well-understood by contemporaries. In sum they provided a framework which made it possible quickly to assess the meaning, implication and degree of menace of a gathering. Set patterns and routines, and deviation from those patterns and routines, invested crowds with extra symbolic significance. From the time and place of a gathering it was possible to infer social composition, degree of marginalisation or integration, threat and anticipated size. Established procedures reflect the integral position of crowd events within the urban environment – in effect the institutionalisation of crowds. Patterns in language of crowd description, meanwhile, reflect the attempt on the part of commentators (consciously or otherwise) to make distinctions between acceptable and unacceptable gatherings, between active and passive crowd membership and between the disruptive or cohesive potential of different crowd events. Of course, these various patterns may operate in conflict with each other: the application of a language of marginalisation may be contradicted by the evidence of well-supported activity suggested by the time, place and procedure of a particular gathering.

In total, the atmosphere of civic rivalry and pride; the potential for personal and corporate self-glorification; the mobilisation of establishment and popular campaigning; the needs of mass consumption and recreation; and the patterns of crowd occurrence together make for an overall framework of crowd activity – frequently with official sanction – which no amount of misrepresentation by contemporary chroniclers could conceal. Nevertheless, whereas some crowds may bear their own messages, others have messages thrust upon them. The extra-politicisation of gatherings – that is, the ascription to them by outsiders of particular meanings or characteristics – is another central theme in the history of mass phenomena. Just as the potential of expression offered by crowds was too important to ignore, so their susceptibility to reinterpretation by commentators gave them an added significance. In other words, if a crowd did not itself offer the mass expression of a desired view, it could nevertheless be ascribed that view, or, alternatively, it could be depicted in such a way as to stigmatise and marginalise its activity. Identifiable and comprehensible through a framework of regular occurrence, crowds could nevertheless individually be made either to transform (by selective reportage), or disappear (by non-reportage).

There is a constant dialectic, therefore, between crowd appearances and what crowds were made to appear to be. The attempt on the part of those in a position to publicise their views to misrepresent crowd activity was sometimes compromised by other sources for information, or by contrary evidence offered by the position of that crowd within an established repertoire of occurrence. But the ever-present possibility of that attempted misrepresentation is at least as important to the history of perceptions of mass phenomena as the crowd occurrences themselves.

Before it is possible to speak with confidence about the form and presentation of crowd activity in the nineteenth century, and indeed the twentieth, at least two further studies are required. One would apply the methods used here to mass activity later in the century and thereby attempt to answer the question: was there in fact a major transformation in the type, frequency and level of violence of mass phenomena in the late Victorian years? And the second study would examine in greater detail the origins and development of prevailing theories of crowd activity. On the basis of evidence offered here it is not possible to talk of a generally understood theory of 'the crowd' in this period. Nevertheless, notions of contagion, regression, criminalisation and susceptibility to suggestion are all episodically present in early nineteenth-century accounts. The formalisation of such views in later years has clearly had an important influence upon present-day perceptions of mass phenomena.

If it is surprising that so few historians have taken up Asa Briggs' initiatives in the discussion of perceptions of 'the human aggregate' in the second half of the nineteenth century, the lack of interest in the perception of mass in the earlier part of the century is bewildering.[2] The development, in the course of the nineteenth century, of a corporate anxiety regarding the supposedly destructive and de-moralising potential of large and densely populated cities, has become, for historians, axiomatic. Yet the normative prescriptions of the poor law commissioners and police and penal reformers have been called into question;[3] the long-term trends in crime and violence

---

[2] Asa Briggs, *The collected essays of Asa Briggs*, vol. 1: *Words, numbers, places and people* (Brighton, 1985).

[3] For example, M. Blaug, 'The myth of the old poor law and the making of the new', *Journal of Economic History*, XXII (1963), pp. 151–84; Ursula Henriques, 'How cruel was the Victorian poor law?', *Historical Journal*, XI, 2 (1968), pp. 365–71; S.E. Finer, *The life and times of Sir Edwin Chadwick* (London, 1952), Wilbur R. Miller, *Cops and bobbies: police authority in New York and London, 1830–70* (Chicago, 1977); Michael Ignatieff, *A just measure of pain: the penitentiary in the industrial revolution, 1750–1850* (London, 1978).

are a matter for dispute;[4] the concept of moral panic has been convincingly applied to the Victorian period;[5] and one influential recent study has exploded as myth successive appeals to a 'golden age' of lower levels of crime, violence and public disorder.[6] Clearly, therefore, there exists the possibility, at the very least, that prominently stated anxieties regarding crowd activity did not express social realities, and indeed may not always have been universally shared.

If there were indeed such discrepancies, then it would seem essential that greater attention be paid to the process of urbanisation in the late eighteenth and early nineteenth centuries. Robert Storch, Hugh Cunningham and others have done much to disentangle the continuities and discontinuities in popular culture in these years.[7] That there has not been a closer and more imaginative focus upon the specific area of mass phenomena and its associated perceptions is probably due in large part to what might be termed the creative stranglehold of the 'crowd historians'. Their illuminating research has been eclipsed by the limitations of their methods, yet their influence has remained overpowering.

The selective characterisation by contemporary observers of the commitment and concern of thousands of people prepared to give their time to the mass demonstration of their opinion, opposition, celebration or fascination has fed nicely the 'enormous condescension' of posterity and modernists alike. The Bristol riot of 1831 – 'the last great urban riot in English history' in the eyes of George Rudé, and of little significance and even less interest to any historian of progressive proletarianism – articulated in drama and fury themes visible to anyone who cares to look behind the rhetoric and representation of crowd activity in the city over the preceding forty

---

4 For example, V.A.C. Gatrell, 'The decline of theft and violence in Victorian and Edwardian Britain', in V.A.C. Gatrell, Bruce Lenman and Geoffrey Parker (eds.), *Crime and the law: the social history of crime in western Europe since 1500* (London, 1980), pp. 238–337; Alan Macfarlane, *The justice and mare's ale: law and disorder in seventeenth-century England* (Oxford, 1981), introduction and conclusion; Lawrence Stone, 'Interpersonal violence in English society 1300–1800', *Past and Present*, no. 101 (Nov. 1983), pp. 22–33.

5 Jennifer Davis, 'The London garotting panic of 1862: a moral panic and the creation of a criminal class in mid-Victorian England', in Gatrell, Lenman and Parker (eds.), *Crime and the law*, pp. 190–213.

6 Geoffrey Pearson, *Hooligan: a history of respectable fears* (London, 1983).

7 Hugh Cunningham, *Leisure and the industrial revolution* (London, 1980); Robert D. Storch (ed.), *Popular culture and custom in nineteenth-century England* (London, 1982).

years and more. The pride, pettiness and priorities of social life in that large town are there in the riot in October – but only for those who have already looked at the coronation celebrations, the meetings and processions and executions.

Something, ironically, has been lost in the attempt to identify faces in the rioting crowd. It has fed the classification of collective activity into protest and change, into the gaining of experience and the putting aside of ideologically puerile ways. There is another irony: it is through the broad picture built up by the patterned occurrence of masses and masses, rather than through the individual in the crowd, that it is possible to gain a glimpse of the meaning and moment of collective diversion and ambition. But it is a picture just visible through successive layers of distortion and defamation. We see far-away people as crowds; and in crowds people seem far away. To the distance of history is added this further distance, the distance of exclusion. Crowds, a part of everyday life, have somehow remained mysterious and mistrusted. Generations of observers and historians have played their part; the crowd is our own invention.

Bibliography

The bibliography has been arranged as follows:

A Manuscript sources
    1 Deposited in Public Records Office, Kew, London
    2 Deposited in Bristol Record Office
    3 Deposited in Bristol Reference Library
    4 Deposited in Bristol University Library
    5 Deposited in Liverpool Records Office
    6 Deposited in Norfolk Record Office

B Printed primary sources
    1 Bristol newspapers
    2 Miscellaneous periodicals relating to Bristol
    3 Other newspapers
    4 General printed material, deposited in Bristol Reference Library
    5 General printed material, deposited in Bristol Record Office
    6 Other printed material
    7 Printed government records

C Secondary sources
    1 Relating to Bristol, published before 1900
    2 Relating to Bristol, published after 1900
    3 Relating to Liverpool, Norwich and Manchester
    4 Selected general secondary sources
    5 Unpublished secondary sources

A MANUSCRIPT SOURCES

1 Deposited in Public Records Office, Kew, London

1831 riots, Bristol

HO 40/28(1)	1831 riots, correspondence
HO 40/28(2)	1831 riots, depositions re prisoners
HO 44/24	Correspondence with counties
HO 52/12	Material relating to trial of Lt Col Brereton
WO 3/83	Entry book, Sept. 1831 to Feb. 1832

Disturbance entry books

HO 41/1   Apr. 1816 to Dec. 1816
HO 41/2   Dec. 1816 to Apr. 1817
HO 41/3   Apr. 1817 to Jan. 1818
HO 41/4   Jan. 1818 to Sept. 1819
HO 41/5   Sept. 1819 to Feb. 1820
HO 41/8   Sept. 1830 to Dec. 1830
HO 41/10   Apr. 1831 to Dec. 1831
HO 41/11   Dec. 1831 to Feb. 1834

Domestic correspondence

HO 42/24   Jan. 1793 to Feb. 1793
HO 42/25   Mar. 1793 to June 1793
HO 42/26   July 1793 to Oct. 1793
HO 42/27   Nov. 1793 to Dec. 1793
HO 42/28   Jan. 1794 to Feb. 1794
HO 42/122   Apr. 1812
HO 42/125   July 1812
HO 42/125   Dec. 1816
HO 42/196   Oct. 1819

Domestic correspondence entry books

HO 43/3   Mar. 1789 to Mar. 1792
HO 43/4   Mar. 1792 to Feb. 1794
HO 43/6   Oct. 1794 to July 1795
HO 43/12   June 1800 to Apr. 1801
HO 43/13   Apr. 1801 to Mar. 1803
HO 43/20   Feb. 1812 to July 1812
HO 43/25   Jan. 1816 to Feb. 1817
HO 43/28   Sept. 1818 to Sept. 1819
HO 43/29   Sept. 1819 to Oct. 1820
HO 43/30   Oct. 1821 to Dec. 1821
HO 43/31   Dec. 1821 to June 1822
HO 43/40   Feb. 1831 to Nov. 1831
HO 43/41   Nov. 1831 to Mar. 1832
HO 43/42   Mar. 1832 to Oct. 1832
HO 43/43   Oct. 1832 to Aug. 1833
HO 43/46   Dec. 1834 to June 1835

2 Deposited in Bristol Record Office

Bristol Corporation records

Assize of bread records, 04350/4a–6a.
Common Council proceedings, 1790–1835.
Common Council letter books, 1791–1813.
Letters and miscellaneous papers, Boxes 1790–1835.
Proceedings of committee of mayor and aldermen, 1790–1836.
Sessions papers, boxes 1787–1800 to '1834 onwards and no date'.

Others:

Bennet, John, Manuscript autobiography of, Portishead, 1853.
Bristol Gas Light Company, Minute books (1815–37).
Butcher MSS, Edmund Butcher and the Bristol riots, 1831–2.
Davis MSS, letters to Rev. C.H. Davis re Bristol riots of 1831.
Greethead's panoramic sketch of the procession to the Bristol Cathedral, Thursday the 8th September 1831 on the coronation day of their majesties William IV and Adelaide.
Gutch, J.M., Letters to, on writing Cosmo's letters; plans for formation of the Chamber of Commerce 1822–25; and other papers.
Hare MSS, John Hare: documents concerning the Bristol election of 1830.
Harford MSS, 28048/c77 (Bristol riots of 1831); and 28048/c62 (Brandon Hill meeting, 1816).
Serjeant's report book, 1832, St Augustine's Parish.
Stedfast Society, Election proceedings, 1806–1812.

3 Deposited in Bristol Reference Library

Baharie, Alexander, An awful brush with the 'old fourteenth'.
Bishop, Betty, Diary, 1779–1801 (vol. III).
Braikenridge, G.W., Collection of letters to (1789–1826).
(Braikenridge, G.W.?), Miscellaneous notes relating to Bristol, 1824 onwards.
Bristol Bridge, Collection of printed and MS material relating to.
Bristol Bridge Trustees, Minutes, 1763–1794.
Bristol history, Volume, chiefly MS, relating to, 1610–1873.
(Bristol history), Register of transactions in and near the city of Bristol, beginning at the year 1799 [–1810].
(Bristol riots of 1831), MS material relating to the Bristol riots of 1831.
(Bristol Volunteers), The mock volunteers, or Bristol heroes; a satire by Peter Pickle, Junior 1794.
Burke, Richard, Letter to John Noble re Bristol Bridge riot: 25 Nov. 1793.

Capper, W., Letter to Mr. Cotterell re Bristol riots of 1831: 13 Aug. 1893.

Committee for investigating the Bridge affairs, minutes of (1793–4).

Dyer, William, Memorable events, extracted from memorandums and diarys, commencing 1744.

Fox, Edward Long, MS draft of notice to appear in *Bristol Gazette*, 24 Oct. 1793.

(Fox, Edward Long), MS draft of letter to appear in *Bristol Gazette*, 7 Nov. 1793 in defence of E.L. Fox.

(Horwood, John), Some account of John Horwood, who was executed at Bristol, April 21st [1821], for the murder of Eliza Balsam at Hanham, Gloucestershire (transcript of materials collected by surgeon Richard Smith, transcribed by George Pryce, Bristol, 1858).

(Invasion), MS pamphlets re the invasion of Bristol by France.

Jefferies, C.T., Collection of MSS of, vols. I–XVI.

Kingsley (Charles?), Letter to Lady Louisa re Bristol riots of 1831, 7 Nov. 1831.

Merchant Venturers Society, Merchants Hall books of proceedings, vols. II–XIV.

Military order book, Bristol, Aug.–Oct. 1804.

Seyer, Rev. Samuel (the younger), Calendar of events in Bristol, 1820–1827.

Seyer MSS, Relating to the history of Bristol: chronicle of events, 1760–1813.

Sharples, Ellen, Diary, 1803–1836.

Vickery, Daniel, A Bristol calendar containing brief notices of such events as have taken place in that city and its neighbourhood July 1824 to the end of the year 1835.

4 Deposited in Bristol University Library

Pinney Papers, Papers relating to the Bristol riots of 1831: S-2(1) and R-5.

5 Deposited in Liverpool Records Office

Liverpool Corporation, Town books, 1790–1835.

Liverpool Corporation, Select finance committee minute books, 1790–1835.

Nicholson Papers.

Underhill, J.G., Underhill MSS, vol. 5: The Liver, a MS history in three parts (1830).

Underhill, J.G., MSS vol. 7: Biography and list of streets.

6 Deposited in Norfolk Record Office

Norwich Corporation, Books of proceedings of the court of mayoralty, 1789–1835.

B PRINTED PRIMARY SOURCES

1 Bristol newspapers

Bonner and Middleton's Bristol Journal
Bristol Gazette and Public Advertiser
Bristol Liberal
Bristol Mercury
Bristol Mirror
Bristol Observer
Felix Farley's Bristol Journal
Sarah Farley's Bristol Journal

2 Miscellaneous periodicals relating to Bristol

Acland's Truth, 5 Feb. 1831
The Age (London), 4 Dec. 1831
Bristol, Bath, Gloucester, West of England and South Wales General Advertiser, 16 and 23 Apr. 1831
Bristol Job Nott or Labouring Man's Friend, Dec. 1831–Dec. 1833
The Bristol Poor Man's Magazine; and Cottager's Friend, 25 July 1829
The Bristol Retaliator, 7 Apr. 1832
Bristol Spectator, 30 Oct. 1800
The Bristolian (James Acland), 1827–9
The Bristolian – Memoirs and correspondence of John Fudge, 7 Nov. 1829
The Christian Guardian: a theological miscellany by a society of clergymen, vol. IV (1803)
The Chronicle of Bristol, July–Oct. 1829
A Conservative Reporter, or Mechanic's Friend, 1834–5
The Country Constitutional Guardian and Literary Magazine, vol. I (Bristol, 1822)
The Discoverer: memoirs and correspondence of a shareholder in the Bristol Bread Association, 1830
A Free Reporter, 29 Sept. 1832
The Morning Chronicle (London), 16 and 17 Aug. 1832
Old Jonathan: the district and parish helper, Feb. 1883
The Sun (London), 10 Oct. 1798
The Taunton and Western Advertiser, for Somerset, Wiltshire, Devon, Dorset, and Cornwall, 2 Nov. 1831

3 Other newspapers

Billinge's Liverpool Advertiser and Marine Intelligencer
Gore's Liverpool General Advertiser

Liverpool Courier and Commercial Advertiser
Liverpool Chronicle
Liverpool Mercury

Norfolk Chronicle and Norwich Gazette
Norwich Mercury

Cowdroy's Manchester Gazette and Weekly Advertiser
Manchester Courier and Lancashire General Advertiser
Manchester Gazette and Weekly Advertiser
Manchester Guardian
Manchester Herald
Manchester Mercury
Manchester Times and Guardian

4 General printed material, deposited in Bristol Reference Library

(Printed in Bristol unless otherwise stated.)

Agg, John, *The lamp trimmed, an address to the public of the city of Bristol* (1807).

A.W., *A letter to Edward Long Fox* (1795).

(Boatmen), *Byelaws, rules and orders for the conduct, management and government of all pilots, watermen and others employed . . . within the port of Bristol*, 2 edns (1810 and 1853).

(Bristol Bridge), *About 400 couples of bloodhounds, the property of L[ord] B[atema]n* (1793).

An address to the citizens, on occasion of the present melancholy state of Bristol (1793).

Cain and Abel Tavern, near Bristol bridge (1793).

A capital selection of Bristol worthies (1793).

A chapter out of the book of Morgan (1793).

Daniel's dream (1793).

Extraordinary gazette, published by authority (1793).

An impartial history of the late riots (1793).

Inquisition for blood shall be made (1793).

The lamentation of Bristolia (1793).

A list of persons killed and wounded (a the late riots in Bristol respecting the Bridge tolls) on the memorable evening of the 30th of September (1793)

Lord B[ateman] otherwise Lord Bodadil (1793).

Notice to fathers and masters from magistrates of Bristol (1793).

Plain truth (1793).

To the public, a notice from Abraham Hiscoxe (1793).

The speech of alderman Twig Pigeon concerning the late riot (1793).

Statement of bridge account by Civis (1793).

Strictures on a pamphlet called Impartial History (1793).

Tragedy called cowardice and murder (1793).

Bristol Bridge Trustees, *Accounts* (1793).

Bristol Constitutional Society for a Parliamentary Reform, *Address to the people of Great Britain* (1794).

Bristol Corporation, *A few facts relating to the present local government of Bristol, and hints for its probable improvement* (1831).

(Bristol Corporation), *Free thoughts on the offices of mayor, aldermen, and common council of the city of Bristol with a constitutional proposition for their annihilation* (1792).

Speech of Balaam's beast (1792).

A small token of admiration at the talents and acquirements of the Corporation of Bristol . . . by two schoolmasters (1824).

Reasons for objecting to the proposed bill of the common council for the reduction and alteration of the town and mayor's dues (1825).

Bristol fragments, A collection of broadsides, 1741–1819.

Bristol General Union, *Rules and orders of the Bristol General Union, established June 7, 1831* (1832).

Bristol riot commissioners, *Bristol riots 1831. Report of the commissioners appointed under the Bristol Damages Compensation Act* (1835).

Bristol Volunteer Association, *Rules and regulations to be observed by the Bristol Volunteer Association* (1797).

Brown, James, *The rise, progress and military improvement of the Bristol volunteers* (1798).

(Burdock, Mary Ann), *Trial, confession and execution of Mary Ann Burdock* (1835).

Carpenter, Lant, *Letter to the editor of the Monthly Repository on the late riots in Bristol* (1831).

Centinel, *The first six letters of Centinel, containing an exposition of the principles of the Trout Tavern dinner club; of Mr H. Hunt, the President; and of Mr Thomas Lee, Vice-President, with occasional incidental remarks* (1807?).

Chamber of Commerce, *Rules and regulations for the establishment of a Chamber of Commerce in Bristol* (1823).

Report . . . to consider a Bill brought into Parliament by the common council on the subject of the town and mayor's duties (1824).

Report . . . on . . . local taxation (1824).

Further reports . . . on local taxation (1824).

Report . . . to consider the facilities which the city and neighbourhood of Bristol afford for the introduction of new and the extension of the existing branches of Manufacture (1828).

Cobbett, William, *Three letters to the independent electors of the city of Bristol* (Bath, 1812).

Coleridge, Samuel Taylor, *An answer to a letter to Edward Long Fox* (1795).

Commercial Coffee Rooms, *An account of the laying of the foundation stone, 1810* (1810).

(Corn Laws), *An address to the free citizens of Bristol* (1815?).

Corry, John and Evans, John, *History of Bristol* (1816).

(Davis, Christopher and Clarke, William), *Narrative of a conversation held with Christopher Davis and William Clarke, who were executed January 27th 1832, for the part they took in the Bristol riots* (1832).

Defoe, Daniel (?), *The Bristol riot containing i) a full and particular account of the riot . . . ii) the whole proceedings relating to the tryal* (London, 1714).

Eagles, John, *The Bristol riots, their causes, progress, and consequences* (1832).

(Elections), Broadsides etc. relating to the parliamentary election of 1796.

An authentic report of the evidence and proceedings before the committee of the House of Commons appointed to try the merits of the Bristol election of Oct. 1812 (1813).

Constitutional resolves, unanimously agreed to by the committee of Friends to Freedom of election, parliamentary reform, and the constitutional rights of Britons (1818).

An authentic report of the evidence and proceedings, before the committee of the House of Commons appointed to try the merits of the Bristol election of June 1818 (1819).

Collection of broadsides, addresses, notices, etc., relating to the election of 1826.

Collection of broadsides, addresses, notices etc., relating to the election of 1830.

Collection of broadsides, addresses, notices, etc., relating to the election of 1831.

Collection of broadsides, addresses, notices, etc., relating to the election of 1832.

Collection of broadsides, addresses, notices, etc. relating to the election of 1835.

Practical instructions for the registration of voters as far as applies to the city and district of Bristol (1835).

Bristol election petition, 1832–3 (1838).

Elton, Charles A., *An apology for Colonel Hugh Baillie* (1819?).

A sequel to the apology for Colonel Hugh Baillie (1819).

(Fairs), *An address to the inhabitants of Bristol, respecting the evils of the fairs* (1815).

The peep-show; a Bristol fairing (1823).

Fox, Edward Long, *Notice to the citizens of Bristol* (1793).

Cursory reflections on the causes and some of the consequences of the stoppage of the Bank of England (1797).

(Fox, Edward Long), *A letter to the citizens of Bristol on the conduct of E.L. Fox* (1793).

Gutch, J.M., *Letters on the impediments which obstruct the trade and commerce of the city and port of Bristol which first appeared in Felix Farley's Bristol Journal under the signature of Cosmo* (1823).

Hobhouse, Benjamin, *Thoughts humbly offered to the mayor and sheriffs of Bristol and to all the other dissenters who accept corporate offices* (1794).

(Hobhouse, Benjamin), 'Mr Hobhouse', extract from *Public characters of 1807* (London, 1807).

(Horwood, John), Newspaper extracts relating to the trial and execution of John Horwood for the murder of Eliza Balsam.

Hunt, Henry, *An address to the public of the city of Bristol* (1807).

(Hunt Henry), *Bristol election: an account of Mr Hunt's public reception in Bristol, May 18, 1812, with a full report of his second address, delivered to the citizens, from the pedestal in front of the exchange* (1812).
A list of the persons who voted for Mr Hunt at the late election (1812).
An account of the public dinner for the friends to purity of election held at the Talbot Inn, Bristol, Jan. 28, 1813 (1813).

Johnson, James, *Transactions of the Corporation of the Poor* (1826).

(Jones, William), *The history of William Jones and his two sisters; with an account of their visits to the Bristol fairs* (1815).

Junius, *A letter to Thomas Daniel, Esq. alderman and magistrate on the loyal address* (1831).

Kentish, Edward, *A narrative of the facts relative to the Bristol election as connected with the meeting on Brandon-hill, June 13, 1818* (1818).

Kington, J.B., *City and port of Bristol: letters, essays, tracts, etc.* (1836).

Lee, Thomas, *Election clubs, late riot at Bristol . . . and dock tax* (1807).
Eyes to the blind! An address to the electors of Bristol, indicating their elective franchise against the endeavours of the Corporation and of certain clubs to render the same a mere nullity (1807).
Trim the lamp! An address to the public of Bristol (1807).

(Lee, Thomas) Anon., *A glance at Dr. Lee in his own looking glass* (1807).

Loyal Union of Britons Benefit Society, *Rules and orders to be observed and kept by the Loyal Union of Britons Benefit Society of handicraft tradesmen, commencing 8th of October 1821* (1821?).

Manchee, Thomas John, *The origin of the riots of Bristol and the causes of the subsequent outrages* (2nd edn, 1831).

Mathews, J., *The Bristol guide 1795* (1795).
The Bristol guide; being a complete ancient and modern history of the City of Bristol, the Hotwells and Clifton (4th edn, 1815).
The Bristol guide; being a complete ancient and modern history of the City of Bristol, the Hotwells and Clifton (5th edn, 1819).

The Bristol guide; forming an ancient as well as a modern history of that opulent provincial metropolis, with its suburbs Clifton and the Hotwells (7th edn, 1829).

Mathews, W., *Mathews's Bristol guide and directory, 1793–4* (1794).

Complete Bristol directory (1803).

Mechanic's Institution, *Rules and orders of the Bristol Mechanic's Institution for the promotion of useful knowledge among the working classes, established June 20, 1825* (1825).

M'Lachlan, Duncan, *The life of Duncan M'Lachlan, written by himself, when under sentence of death in Newgate* (1801).

N.J., *Elegy on the late riots in Bristol* (1793?).

(Pinney, Charles), *Bristol riots. Trial of Charles Pinney, Esq., late mayor; for neglect of duty* (1832?).

(Protestant meeting), *Report of the great Protestant meeting, in defence of the established Church of England and Ireland, held in Bristol, Nov. 26, 1834* (1834).

(Protheroe, Edward), *A summary view of the public conduct of Edward Protheroe, M.P.* (1818).

(Protheroe, Edward, Jnr), *What has Mr. Protheroe done?* (1832?).

Prudent Man's Friend Society, *State of the Society for the year 1814* (1814).

(Reform Bill), *Remarks on the anti-Protestant and democratic tendency of the Reform Bill; an address to the citizens of Bristol* (n.d.).

(Riot, 1714), *The Bristol riot* (London, 1714).

A full and impartial account of the late disorders in Bristol (London, 1714).

The tryals of the rioters at Bristol (London, 1714).

(Riot, 1797), *A statement of facts relative to the riot . . . in Union street . . . 27th and 28th March 1797* (1797).

(Riot, 1831), Collection of newspapers extracts, reports, placards etc. relating to the riots of 1831, BRL B4782.

Collection of newspapers extracts, reports, placards etc. relating to the riots of 1831, BRL B7426.

Miscellaneous illustrations relating to the riots of 1831.

Troubles in Bristol, by politicks, fire and pestilence (collection of broadsides, leaflets and addresses, relating to the riots and elections, etc., 1830–2).

A hint from Bristol; or, what should honest men do now? Containing some remarks on reform, the King's will, and political unions (London, 1831).

A narrative of the dreadful riots and burnings which occurred, on Saturday, Sunday, and Monday the 29th, 30th and 31st October, 1831 and the destruction of property and lives consequent upon them (1831?).

Particulars of the dreadful riots in Bristol on Saturday and Sunday, Oct. 29 and 30, 1831 (1831).

Remarks suggested by recent events, and on the necessity of an efficient police in this city, by a householder (1831).

'Riots at Bristol. By an eye witness' (extract from *New Monthly Magazine*, vol. XXXII, (1831).

Thoughts on education and co-operation suggested by the late riots at Bristol (London, 1831).

A voice to Bristol: the thirtieth and thirty first days of October, 1831 (2nd edn, 1831).

Lamentation of those five unfortunate men now lying under sentence of death in Bristol gaol (n.d., 1832?).

A letter to the judges . . . upon the impropriety of punishing the rioters with death (1832).

The magistrates of Bristol brought to the bar of public opinion. Being a consideration of the charges to which the Mayor and Corporation of this city are liable. As regards their conduct in connexion with the late riots (1832).

The petition to the King on behalf of the prisoners committed under the late special commission at Bristol and Nottingham (London, 1832).

'Trial of the magistrates and reaction among the operatives' (extract from *Blackwoods Magazine*, December 1832).

'What caused the Bristol riots?' (extract from *Blackwood's Magazine*, March 1832).

A whisper from Devonshire: or a dialogue on the Reform Bill (1832).

(Romilly, Sir Samuel) Anon., *An account of the entry of Sir Samuel Romilly into Bristol, on Thursday April 2nd, 1812* (1812).

Freedom of election: correspondence between the mayor of Bristol Mr Protheroe and Sir Samuel Romilly (1812).

Rose, John, *An impartial history of the late disturbances* (1793).

A reply to a Bridge Trustee (1793).

Seyer, Samuel, *Memoirs historical and topographical of Bristol and its neighbourhood, from the earliest period down to the present time*, vol. 2 (1823).

(Smith, Benjamin), *The life and confession of Benjamin Smith, who was executed at Bristol on Friday, April 24, 1795 for forgery* (1795).

Smith, Rev. G.C., *Bristol fair, but no preaching!* (1823).

Somerton, W.H., *Narrative of the Bristol riots on the 29th, 30th and 31st of October, 1831* (4th edn, 1831).

(Somerton, W.H.), *A full report of the trials . . . of the Bristol rioters before the special commission* (1832).

South Gloucestershire Friendly Society, *Explanation of the nature and benefits of the society* (1825).

Rules and regulations (1825).

Fifth report of the Stapleton, Winterbourne, etc. Association of the South Gloucestershire Friendly Society (1831).

(Sport), Volume of miscellaneous sporting notices, 1822–1832.

Telphord, William, *Transparencies exhibited in Bristol and its vicinity on the day of proclaiming peace, Thursday, May 4 1802* (1802).

Thorpe, Rev. W., *A report of the lecture, delivered by the Rev. W. Thorpe, at the Countess of Huntingdon's chapel, on Thursday, Jan. 12, 1832, upon the riots of Bristol* (1832).

'Under five monarchs – Bristol in old days – veteran citizen's reminiscences' (extract from *Bristol Mercury*, 1902?).

Walker, C.H., *An address to the electors of the United Kingdom, but in particular those of Bristol and Colchester* (1812).

An independent address to the electors of Bristol upon the state of the representation of the people (1812).

An address to the honest and conscientious electors of Bristol on the recent election for that city (1819).

A second address to the honest and conscientious electors of Bristol (1819), and *A third address* (1819).

An address to the electors of Bristol showing the ineligibility of Henry Bright Esq. the Whig candidate to represent them in the ensuing parliament (Bristol, 1828).

The petition of William Clarke, convicted at the late special commission at Bristol (London, 1832).

Work in Bristol: a series of sketches of the chief manufactories in the city: reprinted from the Bristol Times and Mirror (1883).

5 General printed material, deposited in Bristol Record Office

Bristol Corporation Printed Orders.

Bristol Parliamentary Elections, 1774–1943: notices, broadsides, etc.

(Coronation of King George IV), *Order of procession on celebrating the coronation of his Majesty King George the Fourth in the city of Bristol, on Thursday, the 19th of July, 1821* (Bristol, 1821).

Evans, John, *Chronological outline of the history of Bristol* (Bristol, 1824).

Friends of Humanity, *Rules, orders, and regulations to be strictly observed by an amicable society, held under the title of Friends of Humanity: Instituted 13th day March 1822* (Bristol, 1831).

Mathews, J., *Mathews's annual Bristol directory for the year 1825* (Bristol, 1825).

6 Other printed material

Anon., *A letter to the Freemen of Norwich, containing brief remarks on the origin, loyalty and practical effects of chartered rights* (Norwich, 1833).

Baines, Edward, *History, directory and gazeteer of the county palatine of Lancaster* (1824; reprinted Newton Abbot, 1968).

Bambridge, J., *Observations on the speech of Mr Edward Taylor on his being returned sheriff* (Norwich, 1819).

Berry, C., *A concise history and directory of the city of Norwich for 1811* (Norwich, 1810).

Bethell's Life in London, and Liverpool Sporting Register (Liverpool, 1827).

Blyth, G.K., *The Norwich guide and directory: an historical and topographical description of the city and its hamlets* (London, 1842).

Browne, P., *The history of Norwich from the earliest records to the present time* (Norwich, 1814).

(Caroline), Collection of handbills, broadsides etc. relating to Queen Caroline (Norwich).

(Coronation of George IV), 'Opening of the Prince's dock, Liverpool', (extract from *The Imperial Magazine*, vol. III, Liverpool, 1821, pp. 780–2).

(Elections), Norfolk and Norwich parliamentary addresses and squibs, relating to contested elections, from 1768 to 1830.

A compendious and impartial account of the election, at Liverpool, which commenced on the first and closed on the eighth of November, 1806 (Liverpool, 1806?).

An impartial collection of addresses, songs, squibs, etc. published during the election of Members of Parliament for the borough of Liverpool, October 1812 (Liverpool, 1812).

An impartial collection of addresses, songs, squibs, etc. published during the election of Members of Parliament for the borough of Liverpool, June 1816 (Liverpool, 1816).

The poll for the election of a member of Parliament for the borough of Liverpool taken between William Ewert, Esq. and John Evelyn Denison, Esq. (Liverpool, 1830).

Report of the proceedings before the select committee of the House of Commons, appointed to try the matter of the petition against the return of William Ewert, Esq. for the borough of Liverpool (Liverpool, 1831).

The poll for the election of members of Parliament for the borough of Liverpool (for 1832) . . . to which is affixed a brief history of the election (Liverpool, 1833).

Result of the evidence given before the select committee to enquire into the petition on Liverpool Borough (London, 1833).

The poll for the election of members of Parliament for the borough of Liverpool . . . on Tuesday the 6th and Wednesday the 7th 1835 (Liverpool, 1835).

Geary, William, *An earnest appeal to the weavers of Norwich on the present awful crisis* (Norwich, 1830).

(George IV), 'Proclaiming his Majesty King George the Fourth, at Liverpool', *Royal Magazine* (Liverpool), no. 1 (March 1820).

Hume, Abraham, *Condition of Liverpool, religious and social; including notices of the state of education, morals, pauperism, and crime* (Liverpool, 1858).

Hunt, Henry, *Memoirs of Henry Hunt written by himself*, 3 vols. (London, 1821).

Kaye, Thomas, *The stranger in Liverpool; or, an historical and descriptive view of Liverpool and its environs* (Liverpool, 1807).

The stranger in Liverpool (6th edn, Liverpool, 1820).

The stranger in Liverpool (10th edn, Liverpool, 1831).

The stranger in Liverpool (11th edn, Liverpool, 1836).

Moss, W., *The Liverpool guide; including a sketch of the environs* (Liverpool, 1797).

The Liverpool guide (4th edn, Liverpool, 1801).

(Norwich Corporation), *The guildhall bulletin; being a faithful and comprehensive account of the intended wonders of this wondrous day* (Norwich, 1800?).

Corporate retribution; or, the unearthing of the foxes! (Norwich, 1835?).

Norwich Patriotic Society, *An address from the Patriotic Society of Norwich to the inhabitants of that city* (Norwich, 1797).

Prentice, Archibald, *Historical sketches and personal recollections of Manchester, intended to illustrate the progress of public opinion from 1792 to 1832* (London, 1851).

(Recreation), 'Ascent of Messrs Livingstone and Sadler in a balloon', *The Imperial Magazine*, vol. I (Liverpool, 1819), pp. 780–2.

Romilly, Samuel, *Memoirs of the life of Sir Samuel Romilly, written by himself*, vol. 3 (London, 1840).

Sharpe, J.J., *Norwich in miniature; containing a brief description of the city; a chronological table of the most remarkable events which have happened therein* (Norwich, 1834).

(Shepherd, W.), *The true and wonderful history of Dick Liver: showing, how from small beginnings he became a man of substance; and how he was robbed while he was asleep; and relating his ineffectual attempts to get into his own house and recover his property* (Liverpool, 1824).

Smithers, Henry, *Liverpool, the commerce, statistics and institutions; with a history of the cotton trade* (Liverpool, 1825).

Taylor, Thomas, *The picture of Liverpool, or stranger's guide; containing a history of the ancient and present state of the town* (Liverpool, 1833).

T.S.N., 'State of society in Norwich', *Monthly Magazine*, 1799.

(Wallace, James?), *A general and descriptive history of the ancient and present state of the town of Liverpool* (Liverpool, 1795?).

Wheeler, James, *Manchester: its political, social and commercial history, ancient and modern* (London, 1836).

7 Printed government records

An Act for preventing tumults and riotous assemblies, and for more speedy and effectual punishing the rioters, 1 Geo. I, st. 2, c. 5 (1715).

An Act for rebuilding and enlarging the bridge over the Avon (Bristol Bridge), 33 Geo. II, c. 52 (1759).

An Act for more effectively preventing seditious meetings and assemblies, 36 Geo. III, c. 8 (1795).

An Act to repeal an Act, passed in the last session of Parliament intitled An Act to prevent unlawful combinations of workmen, and to substitute other provisions in lieu thereof, 39 and 40 Geo. III, c. 106 (1800).

An Act to revive and continue, until six weeks after the commencement of the next session of Parliament, an Act, made in the thirty-sixth year of his present majesty, intitled An Act for the more effectively preventing seditious meetings and assemblies, 41 Geo. III, c. 30 (1801).

An Act for the more effectual preventing seditious meetings and assemblies, 57 Geo. III, c. 19 (1817).

An Act for more effectually preventing seditious meetings and assemblies; to continue in force until the end of the session of Parliament next after five years from the passing of the Act, 60 Geo. III, c. 6 (1819).

An Act to prevent the training of persons to the use of arms and to the practice of military evolutions and exercise, 60 Geo III and 1 Geo. IV, c. 1 (1819).

Journals of the House of Commons: report of the Committee of Secrecy, 1794, vol. XLIX.

Hansard's Parliamentary debates, 1831, vol. VI to vol. IX.

Parliamentary papers: accounts and papers (9) relating to Parliamentary representation, 1831–2, vol. XXXVI, 31.

Parliamentary papers: report of the departmental committee on crowds, 1924, cmnd. 2088, vol. VIII, 225.

Report from the commissioners on municipal corporations in England and Wales, 3 appendix part I, vol. XXIII, 1835.

Report from the commissioners on municipal corporations in England and Wales, 4, appendix part II, vol. XXIV, 1835.

Report from the commissioners on municipal corporations in England and Wales, 6, appendix parts IV and V, vol. XXVI, 1835.

C SECONDARY SOURCES

1 Relating to Bristol, published before 1900

(Published in Bristol unless otherwise stated.)

Barnett, Henry N., *Bristol, past, present and future* (1856).

Beaven, Rev. Alfred B., *Bristol lists: municipal and miscellaneous* (1899).

Braine, A., *History of Kingswood forest* (1891).

British Association, *Bristol and its environs, historical, descriptive and scientific* (London, 1875).

Browne, Latham, *The burning of Bristol: a reminiscence of the first reform bill*, reprinted from *National Review* (Sept. 1884), pp. 45–62.

Graham, Henry, *The annals of the yeomanry cavalry of Wiltshire. Being a complete history of the Prince of Wales' own royal regiment from the time of its formation in 1794 to October, 1884* (Liverpool, 1886).

Hunt and Company's Gloucester and Bristol directory (1849).

Hunt, W., *Bristol* (London, 1887).

Latimer, John, *The annals of Bristol in the eighteenth century* (1893).

The annals of Bristol in the nineteenth century (1887).

Lewis, Harold, *The history of the Bristol Mercury 1715–1886* (1886?).

Nicholls, J.F. and Taylor, John, *Bristol past and present*, vol. III (1882).

Pryce, George, *A popular history of Bristol* (1861).

Sexagenerian, 'Great towns and their public influence – Bristol', (extract from the *Gentleman's Magazine*, new series, V, 13, 1874).

Taylor, John, *A book about Bristol; historical, ecclesiastical and biographical, from original research* (London, 1872).

2 *Relating to Bristol, published after 1900*

(Published in Bristol unless otherwise stated.)

Alford, B.W.E., 'The flint and bottle glass industry in the early nineteenth century: a case study of a Bristol firm', *Business History*, X, 1 (1968), pp. 12–21.

W.D. and H.O. Wills and the development of the U.K. tobacco industry, 1780–1965 (London, 1973).

'The economic development of Bristol in the nineteenth century: an enigma?', in Patrick McGrath and John Cannon (eds.), *Essays in Bristol and Gloucestershire history* (1976), pp. 252–83.

Amey, Geoffrey, *City under fire: the Bristol riots and aftermath* (London, 1979).

Barker, Kathleen, *The Theatre Royal Bristol: the first seventy years* (1961). *Bristol at play: five centuries of live entertainment* (Bradford-on-Avon, 1976).

Bonner, Alphonsus, 'Catholics and the Bristol riots of 1831', *The Month*, CLX (1932), pp. 426–33.

Brace, Keith, *Portrait of Bristol* (London, 1971).

Brown, H.G. and Harris, P.J., *Bristol England* (1946).

Buckley, Francis, 'The early glasshouses of Bristol', *Transactions of the Society of Glass Technology*, IX, 2 (1925), pp. 1–7.

Bush, Graham, *Bristol and its municipal government, 1820–1851* (1976).

Butcher, E.E., *The Bristol Corporation of the Poor, 1696–1898* (1972).

Cannon, John, *The Chartists in Bristol* (1964).

Day, Joan, *Bristol brass: a history of the industry* (Newton Abbot, 1973).

Dowding, W.L., *The story of Bristol: a brief history for young citizens* (1906).

pushed him. Vaughan said he wanted to go home. The officer repeated

Hall, I.V., 'Whitson Court sugar house, Bristol 1665–1824', *Transactions of the Bristol and Gloucestershire Archaeological Society*, no. 65 (1944), pp. 1–97.

'The Daubeny's: the second and third generation of the family at the Holliers Lane refinery under George II and George III. Part II', *Transactions of the Bristol and Glos. Arch. Soc.*, no. 85 (1966), pp. 175–201.

Harvey, Alfred, *Bristol: a historical and topographical account of the city* (London, 1906).

'The Bristol riots', in P.H. Ditchfield (ed.), *Memorials of old Gloucestershire* (London, 1911), pp. 219–32.

Hulbert, Rev. N.F., 'A survey of the Somerset fairs', *Proceedings of the Somerset Archaeological and Natural History Society*, LXXXII (1936), pp. 83–159.

Ison, Walter, *The Georgian buildings of Bristol* (Bath, 1952).

Jenkins, Walter, 'The copper works at Redbrook and at Bristol', *Transactions of the Bristol and Glos. Arch. Soc.*, no. 63 (1942), pp. 145–67.

Jones, S.J., 'The growth of Bristol: the regional aspect of city development', *Transactions of the Institute of British Geographers*, XI (1946), pp. 57–83.

Jones, Philip D., 'The Bristol bridge riot and its antecedents: eighteenth century perceptions of the crowd', *Journal of British Studies*, XIX, 2 (1980), pp. 74–92.

Josephs, Z., 'The Jacobs of Bristol, glassmakers to King George III', *Transactions of the Bristol and Glos. Soc.*, no. 95 (1977), pp. 98–101.

Latham, R.C., *Bristol charters, 1509–1899* (1947).

Little, Bryan, *The city and county of Bristol: a study of Atlantic civilisation* (London, 1954).

'The Gloucestershire spas: an eighteenth century parallel', in Patrick McGrath and John Cannon (eds.), *Essays in Bristol and Gloucestershire History* (1976), pp. 170–99.

McGrath, P.V., *The Merchant Venturers of Bristol* (1975).

MacInnes, C.M., *Bristol and the slave trade* (1963).

MacInnes, C.M. and Whittard, W.F. (eds.), *Bristol and its adjourning counties* (1955).

Malcolmson, Robert W., ' "A set of ungovernable people": the Kingswood colliers in the eighteenth century', in John Brewer and John Styles (eds.), *An ungovernable people: the English and their law in the seventeenth and eighteenth centuries* (London, 1980), pp. 85–127.

Marcy, Peter T., *Eighteenth-century views of Bristol and Bristolians* (1966).

'Bristol's roads and communications on the eve of the industrial revolution, 1740–1780', *Transactions of the Bristol and Glos. Arch. Soc.*, no. 87 (1968), pp. 149–72.

Marshall, Peter, *Bristol and the abolition of slavery: the politics of emancipation* (1975).

Meller, H.E., *Leisure and the changing city, 1870–1914* (London, 1976).

Minchinton, W.E., 'Bristol: metropolis of the west in the eighteenth century', *Transactions of the Royal Historical Society*, 5th series, IV (1954), pp. 69–89.

The port of Bristol in the eighteenth century (1962).

(ed.), *The trade of Bristol in the eighteenth century* (1957).

(ed.), *Politics and the port of Bristol in the eighteenth century: the petitions of the Society of Merchant Venturers, 1698–1803* (1963).

Neve, Michael, 'Science in a commercial city: Bristol 1820–1860', in I. Inkster and J. Morrell (eds.), *Metropolis and province: science in British culture, 1780–1850* (London, 1983), pp. 179–204.

Payne, Herbert, *Bristol riots 1686–1831* (1974).

Powell, Arthur Cecil, 'Glass-making in Bristol', *Transactions of the Bristol and Glos. Arch. Soc.*, no. 47 (1925), pp. 211–57.

Stiles, Robin, 'The Old market sugar refinery, 1684–1908', *Bristol Industrial Archaeological Society Journal* (1969), pp. 10–17.

Stoddard, Sheena, *Mr. Braikenridge's Brislington* (1981).

Thomas, Susan, *The Bristol riots* (1974).

Waite, Vincent, 'The Bristol Hotwell', in Patrick McGrath (ed.), *Bristol in the eighteenth century* (Newton Abbot, 1972), pp. 109–26.

Walters, Roderick, *The establishment of the Bristol police force* (1975).

Ward, J.R., 'Speculative building at Bristol and Clifton, 1783–1793', *Business History*, XX, 1 (1978), pp. 3–18.

Wells, Charles, *Historic Bristol* (1902).

Williams, J., 'Bristol in the general elections of 1818 and 1820', *Transactions of the Bristol and Glos. Arch. Soc.*, no. 87 (1970), pp. 173–201.

3 Relating to Liverpool, Norwich and Manchester

Axon, William E.A. (ed.), *The Annals of Manchester: a chronological record from the earliest times to the end of 1885* (London, 1886).

Brooke, Richard, *Liverpool as it was during the last quarter of the eighteenth century* (Liverpool, 1853).

Checkland, S.G., *The Gladstones: a family biography 1764–1851* (Cambridge, 1971).

Dunckley, Henry (ed.), *Bamford's Passages in the life of a radical, and early days*, 2 vols. (London, 1893).

Edwards, J.K., 'The decline of the Norwich textile industry', *Yorkshire Bulletin of Economic and Social Research*, XVI, 1 (1964), pp. 31–41.

'Communications and the economic development of Norwich, 1750–1850', *Journal of Transport History*, VII, 2 (Nov. 1965), pp. 96–108.

Harris, S.A., 'Early Liverpool workers', *Co-partners Magazine*, VIII, 2 (1945), pp. 28–9.

Jewson, C.B., *The Jacobin city: a portrait of Norwich in its reaction to the French Revolution, 1788–1802* (London, 1975).

Lloyd Prichard, M.F., 'The decline of Norwich,' *Economic History Review*, 2nd series, III, 3 (1951), pp. 371–7.

Marriner, Sheila, *The economic and social development of Merseyside* (London, 1982).

Mathews, Godfrey W., 'Some notes on the Liverpool election of 1806', *Transactions of the Historic Society of Lancashire and Cheshire*, LXXIX (1927), pp. 74–85.

Midwinter, Eric, *Old Liverpool* (Newton Abbott, 1971).

Muir, Ramsey, *A history of Liverpool* (London, 1907).

Muir, Ramsey and Platt, Edith M., *A history of municipal government in Liverpool from the earliest times to the municipal reform Act of 1835* (London, 1906).

Picton, J.A., *Memorials of Liverpool, historical and topographical, including a history of the dock estate*, 8 vols. (Liverpool, 1873).

Read, Donald, *Peterloo: the 'massacre' and its background* (Manchester, 1958).

Redford, Arthur and Russell, Ina Stafford, *The history of local government in Manchester*, 3 vols. (London, 1939).

Sellers, Ian, 'William Roscoe, the Roscoe circle and radical politics in Liverpool, 1787–1807', *Transactions of the Historic Society of Lancashire and Cheshire*, CXX (1968), pp. 45–62.

Tolley, B.H., 'The Liverpool campaign against the Order in Council and the war of 1812', in J.R. Harris (ed.), *Liverpool and Merseyside: essays in the economic and social history of the port and its hinterland* (London, 1969), pp. 98–146.

Touzeau, James, *The rise and progress of Liverpool from 1551 to 1835*, 2 vols. (Liverpool, 1910).

Vigier, François, *Change and apathy: Liverpool and Manchester during the industrial revolution* (Cambridge, Mass., 1970).

4 Selected general secondary sources

(A full list of general secondary sources is provided by the notes to each chapter.)

Bailey, Peter, *Leisure and class in Victorian England* (London, 1978).

Bailey, Victor (ed.), *Policing and punishment in nineteenth-century Britain* (London, 1981).

Barrell, John, *The dark side of the landscape: the rural poor in English painting 1730–1840* (Cambridge, 1980).

Barrows, Susanna, *Distorting mirrors: visions of the crowd in late nineteenth-century France* (New Haven, 1981).

Belchem, John, 'Henry Hunt and the evolution of the mass platform', *English Historical Review*, XCIII (1978), pp. 739–73.

'Republicanism, popular constitutionalism and the radical platform in early nineteenth-century England', *Social History*, VI, 1 (1981), pp. 1–32.

'1848: Feargus O'Connor and the collapse of the mass platform', in James Epstein and Dorothy Thompson (eds.), *The Chartist experience: studies in working-class radicalism and culture 1830–60* (London, 1982), pp. 269–310.

Bienefeld, M.A., *Working hours in British industry: an economic history* (London, 1972).

Borsay, Peter, 'The English urban renaissance: the development of provincial urban culture, c. 1680–c. 1760', *Social History*, II, 2 (1977), pp. 581–603.

Brewer, John, *Party ideology and popular politics at the accession of George III* (Cambridge, 1976).

'Theatre and counter-theatre in Georgian politics: the mock elections at Garrat', *Radical History Review*, no. 22 (1979–80), pp. 7–40.

Brewer, John, and Styles, John (eds.), *An ungovernable people: the English and their law in the seventeenth and eighteenth centuries* (London, 1980).

Briggs, Asa, *Victorian cities* (Harmondsworth, 1963).

The collected essays of Asa Briggs, vol. 1: *Words, numbers, places and people* (Brighton, 1985).

The collected essays of Asa Briggs, vol. 2: *Images, problems, standpoints, and forecasts* (Brighton, 1985).

Burke, Peter, 'Some reflections on the pre-industrial city', *Urban History Yearbook* (1975), pp. 13–21.

Popular culture in early modern Europe (London, 1978).

'The virgin of the Carmine and the revolt of the Masaniello', *Past and Present*, no. 99 (May 1983), pp. 3–21.

Burn, W.L., *The age of equipoise: a study of the mid-Victorian generation* (London, 1964).

Canetti, Elias, *Crowds and power*, trans. Carol Stewart (Harmondsworth, 1973).

Cannadine, David, *Lords and landlords: the aristocracy and the towns, 1774–1967* (Leicester, 1980).

'The transformation of civic ritual in modern Britain: the Colchester oyster feast', *Past and Present*, no. 94 (Feb. 1982), pp. 107–30.

'The context, performance and meaning of ritual: the British monarchy and the "invention of tradition", c. 1820–1977', in Eric Hobsbawm and Terence Ranger (eds.), *The invention of tradition* (Cambridge, 1983), pp. 101–64.

Colley, Linda, 'The apotheosis of George III: loyalty, royalty and the British nation, 1760–1820', *Past and Present*, no. 102 (Feb. 1984), pp. 94–123.

'Whose nation? Class and national consciousness in Britain, 1750–1830', *Past and Present*, no. 113 (Nov. 1986), pp. 97–117.

Cranfield, G.A., *The press and society: from Caxton to Northcliffe* (London, 1978).

Cunningham, Hugh, *Leisure in the industrial revolution* (London, 1980).

Davis, Natalie Zemon, 'The rites of violence: religious riot in sixteenth-century France', *Past and Present*, no. 59 (May, 1973), pp. 51–91.

Donajgrodzki, A.P. (ed.), *Social control in nineteenth-century Britain* (London, 1977).

Durkheim, Emile, *The elementary forms of the religious life*, trans. Joseph Ward Swain (1915; this edn, London, 1976).

Dyos, H.J. and Wolff, Michael (eds.), *The Victorian city: images and realities*, 2 vols. (London, 1973).

Emsley, Clive, *British society and the French wars, 1793–1815* (London, 1979).

Fraser, Derek and Sutcliffe, Anthony (eds.), *The pursuit of urban history* (London, 1983).

Floud, R. and McCloskey, D., *The economic history of Britain since 1700*, vol. 1: *1700 to 1860* (Cambridge, 1981).

Gatrell, V.A.C., 'The decline of theft and violence in Victorian and Edwardian England', in V.A.C. Gatrell, Bruce Lenman and Geoffrey Parker (eds.), *Crime and law: the social history of crime in western Europe since 1500* (London, 1980), pp. 238–337.

George, M. Dorothy, *London life in the eighteenth century* (Harmondsworth, 1966).

Goffman, Erving, *Behaviour in public places: notes on the social organisation of gatherings* (New York, 1963).

Hammerton, Elizabeth and Cannadine, David, 'Conflict and consensus on a ceremonial occasion: the diamond jubilee in Cambridge in 1897', *Historical Journal*, XXIV, 1 (1981), pp. 111–46.

Harrison, Brian, 'Religion and recreation in nineteenth-century England', *Past and Present*, no. 38 (Dec. 1967), pp. 98–125.

Hay, Douglas, Linebaugh, Peter, Rule, G.J., Thompson, E.P. and Winslow, Cal, *Albion's fatal tree: crime and society in eighteenth-century England* (Harmondsworth, 1977).

Hayter, Tony, *The army and the crowd in mid-Georgian England* (London, 1978).

Hobsbawm, E.J., *Primitive rebels: studies in archaic forms of social movement in the nineteenth and twentieth centuries* (Manchester, 1959).

Revolutionaries: contemporary essays (London, 1973).

Hobsbawm, Eric and Ranger, Terence (eds.), *The invention of tradition* (Cambridge, 1983).

Holton, Robert J., 'The crowd in history: some problems of theory and method', *Social History*, III, 2 (1978), pp. 219–33.

Ignatieff, Michael, *A just measure of pain: the penitentiary in the industrial revolution, 1750–1850* (London, 1978).

Jones, David, *Crime, protest, community and police in nineteenth-century Britain* (London, 1982).

Landes, David S., *Revolution in time: clocks and the making of the modern world* (Cambridge, Mass., 1983).

LeBon, Gustave, *The crowd: a study of the popular mind* (London, 1896).

Lefebvre, Georges, 'Revolutionary crowds', in Jeffrey Kaplow (ed.), *New perspectives on the French revolution: readings in historical sociology* (New York, 1965), pp. 173–90.

Le Roy Ladurie, Emmanuel, *Carnival in Romans: a people's uprising at Romans, 1579–80*, trans. Mary Feeney (Harmondsworth, 1981).

Macfarlane, Alan, *The justice and the mare's ale: law and disorder in seventeenth-century England* (Oxford, 1981).

Malcolmson, Robert W., *Popular recreations in English society, 1700–1850* (Cambridge, 1973).

Manchester, A.H., *A modern legal history of England and Wales 1750–1950* (London, 1980).

Marsh, Peter, *Aggro: the illusion of violence* (London, 1978).

Marsh, Peter, Rosser, Elizabeth and Harré, Rom, *The rules of disorder* (London, 1978).

Mather, F.C., *Public order in the age of the Chartists* (Manchester, 1959).

Milgram, Stanley and Toch, Hans, 'Collective behaviour: crowds and social movements', in Gardner Lindzey and Elliot Aronson (eds), *The handbook of social psychology*, vol. 4 (Reading, Mass., 1969), pp. 507–610.

Nye, Robert A., *The origins of crowd psychology: Gustave LeBon and the crisis of mass democracy in the third republic* (London, 1975).

Pearson, Geoffrey, *Hooligan: a history of respectable fears* (London, 1983).

Randall, Adrian J., 'The shearmen and the Wiltshire outrages of 1802: trade unionism and industrial violence', *Social History*, VII, 3 (1982), pp. 283–304.

Read, Donald, *Press and people 1790–1850: opinion in three English cities* (London, 1961).

Reid, Douglas A., 'The decline of St. Monday, 1766–1876', *Past and Present*, no. 71 (May 1976), pp. 76–101.

Rose, Jerry D., *Outbreaks: the sociology of collective behaviour* (New York, 1982).

Rose, R.B., 'Eighteenth-century price riots and public policy in England', *International Review of Social History*, VI, 2 (1961), pp. 277–92.

Rudé, George, *The crowd in history 1730–1848: a study of popular disturbances in France and England* (New York, 1964; revised edn London, 1981). 'English rural and urban disturbances on the eve of the first reform bill, 1830–1831', *Past and Present*, no. 37 (July 1967), pp. 87–102.

Silver, Allan, 'The demand for order in civil society: a review of some themes in the history of urban crime, police and riot', in David J. Bordua (ed.), *The police: six sociological essays* (New York, 1967), pp. 1–24.

Smelser, Neil J., *Theory of collective behaviour* (London, 1962).

Stedman Jones, Gareth, *Outcast London: a study in the relationship between the classes in Victorian society* (Oxford, 1971). 'Class expression versus social control? A critique of recent trends in the social history of leisure', *History Workshop Journal*, IV (1977), pp. 162–70.

'The language of Chartism', in James Epstein and Dorothy Thompson (eds.), *The Chartist experience: studies in working-class radicalism and culture 1830–60* (London, 1982).

Stevenson, John, *Popular disturbances in England, 1700–1870* (London, 1979).

Storch, Robert D. (ed.), *Popular culture and custom in nineteenth-century England* (London, 1982).

Thompson, E.P., *The making of the English working class* (Harmondsworth, 1963).

'Time, work-discipline and industrial capitalism', *Past and Present*, no. 38 (Dec. 1967), pp. 56–97.

'The moral economy of the English crowd in the eighteenth century', *Past and Present*, no. 50 (Feb. 1971), pp. 76–136.

Tilly, Charles, 'Collective violence in European perspective', in Hugh Davis Graham and Ted Robert Gurr (eds.). *The history of violence in America: historical and comparative perspectives* (New York, 1969), pp. 4–45.

'Britain creates the social movement', in James E. Cronin and Jonathan Schneer (eds.), *Social conflict and the political order in modern Britain* (London, 1982), pp. 21–51.

Tilly, Louise A. and Tilly, Charles (eds), *Class conflict and collective action* (London, 1981).

Wearmouth, Robert F., *Methodism and the common people of the eighteenth century* (London, 1945).

Webb, Sidney and Webb, Beatrice, *English local government from the revolution to the municipal corporations act: the manor and the borough*, part II (London, 1908).

Williams, Raymond, *Culture and society 1780–1850* (Harmondsworth, 1963).

Wrigley, E.A. and Schofield, R.S., *The population history of England 1541–1871: a reconstruction* (London, 1981).

Ziegler, Philip, *Crown and people* (London, 1978).

5 Unpublished secondary sources

Hills, D.M. and Atwell, M.E., 'Building operatives in Bristol, 1750–1830', Univ. of Bristol Dept of Adult Education, Notes on Bristol History, 1953, pp. 24–7 (BRL).

Hodgson, Monica, 'The working day and working week in Victorian Britain, 1840–1900', M Phil. thesis, Univ. of London, 1974.

Holford, Elizabeth, 'A man of too much honour', Radio play, broadcast BBC Radio 4, 14 Dec. 1981.

Hulbert, N.F., 'A historical survey of the Somerset and Bristol fairs', MA dissertation, Univ. of Bristol (?), n.d. (1834?) (BRO).

Seal, Helen, 'The gas industry in Bristol, 1815–53', BA dissertation, Univ. of Bristol, 1975 (BRL).

Underdown, P.T., 'The political history of Bristol, 1750–1790', MA dissertation, Univ. of Bristol, 1948 (BRL).

Webb, F.G., 'St. Paul's fair', Univ. of Bristol Dept of Adult Education, Notes on Bristol History, 1953, pp. 15–23.

'Bristol and the rope trade', Univ. of Bristol Dept of Extra-Mural Studies, Notes on Bristol History, no. 5, 1962, pp. 41–51 (BRL).

Index

Past and Present Publications

General Editor: PAUL SLACK, *Exeter College, Oxford*

Family and Inheritance: Rural Society in Western Europe 1200–1800, edited by Jack Goody, Joan Thirsk and E.P. Thompson*
French Society and the Revolution, edited by Douglas Johnson
Peasants, Knights and Heretics: Studies in Medieval English Social History, edited by R.H. Hilton*
Towns in Societies: Essays in Economic History and Historical Sociology, edited by Philip Abrams and E.A. Wrigley*
Desolation of a City: Coventry and the Urban Crisis of the Late Middle Ages, Charles Phythian-Adams
Puritanism and Theatre: Thomas Middleton and Opposition Drama under The Early Stuarts, Margot Heinemann*
Lords and Peasants in a Changing Society: The Estates of the Bishopric of Worcester 680–1540, Christopher Dyer
Life, Marriage and Death in a Medieval Parish: Economy, Society and Demography in Halesowen 1270–1400, Zvi Razi
Biology, Medicine and Society 1840–1940, edited by Charles Webster
The Invention of Tradition, edited by Eric Hobsbawm and Terence Ranger*
Industrialization before Industrialization: Rural Industry and the Genesis of Capitalism, Peter Kriedte, Hans Medick and Jürgen Schlumbohm†*
The Republic in the Village: The People of the Var from the French Revolution to the Second Republic, Maurice Agulhon†
Social Relations and Ideas: Essays in Honour of R.H. Hilton, edited by T.H. Aston, P.R. Coss, Christopher Dyer and Joan Thirsk
A Medieval Society: The West Midlands at the End of the Thirteenth Century, R.H. Hilton
Winstanley: 'The Law of Freedom' and Other Writings, edited by Christopher Hill
Crime in Seventeenth-Century England: A County Study, J.A. Sharpe†
The Crisis of Feudalism: Economy and Society in Eastern Normandy c. 1300–1500, Guy Bois†
The Development of the Family and Marriage in Europe, Jack Goody*
Disputes and Settlements: Law and Human Relations in the West, edited by John Bossy
Rebellion, Popular Protest and the Society Order in Early Modern England, edited by Paul Slack
Studies on Byzantine Literature of the Eleventh and Twelfth Centuries, Alexander Kazhdan in collaboration with Simon Franklin†
The English Rising of 1381, edited by R.H. Hilton and T.H. Aston*

* Published also as a paperback
** Published only as a paperback
† Co-published with the Maison des Sciences de l'Homme, Paris